More C++ GEMS

SIGS Reference Library

1. *Object Methodology Overview CD-ROM* • Doug Rosenberg
2. *Directory of Object Technology* • edited by Dale J. Gaumer
3. *Dictionary of Object Technology: The Definitive Desk Reference* • Donald G. Firesmith and Edward M. Eykholt
4. *Next Generation Computing: Distributed Objects for Business* • edited by Peter Fingar, Dennis Read, and Jim Stikeleather
5. *C++ Gems* • edited by Stanley B. Lippman
6. *OMT Insights: Perspectives on Modeling from the* Journal of Object-Oriented Programming • James Rumbaugh
7. *Best of Booch: Designing Strategies for Object Technology* • Grady Booch (edited by Ed Eykholt)
8. *Wisdom of the Gurus: A Vision for Object Technology* • selected and edited by Charles F. Bowman
9. *Open Modeling Language (OML) Reference Manual* • Donald Firesmith, Brian Henderson-Sellers, and Ian Graham
10. *JavaTM Gems: Jewels from* Java™ Report • Collected and introduced by Dwight Deugo, Ph.D.
11. *The Netscape Programmer's Guide: Using OLE to Build ComponentwareTM Apps* • Richard B. Lam
12. *Advanced Object-Oriented Analysis and Design Using UML* • James J. Odell
13. *The Patterns Handbook: Techniques, Strategies, and Applications* • edited by Linda Rising
14. *Kent Beck's Guide to Better Smalltalk: A Sorted Collection* • Kent Beck
15. *Elements of Java Style* • Vermhelen et al.
16. *More Javatm Gems* • edited by Dwight Deugo, Ph.D.
17. *More C++ Gems* • edited by Robert C. Martin

Additional Volumes in Preparation

More C++ GEMS

edited by
Robert C. Martin

PUBLISHED BY THE PRESS SYNDICATE OF THE UNIVERSITY OF CAMBRIDGE
The Pitt Building, Trumpington Street, Cambridge, United Kingdom

CAMBRIDGE UNIVERSITY PRESS
The Edinburgh Building, Cambridge CB2 2RU, UK http:\\www.cup.cam.ac.uk
40 West 20th Street, New York, NY 10011-4211, USA http:\\www.cup.org
10 Stamford Road, Oakleigh, Melbourne 3166, Australia
Ruiz de Alarcón 13, 28014 Madrid, Spain

Published in association with SIGS Books

First published in 2000

Design and composition by Kevin Callahan/BNGO Books
Cover design by Andrea Cammarata

Printed in the United States of America

A catalog record for this book is available from the British Library.

Library of Congress Cataloging in Publication data is on record with the publisher.

ISBN 0 521 78618 5 paperback

For Daniel Joseph Paz

"So my disability has not been a serious handicap."
Stephen Hawking, 1988

Contents

Foreword

MY FIRST SIGHTING of Bob Martin came in the comp.lang.c++ newsgroup—gosh, but that was a long time ago. Before the *C++ Report*—heck, before even Microsoft had a C++ compiler. Bob was an important voice back then with his detailed postings. Back then, the primary way to get timely information out about C++ was through newsgroups. Back then, that posed a serious problem for working C++ programmers. The *C++ Report* went a long way in providing a solution.

The working C++ programmer was not only the target *audience* for the articles published in the *C++ Report.* The working C++ programmer was also the target *source* for those articles. As Robert Murray, the founding editor of the *C++ Report*, wrote in his foreword to the earlier *C++ Gems* collection[1]:

> When we started the *C++ Report* in late 1989, we decided to target the people who wrote C++ code for a living . . . . To write articles for programmers, we needed to find authors who were programmers.

This philosophy of having authors who preach what they practice set the stage for my second Bob Martin sighting. I had succeeded Rob Murray as editor of the *C++ Report.* When Grady Booch and Mike Violet *retired* as the OO design columnists for the magazine under my watch, I thought well, now I understand how Jefferson Davis felt losing Vicksburg to General Grant. Or

[1] *C++ Gems,* Stanley Lippman, Editor, A SIGS Book imprint, Cambridge University Press, Cambridge, U.K. (1996) ISBN 0-135-70581-9.

was it how Robert E. Lee felt losing Stonewall Jackson to a Confederate sentry's bullet? Or maybe it was like the Spice Girls losing Geri. Or . . . Well, you can see I was really shook up.

[Enter Bob Martin, stage right. Trumpet and general fanfare.] A young boy's voice, frail yet hopeful, cries: "Hail to the new OO design columnist!" Lincoln wanted a Union commander that could do the wartime Union math. I wanted a methodologist who had used his theory in practice and was still able to seriously sling code.

Bob had recently published his excellent *Designing Object-Oriented C++ Applications Using the Booch Method*. Between that and his extensive net postings, he had established himself as an important figure in both the C++ and nascent object community. And so I invited him to become the brand spanking new OO design columnist for the *C++ Report*. My only disappointment back then and now is that it didn't lead to his publishing a second edition of his text.

As Rob Murray notes in his foreword, "The editors really use this stuff. All the editors have been C++ programmers first and editors second." Yep. A first sighting is happenstance. A second, coincidence. A third (or fourth) and the guy must actually be good. Bob Martin has done a fantastic job as editor shepherding the *C++ Report* through the adoption of the standard and the impact of the Java programming language, keeping up a steady flow of articles relevant to the working C++ programmer written by a new generation of C++ programmers. This collection is a testament to that job. I am very pleased to see this new collection of C++ gems. Enjoy!

Stanley Lippman
Dreamworks Feature Animation
and former editor-in-chief of the C++ Report

Acknowledgments

The creator of C++: *Bjarne Stroustrup*

The creator of *C++ Report: Rick Friedman*

The editors of *C++ Report:*
Rob Murray
Stan Lippman
Douglas C. Schmidt

The folks at SIGS Books and Cambridge University Press, especially:
Mick Spillane
Lothlórien Homet

The authors of the articles in this book:

Alberto Antenangeli
Matthew H. Austern
Steve Ball
Chris Cleeland
Dr. James M. Coggins
James O. Coplien
John Crawford
Jerry Fitzpatrick
Richard Gillam
Jeff Grossman
Timothy Harrison
Cay S. Horstmann
Immo Hüneke
John Lakos
Stan Lippman
James W. Newkirk
Nat Pryce
Bhama Rao
Douglas C. Schmidt
Herb Sutter
John Vlissides

Introduction

I HAVE BEEN THE EDITOR of the *C++ Report* for nearly three years; and I really enjoy the work. I get to read all the new papers on C++ long before they make it to print. Indeed, I get to decide which papers make it into print, and which don't. What a hoot! What astounds me is the high quality of the papers that I receive. I can only conclude that the readership of the *C++ Report* (which is the source of the authors) is among the cream of the C++ community.

This book represents the articles that, in my humble (ha!) opinion, are the best of the best. Some of these articles have had a profound effect upon my career as a C++ programmer. Others contain either significant technical insight or significant historical significance. Nevertheless, they are articles that I thought the readership of the *C++ Report* would like to have gathered into a single volume.

What does the future hold for C++? Will Java supplant it? Does it have a place in the .com world of the twenty-first century? Or will it become the next COBOL? How is the future of C++ linked to the future of software engineering in general?

In November 1999 the *C++ Report* ran an article entitled "Wisdom of the C++ Experts: Facing the Millennium." Bjarne Stroustrup's submission to that article was very pertinent. I have reproduced it here with his kind permission:

GETTING FROM THE PAST TO THE FUTURE

BJARNE STROUSTRUP

The main problem for the C++ community today is to use Standard C++ in the way it was intended rather than as a glorified C or a poor man's Smalltalk. Standard C++ offers a balanced set of facilities for efficient, flexible, and type-safe programming; modern implementations offer reasonable —and steadily improving—support for them. Yet, some practical concern and much propaganda discourage people from using these facilities. For example, dire warnings against the evils of multiple-inheritance, templates, exceptions, and the STL are not uncommon. Worse, "coding standards" and "style rules" selectively demonize language features introduced after 1987 or so.

To make major progress and to leave many of the problems of the past behind we must take a different approach. We must emphasize higher-level programming styles and the language features that support them. We must also consider which older styles of programming and which language features have become serious drags on our ability to build efficient and maintainable systems. I do not believe in simple "thou shalt not" style coding rules, but if I did, I'd suggest we start with features that make legacy code hard to deal with. For example:

- Never expose a `T**` to an application programmer.
- Never require an application programmer to write a cast.
- Never expose a `void*` to an application programmer.

I would also have some strong words to say about macros—including macros used to hide such crud.

I'm sure that you have seen libraries and recommended coding practices that force you to break these rules essentially everywhere. Those coding practices are major sources of bad software. For "bad," read unreadable, unmaintainable, unportable, and inefficient.

What is the alternative? Focus on programming and design technique rather than language features and use language features that allow us to express designs directly in code. For example: Containers for holding objects and values, templates for generic programming and type-safe interfaces, concrete types for simple objects. Class hierarchies, preferably based on abstract classes, for generalizations where exact types cannot be known until run time and exceptions for error handling.

We cannot afford to be just starry-eyed idealists. There are millions of lines of ugly but useful code out there, no shortage of C++ implementations that are not up to the level of the standard, and no shortage of interfaces that expose low-level details. However, I do not mind legacy code, I mind legacy interfaces. The problem is not the old code, but the insistence on making new code according to old rules rather than designing and programming using better techniques and providing clean interfaces to code that isn't clean. I am sure that the future belongs to people writing code using these techniques. I am sure that the future belongs to people writing code that is type-safe, uses templates, exceptions, and relies on extensive libraries of concrete types and class hierarchies. I would like those programmers to use C++. They ought to because Standard C++ currently provides a better balance of support for these techniques than any other major programming language. However, the best code will be written by people who use these techniques and language features—in whatever language—rather than people who insist on writing Fortran, K&R C, or whatever in whichever language they (mis)use.

Pay due respect to the lessons of the past and the current-day realities, but face the future. The future will be great; see you there!

The articles reproduced in this book are excellent examples of the "programming and design technique" that Bjarne was talking about. They demonstrate the best uses of C++ and the best design principles to employ.

Analyzing Bjarne's article could be fun. It is clear that he is taking a few lightly veiled pokes at currently popular languages and APIs—and those pokes are certainly appropriate. I happen to like programming in Java from time to time, but I greatly dislike the need for casts whenever I use a container. I happen to think the concept behind COM is cool, but in the C++ API I am horrified by the flagrant use of *void** and unsafe casts to and from various interfaces. These practices represent the worst, not the best, of software engineering in the 90s.

But there is something more profound behind Bjarne's words than simple complaints about languages and APIs. Bjarne says: "Focus on programming and design technique rather than language features and use language features that allow us to express designs directly in code."

Throughout the last three decades, the software industry has been trying to find ways to express designs *outside* the code. Consequently, we invented things like flow charts, data flow diagrams, and UML. Bjarne is saying that we need to express the design directly in the code. This does not preclude diagrams and models, but begs an interesting question. What document is the final authority for the design? Is it the model? Or is it, as Bjarne seems to suggest, the code?

Interestingly enough there is considerable momentum gathering behind a number of lightweight development processes that also claim as a fundamental principle that the design is best expressed in the code. Perhaps the premier of these processes is Extreme Programming (XP). (You can read about XP at http://c2.com/cgi/wiki?ExtremeProgrammingRoadmap.)

What is happening here? Doesn't this contradict the work of the last three decades? Isn't a focus on the code misplaced? Shouldn't code come last, after analysis and design? These folks (and I humbly include myself among them) do not think so. Rather we think that *the code is your product*, and it had better be in the best possible shape at all times. It does not matter how good your analyses and designs are if your code is badly structured. If your code is not as lean, clean, and mean as it can possibly be, if it is not structured to be flexible and maintainable, then your product is inferior.

And this gets me to my pet topic: the nature of the software crisis. Why do so many projects fail? Why is software so hard to maintain? What is wrong with the software industry that we constantly have cost and schedule overruns? Why have we come to accept that a crash once per day is acceptable?

My answer to all these questions is simply this. *As an industry, we do not value the structure of the code we produce*. The only criterion for acceptable code is that it works. If the code works, we ship it. Restructuring and refactoring code *always* takes a back seat to adding new functionality. Yet poorly structured code makes it ever more difficult to add new features. The more the structure of the code falters, the harder new features are to add, and the more likely those new features will further degrade the structure. Eventually the program is so expensive to maintain that release schedules lengthen, development costs soar, and products (and often the companies that make them) fail. The last ten years are littered with such stories.

To make matters worse, users are expecting ever more complexity from the applications we write. There was a time when the average program was less than 10,000 lines. Now the average program is approaching a mega-line. And the big programs are dozens of millions of lines of code.

If we are to survive the next few decades as an industry, our priorities must be reversed. If we are going to succeed in writing the applications for the new millennium, we are going to have to jealously guard the structure of our programs. We are going to have to refactor them mercilessly, in order to keep them clean and well partitioned. We are going to have to absolutely refuse to ship code that is not in the best shape it can be in.

The industry makes lots of noise about architecture. But the industry does not define architecture very well. My definition of architecture is, simply, the structure of the code. If our software has a good architecture, it means that the code has a good clean structure. An architecture-driven project is a project that is driven to keep the structure of the code as clean as possible while adding the features the customers need.

Does that mean we throw out design? Of course not! Rather we express our designs in our code. We make the code be the carrier of the design; and we make the design, and with it the code, clean and well structured.

Does this mean we code instead of building models? No! But it does mean that our models are not the final authority. It also means that our models *are just models* and are not the actual design.

To create well-designed, well-structured code requires good design principles. This book describes a few such principles. More are defined at http://www.objectmentor.com and at http://c2.com/cgi/wiki?PrinciplesOfObjectOrientedDesign. It also requires good design patterns, and you'll find plenty described in the following pages and at http://www.hillside.net. Finally, creating clean code requires good coding techniques. This book contains many articles that discuss such techniques. The reader is also strongly encouraged to read *Refactoring* by Martin Fowler (Addison-Wesley, 1999).

In these pages are some of the best articles on C++ and software engineering that have been published in the last ten years. I am sure many of you will have read them once already in the *C++ Report*. I hope you enjoy reading them again. Some of you may not have read them before. I hope you find them illuminating.

Robert C. Martin
Object Mentor Inc.
www.ObjectMentor.com
Editor-in-Chief
C++ Report

Diamonds from Deep in the Past

Finite State Machines: A Model of Behavior for C++

By Immo Hüneke

In January of 1991, I was working for a telecommunications startup. This was back in the days when the C++ Report *was a plain paper publication with no fancy cover or any of the frills of a 'real' magazine. I was heavily involved with a multitasking system in which the tasks had to communicate with each other using special purpose protocols. These protocols were implemented as finite state machines (FSM).*

I have been using FSMs for many years, and had a standard way of building them. I created data structures that described the state transition table, and then wrote a simple engine that walked and interpreted the table. The table looked something like this:

```
struct Transition
{
  State oldState;
  Event event;
  State newState;
  void (*action)();
};
```

I could then create an array of Transitions, *and when my engine detected an event, it would walk the array, looking for a* Transition *that matched the current state and the event. It would then change the current state to the new state, and call the action function.*

This technique was useful, but also had some disadvantages. Walking the table was slow, especially as the FSM grew in complexity. Using pointers to functions required either ad-hoc arguments, or global functions. This was ugly.

So, one day the C++ Report *landed on my desk. Right on the front cover was the article: "Finite State Machines: A Model of Behavior for C++" by Immo Hüneke. I took the issue down the hall to the only place I could be guaranteed 20 minutes of uninterrupted reading time, sat down on the throne, and started to read.*

By the time I was done, I had a plan. The article described what we now know as the State *pattern from* Design Patterns, *Gamma et al., Addison–Wesley, 1995. I rewrote all my state machines using this format, and was enthralled at how well they worked, and how fast they were.*

But I had many, many more FSMs to write. And the more I wrote, the sicker I got of the entire repeated boiler plate code. I longed for the simplicity of the data table I had discarded.

Then one day, I realized that there was a reason I was disliking all that boiler plate code. Writing it was completely mechanistic. A machine could do it! So I stopped writing that boiler plate code, and instead wrote a little compiler that generated the boiler plate code. The compiler took in a syntax, which was very similar in structure to my old data table, but generated the code as shown in the article.

Thus was born SMC, the State Machine Compiler. I have offered SMC free on my Website for nearly a decade now. It has been downloaded thousands upon thousands of times, and many folks have made good use of it. It is still available on http://www.objectmentor.com.

RALPH HODGSON[1] writes "Reuse depends on the idea of 'plugability.' Compatibility with the architecture of the new application requires our components to behave consistently. . . . Plugablility exists in a framework when there are generalized classes which prescribe a model of behavior . . . for example the Model-View-Controller (MVC) architecture[3,4] . . . Apart from MVC, what other examples of architectures do we know? To progress on methods and reusablility, a taxonomy of components and ways of describing and categorizing architectures are needed."

This paper attempts to provided a partial answer by suggesting an "architecture" for the implementation of Finite State Machines in C++. A small example is given, based on Bill Birch's idea for an FSM parser implemented in LISP with O-O extensions.[2]

Finite State Machines

Finite State Machines are objects characterized by a single state variable which determines all decisions. Incoming events are processed strictly according to the current state of the machine. After each event has been processed, the state is updated. FSMs can be analyzed by various mathematical techniques.

However, once coded, an FSM can be difficult to understand and maintain. Implementations generally resort to nested case statements or employ tables of pointers to functions. In most programming languages, there is no compile-time safeguard that the index into a table or case statement will always be in the correct range.

Object-oriented languages offer a way forward through polymorphism. An FSM can be implemented as an object, which exploits polymorphism to generate different behaviors in response to an event, dependent on the object's current state.

Quote Parser Example

Here is an example of very simple FSM that looks for quoted strings in a character stream, taken from a Bill Birchs paper. It performs the following mapping:

The finite state table for this FSM looks like this:

Events ⇓ *States*⇒	*Inside quotes*	*Outside quotes*
A quote character is received (“”).	Action: output the collected string from the buffer, terminatedby a newline.	Action: reset the collection buffer.
	New state: outside quotes.	New state: Inside quotes.
Any non-quote character is received	Action: add the character to the collection buffer.	Action: none.
	New state: inside quotes.	New state: outside quotes.

The corresponding state transition diagram is shown below.

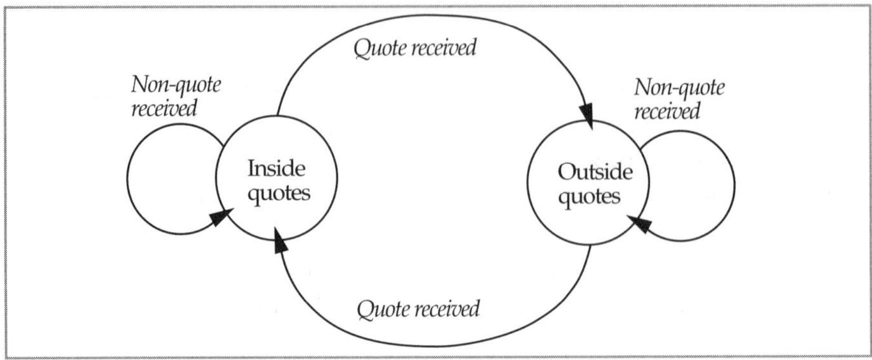

IMPLEMENTATION IN AN OBJECT-ORIENTED LANGUAGE

The language used in the example implementation is C++ release 2.0.

It was decided to represent each FSM and each state by an object. However, multiple instances of the FSM class may co-exist and share a single instance of each state. The states are all subclasses of a single abstract state class. The diagram below attempts to illustrate this idea.

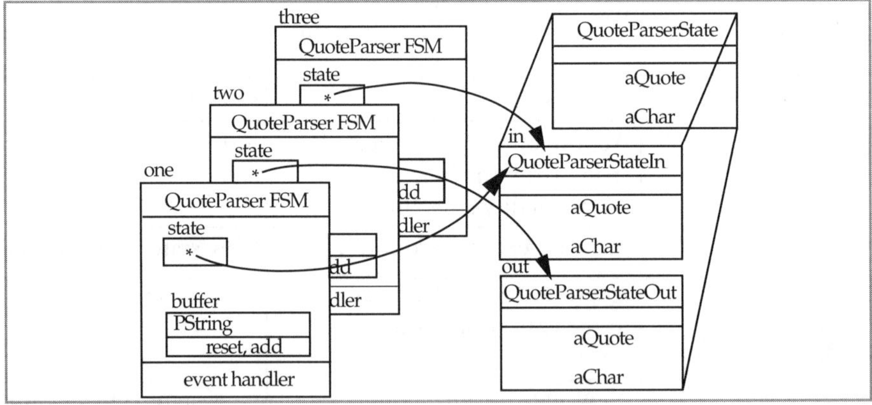

TEST PROGRAM

The program merely has to create an instance of FSM and send a series of events to it. Here it is, in its entirety:

```
# include "qparser.h"
#include "stream.h"
```

```
int main()
{
        char c;
        QuoteParser fsm;

        while (cin.get(c))
                fsm.event(c);
}
```

FSM CLASS

The class is coded in three files. Two of these are headers, the third contains the code for the member functions. First, the class declaration (qparser.h):

```
#ifndef QPARSERH
#define QPARSERH

class QuoteParser {
#include "qparser.hpr" // private/protected members

public:
    QuoteParser();
    virtual void event(char c);
    virtual ~QuoteParser() {delete buffer;}
};

#endif QPARSERH
```

In most practical FSMs, a large proportion of the cells in the tabler contain the entry "error." Such default behavior can be specified once in the abstract class and inherited by all concrete states, overriding only the actions for valid combinations of event and state.

Next the private header file, qparser.hpr:

```
    class QuoteParserState;
    class PString;

protected:
    QuoteParserState* state;
    PString* buffer;
```

The primary interface of QuoteParser to clients is the event handler, QuoteParser : :event ().

Shown below is the implementation of the class, qparser.c. Notice that the event handler first decides what kind of event has been sent to the FSM. It is more usual to identify events outside the FSM itself, and to call a different event handler function for each event type.

Having identified the event, the handler calls the corresponding member function for the current state:

```
     QuoteParserState::aQuote ()
or   QuoteParserState::aChar ().
```

The value returned is the new state (and not just a symbol or code for a state).

Because the member variable state has the type QuoteParserState*, it can store pointers to subclasses of QuoteParserState. It actually points to an instance of either QuoteParserStateIn or QuoteParserStateOut at any particular time. When the call is made, the virtual function table of the called is used to look up the actual function to be executed.

```
#include "qparser.h"
#include "qpstate.h"
#include "pstring.h"

void QuoteParser: : event (char c)
{

        if (c == ' " " ')
                state = state ->aQuote (*buffer);
        else
                state = state ->aChar (*buffer, c);

}
QuoteParser: :QuoteParser ()
{
        state = QuoteParserState: : reset ():
        buffer = new PString;
}
```

The class PString is a "Pascal-like" string, which has better behavior than the standard char*. Not only can characters be added to the end of a PString, other PStrings or characters strings can be appended as well. Moreover, the standard function operator<<() can be used for output, due to the fact that an implicit conversion to char* is provided.

The public declaration of PString is in pstring. h:

```
#ifnedef PSTRINGH
#define PSTRINGH

class Pstring {
#include "pstring.hpr"//private/protected members

public:
        PString();
        virtual void reset(); // empty the string
```

```
        virtual PString& operator+= (char *s);
        virtual operator char* ();
        virtual ~PString ();

};
#endif PSTRINGH
```

Abstract State Class

The abstract state class is required for two reasons.

- It permits the state variable of the FSM to have a polymorphic type which can hold pointers to instances of any state.
- It allows common behavior of the subclasses (i.e. the concrete states) to be generalized to just one place.

The latter point requires some explanation. In most practical FSMs, a large proportion of the cells in the table contain the entry "error." Such default behavior can be specified once in the abstract class and simply inherited by all concrete states, which will override only the actions for valid combinations of event and state.

In some large FSMs it may be useful to generate a hierarchy of abstract states above the concrete states; for example in a communications protocol this would group states which belong to the same phase of a session.

The "public" header file qpstate.h is shown below (notice that no constructor function is needed, as the class contains no non-static member variables):

```
#ifndef QPSTATEH
#define QPSTATEH

class PString;

class QuoteParserState {

#include "qpstate.hpr" // private/protected members
public:
        virtual QuoteParserState* aChar (PString& s, char c)
                {return this;}
        virtual QuoteParserState* aQuote (PString& s)
                {return this;}
        static QuoteParserState* reset() {return out;}
        virtual ~QuoteParserState() {}
};
#endif QPSTATEH
```

Next the "private" header file, qpstate.hpr:

```
protected:
        static QuoteParserState *in, *out;
```

There are two event-handling functions here, both of which define the default behavior (do nothing, keep the same state). The third member function is used to return the initial state for a newly-created FSM.

The purpose of the static member variables is to allow any state to find an instance (the only instance, in fact) of any other state, without resorting to global names. The implementation module for the class, qpstate.c, initializes these member variables:

```
#include "qpstate.h"
#include "qpstin.h"
#include "qpstout.h"

QuoteParserState: : in = new QuoteParserStateIn;
QuoteParserState: : out = new QuoteParserStateOut;
```

No function bodies are required, as all the member functions are coded in line.

CONCRETE STATE CLASSES

The concrete state classes implement the desired behavior of the FSM by redefining the abstract class's event handling functions. The "in quotes" state is presented first. The header file is called qpstin.h:

```
#ifndef QPSTINH
#define QPSTINH
#include "qpstate.h"

class PString;

class Quote ParserStateIn : public QuoteParserState
{

public:
        virtual QuoteParserState* aChar (PString& s, char c);
        virtual QuoteParserState* aQuote (PString& s);
};

#endif QPSTINH
```

This class has no member variables at all. This follows from the fact that the state objects themselves have no state (they are re-entrant), which is a necessary condition if they are to be shared among all FSMs. (Some practical FSMs may incorporate member variables such as statistical counts, so that a management function can check how many times each state has been entered. Such counts would of course represent totals for all FSMs using the state.)

The implementation is in qpstin.c:

```
#include "qpstin.h"
#include "pstring.h"
#include "stram.h"

QuoteParserState*
QuoteParserStateIn::aChar(PString& s, char c)
{
        s += c;
        return this;
}
QuoteParserState*
QuoteParserStateIn::aQuote(PString& s)
{
        cout<< s << "/n";
        return out;
}
```

The “out of quotes” state is even simpler, since it inherits the default action for a non-quote character. The class declaration is in qpstout.h:

```
#ifndef QPSTOUTH
#define QPSTOUTH

#include "qpstate.h"

class PString;

class QuoteParserStateOut : public QuoteParserState {
public:
        virtual QuoteParserState* aQuote (PString& s);
};

#endif QPSTOUTH
```

The implementation is in qpstout.c:

```
#include "qpstout.h"
#include "pstring.h"

QuoteParserState* QuoteParserStateOut: :aQuote(PString& s)
{
        s.reset ();
        return in;
}
```

DISCUSSION

MAINTAINABILITY

This FSM worked first time when it was coded, which may be just a result of its extreme simplicity, but can also be taken as an indication that this approach to the coding of FSMs guards against programming errors.

The fact that each function corresponds to one cell in the table with, action and next-state neatly laid out one after the other, makes it easy to check that the table has been implemented correctly.

The complete absence of programmer-defined symbolic constants makes it possible for the compiler to check the syntactical correctness of the FSM. Errors are still possible, of course:

- Individual action sequences may have been incorrectly coded.
- The table may have been incorrect in the first place.

In the lifetime of an FSM, its behavior may need to be modified in some way. Because a redesign of the table can be laborious using conventional languages, this sometimes leads to code which violates the purely state-driven approach.

The approach described discourages such programming practices, because action routines cannot directly access the internal variables of the FSM class or the buffer.

STORAGE OPTIONS

Data could be stored:

1. In the FSM class (in a member of the FSM object)
2. In the state classes
3. Outside (in some object with global scope).

The static allocation of state objects appears to be the most efficient choice, and has the advantage that there can never be a memory allocation error during a state change. This rules out option (2). Option (3) is ruled out if multiple instances of the FSM are to coexist within a program.

Genericity

It was originally intended to define a generic FSM to act as a base class for more specific FSMs. This class (or set of classes) would therefore be a vehicle for re-use.

In practice, it turns out that C++ does not lend itself easily to this form of re-use. Instead, the most convenient approach is to take an existing FSM class and to use a copy of its source code as the template for a new one.

The reason for this is to be found in the compile-time type checking performed by C++. Unlike Smalltalk-80, in which any message can be sent to any object, C++ checks for type conformance of all arguments and return values.

Because all the member functions of the state classes are application-specific, there is no useful commonality left which could be generalized to an ancestor class. Similarly, the only member function of FSM which could be generalized is `event ()`, but this is of no use because its argument types depend on the application.

Ease of Use

It has been suggested that even with the approach outlined above, large state machines will still be difficult to code and understand. It may therefore be necessary to provide a preprocessor capable of turning input in tabular or state-transition-diagram form into C++ code.

While this may be true, the author believes that a clear object-oriented style of writing FSMs in C++ is nevertheless valuable, irrespective of whether the code was written by machine or by human programmers. For a start, it will aid debugging of the individual action routines.

How does an FSM enter its initial state? For convenience, most state tables contain some event which results in the creation of a new FSM. In reality each FSM is created by some other part of the program in response to an external event. A typical situation is that the program receives a message on a communications link, in response to which a new transaction object is created (an instance of an FSM class).

Provided that this situation is explicitly recognized, a solution can be found in any particular case. In the communications example, a dispatcher object could be created to accept all incoming messages and to create new transaction instances for those messages which do not belong to an existing transaction.

TESTING

Various tools are available for testing FSMs, notably CHOW. These techniques rely on the existence of a state table, which is analyzed in order to generate a list of paths (possible valid sequence of states). Test cases are then generated to force the state machine down each of these paths.

Where such rigorous testing is needed, it is possible (though tedious) to derive a state table in the correct form by inspection of the source code. Given a correct state machine design, however, code written with the technique described can be adequately tested by merely exercising each of the actions.

REFERENCES

1. Hodgson, R. On the Question of the Object-Oriented Method, DRAFT PROCEEDINGS OF **OOPS-30**. March 1990, 50-51.
2. Birch, PW Object-Oriented Finite State Machines. Unpublished paper, March 1990.
3. Knolle, N.T. Variations of Model-View-Controller, **JOOP 2**(3), September 1989, 42-46.
4. Krasner, G.E. and Pope, ST, A Cookbook for Using the Model-View-Controller User Interface Paradigm in Smalltalk-80. **JOOP 1**(3), August 1988, 26-49.

ABSTRACT CLASSES AND PURE VIRTUAL FUNCTIONS

ROBERT C. MARTIN

In August of 1991, I became a consultant. My first client was Rational. I was hired to work on the first release of Rose. By June of '92, the work on Rose was dying down and I had to find other clients. Fortunately, I had begun a campaign of writing many many articles on comp.lang.c++ and comp.object. These articles led to quite a bit of business for me (and still do to this date).

Stan Lippman was the editor of the C++ Report *during this period. I wrote an article entitled "Abstract Classes and Pure Virtual Functions" which I submitted to Stan. He gave me lots and lots (and lots) of editorial feedback, and eventually published it. It was my very first foray into the world of article publishing.*

The article makes use of the original form of Booch's notation (from Object Oriented Design with Applications, *Benjamin Cummings, 1991) But don't fault it for that. The advice it gives is still as true today as it was in '92. In it, you will find the seeds of what eventually became the Dependency Inversion Principle (DIP) (*C++ Report, *May 1996, http://www.objectmentor.com).*

The article also mentions the term "Factoring" as a technique for modifying inheritance hierarchies. Though I am sure that I did not originate the term, this may be one of the first times it appeared in print. Now, of course, we talk more about refactoring, *but the roots are evident.*

Also in this article I discuss the notion of adding an "abstract" keyword to C++, in order to explicitly declare a class abstract. In the article I reject the notion as redundant. Apparently, the Java designers did not agree with me.

Finally, there is an interesting discussion of pure virtual destructors in the article. These bizarre creatures are still part of the C++ syntax, and are very useful, but are often misunderstood.

While it is true that all objects are represented by a class, the converse is not true. All classes do not necessarily represent objects. It is possible, and often desirable, for a class to be insufficient to completely represent an object. Such classes are called abstract classes.

The illustrations used in this article conform to the "Booch Notation" for object-oriented design, a rich and expressive notation that is very useful for presenting OOD concepts. Where necessary, I will digress to explain some of this notation.

What Is an Abstract Class?

Simply stated, an abstract class is a class that does not fully represent an object. Instead, it represents a broad range of different classes of objects. However, this representation extends only to the features those classes of objects have in common. Thus, an abstract class provides only a partial description of its objects.

Because abstract classes do not fully represent an object, they cannot be instantiated. At first, it may seem a little odd that a class is incapable of having any instances. But everyday life is full of such classes. For example, we may describe a particular animal as belonging to the class of all mammals, but we will never see an instance of the class Mammal—at least not a pure instance. Every animal belonging to the class Mammal must also belong to a class which is subordinate to Mammal such as Mouse, Dog, Human, or Platypus. That is because the class Mammal does not fully represent any animal. In object-oriented design, we will never see an instance of an abstract class unless it is also an instance of a subordinate class. This is because the abstract class does not fully represent any object. As Booch says, "An abstract class is written with the expectation that its subclasses will add to its structure and behavior...."[1]

The icon in Figure 1 represents a class. Note the zero in the lower left corner. This represents the cardinality of the class, or the number of instances that the class can support. Since this class can support zero instances, it is abstract.

According to Rumbaugh, "Abstract classes organize features common to several classes."[2] What are the common features mentioned by Rumbaugh? They are features of the class's interface. For example, consider the classes Window and Door. At first glance, these classes may not seem to have any-

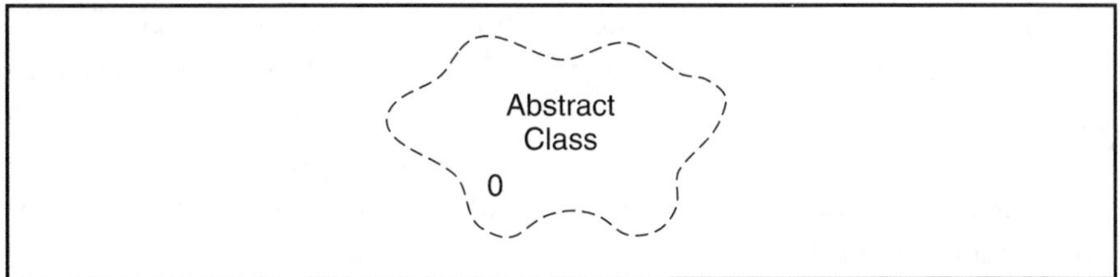

Figure 1. The zero represents the cardinality of the class; this class is abstract, since it can support zero instances.

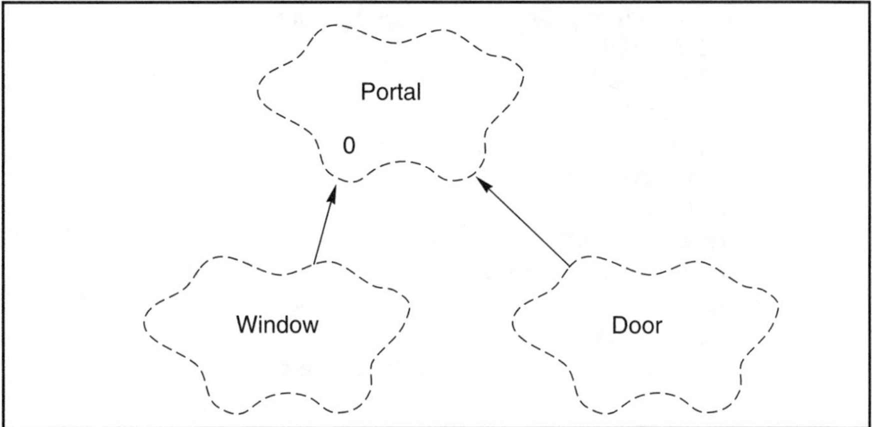

Figure 2. Both Window *and* Door *inherit from a common abstract base.*

thing to do with each other. But both share some interesting common features. They are both holes in a wall. They both have particular locations and sizes with respect to the wall. They both may exist in one of three states: {OPEN, CLOSED, LOCKED}. Finally, they can be sent similar messages: {open, close, lock}. Thus, we can describe both classes as inheriting from a common abstract base, Portal, which contains all the common features of their interface (Figure 2).

Stereotypes and Polymorphism

Notice how this allows Window and Door objects to be stereotyped. They can both be referred to as Portals. While this is an incomplete description of both objects, it is nonetheless accurate and useful. This ability to stereotype an object is a powerful design tool. It allows us to bundle all the common aspects of a set of objects together into an abstract class. As Lippman says, "[An abstract class] provides a common public interface for the entire class hierarchy."[3] This common interface allows us to treat all such objects according to the stereotype. While such treatment may not be socially acceptable when dealing with humans, it provides for great efficiency when dealing with software objects.

For example, consider the Door and Window classes when they do not inherit a common base:

```
class Window
{
 public:
  enum WindowState {open, closed, locked};
      void Open();
      void Close();
      void Lock();
      void GetState() const;
      int GetXPos() const;
      int GetYPos() const;
      int GetHeight() const;
      int GetWidth() const;
private:
      WindowState itsState;
      int itsXpos, itsYpos, itsWidth, itsHeight;
};

class Door
{
 public:
      enum DoorState {open, closed, locked};
      void Open();
      void Close();
      void Lock();
      void GetState() const;
      int GetXPos() const;
      int GetYPos() const;
      int GetHeight() const;
      int GetWidth() const;
 private:
      DoorState itsState;
      int itsXPos, itsYPos, itsWidth, itsHeight;
};
```

These two classes are horribly redundant. They cry for some form of unification. That unification is supplied by creating the abstract base class.

```
class Portal
{
 public:
    enum PortalState {open, closed, locked};
    virtual void Open() = 0;
    virtual void Close() = 0;
    virtual void Lock() = 0;
    void GetState() const;
    int GetXPos() const;
    int GetYPos() const;
    int GetHeight() const;
    int GetWidth() const;
 private:
    PortalState itsState;
    int itsXPos, itsYPos, itsWidth, itsHeight;
};

class Window : public Portal
{
 public:
        virtual void Open();
        virtual void Close();
        virtual void Lock();

};

class Door : public Portal
{
 public:
        virtual void Open();
        virtual void Close();
        virtual void Lock();
};
```

The efficiency that we gained is obvious. Several of the Portal member functions can be reused. The declarations for Door and Window are terse and understandable in terms of the functionality of Portal. Moreover, both Window and Door can be stereotyped as a Portal when convenient. For example:

```
void TornadoWarning(List<Portal*> thePortals)
{
    ListIterator<Portal*> i(thePortals);
    for (; !i.Done(); i++)
    {
```

```
            (*i) ->Open();
        }
    }
```

Forgive the obvious license with the semantics of the ListIterator. Clearly this method for opening all Doors and Windows is superior to handling each type separately. As the application matures, more types of Portals will probably be added. But since the TornadoWarning function deals with all species of Portals, it will not have to change. Thus, the polymorphic behavior of the abstract class Portal provides a more maintainable and robust design.

It should be stressed that forcing Door and Window to inherit from Portal is not necessary to the proper functioning of the application. The application could be designed without the abstract class. However, creating the abstract Portal class results in a superior design that promotes polymorphism and code reuse.

DESIGNING APPLICATIONS WITH ABSTRACT CLASSES

During the first stages of a design, we usually have a good idea of the concrete classes that we need. As the design is refined, we should begin to find common features among some of these classes. These common features are not always obvious. They may come from different parts of the design, and may have different names and configurations. It sometimes takes a careful eye to spot them.

For example, let's say Jim, Bill and Bob are working on the design of the software that will control a car crushing machine. Jim is responsible for the control panel, Bill for the hydraulics control and Bob for the servo motors.

Jim has designed an Indicator class for the control panel. It looks like this:

```
class Indicator
{
 public:
    enum IndicatorState {on,off};
    Indicator(const IndicatorAddress&)
    void TurnOn();
    void TurnOff();
    IndicatorState GetState() const;
};
```

Bill has designed a Valve class for controlling the hydraulics. It looks like this:

```
class Valve
{
 public:
    enum ValveState {open, closed};
    Valve(const ValveAddress&)
    void Open();
    void Close();
    int IsValveOpen() const;
    double GetFlowRate() const;
};
```

Bob has designed a Motor class for controlling the servos. It has the following interface:

```
class Motor
{
 public:
    enum MotorState {running, stopped};
    Motor(const MotorAddress&)
    void SetState(const MotorState);
    MotorState GetState() const;
    Void SetSpeed(int);
    int GetSpeed() const;

};
```

In this simple example, the common features aren't too hard to find. Each of these classes has a binary state, and methods to alter and interrogate that state. The forms and names of these methods are dissimilar, but their functions are common. Thus, we can create an abstract base class Actuator which defines the common points of each:

```
class Actuator
{
 public:
    enum ActuatorState {on, off};
    Actuator();
    virtual void Activate() = 0;
    virtual void Deactivate() = 0;
    ActuatorState GetState() const;
};

class Indicator : public Actuator
```

```
    {
        Indicator(const IndicatorAddress&);
        virtual void Activate();
        virtual void Deactivate();
    };

    class Valve : public Actuator
    {
        Valve(const ValveAddress&);
        virtual void Activate();
        virtual void Deactivate();
        double GetFlowRate() const;
    };

    class Motor : public Actuator
    {
     public:
        Motor(const MotorAddress&);
        virtual void Activate();
        virtual void Deactivate();
        void SetSpeed(int);
        int GetSpeed() const;
};
```

In a more complex application, commonality can be much harder to detect. The names and forms of the methods can disguise the intrinsic similarities. Thus, care should be exercised in the search for commonality. The effort spent in the search will be paid back with a more maintainable design which supports a higher degree of code reuse.

FACTORING

In the **Actuator** example, we found the common features of the concrete classes and promoted them to the abstract base. Rebecca Wirfs-Brock, et al. calls this factoring and goes on to state a profound principle of object-oriented design: Factor common responsibilities as high as possible. The higher in the inheritance hierarchy common features can be factored, the more chances for reuse and polymorphism are engendered.

Have we factored the features in the example high enough? Our example didn't have very many features, but there is still room for some more factoring. It seems unlikely that the **Motor** class will be the only class requiring a speed setting. So we might want to create an abstract subclass of **Actuator** with methods for handling speed. However, speed is just a variable quantity. We can generalize it by creating the abstract class VariableActuator (Figure 3). This provides us with the opportunity to derive other variable-controlled actuators from the common base. For example, we could create a variable brightness lamp or a variable speed fan.

Evolution of Concrete Classes

As the iterative process of design continues to add more and more detail to the application model, classes which had been concrete will tend to become abstract. As we incorporate more of the details of the application into the design, classes which had been specific become the generalities for the new details.

For example, as the car crusher design proceeds, Bill discovers he needs a safety valve that opens automatically when a pressure limit is exceeded. Bill could simply derive SafetyValve from the current Valve class. However, this assumes that the SafetyValve is going to share all the features of the simple valve. This may not be the case. Bill might be better off creating an abstract

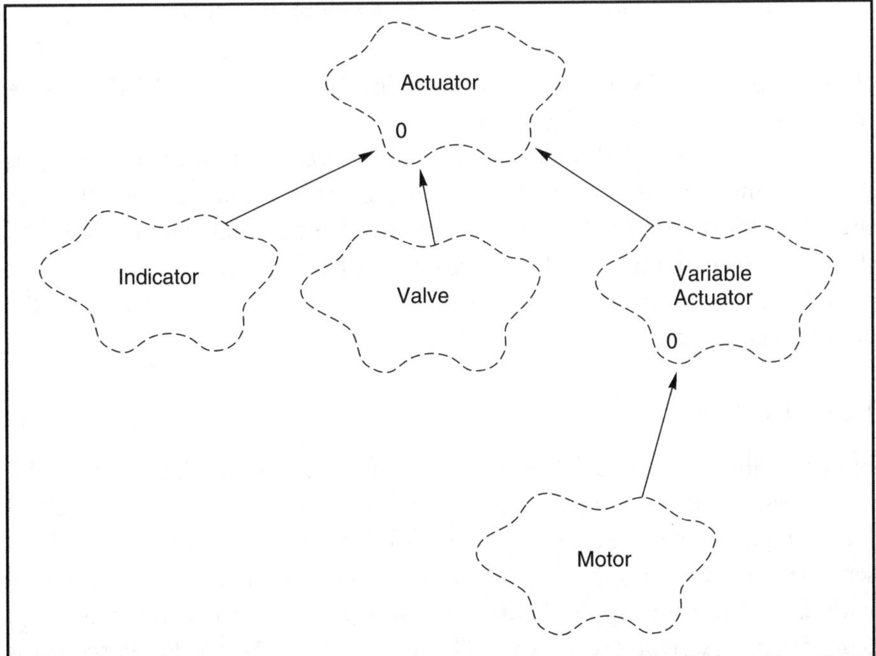

Figure 3. The general features of a variable actuator are factored out of Motor.

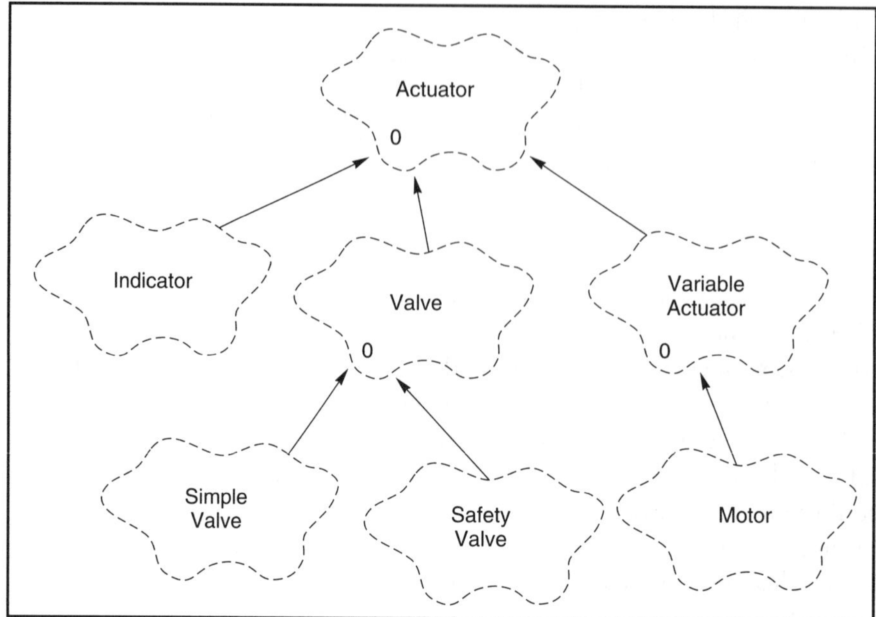

Figure 4. The Valve *class has evolved into an abstract class supplying a common interface for the* SafetyValve *and* SimpleValve *classes.*

class to represent all valves, and then deriving SimpleValve and SafetyValve from that common base (Figure 4).

By taking this tack, Bill has created a generalization that fits not only his existing concrete valve classes, but any new valve class that may be needed in the future. This process of factoring common elements higher and higher into the inheritance hierarchy as the design progresses is typical. As more details are added to the design, more abstract classes are created to deal with the common generalities.

PURE INTERFACES

Note that abstract classes define features common to the interfaces of their derived classes. But what implantation should be provided by the abstract class? For example, what is the implementation for Actuator::Activate()? There is no sensible implementation! It is only the derived classes that know how to deal with the Activate method. Indicator::Activate() turns on a real indicator lamp. SimpleValve::Activate() causes a real life valve to open. Motor:Activate() turns on a real motor. But Actuator::Activate() can't do anything because it doesn't have anything "real" to interface to. Thus, Actuator::Activate() is a pure interface devoid of any implementation. It is the pure interfaces within an abstract class which define the common features encapsulated within it. They are the basis for the polymorphic behavior of abstract classes. The impure interfaces, those interfaces which have implementations, contain the code which is reused by all the derived classes.

Pure Virtual Functions

In C++, pure interfaces are created by declaring pure virtual functions. A pure virtual function is declared as follows:

```
virtual void Activate() = 0;
```

The "=0" on the end of the declaration is supposed to represent the fact that the function has no implementation. However, as we will see, implementations are sometimes provided.

In C++, a class with a pure virtual function is an abstract class. The language provides special semantics for abstract classes. It enforces the constraint that abstract classes cannot have any instances. Thus, the compiler will not allow an instance of an abstract class to be created. If you attempt to declare or create one, the compiler will complain:

```
Actuator myActuator; // error
Actuator* myActuator = new Actuator; // error;
```

This constraint does not, however, prevent you from declaring pointers and references to abstract classes. The compiler allows such constructs, and will allow them to refer to instances of concrete classes which have the abstract class somewhere in their inheritance hierarchy.

```
Actuator* myActuator = new Indicator;
Actuator& anActuator = *(new Indicator);
```

Such pointers and references are very useful for taking advantage of the polymorphic attributes of abstract classes. The pure virtual functions of the abstract class are bound to the implementations defined in the instances to which they refer.

```
myActuator->Activate(); // Turn on indicator.
anActuator.Deactivate(); // Turn off indicator.
```

Including a pure virtual function in a class is the only way to tell the compiler that the class is abstract. This is sometimes considered to be a limitation. It has been suggested that an "abstract" keyword be added to the language so that classes could explicitly be declared abstract.

```
abstract class Actuator; // suggested syntax.
```

However, in my opinion, this would create a redundancy in the language. A truly abstract class must contain a pure interface; otherwise, it would be instantiable.

INHERITING PURE VIRTUAL FUNCTIONS

Pure virtual functions behave differently depending upon the version of the compiler you are using. cfront 2.0 did not allow pure virtual functions to be inherited by derived classes. If the base class had a pure virtual function, then that function had to be declared in the derived classes, either in pure form or in impure form. Thus:

```
class Valve : public Actuator
{
 public:
 virtual void Activate() = 0;
 virtual void Deactivate() = 0;
};
```

This restriction was relaxed in version 2.1 of the compiler, so pure virtual function can be inherited without specifically being declared. If they are not declared in the derived class, they are inherited in pure form, making the derived class abstract.

```
class Valve : public Actuator
{
// This class is abstract.
// It inherits the pure virtual functions
// Activate() and Deactivate()
};
```

INSTANCES OF ABSTRACT CLASSES

Although it is impossible to explicitly create an instance of an abstract class, such instances can temporarily exist during construction or destruction. Instances under construction are only as complete as the currently executing constructor has made them. Instances under destruction are only as complete as the executing destructor has left them. Because these instances are incomplete, the language prevents the virtual mechanism from calling any virtual functions in classes which either have not yet been constructed, or have already been destructed. What might happen if a pure virtual function of such an incomplete object were called?

The language specification (ARM 10.3) says that calling a pure virtual function from a constructor of destructor is undefined. This means that if f() is defined as pure virtual in class C, then calling f() from a constructor or destructor of C is an error.

For example, let us assume that the designer of Actuator wanted to initialize the instance in the deactivated state. To do this he called Deactivate() in the constructor:

```
Actuator::Actuator()
{
   Deactivate();
}
```

But Deactivate() is defined as pure virtual in Actuator. So this is an error. In fact, it is an error that compilers can easily detect, so most will issue some kind of error message. However, it is unreasonable to expect a compiler to detect all the myriad ways in which pure virtual functions can be invoked from constructors or destructors. The error can be hidden by a slight, and very reasonable modification to the example above.

```
class Actuator
{
 public:
  enum ActuatorState {on, off};
        Actuator();
  virtual void Activate() = 0;

   virtual void Deactivate() = 0;
   ActuatorState GetState() const;
 private:
   void Init();
};

Actuator::Actuator()
{
   Init();
}
```

```
void Actuator::Init()
{
   Deactivate();
}
```

Here, the designer has quite reasonably created a **private Init()** function which will be called by the constructor. **Init** calls **Deactivate** in order to initialize the device in the "deactivated" state.

The same bug still exists. **Deactivate()** will still be called within the context of the **Actuator** constructor. But this time, the compiler will probably not complain. Thus, when an **Indicator** is created, the call to **Deactivate** will attempt to invoke a nonexistent implementation, and will very likely crash.

PURE VIRTUAL IMPLEMENTATIONS

Sometimes it is convenient for a pure virtual function to have an implementation. C++ allows this. The implementation is coded in exactly the same way as the implementation of any other member function:

```
void Actuator::Activate()
{
   /* Do something clever here */
}
```

There are not very many good reasons to supply implementations for pure virtual function. After all, a pure virtual function represents a pure interface whose implementation would make no sense in the context of the abstract class. But sometimes there are exceptions.

For example, assume we have a virtual function **IsValid** which checks the instance to see if it is in a valid state. The general form of such a function will be:

```
class MyClass : public MyBase
{
typedef MyBase superclass;
public:
          int IsValid() const;
                    /* ... */
};

int MyClass::IsValid() const
{
  int retval = 0;
  if (superclass::IsValid())
  {
```

```
        if (/* I am valid */)
        {
            retval = 1;
        }
    }

    return retval;
}
```

Note the call to the super class. When IsValid is called for an instance, it checks to see if the portion of the instance which is described by its base class (superclass) is valid. If so it checks its own parts and returns 1 if they are OK, and 0 if they are not. Each IsValid function in each of the base classes repeats this procedure. Thus, when IsValid is called for an instance, the call is passed all the way up the inheritance hierarchy.

Now, let's presume that the base most class of the hierarchy is as follows:

```
class Validatable
{
 protected:
        virtual int IsValid() = 0;
};
```

In other words, the abstract base class describes the set of all classes which have IsValid functions.

Can the immediate derivatives of Validatable obey the IsValid protocol by passing the call up to their superclass (i.e., Validatable)? This would be very desirable since we don't want to have one convention for immediate derivatives of Validatable, and another for its indirect derivatives. If at all possible, we want all the derivatives of Validatable to use the same form for IsValid().

Fortunately, the ARM (10.3) allows implementations of pure virtual function to be called explicitly by using their qualified name, i.e., (Validatable::IsValid()). Thus, if we supply the following implementation for the pure virtual function Validatable:IsValid(), then the immediate derivatives of Validatable can obey the superclass protocol.

```
int Validatable::IsValid()
{
        return 1;
}
```

PURE VIRTUAL DESTRUCTORS

There is one aspect of pure virtual functions which the language specification does not define very well. This is the behavior of pure virtual destructors. Pure virtual destructors are an oddity. They are, I suspect, an accident of syntax rather than a designed feature. They look like this:

```
class OddClass
{
 public:
       virtual ~OddClass()=0; // valid but strange.
};
```

A destructor is not a normal function, it cannot be inherited (ARM 12.4), it cannot be overridden and it cannot be hidden. A virtual destructor is not a normal virtual function. It does not share the same name as the base class destructor, and it is not inherited. A pure virtual function is meant to be inherited, it is the interface for a feature which is to be defined in a derived class. So what is a pure virtual destructor? It is not an interface for a destructor which is to be defined by a derived class, because destructors cannot be inherited. It is not a function without an implementation, because it will be called as the destructor for the class, and so it must be implemented. The only guaranteed feature of a pure virtual destructor is that it makes the class that contains it abstract.

USING ABSTRACT CLASSES

Although programs are not allowed to instantiate abstract classes, in every other way they can be used to manipulate normal objects. Classes may contain pointers or references to abstract classes.

```
class ActuatorTimer
{
 public:
   ActuatorTimer(Actuator&);
   void SetTimer(int);
   int GetTimer() const;
   void Start();
private:
   Actuator& itsActuator;
};
```

This declaration shows the interface of a class which will activate an actuator for a specified period of time, and then turn it off again. Any derivative of Actuator can be used as an argument to the ActuatorTimer constructor. The specified Actuator will be polymorphically activated and deactivated by the ActuatorTimer class.

Summary

Abstract classes provide a powerful design technique which promotes code reuse and polymorphism. According to Coplien, "The power of the object paradigm in supporting reuse lies in abstract base classes."[5] Abstract classes are produced by factoring out the common features of the concrete classes of the application. Although such factorings are sometimes hard to find, the effort put into finding them is usually well worth the benefits of the extra maintainability and reusability. In general, common features should be factored out and moved as high as possible in the inheritance structure.

In C++, pure virtual functions are used to specify the pure interfaces of abstract classes. An abstract class in C++ must have at least one pure virtual function. Although pure virtual functions typically have no implementations, C++ allows implementations to be given to them. The user must take care not to invoke pure virtual functions in the constructors or destructors of an abstract class.

Although abstract classes cannot be instantiated, they can be used in every other way to represent normal objects. They can be contained or passed by reference, and their interface can be used to invoke their intrinsically polymorphic behavior.

References

1. Booch, G. Object-oriented design with applications, Benjamin/Cummings, 1991.
2. Rumbaugh, et al. Object-oriented modeling and design, Prentice-Hall, Englewood Cliffs, NJ, 1991.
3. Lippman, S. C++ Primer, 2d edition, Addison-Wesley, Reading, MA, 1991.
4. Wirfs-Brock, R., et al. Designing object-oriented software, Prentice-Hall, Englewood Cliffs, NJ, 1990.

5. Coplien, J. Advanced C++ programming styles and idioms, Addison-Wesley, Reading, MA, 1992.

MEMORY MANAGEMENT AND SMART POINTERS

CAY S. HORSTMANN

*My consulting business was doing quite well by early 1993, and I was under contract with Prentice Hall to write my first book (*Designing Object Oriented C++ Applications using the Booch Method, *Robert C. Martin, Prentice Hall, 1995). These were exciting times for me. (As are current times). I remember this article quite well, because I had several clients who were complaining to me about the need for smart pointers in C++, and the difficulty of writing them. When I read this article, I immediately forwarded copies to these clients. They found the article quite useful and implemented Cay's ideas.*

This was not the only time I was to be rescued by one of Cay's articles. I remember another article from May of 1994 entitled "Extending the iostream Library". This article showed how to make an iostream that put characters into a scrolling window Windows 3.1. I was deeply immersed in a W3.1 project at the time and immediately grabbed Cay's source code and implemented a nice debug window.

WHEN PROGRAMMING IN a PC environment, memory management is a much greater concern than under UNIX. First of all, there isn't enough of it. The original IBM PC had an address space of one megabyte, of which the lower 640K were made available to the operating system and application programs. The remaining 384K were reserved for graphics adapters, the boot and system ROM and free space for third-party plug-in cards. Sadly, when processors with a larger address space became available in PCs, the operating system never caught up, and to this day, all DOS programmers must cram their code into the dreaded 640K limit. Some relief is available through various "extended" and "expanded" memory schemes.[1] All these schemes are complex and open up a hornet's nest of programming and compatibility problems. In addition, some compilers restrict the total size of the static data to one 64K segment. The situation is only now improving, since Windows (in enhanced mode) and OS/2 offer essentially unlimited address space and virtual memory.

Not only isn't there enough memory, but the available memory is poorly protected. The 80386 processor (and above) implement sensible segment protection. (PC programmers may wince at this endorsement of segments. There is nothing wrong with segments; in fact, they are good since they let the processor watch for transgressions. What is bad about the 8086-style segments is their limitation to 64K bytes. Then again, those 64K segments were introduced, originally, for upward compatibility with the 8080 processor. I guess we C++ programmers can't complain too much about design compromises motivated by compatibility considerations. . . .) But DOS doesn't run in 386 mode, it runs in "real" mode, in which all memory access (within the 1 MB address space) is completely unprotected. A UNIX programmer who mistakenly indirects through an uninitialized pointer has a fair chance of getting a core dump. A debugger such as `dbxtool` can then read the core file and pinpoint the offending line in the source code. In DOS, this is plainly impossible. A wild pointer will simply overwrite memory, maybe crashing the entire system by clobbering an interrupt table, or causing mysterious program behavior many thousands of instructions later.

Many DOS compilers have an amusing strategy to warn against indirection through a null pointer. (Recall that the processor does not protect against that in "real" mode.) The first few bytes of the data segment are preloaded with some pattern by the program entry code, and the exit code checks if the pattern is undistributed. If not, the message "null pointer assignment" is generated. In the old days, my students were much relieved when I told them that the null pointer assignment must have occurred somewhere between the first and last line of `main()`. Nowadays, I can't even tell them that —constructors or destructors of global objects may have been the culprit.

Pointer errors are serious business. Tracking down a subtle pointer error can take days, especially in the DOS environment without sophisticated tools, and cost hundreds or thousands of dollars in programmer time alone, not counting lost profits from the delay. I recently consulted with a group of programmers in C++, and they made the usual pointer errors in program exercises. The manager was very perturbed by that, especially since C++ programs typically perform more free store allocation than C or Pascal programs. They ended up choosing Smalltalk instead. For them, the choice between error-prone manual memory management and slower garbage collection was clear.

In this column, I will not review any commercial products, but will discuss several strategies that are useful in C++ memory management, with special emphasis on the DOS environment.

Smart Pointers

With some effort, it is possible to design C++ classes that behave like pointers to other classes. The key to this is the overloaded -> operator. This operator acts completely differently from all other C++ overloaded operators. At first glance, it seems odd that -> can be overloaded at all. It is not your typical binary operator. Consider an expression

```
p->m
```

where `p` is a "smart pointer" class. Note that `m` is not an object of some class, but the name of a structure member. In fact, in C++ the overloaded -> is a unary operation, returning a pointer to another class, and `p->m` really means

```
(p.operator->())->m
```

Actually, `p.operator->` could return an object of another class for which -> is overloaded, as long as a pointer to a structure is eventually obtained.

In addition, the unary* operator can be overloaded to yield the object to which the smart pointer points (or a reference thereto). In theory, one could overload + and - to achieve pointer arithmetic, but since pointer arithmetic tends to be an error-prone feature of the C language, it seems best not to.

More importantly, smart pointer classes often overload the assignment operator (and the copy constructor) to keep track of the number of smart pointers pointing to an object. We will discuss this in detail in the next section.

As a warm-up for the next section, consider this template for a pointer class. `Pointer<X>` is a somewhat smart pointer to an arbitrary class `X`.

```
template <class X>
struct Pointer
{
    Pointer() : stor(0) {}
    Pointer( X* p) : stor(p) {}
    X* operator->(){assert(stor) ; return stor; }
    X* operator->() const{assert( stor ) ; return stor; }
    X&operator* (){assert( stor ) ; return *stor; }
    const X& operator* () const{assert( stor ); return *stor; }
    operator const void* () const{ return stor ? this : 0; }
private:
    X* stor;
};
```

Except for the type declaration, you use these pointers the same way as regular pointers:

```
Pointer<Employee> pe=
    new Employee ("Harry Hacker", "149-16-2536");
strcpy (s, pe-> name());
Employee harry = *pe;
```

The pointers are smarter for two reasons. First, they are always initialized to 0, not to some random value. And any attempt to indirect through a 0 pointer yields an assertion failure.

Note the type of conversion to const void*. We wish to encapsulate the X* pointer and hence do not provide a conversion to X*. (We hope that nobody will code & *p.) But we still would like to allow Boolean tests:

```
if(p == 0) . . .
```

The const void* conversion merely returns some nonzero pointer if p is conceptually non-null. We return the this pointer rather than the stor pointer to eliminate any attempts at surreptitiously casting the const void* to an X*. (Why not convert to int for Boolean tests and return 0 for null pointers, and 1 otherwise? There are many legal operations on integers, and automatic conversions to int might be invoked although it was not intended. For example, if Array<X> is an array template with a constructor Array<X>(int n) making an array of n elements, then the initialization Array<X> a = p would compile even though it makes no sense—a would have 0 or 1 element.)

How about a ~Pointer<X> destructor? Wouldn't it be desirable if the memory to which p goes out of scope? This question brings us to our next topic.

Reference Counting

When allocating memory from the free store, it is easy to make two common errors. A memory leak occurs if memory is allocated, but not subsequently freed. Memory leaks are particularly serious for programs that run for a long time since they may eventually cause exhaustion of all available memory. Even more serious are dangling pointers. When a memory block is returned to the heap, but a pointer to that block continues to be used at a later time, something catastrophic is bound to happen as that pointer may now point to completely different user data or even an internal part of the heap management data structure. These errors are notoriously difficult to debug.

Reference counting is a simple scheme to minimize allocation errors. Each allocated block keeps a count of the number of pointers that point to it. When copying pointers, the count is incremented. When a pointer goes out of scope, the count is decremented. Only when the count goes to zero is the block recycled to the free store.

If the reference counts had to be kept manually, this mechanism would be somewhat error-prone since the programmer would have to remember to update the reference count every time an object containing a pointer was copied or destroyed. But in C++, the process can be completely automated by defining suitable assignment operators, copy constructors, and destructors. The method has been well publicized for many years,[2,3] but it has had remarkably little impact on commercially available class libraries. It is not clear why. Reference counts are easy to code, and they could have saved both Borland and Microsoft from embarrassing copying problems with their container classes.

It is true that reference counting is somewhat tedious to set up manually. The key to success is to have an automatic delivery mechanism. Templates are ideal for this purpose. Here is a template Rc_Pointer<X> that provides a reference counted pointer to objects of an existing class X:

```
template< class X >
struct Rc_Pointer
{
    Rc_Pointer():stor(0){}
    Rc_Pointer ( x* p ):stor(new Stor(p) ){}
    Rc_Pointer(const Rc_Pointer& b)
        { if (( stor = b.stor )!= 0 ) stor->rc++;}
    const Rc_Pointer& operator= ( const Rc_Pointer& b)
```

```
        {
            if ( b.stor ) b.stor->rc++;
            free ();
            stor = b.stor;
            return *this;
        }
        ~Rc_Pointer () { free (); }
        X* operator->()
            {assert( stor ); return stor->pval; }
        const X* operator*-> () const
            { assert( stor ); return stor->pval; }
        X& operator*( )
            { assert ( stor ); return *(stor->pval);}
        const X& operator* () const
            {assert( stor ) ; return *(stor->pval); }
        operator const void* () const
            { return stor ? this : 0; }
private:
        struct Stor
        {
            unsigned rc;
            x* pval;
            Stor( X* px ) : rc( 1), pval ( px )
                { assert( pval ) ; }
            ~Stor () { delete pval ; }
        };
        void free ()
            { if ( stor && -stor-> rc == 0 ) delete stor; }
        Stor* stor;
};
```

This does look somewhat forbidding (which is exactly why you only want to figure it out only once). But using the template is very easy:

```
Rc_Pointer<Employee> pe =
        new Employee ( "Helmut Hollerith", "135-44-8876");
Rc_Pointer<Employee> qe;
qe = pe;
```

Now qe and pe point to the same block of memory, and the reference count is two. When both pe and qe (and any other copies of the pointer that may have been made later) go out of scope, the **Employee** object is finally deleted from the free store. The copy constructor, assignment operator and destructor of the Rc_Pointer<Employee> structure take care of updating the counts.

The real benefit comes if such a pointer is embedded in another structure. For example:

```
struct Manager
{ // . . .
private:
        Rc_Pointer<Employee> secretary;
        // . . .
};
```

The nontrivial copy semantics of Rc_Pointer<Employee> is automatically preserved by the Manager structure: If objects of type Manager are copied or destroyed, the reference counts of the secretary storage are correctly updated. (This works because of the memberwise definition of copying, assignment, and destruction, a feature present in C++ since release 2.0. Caveat emptor: Early releases of some C++ compilers got this wrong, especially with inline replacements. Of course, this has an absolutely disastrous effect on code relying on this feature and leads to incredibly frustrating debugging sessions. It pays to have test scaffolding, with some classes that print diagnostic messages upon construction and destruction. Hopefully, in the future, there will be validation suites that measure compliance in this subtle area.)

The implementation of the Rc_Pointer template is shown in Figure 1. It would have been tempting to do the simpler layout shown in Figure 2 instead.

That would have saved one level of indirection. But the trouble is that this particular template has the mission of adding reference counts to an existing class X. For example, we added reference counts to a preexisting Employee class with a constructor Employee (const char[], const char[]). And the

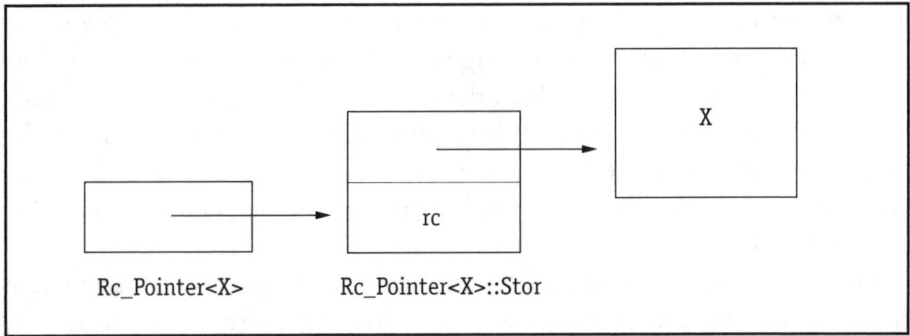

Figure 1. Implementation of the Rc_Pointer *template.*

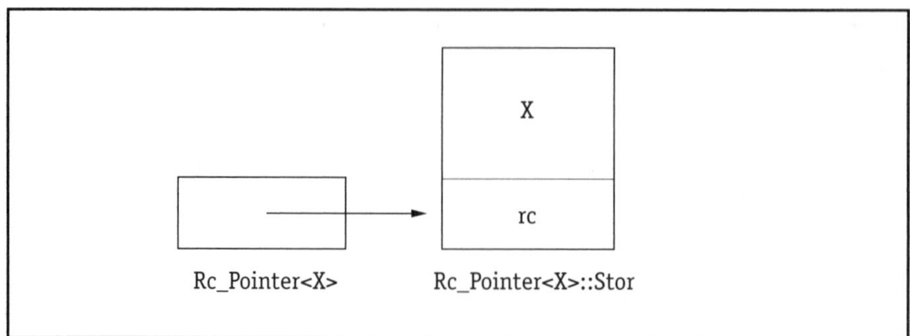

Figure 2. Simplified Layout.

Rc_Pointer<X>::Stor class (which combines the reference count and an X object) cannot pick up constructors (except for the default and copy constructor) from the class X.

If classes are designed with reference counts in mind from the start (rather than having the reference counts added in later), one can do a better job. This can be automated with a slightly different template, as we will see in the next section.

It should be pointed out that reference counting, for all its benefits, suffers from two problems. First, if an object has a very large number of pointers pointing to it, one must take care that the reference count does not exceed the largest representable unsigned integer. One could modify the code updating the reference counts to keep such objects alive forever. Naturally, this problem is rare. The other problem is more serious. Some objects contain counted pointers to other objects of the same type so that the pointers form a cycle. Consider the example given in Figure 3.

Once the pointer on the stack goes out of scope, the reference count of the first object is decremented to one, and the cycle of three objects, which has no external reference any more, is kept alive forever. This illustrates the difference between reference counting and true garbage collection. For some data structures, such as graphs, this is a serious problem, and simple reference counts are not useful for managing such memory configurations. But there are many applications where data is ordered in some hierarchy, with counted pointers only pointing from higher-level objects to lower-level objects, and reference counting is guaranteed to work. In particular, this hierarchical ordering holds for strongly typed container classes (List<X>, HashTable<X>, Array<X>, etc.,).

One note on the implementation of the template. It appears use-full to have classes Handle and Stor that contain all the basic reference count management, and then derive Rc_Pointer<X> from Handle:

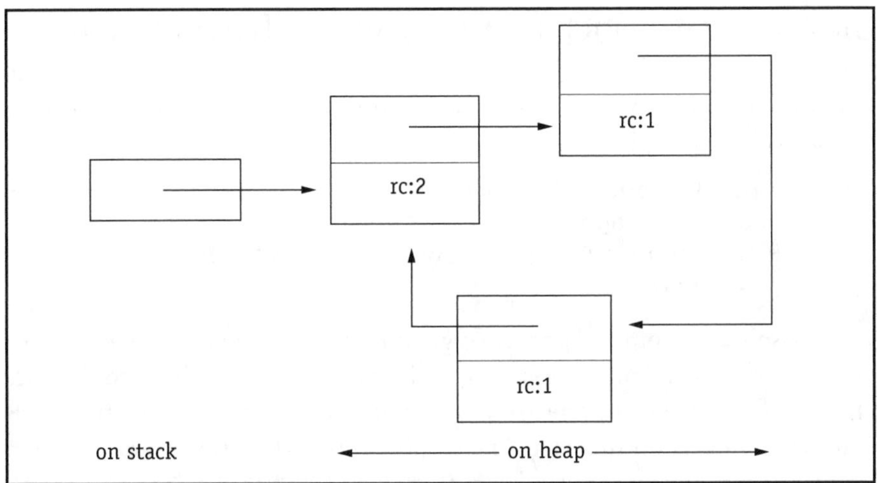

Figure 3. A circular reference.

```
struct Stor
{
   unsigned rc;
   void* pval; // cast by template to X*
};
struct Handle
{
   Handle( const Handle&);
   ~Handle();
   const Handle&operator = (const Handle&);
private:
   Stor* stor;
}
template<class X>
struct Rc_Pointer : Handle
{
      // . . .
};
```

This can indeed be made to work, and it does save some code. But it causes grief with debuggers. The pval pointer in the Stor class is a void* , and inspecting a handle inside the debugger is tedious since it requires manual casting. A golden rule of good template design is not to use pointers to void or to a low-level base class in a smart pointer template, but instead to use pointers to the real type. Otherwise, users will be frustrated during debugging and revert to using dumb pointers in their code.

SMART POINTERS THAT RESPECT INHERITANCE

Smart pointers of any kind have a serious problem. They do not respect inheritance. For example,

```
struct Manager : Employee { /* . . . */};
Pointer<Manager> pm = new Manager ( /* . . . */ );
Pointer<Employee> pe = new Employee( /* . . .*/);
pe = pm; //ERROR!
```

This isn't fair. If pm and pe were regular Manager* and Employee* pointers, the assignment from a pointer to a derived class to a pointer to the base class would have been perfectly legal. In fact, code using virtual functions routinely relies upon this fact. The trouble is that (Pointer<Manager> and Pointer<Employee> are classes, not pointers. And these classes are completely unrelated.

If we could relate the classes by inheritance, we would be in good shape:

```
    //WON'T WORK
struct Pointer<Manager> : Pointer<Employee>
{ /* . . . */}
```

Then the assignment derived class object to base class object would be legal. But, of course, that doesn't work. The classes were generated by templates, and in C++, there is no way of making a template T such that T<D> is derived from B. T<D> and T<B> are simply unrelated classes.

As always, one can fake this with a clever set of macros. It is possible to declare a macro RCI_POINTER(X) resolving to a class name RCI_POINTER_##X and another macro RCI_POINTER-DECLARE (D, B) that produces the class declaration of RCI_POINTER (D) with base class RCI_POINTER(B). We spare the reader the gory details because there is a workaround that uses standard templates.

The key to making inheritance work with smart pointer templates is to provide three operations:

```
Pointer<X> (X* )
Pointer<X>:: operator X* ()
const Pointer<X>&
Pointer<X>::operator=(X* )
```

Now the assignment

```
pe =pm;
```

succeeds. It is

```
pe.operator= (pm. operator Employee*())
```

And the assignment

```
pm = pe;
```

fails, as it should.

There is, of course, no free lunch. The encapsulation of the X* pointer inside the smart pointer class is now broken, and programmers can gain access to that pointer.

```
Employee* dpe = pe;
```

Now dpe is a dumb pointer to the same data, and integrity of the smart pointer pe (for example, the maintenance of reference counts), cannot be guaranteed.

A smart pointer template that respects inheritance is therefore not foolproof, but it nevertheless succeeds admirably as an idiom. With some programmer discipline (namely not to even think about using regular pointers to reference counted objects) one can construct pointers that combine reference counting (or other smart pointer strategies) and casting to base classes.

Locks

As mentioned previously, a major problem for DOS programmers is that there just isn't enough memory available. There are schemes to access so-called extended and expanded memory (if installed on the target machine), but they are cumbersome. There is no support for virtual memory, that is, swapping memory as needed from disk. However, there are commercially available libraries that perform this task, swapping between DOS addressable memory and extended memory, expanded memory, or the hard disk. A typical library has the following calls:

```
typedef unsigned Ds_HandleType
// allocate a block
Ds_HandleType ds_malloc( size_t);
// swap block into DOS memory
// and keep it there
void* ds_lock(Ds_HandleType);
// block can be swapped out if necessary
void ds_unlock(Ds_HandleType );
```

```
void ds_free(Ds_HandleType );
// returns the handle associated
// with a locked block
Ds_HandleType ds_handle(void*);
```

The keys are the ds_lock and ds_unlock functions. To use a memory block, the allocator must check whether it is currently in main memory. If not, some other block (one that is not currently locked) must be swapped out and the requested block swapped in. The ds_lock function performs this task, and it returns a pointer to the location in memory containing the information. It is important to call ds_unlock as soon as possible after ds_lock. If too many pointers are locked, subsequent attempts to swap in other blocks will fail, and the program must come to a halt due to memory exhaustion. Note that the address returned by ds_lock can be different each time for the same memory block, as the requested block is swapped in to replace the least recently used block.

I was involved in a project that used such a system extensively, and we ran into a number of very unpleasant problems. First of all, some programmers on the team were reluctant to use the handles and preferred to lock handles, then copy the pointers around and even stash them into data structures with a long lifetime. It took some aggressive code walkthroughs to stamp out this practice. More seriously, sometimes a handle was locked, a copy of the pointer was made and kept after the original handle was unlocked again. Using such a pointer clobbered the system.

From a code maintenance point of view, the worst aspect of the method was the complete lack of typing. Just about every data item was a Ds_HandleType. Typical code looked like this:

```
Ds_HandleType hfrac = mth_get (/* . . . */);
Mth_Fraction* pfrac = (Mth_Fraction*) dy_lock (hfrac);
```

The programmer had to know the type of the object returned by the function mth_get(). The compiler could not check against coding errors which invariably did happen.

And finally, there was a problem that turned out to be a real nuisance when we tried to replace one library with another. The other library used a different handle type:

```
typedef void* Ds_HandleType;
```

Under DOS, sizeoff(unsigned) and sizeoff(void*) are different, and to my great surprise there were literally hundreds of places in the code that read like

```
unsigned n;
// . . .
Ds_HandleType h = (Ds_HandleType) n;
```

Note the well-intentioned cast that made this code compile (wrongly) even with the new definition. There is a lesson here: Use typedef with extreme caution. In many programming languages (e.g., Pascal), type definitions make new types (and assignments between the old and new type are illegal), whereas in C++ typedef makes a type synonym. This is almost always worthless. In C++, the correct mechanism is the class. In fact, with the definition

```
struct Ds_HandleType
{ unsigned h;} ;
```

the compiler flagged all the bad constructs in the original code.

Let us now see how these problems can be overcome by wrapping the swapping allocator calls inside a set of templates.

The strong typing can be achieved with a template:

```
template<class X>
struct Ds_Handle
{ //. . .
private:
        Ds_HandleType h;

};
```

Now we can describe handles to typed objects by using types such as Ds_Handle<Mth_Fraction>. Let us next turn to the memory allocation. Suppose we want to construct an Employee object. This is actually nontrivial. Even with a constructor Ds_Handle<X>(X*), we can't run

```
Ds_Handle<Employee> he =
        new Employee("Oswald Orr", "195-43-8725");
```

This allocates the employee on the regular heap and does not use the ds_malloc allocator. Conversely, if we allocate the correct amount of memory with the ds_malloc allocator

```
Employee* pe =
        (Employee*) ds_malloc(sizeof(Employee) )
```

how can we now run the constructor? For this purpose, we make use of a little-known C++ feature that allows the definition of specialized operator new functions. The regular global operator new function has the prototype

```
void* operator new (size_t);
```

and terrible things should happen to programmers who replace it with a custom function: If two programmers have that bright idea in two different libraries, gnashing of teeth results. But any number of operator new functions, with more than one argument, can be defined, as long as the first argument is of type size_t. For example, if

```
void* operator new(size_t s, T t);
```

has been defined in some way, then it is invoked by the call

```
T x;
Employee* pe = new (x) Employee( /* . . . */ );
```

with s = sizeof(Employee) and t = x. The following trick is cheap, but effective. Define

```
void*
operator new(size_t s, void* (*a) (size_t ) )
{ return (*a) (s);}
```

Now, if f is any pointer to a function taking a size_t argument and returning a pointer (hopefully to a block of memory of that size), then

```
new (f) Employee( /* . . . */ );
```

allocates sizeof(Employee) bytes using the function f, runs the constructor code on that memory block, and returns the allocated address. In particular, we define

```
void* ds_alloc(size_t s)
{ return ds_lock (ds_malloc(s) ); }
```

and

```
template<class X>
Ds_Handle<X> :: Ds_Handle(x* p):h(ds_handle(p) )
{ds_unlock(h) ;}
```

A typical allocation now looks like

```
Ds_Handle<Employee> h =
        new(ds_alloc) Employee("Oswald Orr", "195-43 8725");
```

There is a danger here. If the ds_ alloc is inadvertently omitted from the call, a regular pointer is returned, and the attempt to unlock it will likely mess up the swap allocator. Unfortunately, I know of no easy way of protecting against that.

Next, how do we turn such a handle into a pointer for a brief time? The obvious idea is to provide an operator->:

```
template<class X> X*
Ds_Handle<X> : : operator->()
{
   X* p = (X*) ds_lock( h );
   ds_unlock( h );
   return p; //DON'T
}
```

For example, if he is a handle to an employee record, then the code

```
int n = he->age;
```

would briefly lock the memory block, thereby obtaining a pointer, and immediately unlock it, then return a pointer to the block which will surely not get swapped out again for some time. This sounds dangerous, and it is. The method will indeed work fine to access a single data member, as in the example above, but it is unpredictable for member functions. A function call

```
he->printTaxForm ( /* . . . */ );
```

could be quite complex and involve sufficient swapping of memory to move the memory block referred to by he out of main memory, making this pointer in the function into a dangling pointer. Instead, it is necessary to make the locking explicit with a second class.

```
template<class X>
struct Ds_Lock
{
    Ds_Lock(const Ds_Handle<X>& d)
    : p( (X*) ds_lock(d.h) )
    { assert (p); }
    ~Ds_Lock () { ds_unlock(ds_handle(p) ) ; }
    X* operator -> () {return p;}
    const X* operator -> () const {return p;}
private:
    // can't assign, copy,
    // take address or allocate on the heap
    void operator=(const Ds_Lock<X>&) {}
    Ds_Lock(const Ds_Lock<X>& b) {}
```

```
        void operator& () {};
        void* operator new (size_t){return 0;}
        x* p;
};
```

With the handle/lock pair, there is only one way to access the information referred to by the handle: Place a lock on it and use the -> operator:

```
Ds_Lock<Employee> le =he;
le->printTaxForm( /* . . . */);
```

When le goes out of scope, its destructor automatically unlocks the handle!

This handle/lock pair perfectly solves our problem. The handle template is for long-term storage of the memory handles, whereas the lock template provides access to the memory and automatically unlocks the block later. There is no way of getting from the handle to the actual pointer without using a lock, and there is no way of keeping the locks for longer than a function call (since the assignment operator, copy constructor, address operator and free store allocation have been defined as private operations).

Since the destructor of the lock so neatly unlocks the handle after the pointer has been used, one may ask whether we can't define an -> operator for the Ds_Handle<X> class that returns a Ds_Lock<X> object. (Recall that -> is applied repeatedly until a pointer to a structure is obtained; applying -> to Ds_Lock<X> yields an X*.) This is indeed a tempting idea, as it makes the Ds_Lock<X> class completely trasparent to the user. For example, the code

```
he->printTaxForm( /* . . . */);
```

would have the following effect:

1. Call Ds_Handle<X> :: operator->
2. Return a temporary Ds_Lock<X> object; call it temp
3. Apply Ds_Lock<X>::operator -> to temp
4. Return an X* pointer; call it p
5. Call p-> printTaxForm (/* . . . */)
6. Destroy temp

The trouble is that this is not necessarily accurate. The ARM is very explicit in warning us to assume nothing about the lifetime of temporaries.[4] It is possible that some compilers transpose steps 5 and 6, first invoking the destructor of temp, then calling the member function with a pointer that is no longer guaranteed to be locked.

It would be very welcome if the C++ standards committee could firm up the lifetime of temporaries. For this particular application, it would be required that any temporaries generated by an operator -> persist until after the member function call on the right hand side of -> is completed. This seems a fairly moderate request, and since -> is such a special operator, it wouldn't bother me if it had some fairly technical conditions attached to its implementation. But until this issue is resolved, I would caution against using code that relies on any particular behavior.

This implementation of the handle/lock pair relied on the existence of a `ds_handle` function that reveals the handle associated with a locked pointer. Not all locking allocators provide such a function. For an allocator that does not, the handle/lock setup is somewhat more complicated. The lock class needs to hang on to the handle, and constructing objects is more cumbersome. We leave this as an exercise to the reader.*

It is possible to combine the locking mechanism with reference counting. In that case, each memory block has two counts associated with it: a reference count specifying how many handles refer to it, and a lock count counting how many of them are currently locked. When the lock count goes to zero, the block can be swapped out of the main memory; when the reference count goes to zero, the block can be removed altogether.

CONCLUSION

Some object-oriented languages, notably Smalltalk and Eiffel, have a uniform memory management model. Neither Smalltalk nor Eiffel ever use explicit pointers. In Eiffel,[5] a variable is either implemented as a reference to a structure (the default) or an actual structure (if it is declared as expanded). The compiler and runtime system know where all pointers are, making modern garbage collection techniques feasible.

C++ has, by default, no memory management support except for the `new/delete` allocator. It is, however, possible, to implement smart pointer classes that relieve the programmer of some of the burdens associated with keeping track of memory allocation. Since C++ is used in a wide range of applications, and different programs have different trade-offs between conve-

---

* Hint: Use a

```
template <class X>
  operator new (size_t, Lock <X>&)
```

nience and efficiency, it is unlikely that one allocation scheme is acceptable to all programmers. Instead, each project should make conscious choices of memory management strategies. One program may actually employ different strategies for different objects.

Certain memory management support schemes can be delivered safely by using a set of well-tested templates. This article introduced two such templates: one for adding reference counting to existing classes, and one to encapsulate a disk swapping allocator. These are good starting points for experimentation. These techniques can be extended to provide runtime type identification and even garbage collection, and I may report on that in a future column.

REFERENCES

1. Duncan, R. EXTENDING DOS, Addison-Wesley, Reading, MA, 1992.
2. Coplien, J.O. ADVANCED C++ PROGRAMMING STYLES AND IDIOMS, Addison-Wesley, Reading, MA, 1992.
3. Horstmann, C.S. MASTERING C++, Wiley, New York, NY, 1990.
4. Ellis, M.A., and B. Sroustrup, THE C++ ANNOTATED REFERENCE MANUAL, Addison-Wesley, Reading, MA, 1991.
5. Meyer, B. EIFFEL—THE LANGUAGE, Prentice Hall, Englewood Cliffs, NJ, 1992.

Pointers vs. References

Stan Lippman

Stan Lippman wrote (and still writes) many articles for the C++ Report. *Stan, of course, is the author of the* C++ Primer. *There have been three editions of this book. The page counts of these three editions have increased geometrically (as have the page counts of all books that attempt to cover C++). Each edition is a masterful presentation of C++ concepts from "asm" to "void" (see page 84 of the third edition).*

In this article, Stan talks about the differences between pointers and references in C++. And, of course, he covers the topic by exploring all the little twisty turns and passages alike that surround that topic.

This article tickles me, not just for its excellent discussion of pointers and references, but because of the sidebar on RTTI. This sidebar is almost as long as the article itself, and provides some intriguing insights to the internals of cfront as well as the thought processes that led to dynamic_cast and RTTI.

Tutorial introductions to references in C++ often speak of them as "simply pointers with object syntax." As with most generalizations, this is both true enough and terribly far from the truth. It is true enough in simple cases, as when contrasting the behavior of a pointer and reference formal argument, such as in the following example:

```
void swap( int *pi, int &ri ) {
    int temp = *pi;
    *pi = ri;
    ri = temp;
```

```
}

int
main() {
     int val1 = 1024;
     int val2 = 2048;

     swap( &val1, val2 );
}
```

It is also true enough to say that class objects addressed by either a pointer or reference both support polymorphism, such as in the following simple example in which the same virtual function rotate() defined within an inheritance hierarchy rooted by the ZooAnimal class is invoked for pooh:

```
extern void rotate( const ZooAnimal *pz);
extern void rotate( const ZooAnimal &rz);

int
main() {
      Teddy pooh ("Winnie");

      //extern void rotate( const ZooAnimal &rz );
      rotate( pooh );

      //extern void rotate( const ZooAnimal *pz );
      rotate( &pooh );
}
```

In a number of fundamental ways, however, references and pointers behave very differently. The obvious distinction is that a reference, once initialized cannot be made to alias another object. As we'll see later, this provides for very different assignment semantics between pointers and references. A second distinction is that a class declaring a reference member must also declare a constructor. A third, and perhaps the most fundamental difference, is that while a pointer can address no object, a reference cannot.

A Reference to No Object?

What would happen were we to invoke rotate() with an argument of 0, such as in the following?

```
rotate( 0 );//which instance?
```

Since the nonmember rotate() is an overloaded function, the instance to be invoked is resolved through argument matching. The first step of the matching algorithm is to look for an exact match. 0 is of type int; obviously, this does not exactly match the formal argument of either instance. Next, the matching algorithm attempts a match through the application of a standard conversion. Through a standard conversion, 0 can be matched to a pointer of any type. Our call, therefore, is resolved:

```
//extern void rotate( const ZooAnimal *pz );
rotate(0);
```

Semantically, however, the call is probably without meaning. In general, when we program with pointers, it is necessary for our code to guard against the possibility of a null pointer. At minimum, then, an implementation of the pointer instance of rotate() might look like the following:

```
void
rotate( const ZooAnimal *pz) {
        if ( pz )
                pz->rotate();
}
```

What about our implementation of the reference instance of rotate()? That is, do we need to guard against the possibility of a null reference?

```
void
rotate( const ZooAnimal &rz ) {
        if ( rz )// necessary?
                rz.rotate();
}
```

That is, can there be a universal reference—a reference that refers to no object of a type? The short answer is no, and this is one way in which a pointer and reference are different. What does it mean, then, to invoke the reference instance of rotate() with 0? For example, let's delete the pointer instance of rotate() and again invoke rotate() with 0. What happens?

There is no standard conversion of a 0 to a reference. Therefore, the 0 is treated as a value of type int. Our first question then is whether there is a way to convert an integer value into a ZooAnimal? A conversion of any built-in type into a particular class type is accomplished by a conversion constructor defined within that class.* Therefore, the call

---

* See Section 6.5 of C++ Primer, for a complete discussion.

```
rotate( 0 );
```

is legal only if the ZooAnimal class defines a constructor of the general form

```
ZooAnimal::ZooAnimal( int );
```

where the int formal argument can actually be any built-in arithmetic type (or that takes a single pointer type!). Okay, so let's presume the constructor is defined; the call is legal. Now what? The compiler constructs an object of class ZooAnimal by invoking the constructor:

```
//compiler generated Zoo Animal temporary
ZooAnimal temp = ZooAnimal( 0 );
```

The call is then rewritten to pass the temporary class object to the reference instance of rotate() being invoked:

```
//replaces user's rotate( 0 );
rotate( temp );
```

Remember that passing an actual argument to a function invocation is viewed as an initialization of that function's formal argument. That is, passing a 0 to rotate() is the same as explicitly initializing a reference with 0, such as:

```
ZooAnimal &ref = 0;
```

In both cases, a compiler generated temporary object of type ZooAnimal is constructed. The reference is initialized to address that object. That is, for a reference, 0 simply represents an integer value no different than that of 1 or 1024. Unlike a pointer, there is no built-in value a reference can be initialized to indicate that it is a reference that refers to no object. Our code, therefore, does not need to guard against the possibility of a reference being null. The reference implementation of rotate() can dispense with such a check:

```
void
rotate( const ZooAnimal &rz )
{
        rz.rotate();
}
```

This difference between a pointer and reference is perhaps most apparent in the semantics of the dynamic_cast operator supporting runtime type identification. (For those of you unfamiliar with the dynamic_cast operator and runtime type identification, see the sidebar accompanying this article.)

REFERENCE VS. POINTER ASSIGNMENT

One characteristic of polymorphic objects is that they are initialized by reference rather than value; that is, the initialized pointer or reference serves as an alias or second handle to the actual class object. For example, in the following code fragment:

```
Toy_bear Winnie( "Pooh" );

Bear&Pooh_bear = Winnie;
Bear*Piglets_friend = &Winnie;
Bear Honey_gobbler = Winnie;
```

neither Pooh_bear nor Piglets_friend introduce additional Bear objects; rather, they serve as alternative methods of manipulating Winnie through the class Bear public interface. Honey_gobbler, however, defines a second class object initialized by the class Bear copy constructor. The values of Winnie's Bear subobject are copied into Honey_gobbler; the Toy_bear portions of Winnie (and any intermediate class derivations) are not present within Honey_gobbler. Honey_gobbler, unlike Pooh_bear and Piglets_friend, is not a polymorphic object but simply a Bear.†

The assignment of pointers in effect behaves similarly; that is, although pointers are copied by value, the effect of pointer assignment is to have two pointers addressing the same object. Thus, given the assignment:

```
Tiggers_friend = Piglets_friend;
```

both Tiggers_friend and Piglets_friend at the completion of the assignment address Winnie.

It is this aspect of pointer semantics that complicates class object management: by default, assignment of one class object with another results in the *shallow* copy (or aliasing) of its pointer members with those of the source class object. In general, however, class object management requires *deep* copy (the recursive construction of a new object given the same values as that being addressed) of its pointer members (or, alternatively, some strategy of reference counting). The following simple example illustrates the distinction between shallow and deep copy. Given the following pair of pointers:

† For a detailed discussion of this behavior, see the C++ PRIMER column in C++ REPORT (6[5]).[1]

```
char*s1,*s2;
```

the assignment:

```
s1=s2;
```

results in a shallow copy (s1 now addresses the same "object" as s2). Shallow copy occurs by default with pointers in C and is the inherited behavior of pointers in C++. Programmer intervention is required to effect deep copy (that is, to provide s1 with the address of a new object that is a copy of the object s2 addresses):

```
s1=new char[strlen(s2)];
strcpy( s1,s2 );
```

Programming deep copy is necessary in the copy constructor and assignment operator of a class, in general, if a pointer member:

- addresses heap memory allocated by the class and is deallocated by the class (perhaps in the constructor and destructor)—reference counting is an alternative strategy.
- is going to be altered during the lifetime of an object to uniquely reflect its state, which would then reflect an invalid state for a second or subsequent object—copy on write is an alternative strategy.

What about the assignment of one reference with another? Is that carried out with value or reference semantics? That is, given the following code fragment:

```
void
foo( Bear &b1, const Bear &b2 )
{
        b1=b2;
}
```

is `b1` now an alias for `b2`? Do both now refer to the same object, or is memberwise copy applied? That is, is the assignment operator for Bear applied—or, if the assignment operator is virtual, for the type of object `b1` actually refers to? Again, think about it a minute before reading on.

The answer is that reference semantics (shallow copy) do not hold for the assignment of one reference either with another reference or with an object; rather, copy by value is effected the same as if the reference to be assigned to were an object. In this case, pointers and references couldn't behave more differently, and we see that what is true enough in the simplest cases is really terribly far from the truth.

REFERENCES

1. Lippman, S.C++ PRIMER, second ed., Addison-Wesley, Reading, MA, 1991.
2. Lajoie, J. New operators for array `new` and `delete`...and more C++ REPORT, 5(4), 1993.
3. Stroustrup, B. THE DESIGN AND EVOLUTION OF C++, Addison-Wesley, Reading, MA, 1994.

RUNTIME TYPE IDENTIFICATION

IN cfront, Stroustrup's original implementation of C++, a portion of the internal type hierarchy to represent programs looks as follows:

```
class node {...};
class type: public node {...};

class classdef : public type {...};
class fct : public type {...};
class gen : public type {...};
```

where gen is short for generic and represents an overloaded function.

Thus, whenever one had a variable or member of type* and knew it represented a function, one still had to determine whether its specific derived type was a fct or gen. Except, that is, in one particular instance. Or at least in one particular instance for one particular span of time: that of conversion operators, such as

```
class String {
public:
        operator char*();
        //...
};
```

Prior to the introduction of const member function in Release 2.0, conversion operators, since they do not take arguments, could not be overloaded. Subsequent to their introduction, declarations like the following now become possible:

```
class String {
public:
        //ok with Release 2.0
        operator char*();
        operator char*() const;
        // ...
};
```

Therefore, it was always safe (and faster), prior to the internal version of Release 2.0 supporting const member functions, anyway, to short-circuit access of the derived object by an explicit cast (note: after the introduction of const member functions, the explicit cast remained faster, albeit less safe):

```
typedef type *ptype;
typedef fct *pfct;

Simplify_conv_op( ptype pt ) {
        // ok: conversion operators can only be
        // fcts, never gens
                pfct pf = pfct( pt );
        //...
```

This code,[†] then, is tested and correct prior to the introduction of const member functions. There is even a programmer comment, notice, documenting the safety of the cast. Of course, subsequent to the introduction of const member functions, both the comment and code are no longer correct: this code fails miserably with the revised String class declaration above since the char* conversion operator is now stored internally as a gen.

A cast of the form

```
pfct pf = pfct( pt );
```

is spoken of as a *downcast* because it effectively casts a base class down its inheritance hierarchy, forcing it into one of its more specialized derived classes. Downcasts are potentially dangerous since they circumvent the type-system, and, when incorrectly applied, may misinterpret or corrupt program memory. In our code example, we incorrectly downcast the pointer pf to a gen object into a pointer to an object of type fct. All subsequent use of pf in our program, except for a test of whether it is nil or not, is likely to be invalid.

INTRODUCING A TYPE-SAFE DOWNCAST

One of the criticisms of C++ had been its lack of support for a type-safe downcast mechanism—one that performs the downcast only if the actual

[†] Of course, now that the actual type of pt can be either a fct or gen, the preferred programming method is a virtual function. In that way, the actual type of the argument is encapsulated: the program is both clearer and more easily extended to handle additional types.

(Continued)

type being cast is appropriate. The problems with support for a type-safe downcast mechanism are the following:

- it requires additional space to store type information—usually a pointer to some type information node; and,
- it requires additional time to determine the runtime type since, as the name makes explicit, it can be done only at runtime.

What would a such mechanism do to the size, the performance, and the link compatibility of such common C constructs as the following?

```
char*str_tbl[] = {"phooey", "oh, bother","etc."};
```

Obviously, there would be a considerable space and efficiency penalty placed on programs that made no use of the facility. The conflict, then, is between two sets of users:

- programmers heavily using polymorphism and therefore with a legitimate need of a type-safe downcast mechanism; and,
- programmers using the built-in data types and nonpolymorphic facilities, and therefore with a legitimate need not to be penalized by the overhead of a mechanism that does not come into play in their code.

The solution is to provide for the legitimate needs of both parties, although perhaps at the expense of a "pure" design.

The C++ runtime type identification mechanism provides a type-safe downcast facility but only for those types exhibiting polymorphism—that is, those types that make use of inheritance and dynamic binding. How does one recognize that? That is, how can a compiler look at a class definition and determine whether this class represents an independent abstract data type or an inheritable subtype supporting polymorphism? One strategy, of course, is the introduction of a new keyword. This has the advantage of clearly identifying types that support the new feature; the disadvantage is that old code would then need to retrofit the keyword into their programs. An alternative strategy is to distinguish between class declarations by the presence of one or more declared or inherited virtual functions. This has the advantage of transparently transforming existing programs that are re-compiled; it has the disadvantage of possibly forcing the introduction of an otherwise unnecessary virtual function into the base class of an inheritance hierarchy. No doubt you can think of a number of additional strategies. In any case, this latter strategy of (requiring the presence of either an inherited or declared virtual function) is the one supported by the runtime type identification mechanism.

A Type-Safe Dynamic Cast

The dynamic_cast operator determines at runtime the actual type being addressed. If the downcast is safe (that is, if the base type pointer actually addresses an object of the derived class), it returns the appropriately cast pointer. If the downcast is not safe, it returns 0. For example, here is how we might rewrite our original cfront downcast (if we had a compiler that supported the dynamic-cast)††

```
typedef type *ptype;
typedef fct *pfct;

Simplify_conv_op( ptype pt ) {
        if ( pfct pf= dynamic_cast<pfct>( pt ) ) {
                //...process pf
        }
        else {...}
}
```

The additional ability to place a declaration within the test of the if-statement is a notational convenience.

References Are not Pointers

The dynamic_cast of a class pointer type provides a true/false pair of alternative pathways during program execution:

- by returning an actual address, the dynamic type of the object is confirmed, and type-dependant actions may proceed;
- by returning 0, the universal address of no object, alternative logic can be applied to an object of uncertain dynamic type.

†† This code, of course, is not real cfront code, but simply made up for this example. In general, it is better to encapsulate castings within inline member functions.

(Continued)

The dynamic-cast operator can also be applied to a reference. The result of a non-type-safe cast, however, cannot be the same as for a pointer. Why? As we have seen in the main portion of this article, a reference cannot refer to "no object" the way a pointer can by having its value be set to 0. Initializing a reference with 0 causes a temporary object of the referred to type to be generated. This temporary is initialized with 0. The reference is then initialized to alias the temporary. Thus, the dynamic_cast operator, when applied to a reference, cannot provide an equivalent true/false pair of alternative pathways as it does with a pointer. Rather, the following occurs:

- if the reference is actually referring to the appropriate derived class, or an object of a class subsequently derived from that class, the downcast is performed and the program may proceed.
- if the reference is not actually a kind of the derived class, since returning 0 is not viable, an exception is thrown.

Here is our simplify_conv_op() function reimplemented with a reference argument:

```
simplify_conv_op( const type &rt) {
        try{
                fct &rf = dynamic_cast<fct&>( rt );
                //...
        }
        catch( Bad_cast ) {
                //...mumble...
        }
}
```

where the action to perform ideally indicates some sort of exceptional failure rather than simply a flow-of-control transfer.

Typeid Operator

It is possible to achieve the same runtime "alternative pathway" behavior with a reference by using the typeid operator:

```
simplify_conv_op( const type &rt ) {
        if ( typeid( rt ) ==typeid( fct ))
```

```
        {
            fct&rf=static_cast<fct&>( rt );
            //...
        }
        else {...}
    }
```

although clearly at this point the better implementation strategy is to introduce a virtual function common to both the gen and fct classes.

The typeid operator returns a const reference of type typeinfo. In the above test, the equality operator is an overloaded instance:

```
int typeinfo::
operator==( const typeinfo& ) const;
```

and returns 1 if the two typeinfo objects are the same. More detailed explanations of runtime type identification are given in Lajoie[2] (5[4]) and Stroustrup.[3]

Much Ado about Null

Dr. James M. Coggins

In the early years of the C++ Report, *there was a column entitled "Best of comp.lang.c++." James was one of the authors of this column. This was a great column because it summarized the best threads on, what was then, the best newsgroup on the net, bar none. Since then, of course, comp.lang.c++ has become a noise factory, and those of us who wish a purer environment hang out on comp.lang.c++.moderated.*

Notice the names that appear in this article. Scott Meyer, Steve Clamage, Desmond D'Souza, and Cay Horstmann, to mention a few. Though I was posting quite often at this time, apparently I did not have an awful lot to say about NULL.

This is a great discussion, it shows how a simple concept like:

```
#define NULL 0
```

Can become a very complicated issue when put in the context of multiple platforms and compilers. And the solutions these guys come up with are amazing in some cases. The lengths we will go to define nothing are amazing.

Compare this article to Bobby Wolf's NULL Object Pattern *in* Pattern Languages of Program Design 3, *Robert C. Martin, et al., Addison–Wesley, 1996.*

THIS MONTH WE WILL EXAMINE the different ways to represent Nothing in C++. This is worthy of discussion because the representation of Nothing must have a type and, well, what type is Nothing? Before you decide to forward this column to the Philosophy Department for interpretation, let's begin with a seemingly straightforward inquiry from Scott Meyers who asks the Net about the semantics of '0'. This question eventually reaches into areas such as automatic type conversion rules, interactions of preprocessor symbols with the type system, compatibility problems among C++ implementations, standardization concerns, and the interaction of classes with basic types.

> **What is the type of the constant '0', independent of any context? If there is such a default type, call it T. Then are there any conversions in any of the following?**
>
> ```
> int I       =0;      // conversion from T to int?
> int ip      =0;      // conversion from T to int?
> double d  =0;        //conversion from T to double?
> ```
>
> **The reason for asking is that it would be nice to avoid the following ambiguity:**
>
> ```
> void f(int x);        //parameter of a numerical type
> void f(char *s);      //parameter of a pointer type
> f(0);                 //ambiguous call – is 0 an
>                       //int or a char*?
> ```
>
> **I would prefer that the default type for 0 be int, in accord with the default type of functions and consts. Then the call to f(0) would resolve to calling f(int) and there would be no ambiguity. It would of course still be possible to call f(char*) via an explicit cast of, more palatably, by declaring a const null pointer of the appropriate type, e.g.,**
>
> ```
> const char *NULLSTRING = 0;
> f(NULLSTRING);
> ```
>
> **Unfortunately, we'd have to augment the rules for disambiguating overloaded functions described in section 13.2 of the ARM (pp.3112ff of the American edition). There are currently five rules. I'd add the conversion of '0' to 'null pointer' to rule 3, on standard conversions.**
>
> **I suspect the matter is substantially more comlicated and subtle than I've described here. Comments?**

The matter was indeed more complicated and subtle than it appeared, Before we peel away a few layers of this technophilosophical onion, we get an answer to the surface question from Stephen Clamage:

A literal zero has type int. It can also serve as a null pointer constant when initializing a pointer.

```
int i = 0;              // 0 has type int
double d = 0;           // 0 implicitly converted to type double
T* t = 0;               // 0 implicitly converted to type T*
T* u = i;               // illegal, since i is not a null pointer constant
```

The function call example is not ambiguous. The zero is an exact match to f(int), but requires a conversion to f(char*). If your compiler calls it ambiguous, this is a bug.

Anders Juul Munch provides a test for determining the type of '0' and then peels away a layer of the onion:

Try:

```
printf(8%d,%d,%d\n*, sizeof(int),
sizeof(void*), sizeof(0));
```

on a system with different sizes for int and pointers. What you'll find is that "0" is foremost an integer (which incidentally may be used in place of a pointer).

But I wonder, if we have

```
#define NULL 0
```

(which is ANSI C compliant, I don't know if C++ is any different), then f(NULL) would call f(int)?! This seems highly unreasonable to me, and it looks like yet another good reason why the implicit conversion of 0 to the null pointer should be disallowed. Instead, NULL should be used whenever a null pointer is needed. NULL being defined as

```
#define NULL ((void*)0)
```

And

```
int* ip = NULL;
```

would then be illegal, and replaced by

```
int* ip = NULL;
```

Cay Horstmann reveals one practical problem with using defined NULL symbols:

Beware of DOS header files that define NULL as `0L` in the large memory model!!! `0L` is NOT convertible to a pointer. I got bitten by that one when switching from Glockenspiel to Borland C++.

Chip Salzenberg replied:

When in doubt, cast...[It's] too late [to disallow] implicit conversion of `0` to a pointer. It isn't even a C++ invention. As an ANSI C feature, I doubt it will disappear.

Regarding March's suggested definition of NULL, Salzenburg adds:

Sorry, that won't work. The ARM explicitly disallows automatic (castless) conversion of a void* to another pointer type.

Thomas M. Breuel replied to Salzenburg:

A possible fix to this mess might be to introduce a new value 'nil' that behaves mostly like '`0`', but is not an integer.

Bruel's suggestion struck a responsive chord with Joseph Breckenbach:

I've stopped using `0` (as pointer) and NULL directly in my C code, and have finessed the problem with

```
#define NIL(type) ((type)NULL)
```

For me it's the easiest solution, since I tend not to think of a generic 'nil' pointer but of a 'nil pointer of type T'.

What other reasonable schemes can be used for the same effect?

Chip Sazenberg replied:

I like it. It's too late to save ANSI C, but C++ could finally provide the vehicle to end the NULL wars.

In a later discussion, Scott Meyers updates his thoughts about implementing NULL:

I've been doing some thinking lately about how to implement NULL such that NULL is distinguishable from the integer `0`, i.e., given functions

```
f(int x);
f(T *x); //T is any type; what's
         //important is that x is a pointer
```

a call to f(0) will call the former (as currently happens) and f(NULL) will call the latter. This precludes the old #define approach. The motivation for this, by the way, is that when you have overloaded functions such as the above, it's clumsy and error-prone to invoke f with the null pointer, since you have to say f((T*) 0) in order to be sure to get the right function.

As I see it, the problem boils down to the fact that NULL must be of pointer type, but type compatible with all pointers without a cast.

So here's my latest though, but since I don't have a compiler supporting templates, I don't know if it will work:

```
class NullClass {
   public:
      template <class T> operator T* () const
      { return 0; }
};

extern Nullclass NULL;
```

The idea here is that given a call to f(NULL), the compiler will try to convert the object NULL into either an int or a pointer-to-T, and since there's no defined conversion to an int, it'll invoke the appropriate conversion operator to a pointer. The attractive thing about it is that the compiler instantiates template functions upon implicit demand, so the NULL object should be silently convertible into a pointer of any type.

Anybody know if this will work or not? Are template member functions allowed inside non-template classes?

Chip Salzenberg reveals one hole in the proposal (there must be a serious problem if you can find a hole in Nothing):

[Defining a NullClass] loses when NULL is used for a non-class pointer. For example, this code fragment won't work with NullClass:

```
extern time_t time(time_t *t);
main()
{
   time_t t =time(NULL);
}
```

Desmond Dsouza also points out a problem:

> **Nice idea, but: ARM, p 342: A template declaration can only appear as a global declaration.**

A related discussion occurred in the standards group discussions. Jerry Schwarz, in a list of outstanding issues to be decided, adds the following comment:

> **I think the crunch comes with regard to header files. I assume that vendors who currently define NULL as (void*)0 in their C headers will continue to do so. Can they switch to 0 in the C++ headers? This isn't a technical question, they obviously have an #ifdef_cplusplus. It's a pragmatic question having to do with how hard it is to transform C code to C++ code. Perhaps some vendor who currently has header files with (void*)0 will comment?**

Steve Clamage replied:

> **OK. I'll comment. All our implementation use something like**

```
#ifdef_cplusplus
#define NULL 0
#else
#define NULL (void*) 0
#endif
```

> **(I'm beginning to think we may need to include a preceding "#undefNULL" as well, because of miscellaneous C headers lurking about which blithely #define their own version of NULL.)**
>
> **I have seen that other C++ vendors do the same thing.**
>
> **We supply versions of all the ANSI C headers configured to work in both C and C++ modes. We also have to supply version of other host systems header files configured to work with C++. (There are few systems whose default C compilers accept prototypes, for example.) "Have to supply," because customers are otherwise not eager to buy our products.**
>
> **As others have pointed out, it is a rare C header file which works at all with a C++ compiler. That is to say,**

```
extern "C"
{
#include <someheader.h>
}
```

is almost never sufficient. The problem of `(void*) 0` vs `0` is a very tiny part of header file compatability. I don't see how it can justify making a special case in the language.

Setting the Stage

James O. Coplien

1994 was quite a year. I was in the final throes of finishing my book. The final drafts of the Design Patterns book were up on the net and available for download. Many of us were devouring these chapters and sending comments back to the authors. The times were frenetic! (And they still are!!)

I ran into Jim Coplien, the renowned author of Advanced C++ Programming Styles and Idioms, *Addison–Wesley, 1992 (which, by the way, is still one of the best C++ books around) at C++ World a few months earlier. He had a note pinned on his lapel: "Ask me about patterns." I had never heard of patterns, so I asked. He told me. Wow!*

The article you are about to read is the first in a column that still continues to this day. It is "The Column Without A Name." In this article Cope describes the history of patterns, and the formation of the important political entities that continue to drive patterns today. Once again, the names he mentions in this article are telling: Grady Booch, Kent Beck, Ken Auer, Bruce Anderson, Voltaire, Lau-Tzu, the GOF (Gang-of-Four (Gamma, Johnson, Vlissides, Helm)), etc. Another name he mentions is the "Hillside" group (http://www.hillside.net).

You've always counted on the C++ *Report* to bring you the latest tips and advice on C++. Among such articles, I consider the material on architecture and design to be the most important to the long-term success of a software project. Design encompasses all those things that help reduce the understanding of a problem to implementation (including the modified understanding along the way). Most of these tips and guidelines come in object-oriented packaging.

In the July–August 1994 issue, something decidedly un-object-oriented invaded the C++ *Report* landscape. The article "Generative pattern languages" appeared on the scene[1] taking a niche in well-established object territory. Many of you probably wondered, "Why does the *C++ Report* have a column on *patterns*?" This month, we introduce "The Column Without a Name" (more about that later), where the theme of patterns will be taken up in coming months. Are patterns object-oriented? Just what are they doing here in the *C++ Report*, anyhow? And what do they mean to you and me?

In this column, I offer one perspective on how patterns fit in the progression of design techniques that have evolved from procedural design through object-oriented techniques in recent years. I also relate how I became interested in patterns, and why I think they show promise for a new generation of software architecture.

RISING TO THE ABSTRACTION LEVEL OF PATTERNS

For years, software designers have focused on finding good classes that are understandable, useful units of software packaging. But in large systems, many important design abstractions cannot be captured within a single class, but cut across classes; the same is true in the parallel world of object instances and the relationships between them. Just as designers of the 1960s and 1970s raised the level of abstraction from procedures to procedural hierarchies and modules, so we find power in inheritance hierarchies and in object implementation hierarchies. These design techniques reflect relationships *between* classes or *between* objects, respectively. They speak more to system structure than do objects or classes alone. For example, class `String` or class `Number` offer limited understanding about the workings of a compiler that comprises them; understanding the `Symbol` class hierarchy offers more insight about how the compiler works. By their nature, hierarchies are more abstract than individual classes, and allow us to reason about more of the system at once. They also tell us about the *structure* of the system along lines of inheritance.

But for complex systems, even these techniques aren't enough. Individually, a given hierarchy is one-dimensional, and few design techniques integrate multiple perspectives into a single, unified design view. But more importantly, other important hierarchies abound in complex systems. Booch's mechanisms cut across classes and objects alike. Object communities are a common design abstraction: container and iterator; handle and body; model, view, and controller. While hierarchies are a powerful abstraction construct, the world is not fundamentally hierarchical. At best, a good world-model comprises multiple, interwoven hierarchies, tangled with flat clusters of related abstractions.

To me, one of the most important benefits of design patterns is that they capture not only system parts, but rich relationships between them. Together, these describe a system architecture that is broader than any object or class hierarchy. With the architectural tools that patterns provide, we can describe important structures and relationships at the system level, and can instruct designers and implementors how to use them. Another major benefit of patterns is that they capture emerging experience in a young domain—such as the object paradigm—so inexpert practitioners can avoid re-inventing the wheel. Pattern languages are an ideal form of documentation for frameworks, which are an important and increasingly popular software architectural packaging technique.

As described in my previous article, patterns are structured prose documents that present a solution to a problem that occurs in a given context. They describe the forces present in the problem, and describe how and to what degree the pattern resolves those forces. They provide a rationale for their structure and application. The "pattern form" comes from Christopher Alexander, who uses such formulations for the architectures of buildings and towns.

Growing into Patterns

The work of Christopher Alexander is broadly hailed as the catalyst that precipitated the contemporary software patterns movement. However, most people involved in patterns discovered them through their experience in programming, and Alexander is regarded today as an almost quixotic guide and inspiration to the software patterns movement. Grady Booch came to patterns through his work with mechanisms (a group of objects working together on the system's behalf); Kent Beck discovered them in the elegant interworkings within Smalltalk programs.* An important aspect of patterns is their concreteness, and their preoccupation with what we have come to refer to as *Stoff*—"real stuff," not platitudes and theories.

My own experience with patterns goes back to architecture work I did with my colleague, Tom Burrows, at Bell Laboratories in the early 1980s. Tom assembled architectural principles that integrated demand-driven data flow and objects. We felt that his vision was well-suited to the problems of

* Such motivations have been explored in several forums, including "Coping with Grady and Kent" at the Borland International Conference, Orlando, FL, June 6, 1994.

high-availability systems. We developed software and hardware designs in parallel to support that vision.[2] We often had difficulty allocating a given architectural feature to hardware or software. Each of these media had its respective building blocks (objects in software; modular subassemblies in hardware) and integration fabric (backplanes in hardware and data flow "ports" in software): in Tom's paradigm, the design rules for both were the same. In both domains, objects were of secondary interest for real-time and high availability: the important functionality was in the connection between them. As with most data flow architectures, the focus was on the flow of information through the system as a whole. The scheduling of real-time events, and propagation of changes, entailed other important nonmodular abstractions. The term "pattern" was not yet in popular use;† we gave the name foils to these recurring interconnecting structures. The term comes from the patterns of connecting metal on printed-circuit boards, a metaphor for the backplane interconnect of a hardware bus architecture. We had several pet names for this non-object-based approach to design, many of them (curiously enough, as we will see later) with roots in Eastern schools of thought. One such term was *Madhyamika*, a "middle way" of thinking, intermediate between a highly unified world-view, and a world reduced to a rubble of objects.

As the data flow work reached its peak in about 1988, I had already been an active user of C++ for five years. Object-oriented programming had been the focus of many C++ users from the start, and object-oriented design started making inroads into the C++ community in about 1986. Even before published object-oriented design techniques saw wide use, programmers across the industry were discovering techniques to solve specific C++ design problems. I saw the same tricks recurring in the work of my colleagues, in early papers on C++, and in my own work. It struck me that what it took to be a professional C++ programmer wasn't in any of the books yet, and that any project that started off without knowing how to use simple constructs like handle and body classes would soon be struggling. I prepared notes on effective use of such "tricks," and used them to bring new projects up to speed as they anticipated using C++. The notes grew into a comprehensive collection of the constructs whose use separated "native speakers" of C++ from those who were just learning it as a second (or first) language. After much polishing and review, the notes appeared as *Advanced C++ Programming Styles and Idioms* in 1991.[3]

† Tom, in his discussions and writings, employed analogies between this work, and creations made on the loom that fills one of the rooms of his home: a harbinger of patterns?

The constructs were called idioms because, again, the term "patterns" was not yet in vogue. Furthermore, idioms aren't "full-fledged" patterns. Idioms are language-specific; patterns are broader design constructs with broader applicability across programming languages. Yet idioms captured design practices necessary to effective C++ programming; they described how to build abstractions that don't just fall out of an object-oriented analysis; most of them described symbiotic relationships between several objects. These characteristics of idioms foreshadowed what was to come in patterns.

About this time, my career focus turned from object-oriented technology to software development organization and process. Rather than follow the prevailing focus of the process community on process sequencing and intervals, I chose to assess processes indirectly by studying the architecture of their organizations. Key to this technique was the use of visual patterns (yes, there's that word) to identify instrumental organizations in development cultures. An instrumental organization is a self-organizing group of people with close ties and mutual interests, which may (and usually does) cut across institutional organization boundaries. The concept is known to cultural anthropology, which, after all, concerns itself largely with patterns of interaction in a culture. Cultural interaction patterns throw a powerful spotlight on the organization and its processes.

Kent Beck invited me into the patterns dialogue in mid-1993. At that time, a small patterns movement had already established its identity through the Software Architecture Workshop at OOPSLA, under the direction of Bruce Anderson and Peter Coad. I joined a subset of that group that met in Colorado in August 1993, to lay the groundwork for generative software patterns based on Alexander's work. Members of that group, which took the name "The Hillside Group," continue to foster and shepherd software design patterns today through electronic forums, a conference, talks, and publications.

I started digesting the works of Christopher Alexander in earnest, and exchanging patterns and pattern critiques through an ever-growing electronic mailing list. I saw the Hillside Group's patterns not only as the extrapolation of idioms into something much broader—like Burrows' data flow architecture vision—but also as a perfect expression of the recurring structures, practices, and interactions I found in software development organizations. Furthermore, I saw the opportunity to use patterns not only for analysis, but for synthesis as well. Today, I study patterns not only as a means to capture and shape software architecture, but as a way to understand and shape organizational architecture. I may address both in this column, but will focus on software patterns relevant to programmers using C++ (and other programming languages).

THE COLUMN WITHOUT A NAME

I decided to call this column "The Column without a Name" after a suggestion made by Ken Auer of KSC,[Δ] a member of the Hillside Group. The name clearly takes it cue from Alexander's writings, and his quest for "The Quality Without a Name." Alexander measures architecture by this Quality, which applies to the result of any creative process. He describes the Quality in broad terms of systems' ability to "be alive": to be a part of, and to support, our lives. This Quality happens when the forces in a system are resolved. At a cruder level, this Quality is utilitarian, aesthetically pleasing, robust, and whole. But Alexander notes that any attempt to name or measure the Quality is futile: that all words confuse more than they explain.[4] (Can you think of any programming language which, at some time, was not the subject of an obfuscation contest?)

Alexander in turn draws on more ancient sources for this phrase. The intrigue of names is an important aspect of our fascination with human language, and has been throughout history. In some cultures, names and their invocation have the power to invoke their subject; the name and the thing are inseparable. In other cultures and world-views, names are ephemeral, human creations, conventions by which we understand an amorphous reality. The classic Chinese writer Lao-Tzu notes that "the Tao which can be named is not the true Tao."[5] Indeed, the role that language itself plays in communication can be brought into question. Voltaire wryly notes that "mankind was given speech so that he may better hide his thoughts." We must look beyond language to find the expressions that separate survival from greatness. In architecture, for example, we need to capture the architectural intent that goes beyond the language of the blueprints if we are to build great buildings.

If this is so with natural language, why not view computer languages with the same suspicion? Each language has its own modes of expression—both its native, "primer" forms of expression, and its idioms, as discussed earlier. But such expression goes only so far. C++ can't tell us why the designer chose a given idiom, what problem it solves, what other idioms might apply if circumstances

Δ The naming of things is likely to be a recurring theme in future installations of this column.

change, or indeed whether a given collection of code is idiomatic at all. These are crucial design considerations that deserve structured linguistic expression.

Pattern languages provide a framework to capture such design considerations. A pattern language is not a programming language, but a structured collection of natural language blocks that give the inexpert designer some modest expert insights. For me, patterns are an opportunity to take the next logical step in the progression from C++, past object-oriented design, through idioms, and into the next generation of software design. This column is both a vehicle to share such patterns, and a prod to think about design and programming in new ways. It is no less so for you than it will be for me. Our search for patterns in our respective realms of expertise will be a search within ourselves, to understand how we think about design, and to find expression for those thoughts so others can take advantage of our experience. If this column succeeds, it will help the experts among you discover and articulate the magic already within you that makes your great software great. If you do not consider yourself a software virtuoso, then this column might take you to a new level of design understanding, particularly for the systems you implement in C++.

Those who follow this column should understand that this is new terrain. We have witnessed some small successes with patterns ("small" in the sense of either scope or scale), but a full-fledged endorsement and blueprint of patterns would be premature at this point. Through this column, I wish to broaden the scope of the dialogue about patterns in the industry, hoping that the dialogue that follows will hone and shape the direction of patterns. It is my wish not to incite readers to premature practice. It is important to let the dialogue educate us, as an industry, to the point where development projects can invest in their use with confidence.

Mapping Out the Patterns Column

I could continue to tell you about patterns in future appearances of this column (as I have done so far in this issue): Much is being said these days about the value of context and history in understanding new software languages and tools. At the Conference on Pattern Languages of Programming in Illinois this past August, attendees had the opportunity to relive some of the same experiences that shaped the philosophy of the Hillside group. But just as the best way to learn a new programming language is by writing programs in it, the best way for you and I to learn patterns together is to write patterns instead of just writing or reading about patterns. Many in the Hillside Group—and Kent Beck in particular—have established a stigma against "going meta." We want to grapple with the *Stoff* of patterns before moving on to generalities and platitudes.

I resolve these forces by making this a dual-purpose column. The first part of the column will be about patterns, including tips and techniques, new developments, answers to commonly asked questions, and much about the relationship between software patterns and techniques from other disciplines. The second part of the column will contain one or more patterns. These will almost always be software patterns, and almost all of them will have direct applicability for C++ programmers.

As opportunities arise to do so, I would like to use the column as a forum for two-way dialogue. If you have thoughts or questions on patterns, send them to me. I will consider reprinting questins or discussions on issues of sufficiently broad interest.

A PATTERN AS PROMISED

Over the next few months, I will present a series of patterns that build a simple pattern language. These patterns are all relevant to C++, and they come from the established body of idioms currently in common use in the C++ community. One might jump to the conclusion that little is to be gained from recasting well-known idioms as patterns. My experience suggests that the exercise is worthwhile. It reinforces the pattern form, building on what people know about the techniques to extrapolate to what they may not know about the form. And, for some, the light will come on, and they will see the patterns' applicability and purpose for the first time, or they may see it in a new light: Experience has borne this out.

In last month's article, we started this trend with the pattern C++ Type Promotion. I end this month's column with a pattern called The Counted Body Pattern.§ This pattern applies to classes to which the basic handle/body pattern has been applied. It forms the basis for patterns that will follow in future columns.

Name: Counted Body Pattern
Problem: Naive implementations of assignment in C++ are often inefficient or incorrect.

§ In their forthcoming book, Gamma, Helm, Johnson, and Vlissides describe related patterns based on their Bridge pattern. Watch for this book at a technical bookstore near you soon this fall.

Context: A design has been transformed into body/handle C++ class pairs (Handle/Body pattern). The pattern may be relevant to other object-based programming languages.
Forces: Assignment in C++ is defined recursively as member-by-member assignment with copying as the termination of the recursion; it would be more efficient and more in the spirit of Smalltalk if copying were rebinding.

- Copying of bodies is expensive.
- Copying can be avoided by using pointers and references, but these leave the problem of who is responsible for cleaning up the object, and leave a user-visible distinction between built-in types and user-defined types.
- Sharing bodies on assignment is usually semantically incorrect if the shared body is modified through one of the handles.

Solution:

- A reference count is added to the body class to facilitate memory management.
- Memory management is added to the handle class, particularly to its implementation of initialization, assignment, copying, and destruction.
- It is incumbent on any operation that modifies the state of the body to break the sharing of the body by making its own copy. It must decrement the reference count of the original body.

Forces Resolved:

- Gratuitous copying is avoided, leading to a more efficient implementation.
- Sharing is broken when the body state is modified through any handle. Sharing is preserved in the more common case of parameter passing, etc.
- Special pointer and reference types are avoided.
- Smalltalk semantics are approximated; garbage collection is driven off of this model.

Design Rationale: Reference counting is efficient and spreads the overhead across the execution of real-time programs. This implementation is a variation of shallow copy with the semantics of deep copy and the efficiency of Smalltalk name-value pairs.

Example:

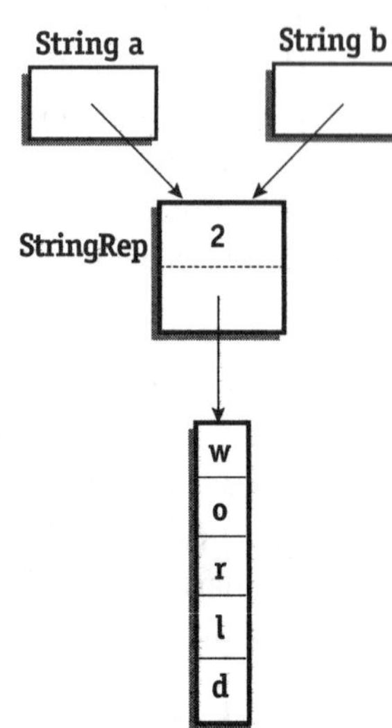


```
class String {
private:
    class StringRep {
    friend class String;
        StringRep(const char *s):count(1)
        {
            strcpy(rep=new char[strlen(s)+1], s);
        }
        ~StringRep() { delete rep; }
        int count; char *rep;
    } *rep;
public:
    String():rep(new StringRep("")) { }
    String(const String &s):
        rep(s.rep) { rep->count++; }
    String &operator=(const String &s){
        s.rep->count++;
        if(--rep->count <= 0) delete rep;
        rep = s.rep;
        return *this;
    }
    ~String() {
        if(--rep->count <= 0) delete rep;
    }
    String(const char *s):
        rep(new StringRep(s)) { }
    . . . .
};

int main() {
    String a = "hello", b = "world";
    a = b;
    return 0;
}
```

REFERENCES

1. Coplien, J. O. Generative pattern languages, *C++ Report,* 6(6), 1994.
2. Coplien, J. O. *ISHMAEL:* An integrated software/hardware maintenance and evaluation system, *AT&T Technical Journal,* 70(1), 1991.
3. Coplien, J. O. *Advanced C++ Programming Styles and Idioms,* Addison-Wesley, Reading, MA, 1992.

4. Alexander, C. *The Timeless Way of Building*, Oxford University Press, New York, 1979, p. 38.
5. Cheng, M.-J. My words are very easy to understand, *Lectures on the Tao Teh Ching* (translated from the Chinese by T.C. Gibbs). North Atlantic Books, Richmond, CA, 1981, ch. 1.
6. Gamma, E., R. Helm, R. Johnson, and J. Vlissides, *Design Patterns: Elements of Reusable Object-Oriented Software,* Addison-Wesley, Reading, MA, forthcoming.

PERSPECTIVES FROM THE "GANG OF FOUR"

JOHN VLISSIDES

This article marks the first installment of another column that still runs to this day: "Pattern Hatching" by John Vlissides. Over the years, John has provided us with a wealth of great material in this column. He has given us insight into the process by which patterns are 'hatched' from existing applications, and has exposed quite a few great patterns while we watched.

In this article, John talks about patterns in general, the format of the pattern form used in Design Patterns, *and then focuses in upon an investigation of the* Composite *pattern.*

JIM COPLIEN has laid the groundwork for all sorts of discussions on software patterns in "The Column Without a Name." In this column I'll offer another perspective on this emerging discipline, one that reflects my experience as a member of the "Gang of Four." I'm referring not to some group of malefactors, I think, but to Erich Gamma, Richard Helm, Ralph Johnson, and myself. Together we authored *Design Patterns: Elements of Reusable Object-Oriented Software*, a book of 23 patterns distilled from numerous object-oriented software systems.[1]

In *Design Patterns* we've tried to describe recurring snippets of object-oriented design that impart those elusive properties of good software: elegance, flexibility, extensibility, and reusability. We've recorded these snippets in a form that, although different from Alexander's,[2] is nevertheless faithful to pattern ideals. More on our pattern form later.

The patterns in the book come from many application domains, including user interfaces, compilers, programming environments, operating systems, distributed systems, financial modeling, and computer-aided design. That's not to say design patterns are domain-specific, however. We were careful to include only proven designs we'd seen again and again across domains.

We call our patterns "design patterns" for at least a couple of reasons. Our work has its roots in Erich Gamma's doctoral dissertation, where he coined the term.[3] He wanted to emphasize that he was capturing *design* expertise as opposed to other software development skills, such as domain analysis or implementation. Another reason is that "pattern" alone means different things to different people, even among pattern aficionados. Prepending "design" provides some needed qualification. But since I'll be talking mostly about design patterns in this column, I'll dispense with the "design" prefix whenever I can get away with it.

As for the title of this column, I chose "Pattern Hatching" initially for its similarity to a familiar concept in computer science. (Besides, all the good titles were taken.) But I've come around to thinking that it captures my intent for this column rather well. "Hatching" doesn't suggest that we are creating anything. It implies development from preexisting rudiments. That happens to be appropriate: *Design Patterns* is our incubator of eggs, as it were, from which much new life will hopefully emerge. (I trust we won't have opportunity to take this analogy too much further.)

The "Pattern Hatching" column will not merely echo the book. My aim is to build on what's in the book, to leverage its concepts so that we can learn from them and improve on them.

DESIGN PATTERNS VERSUS ALEXANDER'S PATTERNS

Design patterns have a substantially different structure from Alexander's patterns. Basically, Alexander starts with a short statement describing the problem, followed by an example that explains and resolves the forces behind the problem, and culminates in a succinct statement of the solution. Except for a few typographical embellishments, the pattern looks much like conventional prose. It invites reading through from start to finish. The down side is that this structure is rather coarse; there's no structure at a finer level, just narration. If for example you need detailed information about a particular "force" in the pattern, you have to scan through a lot of text.

Design patterns are more highly structured by comparison. They have to be.

They contain more material than Alexander's patterns: the average design pattern is 10 pages, compared to four (smaller) pages for its Alexandrian counterpart. Design patterns also describe in detail how you might implement the pattern, including sample code and a discussion of implementation trade-offs. Alexander seldom deals with construction details on a comparable level.

We could have presented this material using a more Alexander-like structure, but we wanted to allow quick reference in the heat of design or implementation. Since we don't prescribe an order in which to apply the patterns (as would a true pattern language in the Alexandrian tradition), there's less to guide you to the right pattern. Even if you know which pattern you want, its size could make it hard to find the detail that interests you. We had to make it fast and easy for designers to find the patterns that are appropriate to their problems. That led us toward a finer-grained pattern structure.

Design Pattern Structure

A design pattern has the following 13 sections:

1. Name
2. Intent
3. Also Known As
4. Motivation
5. Applicability
6. Structure
7. Participants
8. Collaborations
9. Consequences
10. Implementation
11. Sample Code
12. Known Uses
13. Related Patterns

The first three sections identify the pattern. Section 4 approximates the content of an Alexandrian pattern: It gives a concrete example that illustrates the problem, its context, and its solution. Sections 5–9 define the pattern abstractly. Most people seem to understand things better when they're explained in concrete terms first, followed by more abstract terms. That's why a design pattern considers the problem and its solution concretely before describing them in the abstract. Section 10 gets concrete again, and section 11 is the most concrete of all. Section 12 is bibliographic, and section 13 provides cross-references.

BUILDING WITH COMPOSITES

Let's take the **Composite** pattern as an example. Its intent is twofold: Compose objects into tree structures to represent part–whole hierarchies, and give clients a uniform way of dealing with these objects whether they are internal nodes or leaves. To motivate the pattern, let's consider how we might design a hierarchical file system. For now I'll focus on just two particularly important aspects of the design. I'll build on this example in subsequent columns as a way of showing you how other patterns address design issues.

From the user's perspective, the file system should handle file structures of arbitrary size and complexity. It shouldn't put arbitrary limits on how wide or deep the file structure can get. From the implementor's perspective, the representation for the file structure should be easy to deal with and extend.

Suppose you are implementing a command that lists the files in a directory. The code you write to get the name of a *directory* shouldn't have to be different from the code you write to get the name of a *file*—the same code should work for both. In other words, you should be able to treat directories and files uniformly with respect to their names. The resulting code will be easier to write and maintain. You also want to accommodate new kinds of files (like symbolic links, for example) without reimplementing half the system.

It's clear that files and directories are key elements in our problem domain and that we need a way of introducing specialized versions of these elements after we've finalized the design. An obvious design approach would be to represent these elements as objects, as shown in Figure 1.

How do you implement such a structure? The fact that we have two kinds of objects suggests two classes, one for files and one for directories. We want to treat files and directories uniformly, which means they must have a common interface. In turn, that means the classes must be derived from a common (abstract) base class, which we'll call "`Node`." We also know that directories aggregate files. Together, these constraints essentially define the class hierarchy for us:

```
class Node {
public:
    // declare common interface here
protected:
    Node();
};
```

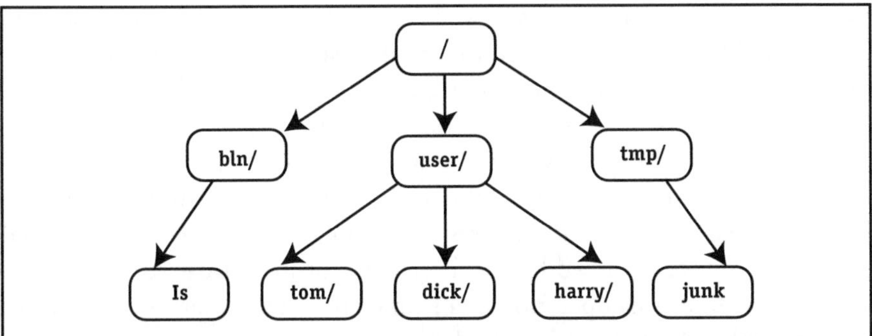

Figure 1.

```
class File : public Node {
public:
    File();

    // redeclare common interface here
};

class Directory : public Node {
public:
    Directory();

    // redeclare common interface here
private:
    List<Node*> _nodes;
};
```

The next question to consider concerns the makeup of the common interface. What are the operations that apply equally to files and directories? Well, there are all sorts of attributes of interest, like name, size, protection, and so forth. Each attribute can have operations for accessing and modifying its value(s). Operations like these that have clear meaning for both files and directories are easy to treat uniformly. The tricky issues arise when the operations don't seem to apply so clearly to both.

For example, one of the most common things users do is ask for a list of the files in a directory. That means that Directory needs an interface for enumerating its children. Here's a simple one that returns the *n*th child:

```
virtual Node* GetChild(int n);
```

GetChild must return a Node*, because the directory may contain either File objects or Directory objects. The type of that return value has an important ramification: It forces us to define GetChild not just in the Directory class but in the Node class as well. Why? Because we want to be able to list the children of a subdirectory. In fact, the user will often want to descend the file system structure. We won't be able to do that unless we can call GetChild on the object GetChild returns. So, like the attribute operations, GetChild is something we want to be able to apply uniformly.

GetChild is also key to letting us define Directory operations recursively. For example, suppose Node declares a Size operation that returns the total number of bytes consumed by the directory (sub)tree. Directory could define its version of this operation as a sum of the values that its children return when their Size operation is called:

```
long Directory::Size () {
    long total = 0;
    Node* child;

    for (int i = 0; child = GetChild(i); ++i) {
        total += child->Size();
    }

    return total;
}
```

Directories and files illustrate the key aspects of the Composite pattern: It generates tree structures of arbitrary complexity, and it prescribes how to treat those objects uniformly. The Applicability section of the pattern echoes these aspects. It states that you should use Composite when

- you want to represent part–whole hierarchies of objects.
- you want clients to be able to ignore the difference between compositions of objects and individual objects. Clients will treat all objects in the composite structure uniformly.

The pattern's Structure section presents a modified OMT diagram of the canonical Composite class structure (see Fig. 2). By "canonical" I mean simply that it represents the most common arrangement of classes that we (the Gang of Four) have observed. It can't represent the *definitive* set of classes and relationships, because the interfaces may vary when we consider certain design or implementation-driven trade-offs. (The pattern will spell those out, too.)

Figure 2 shows the classes that participate in the pattern and their static relationships. Component is the abstract base class to which our Node class corresponds. Subclass participants are Leaf (which corresponds to File) and Composite (corresponding to Directory). The arrowhead line

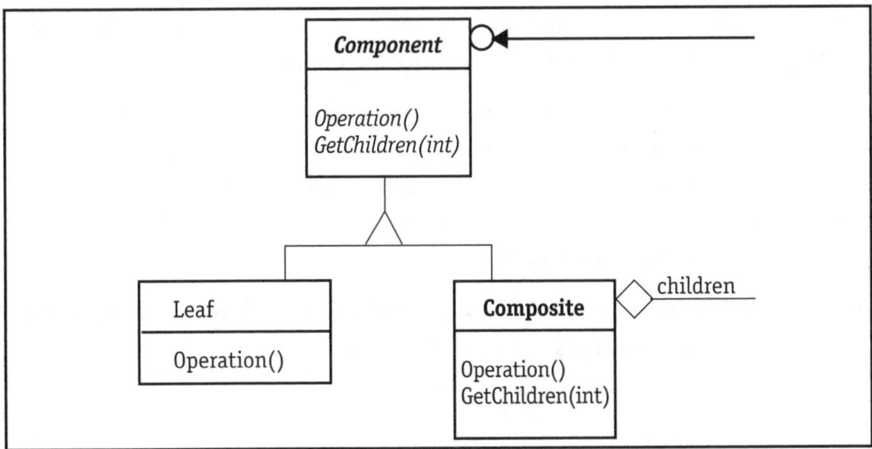

Figure 2. OMT structure diagram for Composite.

going from Composite to Component indicates that Composite contains instances of type Component. The ball at the tip of the arrowhead indicates more than one instance; if the ball were omitted, it would mean *exactly* one instance. The diamond at the base of the arrowhead line means that the Composite aggregates its child instances, which implies that deleting the Composite would delete its children as well. It also implies that components aren't shared, thus assuring tree structures. The Participant and Collaboration sections of the pattern explain the static and dynamic relationships, respectively, among these participants.

Composite's Consequences section sums up the benefits and liabilities of the pattern. On the plus side, the pattern supports tree structures of arbitrary complexity. A corollary of this property is that a node's complexity is hidden from clients: they can't tell whether they're dealing with a leaf or a composite component, because they don't have to. That makes client code more independent of the code in the components. The client is also simpler, because it can treat leaves and composites uniformly. No longer do clients have to decide which of multiple code paths to take based on the type of component. Best of all, you can add new types of components without touching existing code.

Composite's down side, however, is that it can lead to a system where the class of every object looks like the class of every other. The significant differences show up only at run-time. That can make the code hard to understand, even if you are privy to class implementations. Moreover, the number of objects may become prohibitive if the pattern is applied at a low level or at too fine a granularity.

As you might have guessed, implementation issues abound for the `Composite` pattern. Some of the issues we address include:

- when and where to cache information to improve performance,
- what if any storage the Component class should allocate,
- what data structure(s) to use for storing children, and
- whether or not operations for adding and removing children should be declared in the Component class.

Since I'm rapidly running out of space, I'll take a closer look at these and other implementation questions in future columns.

WINDING DOWN

People tend to react to design patterns in one of two ways, which I'll try to describe by way of analogy.

Picture an electronics hobbyist who, though bereft of formal training, has nevertheless designed and built a slew of useful gadgets over the years: a ham radio, a Geiger counter, a security alarm, and many others. One day the hobbyist decides it's time to get some official recognition for this talent by going back to school and earning a degree in electronics. As the coursework unfolds, the hobbyist is struck by how familiar the material seems. It's not the terminology or the presentation that's familiar but the underlying concepts. The hobbyist keeps seeing names and rationalizations for stuff he's used implicitly for years. It's just one epiphany after another.

Cut now to the first year undergraduate taking the same classes and studying the same material. The undergrad has no electronics background—lots of rollerblading, yes, but no electronics. The stuff in the course is intensely painful for him, not because he's dumb, but because it's so totally new. It takes quite a bit more time for the undergrad to understand and appreciate the material. But eventually he does, with hard work and a bit of perseverance.

If you feel like a design pattern hobbyist, then more power to you. If on the other hand you feel more like the undergrad, take heart: the investment you make in learning good patterns will pay for itself each time you apply them in your designs. That's a promise.

But maybe electronics, with its "techie" connotations, isn't the best analogy for everyone. If you agree, then consider something Alfred North Whitehead said in 1943, admittedly in a different context, which might nonetheless make a more appealing connection:

Art is the imposing of a pattern on experience, and our aesthetic enjoyment in recognition of the pattern.

References

1. Gamma, E., R. Helm, R. Johnson, J. Vlissides. *Design Patterns: Elements of Reusable Object-Oriented Software*, Addison-Wesley, Reading, MA, 1995.
2. Alexander, C., *et al. A Pattern Language,* Oxford University Press, New York, 1977.
3. Gamma, E. *Object-Oriented Software Development Based on ET++: Design Patterns, Class Library, Tools*, (in German), PhD thesis, University of Zurich Institut für Informatik, 1991.

Present Day Industrial Diamonds

The Open–Closed Principle

Robert C. Martin

It was probably in 1995, just after the publication of my book. I was posting heavily on comp.lang.c++ that year. A fellow by the name of Jim Flemming started a tirade against C++, and promoted a language named C+@ (Pronounced "CAT"). His posts were incendiary, and sometimes rather personal.

At one point he posted "The Ten Commandments of Object-Oriented Programming" which consisted of simple heuristics such as making sure your variables were private, etc. I considered the post a refreshing change from his otherwise argumentative postings, but also thought the list of commandments to be a bit naive.

I had been thinking quite a bit about design principles during that time, and something about Flemming's article crystallized the concept in my mind. I responded to his post with another article that I called the Principles of Object-Oriented Design.

Over the months, these concepts grew and flourished, until I was ready to publish a series of articles about them. This article is the first of that series. "The Open-Closed Principle."

The other articles are all in the publication section of http://www.-objectmentor.com. They are entitled:

The Liskov Substitution Principle
The Dependency Inversion Principle
The Interface Segregation Principle
Granularity
Stability

Whereas the techniques of refactoring tell us the mechanism for changing code from one form to another, the principles give us guidance as to what form the eventual code should take. They help to define the "Normal Form" of well-structured code.

In this article I mention the upcoming book Advanced Principles and Patterns of OOD. *Sigh, I am still writing that book. But now, it has mu-*

tated into the second edition of my first book, and is entitled: "Designing Object Oriented Applications with UML".

THIS IS THE FIRST of my Engineering Notebook columns for the *C++ Report.* The articles that will appear in this column will focus on the use of C++ and object-oriented designs (OOD), and will address issues of software engineering. I will strive to write articles that are pragmatic and directly useful to the software engineer in the trenches. In these articles I will make use of Booch's notation for documenting OODs.

There are many heuristics associated with OOD. For example, "all member variables should be private," or "global variables should be avoided," or "using runtime type identification (RTTI) is dangerous." What is the source of these heuristics? What makes them true? Are they *always* true? This column investigates the design principle that underlies these heuristics—the open-closed principle.

As Ivar Jacobson said: "All systems change during their life cycles. This must be borne in mind when developing systems expected to last longer than the first version."[1] How can we create designs that are stable in the face of change and that will last longer than the first version? Bertrand Meyer[2] gave us guidance as long ago as 1988 when he coined the now famous open-closed principle. To paraphrase him:

> *Software entities (classes, modules, functions, etc.) should be open for extension, but closed for modification.*

When a single change to a program results in a cascade of changes to dependent modules, that program exhibits the undesirable attributes that we have come to associate with "bad" design. The program becomes fragile, rigid, unpredictable and unreusable. The open-closed principle attacks this in a very straightforward way. It says that you should design modules that *never change*. When requirements change, you extend the behavior of such modules by adding new code, not by changing old code that already works.

DESCRIPTION

Modules that conform to the open-closed principle have two primary attributes.

1. They are "Open for Extension." This means that the behavior of the module can be extended. Thus we can make the module behave in new

and different ways as the requirements of the application change, or to meet the needs of new applications.

2. They are "Closed for Modification." The source code of such a module is inviolate. No one is allowed to make changes to it. It would seem that these two attributes are at odds with each other. The normal way to extend the behavior of a module is to make changes to the module. A module that cannot be changed is normally thought to have a fixed behavior. How can these two opposing attributes be resolved?

Abstraction Is the Key

In C++, using the principles of OOD, it is possible to create abstractions that are fixed and yet represent an unbounded group of possible behaviors. The abstractions are abstract base classes, and the unbounded group of possible behaviors is represented by all the possible derivative classes. It is possible for a module to manipulate an abstraction. Such a module can be closed for modification since it depends upon an abstraction that is fixed. Yet the behavior of that module can be extended by creating new derivatives of the abstraction.

Figure 1 shows a simple design that does not conform to the open-closed principle. Both the Client and Server classes are concrete. There is no guarantee that the member functions of the Server class are virtual. The Client class *uses* the Server class. If we wish for a Client object to use a different server object, then the Client class must be changed to name the new server class.

Figure 2 shows the corresponding design that conforms to the open-closed principle. In this case, the AbstractServer class is an abstract class with pure-virtual member functions. The Client class uses this abstraction. However, objects of the Client class will be using objects of the derivative Server class. If we want Client objects to use a different server class, then a new derivative of the AbstractServer class can be created. The Client class can remain unchanged. This design is an example of the bridge pattern form *Gamma et al.*[3]

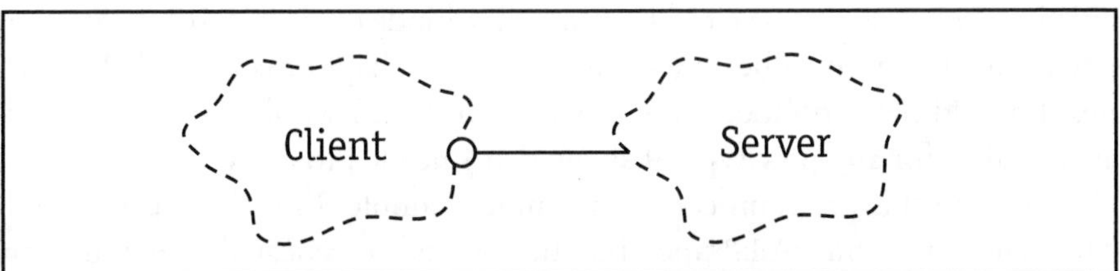

Figure 1. Closed Client.

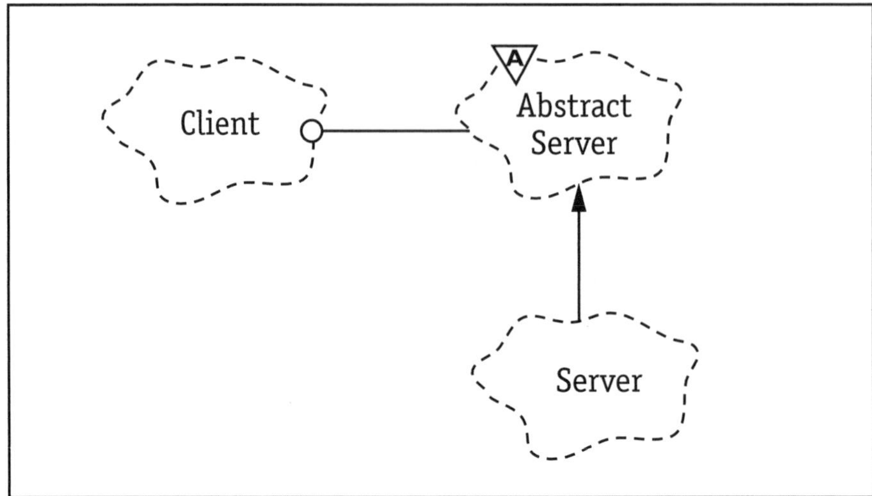

Figure 2. Open Client

THE Shape ABSTRACTION

Consider the following example. We have an application that must be able to draw circles and squares on a standard GUI. The circles and squares must be drawn in a particular order. A list of the circles and squares will be created in the appropriate order and the program must walk the list in that order and draw each circle or square.

In C, using procedural techniques that do not conform to the open-closed principle, we might solve this problem as shown in Listing 1. Here we see a set of data structures that have the same first element, but are different beyond that. The first element of each is a type code that identifies the data structure as either a circle or a square. The function DrawAllShapes walks an array of pointers to these data structures, examining the type code and then calling the appropriate function (either DrawCircle or DrawSquare).

The function DrawAllShapes does not conform to the open-closed principle because it cannot be closed against new kinds of shapes. If I wanted to extend this function to be able to draw a list of shapes that included triangles, I would have to modify the function. In fact, I would have to modify the function for any new type of shape that I needed to draw.

Of course this program is only a simple example. In real life the switch statement in the DrawAllShapes function would be repeated over and over

Listing 1. Procedural Solution to the Square/Circle Problem.

```
enum ShapeType {circle, square};

struct Shape
{
ShapeType itsType;
{;

struct Circle
{
    ShapeType itsType;
    Double itsRadius;
    Point itsCenter;
{;

struct Square
{
    ShapeType itsType;
    Double itsSide;
    Point itsTopLeft;
};

//
// These functions are implemented elsewhere
//
void DrawSquare(struct Square*)
void DrawCircle (struct Circle*);
typedef struct Shape *ShapePointer;

void DrawAllShapes(ShapePointer list[ ], int n)
{
    int i;
    for (i=0; i<n, i++)
    {
        struct Shape* s=list[ i ];
        switch (s->itsType)
        {
        case square:
            DrawSquare((struct Square*)s);
        break;

        case circle:
            DrawCircle((struct Circle*)s);
        break;
        }
    }
}
```

Listing 2. OOD solution to Square/Circle problem.

```
class Shape
{
public:
        virtual void Draw ( ) const = 0;
};

class Square : public Shape
{
public:
        virtual void Draw ( ) const;
};
class Circle : public Shape
{
public:
        virtual void Draw ( ) const;
};
void DrawAllShapes (set<Shape*>& list)
{
    for (Iterator<Shape*>(list); i; i++)
        (*i)->Draw( );
}
```

again in various functions all over the application; each one doing something a little different. Adding a new shape to such an application means hunting for every place that such switch statements (or if/else chains) exist, and adding the new shape to each. Moreover, it is very unlikely that all the switch statements and if/else chains would be as nicely structured as the one in DrawAllShapes. It is much more likely that the predicates of the if statements would be combined with logical operators, or that the case clauses of the switch statements would be combined so as to "simplify" the local decision making. Thus the problem of finding and understanding all the places where the new shape needs to be added can be nontrivial.

Listing 2 shows the code for a solution to the square/circle problem that conforms to the open–closed principle. In this case an abstract Shape class is created. The abstract class has a single pure-virtual function called Draw. Both Circle and Square are derivatives of the Shape class.

Note that if we want to extend the behavior of the DrawAllShapes function in Listing 2 to draw a new kind of shape, all we need do is add a new derivative of the Shape class. The DrawAllShapes function does not need to change. Thus DrawAllShapes conforms to the open-closed principle. Its behavior can be extended without modifying it.

In the real world the Shape class would have many more methods. Yet adding a new shape to the application is still quite simple since all that is required is to create the new derivative and implement all its functions. There is no need to hunt through all of the applications looking for places that require changes.

Since programs that conform to the open-closed principle are changed by adding new code, rather than by changing existing code, they do not experience the cascade of changes exhibited by nonconforming programs.

Strategic Closure

It should be clear that no significant program can be 100% closed. For example, consider what would happen to the DrawAllShapes function from Listing 2 if we decided that all Circles should be drawn before any Squares. The DrawAllShapes function is not closed against a change like this. In general, no matter how "closed" a module is, there will always be some kind of change against which it is not closed.

Since closure cannot be complete, it must be strategic. That is, the designer must choose the kinds of changes against which to close his design. This takes a certain amount of prescience derived from experience. The experienced designer knows the users and the industry well enough to judge the probability of different kinds of changes. He then makes sure that the open-closed principle is invoked for the most probable changes.

Using Abstraction to Gain Explicit Closure

How could we close the DrawAllShapes function against changes in the ordering of drawing? Remember that closure is based upon abstraction. Thus, in order to close DrawAllShapes against ordering, we need some kind of "ordering abstraction." The specific case of ordering above had to do with drawing certain types of shapes before other types of shapes.

An ordering policy implies that, given any two objects, it is possible to discover which ought to be drawn first. Thus, we can define a method of Shape named Precedes that takes another Shape as an argument and returns

Listing 3. Shape with ordering methods.

```
class Shape
{
public:
    virtual void Draw( ) const = 0;
    virtual bool Precedes(const Shape&) const =0;

    bool operator<(const Shape& s) {return Precedes(s); }
};
```

Listing 4. DrawAllShape with Ordering.

```
void DrawAllShapes(Set<Shape*>& list)
{
    // copy elements into
    // OrderedSet and then sort.
     OrderedSet<Shape*> orderedList = list;
        orderList.Sort( );

    for (Iterator<Shape*> i(orderedList); i; i++)
        (*i)->Draw( );
```

a bool result. The result is true if the Shape object that receives the message should be ordered before the Shape object passed as the argument.

In C++ this function could be represented by an overloaded operator< function. Listing 3 shows what the Shape class might look like with the ordering methods in place.

Now that we have a way to determine the relative ordering of two Shape objects, we can sort them and then draw them in order. Listing 4 shows the C++ code that does this. This code uses the Set, OrderedSet and Iterator classes from the Components category developed in my book.[4]

This gives us a means for ordering Shape objects, and for drawing them in the appropriate order. But we still do not have a decent ordering abstraction. As is stands, the individual Shape objects will have to override the Precedes method in order to specify ordering. How would this work? What kind of code would we write in Circle::Precedes to ensure that Circles were drawn before Squares? Consider Listing 5.

It should be very clear that this function does not conform to the open-closed principle. There is no way to close it against new derivatives of Shape. Every time a new derivative of Shape is created, this function will need to be changed.

Listing 5. Ordering a Circle.

```
bool Circle::Precedes(const Shape& s) const
{
    if (dynamic_cast<Square*>(s))
        return true;
    else
        return false;
]
```

Using a "Data Driven" Approach to Achieve Closure

Closure of the derivatives of Shape can be achieved by using a table driven approach that does not force changes in every derived class. Listing 6 shows one possibility.

By taking this approach we have successfully closed the DrawAllShapes function against ordering issues in general and each of the Shape derivatives against the creation of new Shape derivatives or a change in policy that reorders the Shape objects by their type. (e.g. Changing the ordering so that Squares are drawn first.)

The only item that is not closed against the order of the various Shapes is the table itself. And that table can be placed in its own module, separate from all the other modules, so that changes to it do not affect any of the other modules.

Extending Closure Even Further

This isn't the end of the story. We have managed to close the Shape hierarchy, and the DrawAllShapes function against ordering that is dependent upon the type of the shape. However, the Shape derivatives are not closed against ordering policies that have nothing to do with shape types. It seems likely that we will want to order the drawing of shapes according to some higher level structure. A complete exploration of these issues is beyond the scope of this article; however, the ambitious reader might consider how to address this issue using an abstract OrderedObject class contained by the class OrderedShape, which is derived both from Shape and OrderedObject.

Listing 6. Table driven type ordering mechanism

```
#include <typeinfo.h>
#include <string.h>
enum {false, true};
typedef int bool;

class Shape
{
public:
    virtual void Draw ( ) const = 0;
    virtual bool Precedes (const Shape&) const;

    bool operator<(const Shape& s) const
    {return Precedes(s);}

private:
    static char* typeOrderTable [ ];
};

char* Shape::typeOrderTable[ ] =
{
    "Circle,"
    "Square,"
    0
};

//This function searches a table for the class names. The table defines
// the order in which the shapes are to be drawn. Shapes that are not
//found always precede shapes that are found.

bool Shape::Precedes(const Shape& s) const
{
    const char* thisType = typeid(*this).name( );
    const char* argType = typeid(s). name( );
    bool done = false;
    int thisOrd = -1;
    int argOrd = -1;
    for (int i=0; !done; i++)
    {
        const char* tableEntry = typeOrderTable[i];
        if (tableEntry !=0)
        {
            if (strcmp(tableEntry, thisType) ==0)
            thisOrd = i;
```

Listing 6. (continued)

```
            if (strcmp(tableEntry, argType) ==0)
                argOrd = i;
            if ((argOrd > 0) && (thisOrd > 0))
                done = true;
            }
            else //table entry == 0
                done = true;
        }
    return thisOrd < argOrd;
}
```

Heuristics and Conventions

As mentioned at the beginning of this article, the open–closed principle is the root motivation behind many of the heuristics and conventions that have been published regarding OOD over the years. Here are some of the more important of them.

Make All Member Variables Private

This is one of the most commonly held of all the conventions of OOD. Member variables of classes should be known only to the methods of the class that defines them. Member variables should never be known to any other class, including derived classes. Thus they should be declared private, rather than public or protected.

In light of the open–closed principle, the reason for this convention ought to be clear. When the member variables of a class change, every function that depends upon those variables must be changed. Thus, no function that depends upon a variable can be closed with respect to that variable.

In OOD, we expect that the methods of a class are not closed to changes in the member variables of that class. However we *do* expect that any other class, including subclasses *are closed* against changes to those variables. We have a name for this expectation, we call it: *encapsulation.*

Now, what if you had a member variable that you knew would never change? Is there any reason to make it private? For example, Listing 7 shows a class Device that has a bool status variable. This variable contains the status of the last operation. If that operation succeeded, then status will be true; otherwise it will be false.

Listing 7. nonconst public variable.

```
class Device
{
public:
    bool status;
};
```

Listing 8.

```
Class Time
{
public;
   int hours, minutes, seconds;
   Time& operator-=(int seconds);
   Time& operator+=(int seconds);
   bool  operator< (const Time&);
   bool  operator> (const Time&);
   bool  operator==(const Time&);
   bool  operator!=(const Time&);
};
```

We know that the type or meaning of this variable is never going to change. So why not make it public and let client code simply examine its contents? If this variable really never changes, and if all other clients obey the rules and only query the contents of status, then the fact that the variable is public does no harm at all. However, consider what happens if even one client takes advantage of the writeable nature of status, and changes its value. Suddenly, this one client could affect every other client of Device. This means that it is impossible to close any client of Device against changes to this one misbehaving module. This is probably far too big a risk to take.

On the other hand, suppose we have the Time class as shown in Listing 8. What is the harm done by the public member variables in this class? Certainly they are very unlikely to change. Moreover, it does not matter if any of the client modules make changes to the variables, the variables are supposed to be changed by clients. It is also very unlikely that a derived class might want to trap the setting of a particular member variable. So is any harm done?

One complaint I could make about Listing 8 is that the modification of the time is not atomic. That is, a client can change the minutes variable without changing the hours variable. This may result in inconsistent values for a Time object. I would prefer it if there were a single function to set the time that took three arguments, thus making the setting of the time atomic. But this is a very weak argument.

It would not be hard to think of other conditions for which the public nature of these variables causes some problems. In the long run, however, there is no *overriding* reason to make these variables private. I still consider it bad *style* to make them public, but it is probably not bad *design*. I consider it bad style because it is very cheap to create the appropriate inline member functions; and the cheap cost is almost certainly worth the protection against the slight risk that issues of closure will crop up.

Thus, in those rare cases where the open-closed principle is not violated, the proscription of public and protected variables depends more upon style than on substance.

No Global Variables—Ever

The argument against global variables is similar to the argument against public member variables. No module that depends upon a global variable can be closed against any other module that might write to that variable. Any module that uses the variable in a way that the other modules don't expect, will break those other modules. It is too risky to have many modules be subject to the whim of one badly behaved one.

On the other hand, in cases where a global variable has very few dependents, or cannot be used in an inconsistent way, they do little harm. The designer must assess how much closure is sacrificed to a global and determine if the convenience offered by the global is worth the cost.

Again, there are issues of style that come into play. The alternatives to using globals are usually very inexpensive. In those cases it is bad style to use a technique that risks even a tiny amount of closure over one that does not carry such a risk. However, there are cases where the convenience of a global is significant. The global variables cout and cin are common examples. In such cases, if the open-closes principle is not violated, then the convenience may be worth the style violation.

RTTI Is Dangerous

Another very common proscription is the one against dynamic_cast. It is often claimed that dynamic_cast, or any form of run-time type identification

Listing 9. RTTI violating the open-closed principle.

```
class shape { };

class Square : public Shape
{
private:
   Point  itsTopLeft;
   Double itsSide;
   friend DrawSquare(Square*);
};

class Circle : public Shape
{
private:
   Point  itsCenter;
   Double its Radius;
   friend DrawCircle(Circle*);
};

void DrawAllShapes(Set<Shape*>& ss)
{
   for (Iterator<Shape*>i(Ss); i;i++)
   {
         Circle* c = dynamic_cast<Circle*>(*i);
         Square* s = dynamic_cast<Square*>(*i);
         if (c)
              DrawCircle(c);
         else if (s)
              DrawSquare(s);
   }
}
```

(RTTI) is intrinsically dangerous and should be avoided. The case that is often cited is similar to Listing 9 which clearly violates the open-closed principle. However Listing 10 shows a similar program that uses dynamic_cast, but does not violate the open-closed principle.

The difference between these two is that the first, Listing 9, *must* be changed whenever a new types of Shape is derived. (Not to mention that is just downright silly.) However, nothing changes in Listing 10 when a new derivative of Shape is created. Thus, Listing 10 does not violate the open-closed principle.

As a general rule of thumb, if a use of RTTI does not violate the open-closed principle, it is safe.

Listing 10. RTTI that does not violate the open-closed principle.

```
class Shape
{
public:
  virtual void Draw( ) const = 0;
};

class Square : public Shape
{
      // as expected.
};

void DrawSquareOnly(Set<Shape*>& ss)
{
  for (Iterator<Shape*>i(ss); i; i++)
  {
      Square* s=dynamic_cast<Square*>(*i);
      if (s)
          s->Draw ( )

  }
}
```

Conclusion

There is much more that could be said about the open-closed principle. In many ways this principle is at the heart of OOD. Conformance to this principle is what yields the greatest benefits claimed for object-oriented technology, i.e., reusability and maintainability. Yet conformance to this principle is not achieved simply by using an object-oriented programming language. Rather, it requires a dedication on the part of the designer to apply abstraction to those parts of the program that the designer feels are going to be subject to change.

This article is an extremely condensed version of a chapter from my forthcoming book, *The Advanced Principles and Patterns of OOD.* In subsequent articles we will explore many of the other principles of OOD. We will also study various design patterns, and their strengths and weaknesses with regard to implementation in C++. We will study the role of Booch's class categories in C++, and their applicability as C++ namespaces. We will define what "co-hesion" and "coupling" mean in an OOD, and we will develop metrics for measuring the quality of an OOD., and after that, many other interesting topics.

REFERENCES

1. Jacobson, I. OBJECT ORIENTED SOFTWARE ENGINEERING A USE CASE DRIVEN APPROACH, Reading, MA Addison-Wesley, 1992, 21.
2. Meyer, B. OBJECT ORIENTED SOFTWARE CONSTRUCTION. Prentice Hall, 1988, p. 23.
3. Gamma, E., R. Helm, R. Johnson, J. Vlissides, DESIGN PATTERNS: ELEMENTS OF REUSABLE OBJECT-ORIENTED SOFTWARE, Reading, MA, Addison-Wesley, 1995.
4. Martin, R.C. DESIGNING OBJECT ORIENTED C++ APPLICATIONS USING THE BOOCH METHOD. Prentice Hall, 1995.

LARGE-SCALE C++ SOFTWARE DESIGN

PART 1: MENTOR GRAPHICS EXPERIENCES USING C++ FOR LARGE SYSTEMS

JOHN LAKOS

In 1996, John Lakos wrote a book entitled Large Scale C++ Software Design, *published by Addison-Wesley. This book recounts John's experiences with using C++ in very large applications. It also talks of his strategies for dealing with huge compile, link, and release times. The book develops metrics for measuring the structure of the software, and techniques for refactoring the software to improve its structure and decrease compile, link, and release times. The book is a masterpiece.*

The next three articles are a kind of summary of that book. They were published in the C++ Report *over a 6-month period in 1996. They are a* must read *for any serious C++ engineer.*

MANY TECHNIQUES AND PRACTICES learned through experiences with smaller C++ projects simply do not scale well compared to larger development efforts. Naïve use of familiar ad hoc practices in larger projects invariably results in systems of low quality that are painful expensive to maintain. In 1985, Mentor Graphics (a leader in the Electronic Design Automation industry) became one of the first companies to attempt a truly large project in C++. At that time, no one anticipated the cost overruns, slipped schedules, huge executables, poor performance, and incredibly expensive build times that a naïve approach produces.

Valuable lessons were learned along the way—knowledge obtained through bitter experience. There were no books to help guide the design process; object-oriented designs on this scale had never before been attempted. Eight years later, with a wealth of valuable experience under its belt, Mentor Graphics produced several truly large software systems written in C++, and paved the way for others to do the same.

Achieving quality is an engineering responsibility; it must be actively sought from the start. Designing large, high-quality systems requires decomposing them into physical (not inheritance) hierarchies of smaller, more manageable components. Such systems with their acyclic physical dependencies are fundamentally easier and more economical to maintain, test, and reuse than tightly interdependent systems. Physical design quality is not something that can be added after a project is largely complete.

My book *Large Scale C++ Software Design* was written explicitly for experienced C++ software developers, system architects, and proactive quality assurance professionals involved in the development of very large scale C++ software systems and covers all aspects of large-scale development. Here, I limit my discussion to physical design concepts essential for success with larger projects, yet applicable to moderate size systems.

OVERVIEW

It would be ludicrous to attempt to erect a 50-story office building using the same materials and techniques a carpenter would use to build a single-family home. As it is in the construction industry, so it is in software: knowledge and experience gained from small projects are simply not adequate for building larger systems. Unfortunately, this truth is often not immediately apparent to those first attempting a large C++ project.

> *Experience gained from small projects does not always extend to larger development efforts.*

Just like C, even a small, poorly written C++ program can be very hard to understand and maintain. If interfaces are not fully encapsulating, it will be difficult to tune or to enhance implementations. Poor encapsulation will hinder reuse, and any advantage in testability will be eliminated.

Contrary to popular belief, object-oriented programs—in their most general form—are fundamentally more difficult to test and verify than their procedural counterparts.[1]

The ability to alter internal behavior via virtual functions can invalidate class invariants essential to correct performance. Further, the potential number of control flow paths through an object-oriented system can be explosively large.

Fortunately, it is not necessary to write such arbitrarily general (and untestable) object-oriented programs. Reliability can be achieved by restricting our use of the paradigm to a more testable subset without sacrificing performance, functionality, or creativity.

As programs get larger, forces of a different nature come into play. Most notably, larger projects can fail due to a poor physical design. We now examine specific instances of some of the kinds of problems that we are likely to encounter.

Cyclic Link-Time Dependencies

Most likely you have been in a situation where you were looking at a software system for the first time and you could not seem to find a reasonable starting point or a piece of the system that made sense on its own. Not being able to understand or use any part of a system independently is a symptom of a cyclically dependent design.

C++ objects have a phenomenal tendency to get tangled up in each other. This insidious form of tight physical coupling is illustrated in Figure 1. A circuit is a collection of elements and wires. Consequently, a `Circuit` knows about the definitions of both `Element` and `Wire`. An element knows the circuit to which it belongs, and can tell whether or not it is connected to a specified wire. Hence, an `Element` also knows about both `Circuit` and `Wire`. Finally a wire can be connected to a terminal of either an element or a circuit. To do its job, a `Wire` must access the definitions of both `Element` and `Circuit`.

The definition for each of these types reside in a separate physical component (translation unit) to improve modularity. But even though the implementations of these individual types are fully encapsulated by their interfaces, the `.c` files for each component are forced to include the header files of the other two. The resulting dependency graph for these three components is cyclic. That is, no one component can be used or even tested without the other two.

Large systems that are naively architected tend to become tightly coupled by cyclic dependencies and fiercely resist decompositions. Supporting such systems can be a nightmare, and effective modular testing is often impossible. A case in point is an early version of an electronic design database. At the time, its authors did not realize the need for avoiding cyclic dependencies in the physical design. The result was an interdependent collection of

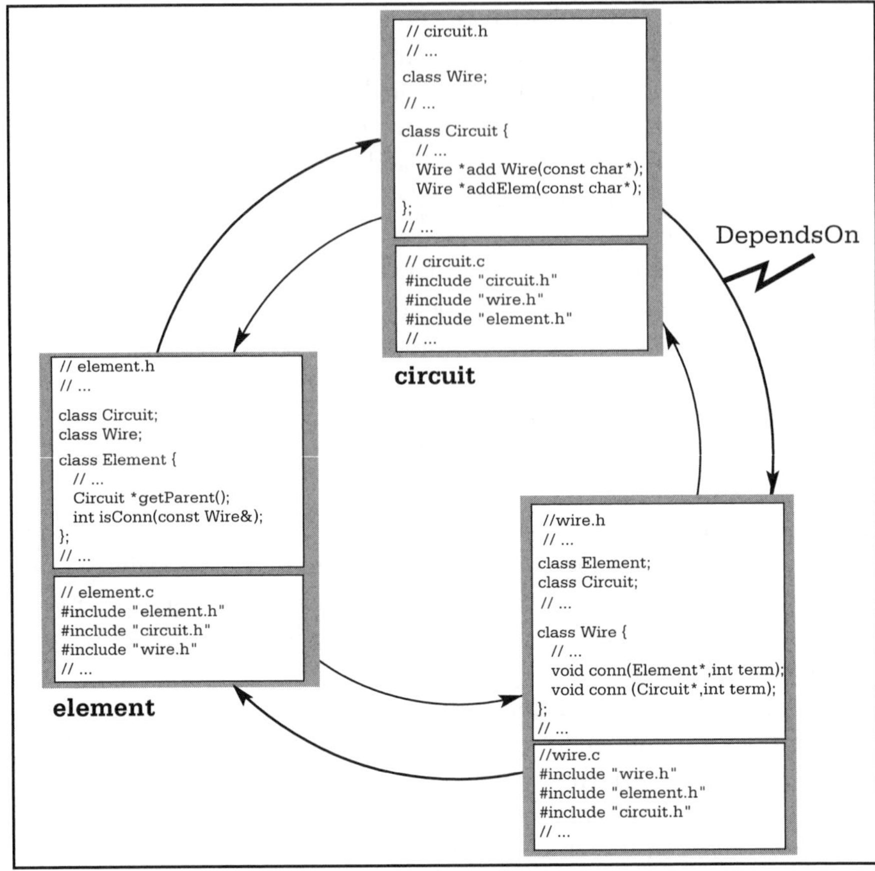

Figure 1. Cyclically dependent components.

files containing hundreds of classes with thousands of functions, and no way to use or even test it except as a single module. This system had very poor reliability, proved impractical to extend or maintain, and ultimately had to be thrown out and rewritten from scratch.

By contrast, hierarchical physical designs (i.e., without cyclic interdependencies) are relatively easy to understand, test, and reuse incrementally.

EXCESSIVE LINK-TIME DEPENDENCIES

If you have attempted to link to a small amount of functionality in a library and found that your time to link has increased disproportionately to the benefit you are deriving, then you may have been trying to reuse heavy-weight rather than light-weight components.

One of the nice things about objects is that it is easy to add missing functionality as the need presents itself. This almost seductive feature of the paradigm has tempted many conscientious developers to turn lean, well-thought-out classes into huge dinosaurs that embody a tremendous amount of code—most of which is unused by most clients.

Figure 2 shows what can happen when the functionality in a simple string class is allowed to grow to fill the needs of all clients. Each time a new feature is added for one client, it potentially costs the rest of the clients increased instance size, code size, runtime, and physical dependencies.

C++ programs are often somewhat larger than necessary. But if care is not taken, the executable size for a C++ program could be much larger than it would be if the equivalent program were written in C. By ignoring external dependencies, over-ambitious class developers have created sophisticated classes that directly or indirectly depend on enormous amounts of code. A "Hello World" program employing one particularly elaborate `String` class produced an executable size of 1.2 Megabytes!

Overweight components such as this `String` class not only increase executable size but can make the linking process unduly slow and painful. If the time necessary to link in `String` (along with all of its implementation dependencies) is large relative to the time it would otherwise take to link your subsystem, it is less likely that you would bother to reuse `String`.

Fortunately, techniques exist for avoiding these and other forms of unwanted link-time dependencies.

Excessive Compile-Time Dependencies

If you have ever tried to develop a multi-file program in C++ then you know that changing a header file can potentially cause several translation units to recompile. During early stages of system development making a change that forces the entire system to recompile presents no significant burden. As you continue to develop your system, however, the idea of making a change to a low-level header file becomes increasingly distasteful. Not only is the time to recompile the entire system increasing, but so is the time to compile even individual translation units. Sooner or later, you will simply refuse to modify a low-level class because of the cost to recompile. If this sounds familiar, then you may have experienced excessive compile-time dependencies.

Excessive compile-time coupling (virtually irrelevant for small projects) can grow to dominate the development time for larger projects. Figure 3 shows an example of what appears to be a good idea at first but turns bad as the size of a system grows. The **myerror** component defines a struct **MyError** which contains an enumeration of all possible error codes. Each new component added to the system naturally includes this header file. Unfortunately, each new component may have its own error codes that have not already been identified in the master list (see Figure 4).

```
// str.h
#ifndef INCLUDED_STR
#define INCLUDED_STR

class String {
    char  *d_string_p;
    int d_length;
    int d_size;
    int d_cound;
    // ...
    double d_creationtime;

  public:
    String();
    String(const String& s);
    String (const char *cp);
    String(const char c);
    // ...
    ~String();
    String &operator=(const.String& s);
    String &operator+=(const String& s);
    // ...
    // (27 pages omitted!)
    //
    int isPalindrome() const;
    int isNameOfFamousActor() const;
};
// ...
#endif
```

```
// str.c
#include "str.h"
#include "sun.h"
#include "moon.h"
#include "stars.h"
//...
// (lots of dependencies omitted)
// ...
#includes "theirbrother.h"

String:String()
: d-string_p(0)
, d_length (0)
, d-size(0)
, d_count(0)
// ...
// ...
// ...
```

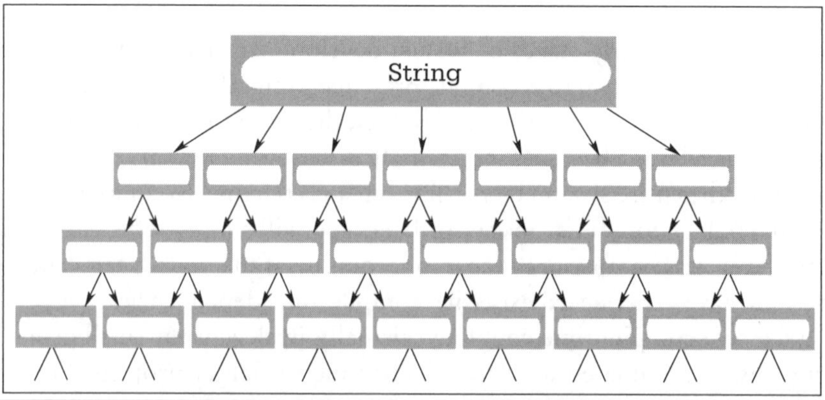

String

Figure 2. Oversized, heavy-weight, nonreusable String class.

As the number of components gets larger, our desire to add to this list will wane and will be a tempted to reuse existing error codes that are, perhaps, only roughly appropriate just to avoid changing myerror.h. Eventually, we will abandon any thought of adding a new error code, and simply return ERROR or WARNING rather than change myerror.h. By the time we reach this point, the design is unmaintainable and practically useless.

```
//myerror.h
#ifndef INCLUDED_MYERROR  //standard (internal)
#define INCLUDED_MYERROR  //include guard

struct MyError {
  enum Codes {
    SUCCESS = 0,
    WARNING,
    ERROR,
    IO_ERROR,
    // ...
    READ_ERROR,
    WRITE_ERROR,
    // ...
    // ...
    BAD_STRING,
    BAD_FILENAME,
    // ...
    // ...
    CANNOT_CONNECT_TO_WORK_PHONE,
    CANNOT_CONNECT_TO_HOME_PHONE,
    // ...
    // ...
    MARTIANS_HAVE_LANDED,
    // ...
  };
};

#endif
```

Figure 3. An insidious source of compile-time coupling.

Unnecessary Compile-Time Dependencies

There are many other causes of unwanted compile-time dependencies. A large C++ program tends to have more header files than an equivalent C program. The unnecessary inclusion of one header file by another is a common source of excessive coupling in C++ (See Listing 1).

Consider the example in Listing 1. A Bank class uses a BankCard class and a variety of currency classes in its interface. The Bank class does not inherit from any other class. Let us assume that Bank does not have any inline function that make substantive use of class BankCard or any of the currency classes and that class Bank does not embed instances of any user-defined class (HasA) in its own definition.

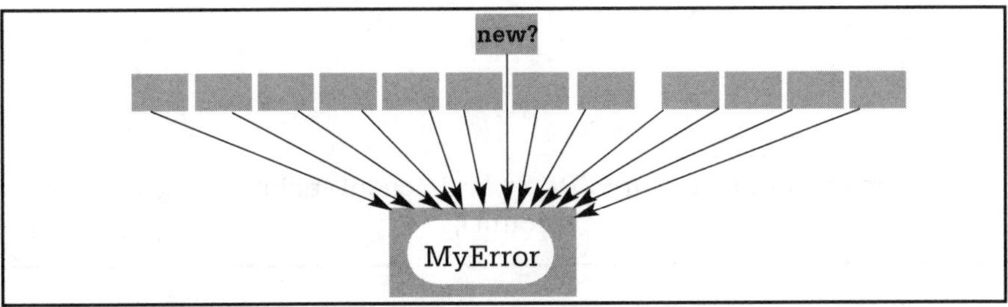

Figure 4. Adding yet another component with new error codes.

Listing 1. Class Using Many Types in the Interface.

```
//bank.h
#ifndef INCLUDED_BANK                       //standard (internal)
#define INCLUDED_BANK                       // include guard

#ifndef INCLUDED_BANKCARD                   // redundant (external)
#include "bankcard.h"                       // include guard
#endif

#ifndef INCLUDED_GERMANMARKS
#include "germanmarks.h"
#endif

#ifndef INCLUDED_JAPENESEYEN
#include "japeneseyen.h"
#endif

#ifndef INCLUDED_UNITEDSTATESDOLLARS
#include "unitedstatesdollars.h"
#endif

#ifndef INCLUDED_ENGLISHPOUNDS
#include "englishpounds.h"
#endif

// ...
// ...
// ...

#ifndef INCLUDED_LAKOSIANFOOBARS
#include "lakosianfoobars.h"
#endif

class Bank {
    // ...
    Bank(const Bank&);                      //We don't want to copy
    Bank& operator=(const Bank&);           // or assign banks.

    public:
      //CREATORS
      Bank();
      ~Bank ();

      //MANIPULATORS
      GermanMarks getMarks(BankCard *cashMachineCard, double
                                amount);
```

(continued)

Listing 1. (continued)

```
        JapeneseYen getYen(BankCard *cashMachineCard, double
                                        amount);
        UnitedStateDollars getDollars(BankCard *cashMachineCard,
                                                double amount);
    EnglishPounds getPounds(BankCard *cashMachineCard, double
                                        amount);
        // ...
        // ...
        // ...
        LakosianFooBars getFooBars(BankCard* cashMachineCard,
    double amount);
};

#endif
```

Now consider a client of this bank in the United States. This person is typically interested in going to the bank with his or her bank card and withdrawing money in United States dollars. A toy implementation of a Person's withdraw member function is implemented as follows:

```
// person.c
#include "person.h"
#include "bank.h"

//...

void Person::withdraw(double amount)
{
        d_wallet_p->putIn(d_bank_p->getDollars
        (d_cashMachineCard_p, amount));
}
```

Picture if you will the fictitious island republic of Lakos; its national unit of currency, the *FooBar*, is notoriously unstable and subject to change without notice. Today, this country has again announced its intention to make an uninsulated change to its implementation of FooBar. The world financial community is demanding to know who will be forced to recompile.

Not only will all actual clients of LakosianFooBars have to recompile but so would all other clients of Bank. That is, if you banked at this bank, whether or not you ever cared or had even heard about LakosianFooBars, any change to lakosianfoobar.h will cause software configuration management tools (such as *make*) to recompile you automatically.

To add insult to injury, there is no need for you to be compile-time dependent on that currency! None of your code depends on that currency at compile time. So why did the Bank's author decide to include all these header files in bank.h (instead of bank.c)? The answer you might receive is, "for the convenience of the bank's clients."

The author of the bank component believes that just in case you might need some class definition, we'll include it for you. This approach has the relatively small advantage that, as long as you include bank.h, you will never need to include the header for UnitedStatesDollars or your BankCard. This approach has the relatively large disadvantage that you will forever be at the mercy of a potentially large number of header files that you neither control nor otherwise care about.

It is not necessary to include the definition of objects in the Bank's header file just because a client of Bank may find these definitions useful. Doing so forces the client to depend on all such components at compile-time whether or not they are actually used. Excessive #include directives not only increase the cost of compiling the client, but increases the likelihood that the client will need to be recompiled as a result of a low-level change to the system.

By ignoring compile-time dependencies, it is possible to cause each translation unit in the system to include nearly every header file reducing compilation speed to a crawl. One of the first truly large C++ projects (literally thousands of man-years) was a CAD framework product developed at my company. The developers initially had no idea of how much compile-time dependencies would impede their efforts. Even using our large network of workstations, recompiling the entire system was taking on the order of a week!

The problem was due to organizational details illustrated in part by the bank component shown in Listing 1. Each header file was including one or more header files that, in turn, include one or more other header files, until eventually virtually every header file in the system has been included. Cosmetic techniques (e.g., redundant, external include guards) were developed to mitigate the problem, but the real solution came when the unnecessary compile-time dependencies were eliminated entirely.

As with link-time dependencies, there are several specific techniques available for eliminating compile-time dependencies.

REUSE

The term *reuse* means different things to different people. Object-oriented design touts reuse as an incentive, yet like many other benefits of the paradigm, it is not without cost. Although reuse of objects and functions within a single physical unit is almost always desirable, reuse across physical boundaries implies coupling, and coupling in itself is undesirable. If several programmers are attempting to use the same standard component without demanding functional changes, the reuse is probably reasonable and justified.

But consider the scenario where there are several clients working on different programs, and each is attempting to "reuse" a common component to achieve a somewhat different purpose. If those otherwise independent clients are actively seeking enhancement support, they could find themselves at odds with one another as a result of the reuse. An enhancement for one client could disrupt the others (as we saw with the shared enumeration in Figure 3). Worse, we could wind up with an overweight class (like the String class of Figure 2) that serves the needs of no one.

Unlike a program (see Figure 5), a system has no top—no one main program that executes all its functionality. Instead, a system (see Figure 6) is comprised of a collection of interdependent components that support a particular application domain. Reuse is often the right answer. But for a component or subsystem to be reused (or tested) effectively in separate programs, it must not be tied to a large block of unnecessary code. That is, it must be possible to reuse the part of the system that is needed to implement a particular program without having to link in the rest of the system.

> *Reuse is not without cost; reuse implies coupling and coupling can be undesirable.*

Not all code an be reusable. Attempting to implement excessive functionality or robust error checking for implementation objects can add unnecessarily to the development and maintenance cost as well as to the size of the executable. Large projects stand to benefit from its implementors' knowing both when to reuse components and when to make components reusable.

OBSERVATIONS

Reduced reliability, increased maintenance costs, increased executable size, and reduced runtime performance are among the likely consequences of a poor sys-

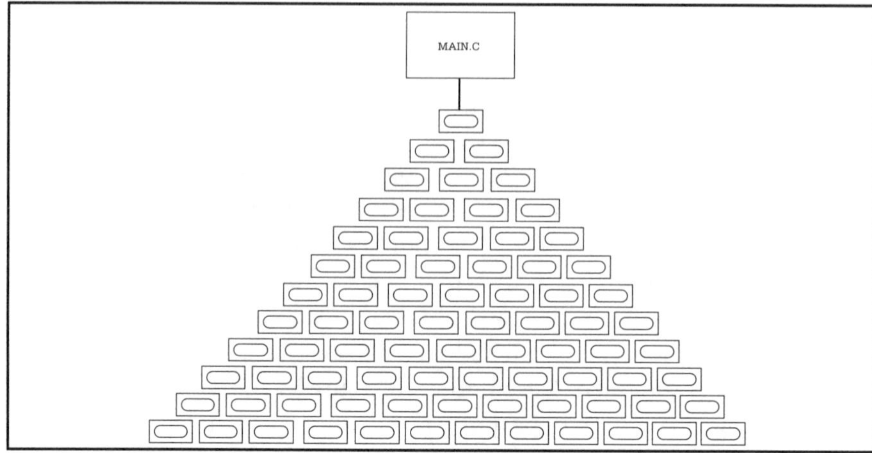

Figure 5. A large program

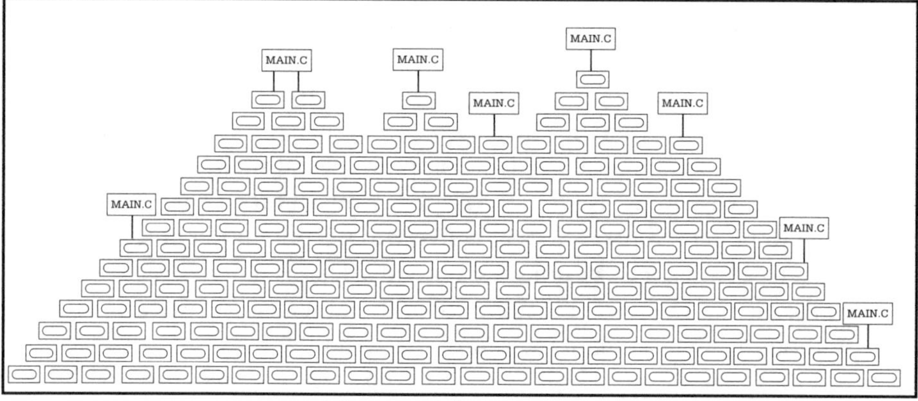

Figure 6. A large system.

tem architecture. Reduced testability, reduced usability, and reduced modifiability are important primary causes. Secondary causes include increased link time, reduced understandability, and increased compile-time. But the root cause of these problems can often be traced to excessive link-time and compile-time dependencies among the physical components of a system (see Figure 7).

Both compile-time and link-time dependencies affect physical design quality, by increasing the time needed to compile and link programs. But more importantly, excessive physical dependencies compromise understandability, and therefore both usability and maintainability. Moreover, excessive physical dependencies can undermine successful reuse in separate executables. It

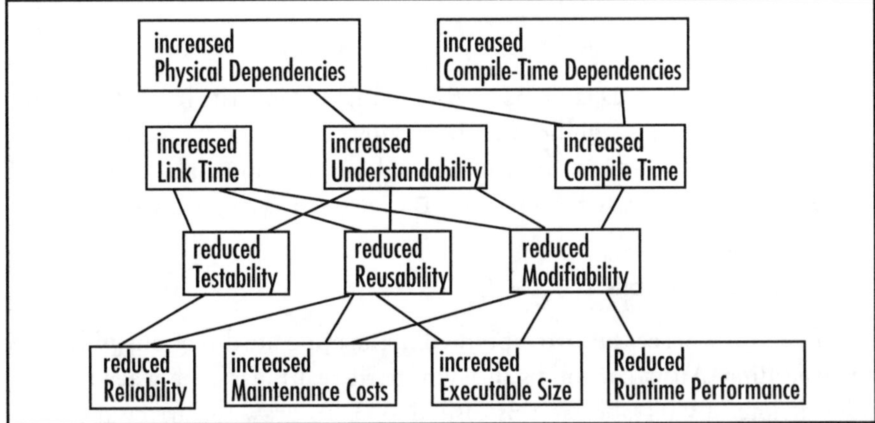

Figure 7. Root causes of poor quality in large systems.

Definition:

NOTATION	MEANING
X	X is a logical entity (e.g., class).
x	x is a physical entity (e.g., file).
B —IsA→ *A*	*B* is a kind of *A*.
B ○—Uses-In-The-Interface— *A*	*B* uses *A* in *B*'s interface.
B ●—Uses-In-The-Implementation— *A*	*B* uses *A* in *B*'s implementation.

Figure 8. Notations and their meanings.

is by minimizing these physical interdependencies that we achieve fundamental quality in our software designs.

Logical Design Notation

Object-Oriented design lends itself to a rich set of notations.[2] Most of these notations denote relationships between the logical entities of a design (see Fig. 8).

If there is ever a need for additional logical notation, a labeled arrow explicitly identifying the relationship will suffice.

ISA

D ──► *B* means that "*D* is a kind of *B*" and that "D inherits from *B*". The direction of the arrow is significant; it points in the direction of implied dependency. Class D depends on B because D is derived from B. The definition of class B must have already been seen for D to name B as a base class:

```
class B {/*...*/}
class D : public B {/*...*/};
```

Often you will see the arrow pointed in the opposite direction, which can be misleading. An arrow shows an asymmetric realtionship between two entities denoted by its label (in this case "IsA"). To draw the arrow the other way, we would logically have to call the relation something else, such as "Derives" or "Is-A-Base-Class-Of":

(D) ◄─Derives─ (B) (less useful)

This alternative notation is less desirable because the arrow points in the direction opposite to that of implied dependency.

USES-IN-THE INTERFACE

*B*o———*A* means, "*B* uses *A* in *B*'s interface." We will sometimes be sloppy and say, "*B* uses *A* in its interface," but we will always mean *B* uses *A* in *B*'s interface, and never *B* uses *A* in *A*'s interface.

Whenever a function names a type in its parameter list or names a type as a return value, that function is said to use that type in its interface. For example, the free function

```
int operator==(const IntSet&, const IntSet&);
```

clearly makes use of class IntSet in its interface. This function happens to return an int, so int also would be considered part of this function's interface. However, fundamental types are ubiquitous andomitted from such consideration in practice.

A type is used in the (public) interface of a class if the type is used in the interface of any (public) member function of that class.

For example, the construcor for class IntSetIter:

```
IntSetIter::IntSetIter(const IntSet&),
```

Table 1. Ways a Class Can use a Type in Its Implementation.

Name	*Meaning*
Uses	The class has a member function that names the type.
HasA	The class embeds an instance of the type.
HoldsA	The class embeds a pointer (or reference) to the type.
WasA	The class privately inherits from the type.

uses class IntSet in its interface, therefore, IntSet is used in the interface of IntSetIter.

You can think of the o—— symbol as an arrow with its tail at the bubble and the head missing (or as a conductor's baton pointing at a member of the orchestra). The direction of the implied arrow is important—it points in the direction of implied dependency, i.e., if *B* uses *A*, then *B* depends on *A* and not vice versa.

Uses-in-the-Implementation

B•————*A* means *A* is used in the implementation of B. Like its counterpart, "Uses-In-The-Implementation" suggests a physical dependency between two logical entities, while implicitly denying an interface dependency. A type is used in the implementation of a function if the type is referred to in the definition of that function.

Figure 9 shows the logical view of the intset component along with both kinds of uses relationships. In particular we see that

```
int operator==(const IntSet&, const IntSet&)
```

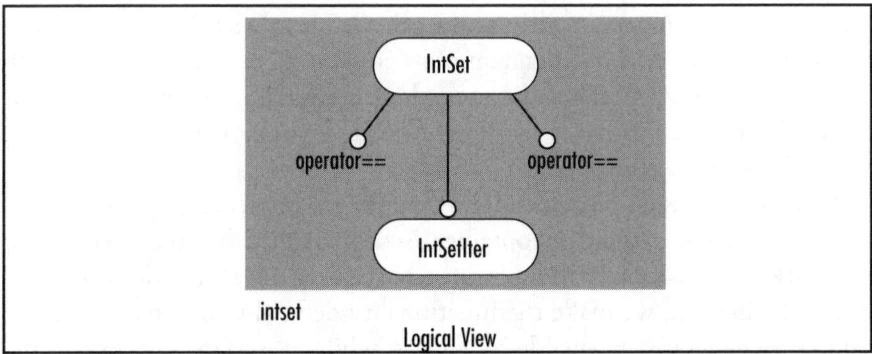

Figure 9. Logical view of component intset.

uses class IntSet in its interface and class IntSetIter in its implementation. We can also infer directly from Figure 9 that operator!= does *not* use IntSetIter in its interface. Although operator!= is shown implemented symmetrically to operator==, operator!= would probably be implemented in terms of operator== in practice.

> *A type is used in the implementation of a class if that type (1) is used in a member function of the class, (2) is referred to in the declaration of a data member of the class, or (3) is a private base class of the class.*

Layering is the process of building upon smaller, simpler, or more primitive types to form larger, more complex, or more sophisticated types. Often layering occurs through composition (e.g., HasA or HoldsA), but any form of substantive use (i.e., that would induce a physical dependency) would qualify as layering. The particular way in which our class uses a type will affect not only how our class depends on that type but also to what extent clients of our class will be forced to depend on that type. Here, we simply enumerate the different ways in which a class can use a type in its implementation.

Although a class can use a type in its implementation in several ways, the notation used to represent each of the variations identified in Table 1 is the same.

COMPONENTS

A component is not a class and vice versa. Conceptually, a component embodies a subset of the logical design that makes sense to exist as an independent, cohesive unit. Classes, functions, enumerations, and so on are the logical entities that make up these components. In particular, every class definition resides in exactly one component.

Structurally, a component is an indivisible, physical unit, none of whose parts can be used independently of the others. The physical form of a component is standard and independent of its content. A component consists of exactly one header (.h) file and one implementation (.c) file. We will ignore extraordinary circumstances that might justify a component's having more than a single .h or .c file.

As a concrete example, consider a component implementing a stack abstraction. A stack is a kind of container. Access to other than the top element of a stack is not normally thought of as part of a stack abstraction. By providing the iterator, we make the functionality defined in this stack component more generally extensible by clients, while preserving encapsulation.

Listing 2. Header file stack.h for a stack component.

```
// stack.h
#ifndef INCLUDED_STACK
#define INCLUDED_STACK

    class StackIter;

    class Stack {
        int *d_stack_p;                 // pointer to array of int
        int d_sp;                       // stack pointer (index)
        int d_size;                     // size of current array of int
        friend StackIter;

    public:
        //CREATORS
        Stack();                        // create an empty Stack
        Stack(const Stack& stack);
        ~Stack();

        //MANIPULATORS
        Stack& operator=(const Stack& stack);
    // copy Stack from Stack
        void push(int value);           // push integer onto this Stack
        int pop();                      // pop integer off this Stack
                                        // undefined if Stack empty

        //ACCESSORS
        int isEmpty()const;             // 1 if empty else O
        int top() const;                // integer on top of this Stack
                                        // undefined if Stack empty
};
```

(continued)

Listing 2 shows the header file for a stack component containing two classes defined at file scope, namely **Stack** and **StackIter**. We also see that there are two free (i.e., not member) operator functions implementing == and != between two **Stack** objects. Peeking at the implementation, we would discover that **operator==** uses **StackIter**, and that **operator!=** is implemented in terms of **operator==**. The complete set of logical entities at file scope in component **stack** is pictured in Figure 10a. The physical entities (**stack.h** and **stack.c**) along with their canonical physical relationship are depicted in Figure 10b.

A component will typically define one or more closely related classes and any free operators deemed appropriate for the abstraction it supports. Basic types (e.g., **Point**, **String**, **BigInt**, etc.) will each be implemented in a component containing a single class (Figure 11a). Container classes (e.g., **IntSet**, **Stack**, **List**) will typically be implemented in a component containing (at least)

Listing 2. (continued)

```
int operator==(const Stack& lhs, const Stack& rhs);
    //1 if two stacks contain identical values else 0

int operator!=(const Stack& lhs, const Stack& rhs);
    //1 if two stacks do not contain identical values else 0

class StackIter {                        // iter order: top to bottom
    int *d_stack_p;                      // points to orig. stack array
    int d_sp;                            // local stack pointer (index)
    StackIter(const StackIter&);         // not implemented
    StackIter& operator=(const StackIter&);

    public:
      //CREATORS
      StackIter(const Stack& stack); //initialize to top of Stack
      ~StackIter();

    //MANIPULATORS
      void operator++();                 //advance state of iteration
    //undefined if done
      //ACCESSORS
      operator const void *() const;     //non-zero if not done else 0
      int operator ()() const;           //value of current integer
    //undefined if done
};

#endif
```

the principle class and its iterator (Fig. 11b). More complex abstractions involving multiple types (e.g., Graph) can embody several classes in a single component (Fig. 11c). Finally, classes that provide a wrapper for an entire subsystem may form a thin encapsulating layer consisting of one or more principle classes and many iterators (Fig. 11d).

Each of the components in Figure 11 (like every other component) has a physical as well as a logical view. The physical view consists of the .h file and the .c file, with the .h file included as the first substantive line of the .c file. The physical implementation of a component always depends on its interface at compile time. This internal physical coupling contributes to the need to treat these two files as a single physical entity.

A component (and not a class) is the appropriate fundamental unit of both logical and physical design for at least three reasons:

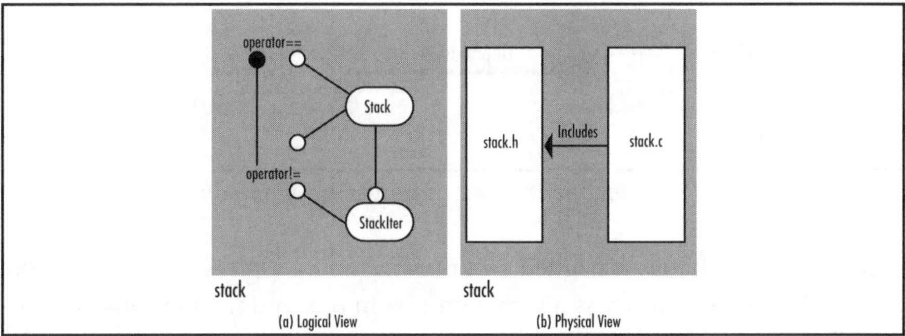

Figure 10. Two view of a stack *component: (a) Logical view; (b) Physical view.*

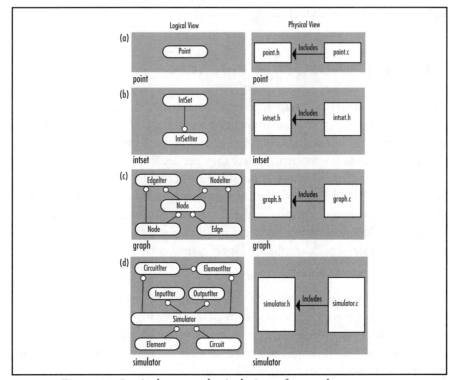

Figure 11. Logical versus physical view of several components.

1. A component bundles a manageable amount of cohesive functionality that often spans several logical entities (e.g., classes and free operators) into a single physical unit.
2. Not only does a component capture an entire abstraction as a single entity, but it allows for consideration of physical issues not addressed by class-level design.

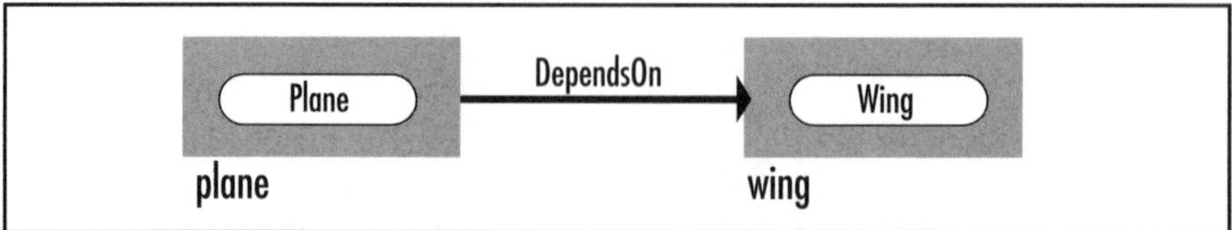

Figure 12. Component plane depends on *Component wing.*

3. An appropriately designed component (being a physical entity unlike a class) can be lifted as a single unit from one system and reused effectively in another system without having to rewrite any code.

Throughout this article, the need to consider physical as well as logical design issues will become increasingly evident.

THE "DEPENDSON" RELATION

Physical dependencies among the components that make up a system will affect its development, testing, maintenance, and independent reuse. The logical relations among classes and free (operator) functions imply physical dependencies among the components where they reside.

The DependsOn relation is quite different from the relations we have already seen. IsA and Uses are logical relations because they apply to logical entities, irrespective of the physical components in which those logical entities reside. DependsOn is a physical relation because it applies to components as a whole, which are themselves physical entities.

A component y *DependsOn a component* x *if* x *is needed to compile or link* y.

The notation used to represent the dependency of one physical unit on another is a (fat) arrow. For example, the diagram in Figure 12 illustrates how the component plane depends on component wing. That is, component plane cannot be used (i.e., it cannot be linked into a program or possibly even compiled) unless component wing is also available.

As has been our convention, logical entities are represented by ellipses, and physical entities are represented by rectangles. Notice that the arrow used to indicate physical dependency is drawn between components and not individual classes. The (fat) arrow notation used to denote physical dependency should never be confused with the arrow notation used to denote inheritance. An inheritance arrow always runs between two classes (which are logical entities); a DependsOn arrow connects physical entities (e.g., files, components, and packages).

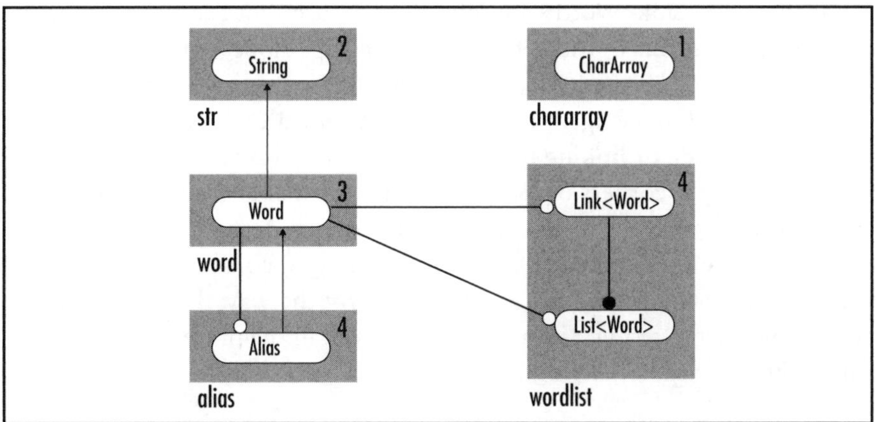

Figure 13. Component diagram showing only direct dependencies.

Implied Dependency

Logical designs imply certain physical characteristics. We would like to take full advantage of known logical relationships to predict the physical implications of our logical design *before* it is implemented. Resulting undesirable physical characteristics will often force us to alter or even rework our logical designs. Inferring physical dependencies at the design stage enables us to achieve a sound physical architecture much earlier in the development process. We now consider the implications of logical design on physical dependency, beginning with the Uses relation.

The Uses relationship between classes in separate components implies a physical dependency between these components (unless the dependency is in name only). According to Figure 13, class String uses class CharArray in its implementation. Assuming the use is substantive, this use implies that either string.h or string.c includes chararray.h. In either case, we will not be able to compile string.c without access to chararray. Thus component str DependsOn component chararray.

The IsA relation between classes in separate components always implies a compile-time dependency between the components that contain them. Figure 13 shows that class Word is a kind of String; hence, component word depends on component str.

Similarly, an Alias is a kind of Word that also uses Word in its interface. Fortunately, the physical dependency implied by both notations is in the same direction: alias depends on word. That is, we can test and reuse word independently of alias, but not vice versa.

Finally, both Link<Word> and List<Word> use Word in their respective interfaces. Either one of these logical relationships alone would be sufficient for us to infer a (likely) physical dependency of the entire wordlist component on word. Notice again that component word can exist in a program without including or linking to wordlist, but not vice versa. (The numbers in the upper right corners of the component boxes are called level numbers, and are explained in the next installment coming in August.)

To illustrate the DependsOn relation in action, consider the following skeleton header file for a string component. By the way, don't try to name your component "string"; it may not work well in the presence of the standard C library header <string.h>:

```
// str.h
#ifndef INCLUDED_STR
#define INCLUDED_STR

#ifndef INCLUDED_CHARARRAY          // redundant (external)
#include "chararray.h"              // include guard
#endif
class String {
            CharArray d_array: //HasA
        // ...
  public:
        //...
};
// ...
#endif
```

There is just enough information visible for us to see that class String has a data member of type CharArray. We know from C that if a struct has an instance of a user-defined type as a data member, it will be necessary to know the size and layout of that data member even to parse the definition of the struct.

> *A component* y *exhibits a compile-time dependency on component* x *if* x.h *is needed to compile* y.c.

More specifically, it is not possible to compile any file that needs the definition of String without first including chararray.h. (For that reason we are justified in nesting #include "chararray.h" in the header file of component str along with the concomitant redundant include guards.)

Figure 14 illustrates the physical dependency of component str on component chararray. A component's .c file must always depend on its .h file at com-

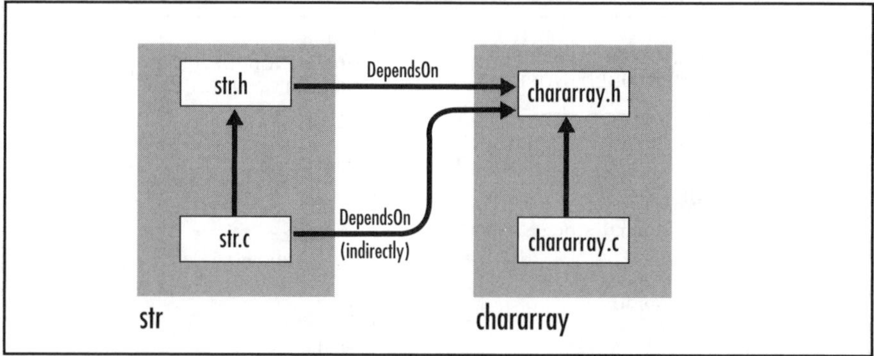

Figure 14. Indirect compile-time dependency of str.c *on* chararray.h.

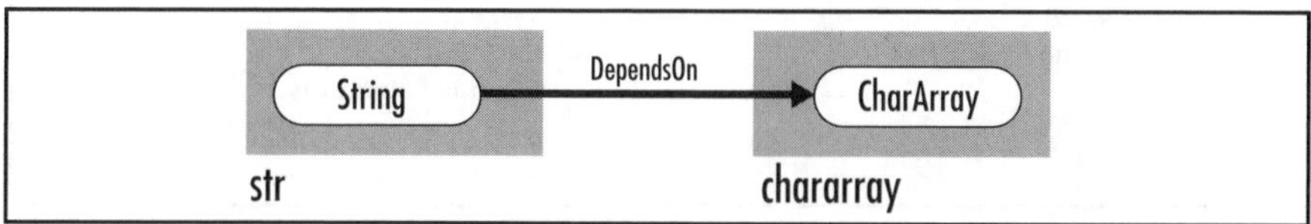

Figure 15. Abstract representation of component dependency.

pile time. Since str.c will not compile without str.h, and str.h will not compile without chararray.h, str.c has an indirect compile-time dependency on chararray.h. Notice that the arrow used to indicate the physical dependency is drawn between two physical entities (in this case, files). A more abstract representation of physical dependency at the component level is shown in Figure 15.

A component need not be dependent on another at compile time to be dependent on it at link time. Consider the implementation for component word and the alternate implementation of component str show in Figure 16.

Compiling chararray.c of course requires chararray.h. Both str.h and chararray.h are needed to compile str.c. Finally, both word.h and str.h are needed co compile word.c. Notice that chararray.h is not needed to compile word.c. There is no compile-time dependency of component word on the component chararray. However, word still exhibits a physical dependency on chararray, which will become obvious as soon as we try to link word.o to a test driver.

> *A component* y *exhibits a link-time dependency on component* x *if the object file* y.o *(produced by compiling* y.c*) contains undefined symbols for which* x.o *may be called upon either directly or indirectly to help resolve at link time.*

```
// word.h
#ifndef INCLUDED_WORD
#define INCLUDED_WORD

#ifndef INCLUDED_STR
#include "str.h"
#endif

class Word {
        String d_string;  //HasA
        // ...
      public:
        Word();
        // ...
};

#endif
```

```
// str.h
#ifndef INCLUDED_STR
#define INCLUDED_STR

class CharArray:

class String {
      CharArray *d_array_p; //HoldsA
        // ...
    public:
        String();
        // ...
};

#endif
```

```
//word.c
#include "word.h"

// ...
```

```
//str.c
#include "str.h"
#include "chararray.h"

// ...
```

Figure 16. Implementation of word *and alternate implementations of* str.

Except for inline functions, all class member functions and static data members in C++ have external linkage. For all practical purposes we can say that if a component needs to include another component to compile, it is going to depend on that component at link time to resolve undefined symbols at the object-code level.

> *A compile-time dependency almost always implies a link-time dependency.*

As Figure 17 shows, word.o depends on external names defined in str.o. Even if word.o does not directly use names defined in chararray.o, it does use names defined in str.o. The names used in str.o to resolve these undefined symbols will probably introduce new undefined symbols whose definitions must be supplied by chararray.o, which leads us to an interesting and important conclusion.

> *The DependsOn relation for components is transitive.*

For example, assume x, y, and z are components. If x depends on y and y depends on z, then x depends on z. The transitive property of dependency among components makes no mention of which file in one component is dependent on which file in the other. Any such file-level dependency is sufficient to produce an implementation dependency for the components as a

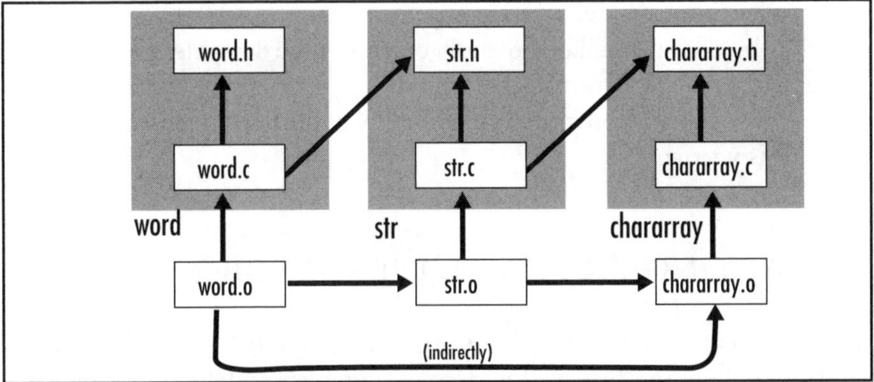

Figure 17. Link-time dependency of word on chararray.

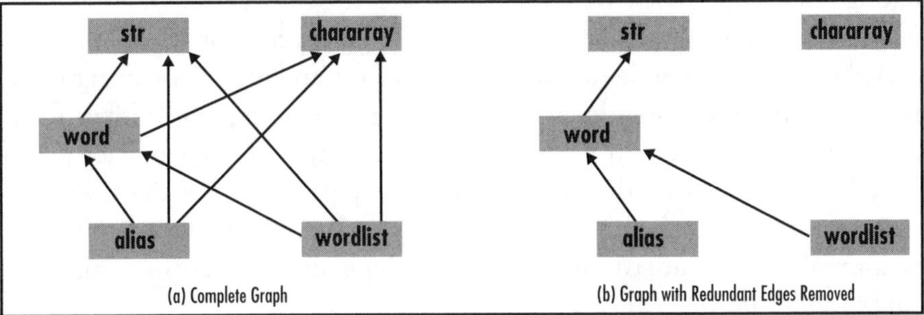

Figure 18. Transitive closure of direct dependency graph. (a) Complete graph. (b) Graph with redundant edges removed.

whole. The compile-time dependencies of word on str and of str on chararray have produced the indirect link-time dependency of word on chararray.

The transitive closure of the dependency graph in Figure 13b is shown in Figure 18a. All the edges in this graph labeled with a "t" are called *transitive edges* because their existence is implied by other edges which represent "direct" dependencies. Removing these redundant transitive edges does not lose any information but reduces clutter and makes the graph easier to understand.

Figure 18b shows that word depends indirectly on chararray and that wordlist depends directly on word. In general, a component x DependsOn component y if and only if there is a path in the dependency graph from x to y.

To recap: the DependsOn relation is important to physical design because it indicates all of the components needed for the functionality in a given component to be maintained, tested, and reused. As we have seen, it is possible to infer physical dependency directly from abstract logical relationships. IsA and HasA between logical entities will always imply compile-time dependencies when implemented across component boundaries. Relationships such as HoldsA and Uses are likely to imply compile-time dependencies when implemented across components. By considering implied dependencies at design-time, we can evaluate the physical quality of our architecture long before any code is written.

EXTRACTING ACTUAL DEPENDENCIES

Suppose now that we are designing a large project, guided only by implied dependencies. After the design stage is largely complete and development is under way, we would like to have a tool that can extract the physical dependencies among our components. We could then track the actual component dependencies and compare them with our initial design expectations.

Although it is possible to parse the source for an entire C++ program to determine the exact component dependency graph, doing so is both difficult and relatively slow. It is possible to extract the component dependency graph directly from the components' source files by parsing only the C++ preprocessor #include directives. Such processing is relatively fast and is done by a number of standard, public-domain dependency analysis tools (e.g., gmake and mkmf).

There are a few physical design rules that we must follow for this strategy to work:

1. All constructs with external linkage defined in a .c file must be declared in that component's .h file.
2. All construct declared in a component's .h file (if defined at all) are defined in that component as well.
3. There are no local copies of a declaration for a construct with external linkage that is defined in another component; instead, the header file for that component is included to obtain the declaration.

Following each of these rules has obvious benefits of modularity and maintainability, but collectively they lead to the following proposition:

> *The include-graph generated by C++ preprocessor #include directives should alone be sufficient to infer all physical dependencies within a system, provided the system compiles.*

To see why this claim is true, consider the following line of reasoning. If component x makes direct substantive use of component y, then to compile x, the compiler will have to see the definition supplied in y.h. The only way

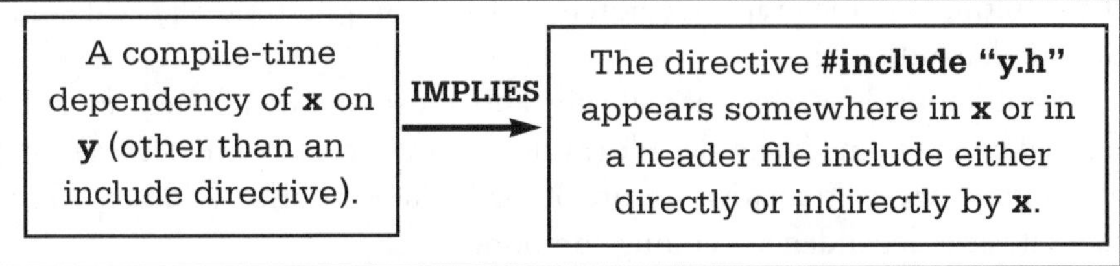

Figure 19. Compile-time dependency implies #include *directive.*

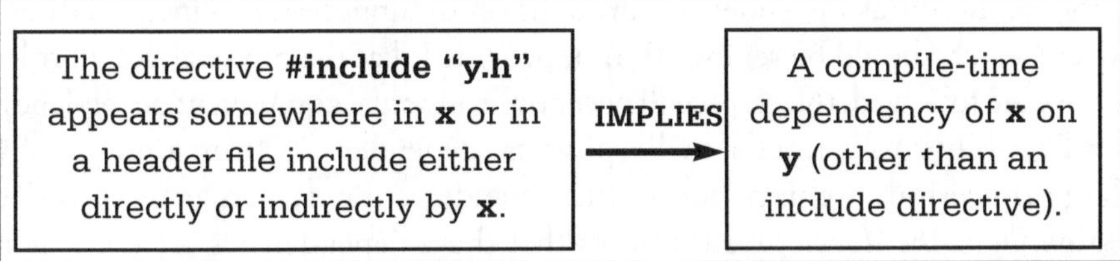

Figure 20. The #include *directive* should *imply intrinsic compile-time dependency.*

this can happen is for component x to directly or indirectly include y.h. But assuming the design rules have been followed, any such direct substantive use is synonymous with a compile-time dependency (see Figure 19).

The contrapositive (that if x does *not* include y.h then x does *not* have a compile-time dependency on y) is certainly true, provided x compiles.

Going the other way, the only reason component x would legitimately include the header file of component y is if component x did in fact make direct substantive use of component y. Otherwise, the inclusion itself would be superfluous and introduce unwanted compile-time coupling (See Fig. 20).

The contrapositive (that if x does *not* have an intrinsic compile-time dependency on y then x does *not* include y.h) should always be true—but occasionally, through human oversight, it is not.

The very fact that one component includes the header of another forces a compile-time dependency whether or not one previously existed. If we assume that all #include directives in a component are necessary, then it is likely that the compile-time dependency will be accompanied by a link-time dependency (which we already know is transitive). In other words, *substantive use* should equate to *header file inclusion*, and that substantive use almost always implies a kind of physical dependency that is transitive.

The #include graph for a set of components is just another relation that happens to reflect the dependency among components quite accurately. If we interpret "component x (either x.h or x.c) Includes y.h (either directly or indirectly)" as "component x DependsOn component y directly", then the resulting include graph accurately reflects compile-time physical component dependencies.

The design rule stating that all substantive use of a component must be flagged by including its header file (rather than via local extern declarations) guarantees that the transitive closure of the Includes relation indicates all actual physical dependencies among components.

These extracted dependencies will occasionally err on the side of being too conservative. The dependency graph extracted in this manner may indicate additional, fictitious dependencies brought on by unnecessary `#include` directives (which should be removed). But, provided that the physical design rules above are followed, the graph will never omit an actual component dependency.

The ability to extract actually physical dependencies from a potentially large collection of components quickly and accurately allows us to verify *throughout the development process* that these dependencies are consistent with our overall architectural plan. (A complete specification of a suite of tools to extract physical dependencies is provided in Appendix C of the book.)

SUMMARY SO FAR

Small project experience simply does not scale to larger projects, and this is especially true of C++ software development. Physical design is an important consideration from the very start. By ignoring physical issues during the design stage, we can easily wind up with excessive compile-time and cyclic link-time dependencies that could cripple the maintainability of our system.

Classes and functions are logical design entities. We identified the component as the atomic unit of physical design. We then argued that the component, and not the class, is the appropriate fundamental unit of design because it captures a complete abstraction (which may span several logical entities) in a single physical unit that can readily be lifted from one system and reused in another without modification.

Inferring physical dependencies among components from logical relationships (such as IsA and Uses) at design time enables us to detect/prevent excessive physical dependencies early in the development process. By following a few common-sense physical design rules, we are also able to extract all actual physical dependencies among the components in a system, just by analyzing the component `#include` graph.

In the August issue, we will continue our discussion of physical design by introducing the notion of physical hierarchy and demonstrating how it enables effective testing, significantly improves maintainability, and allows for independent reuse—all without violating encapsulation.

References

1. Perry, D.E., and G. Keiser. "Adequate Testing and Object-Oriented Programming," *Journal of Object-Oriented Programming*, 2 (5), Jan./Feb. 1990, pp. 13-19.
2. Booch, G. *Object-Oriented Analysis and Design with Applications* 2nd. Ed., Benjamin/Cummings, Redwood City, CA, pp. 171-228.

Part 2: Effective Testing, Improved Maintainability, Independent Reuse

In my previous article,[1] I claimed that small project experience does not necessarily scale to larger projects, and that this is especially true of C++ software development. I introduced the notion of physical design (involving files, directories, and libraries) in contrast to logical design (involving classes, functions, and operators) as an essential consideration of large-scale C++ software design. I introduced the component (a corresponding pair of .h and .c files) as the atomic unit of physical design and then argued that the component, not the class, is the appropriate fundamental unit of design because it captures a complete abstraction (which may span several logical entities) in a single physical unit that can readily be lifted from one system and reused in another without modification.

Two distinct kinds of physical dependency were discussed and it was demonstrated that compile-time dependency almost always implies link-time dependency and that the physical dependency relation DependsOn among components is transitive.

Inferring physical dependencies among components from logical relationships (e.g., IsA and Uses) at design time enables us to detect/prevent excessive physical dependencies early in the development process. By following a few common-sense physical design rules, we are also able to extract all actual physical dependencies among the components in a system, just by analyzing the component `#include` graph (including both `.c` and `.h` files).

In this second of three parts, our discussion of physical design continues by introducing the notion of physical hierarchy and demonstrating how it enables effective testing, significantly improves maintainability, and allows for independent reuse—all without violating encapsulation.

The application of the material in this part is not limited to C++, and applies to any compiled language with separate translation units. These principles do not necessarily apply to an interpreted language (e.g., Smalltalk or CLOS) that has a single monolithic environment. What makes C++ an ideal context for discussing physical design concepts is that, unlike Ada or Java, C++ enables compile-time coupling in the name of runtime efficiency. Finally, the material in this part is prerequisite to the C++-specific discussion (coming in part III) of techniques to eliminate excessive compile-time and link-time physical dependencies.

PHYSICAL HIERARCHY

The hierarchy among components as defined by the DependsOn relation is analogous to the logical hierarchy implied by layering. (Physical hierarchy among components should not be confused with logical inheritance among classes, although inheritance implies physical dependencies.) Avoiding cyclic physical dependencies is central to effective comprehension, maintainability, testing, and reuse. Well-designed interfaces are small, easy to understand, and easy to use, yet these kinds of interfaces make user-level testing expensive.

A Metaphor for Software Testing

When a customer test-drives a car, he or she is looking to see how well the car performs as a unit—how well the car handles, corners, brakes, etc. The customer is also interested in subjective usability—how "nifty" the car looks, how comfortable the seats are, how plush the interior is, and, in general, how satisfying the car would be to own. Typical customers do not test the air-bags, ball-joints, or engine mounts to see whether they will perform as expected in all circumstances. When buying a new car from a reputable manufacturer, this important low-level reliability is simply taken for granted.

For the car to function properly, it is important that each of the objects on which the car depends works properly as well. Customers do not test each part of the car individually—but somebody does. It is not the responsibility of the customer to "QA" the car. The customer is paying for a quality product, and part of that quality is the satisfaction of knowing that the car works properly.

In the real world, each part of a car has been designed with a well-defined interface and has been tested in isolation under extreme conditions to ensure that it meets its specified tolerances long before it is ever integrated into a car. To maintain a car, mechanics must be able to gain access to its various parts from time to time in order to diagnose and fix problems.

In this respect, complex software systems are like cars. Each of the low-level parts are objects with well-defined interfaces. Each part (i.e., each component) can be stress tested in isolation. These parts can then be integrated (via layering) into a sequence of increasingly complex subsystems—each subsystem with a test suite to ensure that the incremental integration has occurred properly. This layered architecture enables test engineers to access the functionality implemented at lower levels of abstraction without exposing clients of the product to these lower-level interfaces. The final product is also tested to ensure that it meets customer expectations.

The Difficulty in Testing "Good" Interfaces

A truly effective use of object-oriented technology is to hide tremendous amounts of complexity behind a small, well-defined, easy-to-understand, and easy-to-use interface. Yet it is precisely these kinds of interfaces that, if naively implemented, can lead to the development of subsystems that are exceedingly difficult to test.

Pretend for a moment that you are a quality assurance engineer. You are given the oracle component shown in Figure 1 and asked to devise a test strategy that guarantees its reliability. How would you proceed?

Even with ample documentation, the obviously enormous amount of implementation complexity hidden behind oracle's tiny interface makes guaranteeing reliability using only its interface absurd. Effective testing of such a component demands that developers have direct access to the lower levels of the implementation. At the same time, we must not compromise encapsulation by exposing implementation details through the interface of the component.

Providing sufficient but minimal interfaces is a cornerstone of good software engineering. Yet these very interfaces that we strive so hard to achieve can present a formidable barrier to conventional testing techniques. Fortunately, there are effective strategies to overcome these testing problems.

DESIGN FOR TESTABILITY

A major component of designing in quality is Design For Testability (DFT). The importance of DFT is well recognized in the Integrated Circuit (IC) industry. In many cases it is impractical to test IC chips, some with over a million transistors, from the outside pins alone.

When an IC chip is fabricated, it acts as a "black box" and can be tested only from the external inputs and outputs (pins). Figure2(a) illustrates the process of trying to test a hardware subsystem W using only the interface

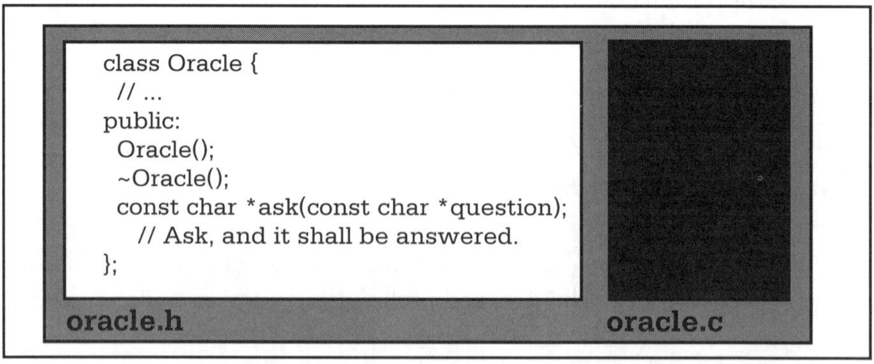

```
class Oracle {
  // ...
public:
  Oracle();
  ~Oracle();
  const char *ask(const char *question);
    // Ask, and it shall be answered.
};
```

oracle.h

oracle.c

Figure 1. oracle component with minimal interface

provided to regular clients of the chip itself. In order to test W, it is necessary not only to figure out what would make a good test suite for W, but also how to propagate that test suite through the chip to reach the inputs of W. As if that weren't bad enough, each result that W produces must then be propagated from the output of W to some output of the chip itself in order to observe and verify that W has behaved correctly. Ensuring propagation of this information requires detailed knowledge about the entire chip—knowledge that has nothing to do with the correct functionality of W.

One form of DFT for IC chips called "scan" is accomplished with extra pins and additional internal circuitry provided solely for testing purposes. Using these special features, test engineers are able to isolate the various subsystems within the chip. In so doing they are able to gain direct access to the inputs and outputs of internal subsystems and to exercise their functionality in isolation. In other words, this DFT approach attempts to grant the tester direct access to a subsystem, thereby eliminating the cost of propagating signals through the entire chip. In this way, the full functionality of the subsystem can be explored efficiently as illustrated in Figure 2(b), without regard to the details of how the subsystem is used in the larger system.

> *With respect to testing, a software* class *is analogous to a real world* instance.

Like IC design, object-oriented software involves the creation of a relatively small number of types, which are then instantiated repeatedly to form a working system. For example, a String class is a primitive type in many software systems, Many instances of this class may be created during a typical invocation of the system.

Both disciplines require that the functionality in these types be tested thoroughly to ensure correct behavior when instantiated. But, unlike IC design where each individual instance of a type must be tested for physical defects,

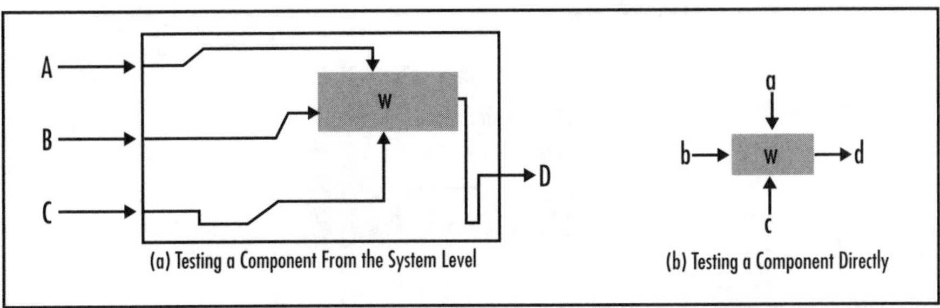

Figure 2. Design for testability in integrated circuits.

software objects are immune to such defects. If a class is implemented correctly, then, by definition, all instances of that type are correctly implemented as well.

From the point of view of testing, each software type is like a real-world instance. Testing the functionality of a String class is easiest and most effective if done directly, rather than by attempting to test it as part of a larger system. And, unlike IC testing, we automatically have direct access to the interface of the software subsystem - i.e., the String class.

> *Distributing system testing throughout the design hierarchy can be much more effective per testing dollar than testing at only the highest level interface.*

Put another way, if we have only *X* dollars to spend on testing, we can get more thorough coverage if we distribute the testing effort throughout the system, thus testing the individual component interfaces directly, than we can by testing from the end-user's interface alone.

Consider again the oracle component of Figure 1. Even assuming entirely predictable behavior, it would be ineffective to attempt to test this component entirely from the highest level, especially given its tiny interface. In analogy to IC testing (see Figure 3), this would be like trying to test a one-million transistor microprocessor chip with only two pins!

Software testing is inherently easier than hardware testing because instances of a class created *within* a system are no different than instances of the same class created independently outside that system. If a complex software subsystem were truly analogous to an TC chip, the implementation would reside entirely within a single physical component. If the functionality declared in oracle.h were implemented entirely within oracle.c, we would probably be forced to violate encapsulation by providing extra functionality in the public interface—just to enable effective testing.

Fortunately, the implementation of Oracle does not live in a single component. Instead the implementation is deliberately distributed throughout a phys-

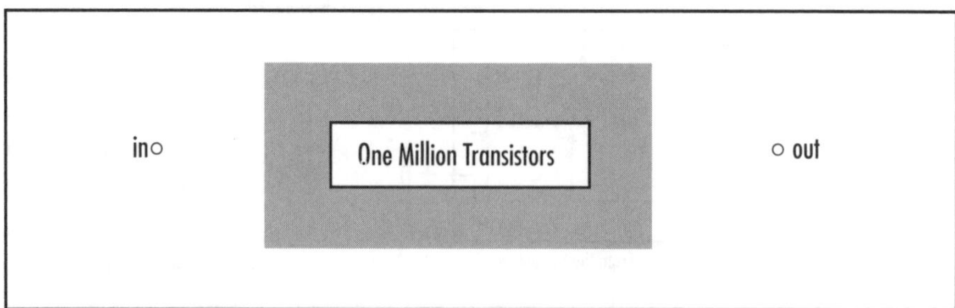

Figure 3. Fictitious, highly test-resistant IC chip with only two pins.

ical hierarchy of components. Even though the client of an Oracle object has no programmatic access to the layered objects that make up the Oracle, it is still possible for test engineers to identify subcomponents with predictable behavior that can be tested and verified much more efficiently in isolation.

Testing in Isolation

In a well-designed modular subsystem, many components can be tested in isolation. Consider a String class that is developed as part of an interpreter. The interpreter never sees a zero-length identifier, so it never tries to create an empty String to represent one. (This boundary condition would certainly be addressed by a thorough test designed specifically for the string component.)

As our system evolves, we may at some later point reuse the String class in other parts of the same system but in new ways (e.g., to hold String variables). At this point, an instance of an empty String *can* occur within this system. The enhancement may have been made at a fairly high level in the system, but the potential bug exists at the lowest level—in the String class—which has been working "perfectly" for quite some time!

In a large project, the author of the String class is probably not the same individual as the one whose valid enhancement exposes the problem. Detecting and then repairing such bugs, not to mention the frustration that ensues, is far more expensive than simply avoiding them in the first place through early, component-level testing in isolation.

> *Testing a component in isolation is an effective way for ensuring reliability.*

It would be redundant and unnecessarily costly for every system that uses a library facility such as iostream to have tests to verify that the needed iostream functionality is working properly. People have come to assume that iostream does work as intended. For large systems there will probably be many application libraries developed in house. No single executable will make use of all this functionality, yet all of it should be tested thoroughly *in isolation*.

We can avoid the redundancy by grouping the testing effort with the components themselves. In so doing one extends the notion of object-oriented design to include, as a single unit, not only the component but also the supporting tests and documentation. Furthermore, well-written, component-level tests can facilitate reuse by providing prospective users with a suite of small but comprehensive examples. The functionality supplied by each com-

```
//c1.h
#indef INCLUDED_C1
#define INCLUDED_C1


class C1 {
  // ...
 public:
  C1 f();
};

#endif
```

```
//c2.h
#indef INCLUDED_C2
#define INCLUDED_C2
class C1;


class C2 {
  // ...
 public:
  C1 g();
};

#endif
```

```
//c3.h
#indef INCLUDED_C3
#define INCLUDED_C3
class C2;


class C3 {
  // ...
 public:
  C1 h()(const C2& arg);
};

#endif
```

Figure 4. Components with acyclic implied dependencies.

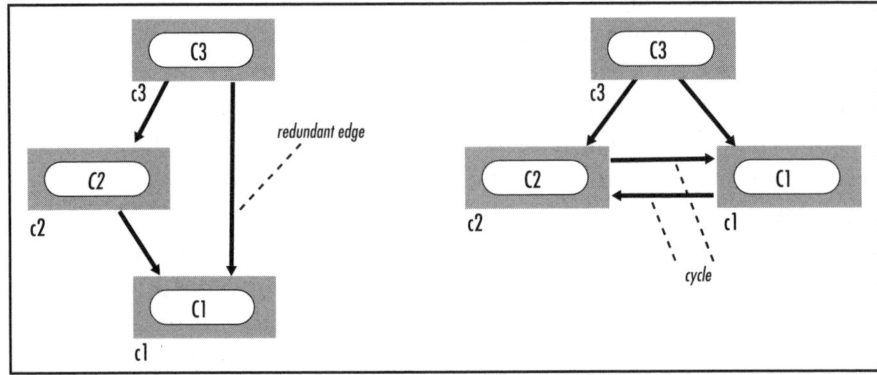

Figure 5. Acyclic versus cyclic physical dependencies.

ponent can now be tested thoroughly in a single place; clients who depend on these components may reasonably assume they are reliable.

ACYCLIC Physical DEPENDENCIES

For a design to be tested effectively, it must be possible to decompose the design into units of functionality whose complexity is manageable. A component is ideal for this purpose. Consider the header files for three components: c1, c2, c3 depicted in Figure 4. Note that we have declared class C1 in component headers c2.h and c3.h without providing its definition because it is not necessary to define a class that is returned by value in order to declare that function.

We observe that there is no implied dependency of c1 on any other component. Class C2 uses class Cl in its interface. Therefore, it is likely that component c2 depends on component c1 but we hope not on c3. Class C3 uses both C2 and Cl in its interface and so c3 is likely to depend on both c2 and c1. The implied dependencies in this system form a directed acyclic graph (DAG) as shown in Figure 5(a).

Component dependency graphs that contain no cycles have very positive implications for testability, but not all component dependency graphs are acyclic. To see why, consider what would happen if we changed the return type of Cl::f from a Cl to a C2 as shown in Figure 6.

```
class C1 {#indef INCLUDED_C1
    // ...
    public:
        // C1 f();  // old
        C2 f();     // new
};
```

Figure 6. Modification to class Cl.

Now Cl uses C2 in its interface and (probably) depends on it. The implied component dependency graph for this modified system now has a *physical* cycle, and is shown in Figure 5(b).

Systems with acyclic physical dependencies are far easier to test effectively than those with cycles. Whenever the component dependencies in a system are acyclic, there is at least one reasonable order to go about testing the system. Since component c1 depends on nothing else, tests to verify its functionality in isolation can be written first. Next we see that component c2 depends only on component c1. Because we were able to write effective tests for c1, we may presume c1 to be functioning properly. We can now write tests for the functional value added by c2. We need not retest the contribution of c1 since that functionality is already covered. Then we look at c3, which depends on both c1 and c2. Because we presumably have already written tests to verify the functionality supplied by both c1 and c2, we need address only the additional functionality implemented in c3.

Level Numbers

I now describe a method for partitioning components into equivalence classes called *levels*, based on their physical dependencies. Each level is associated with a non-negative integer index, referred to as the *level number*. If the component dependencies in a software system happen to form a DAG, we can define the level of each component as shown in Table 1.

In this definition, we assume all components (e.g., iostream) outside our current package (assume for now that *package* means the current project directory) have already been tested and are known to function properly. These components are treated as "given" and have a level of 0. A component with no local physical dependencies is defined to have a level of 1. Otherwise, a component is defined to have a level one more than the maximum level of the components upon which it depends.

> *A physical dependency graph that can be assigned unique level numbers is said to be* **levelizable.**

Every directed acyclic graph can be assigned unique level numbers; a graph with cycles cannot. Figure 7 repeats the component dependency diagram in Figure 13 from Part 1 of this article, which has no cycles and hence is levelizable. The level number of each component is shown in its upper right corner. Component chararray does not depend on any other components locally

Table 1. Definition of Level Numbers.

level	*Definition*
level 0	A component that is external to our package.
level 1	A component that has no local physical dependencies.
level N	A component that depends physically on a component at level N-1, but not higher.

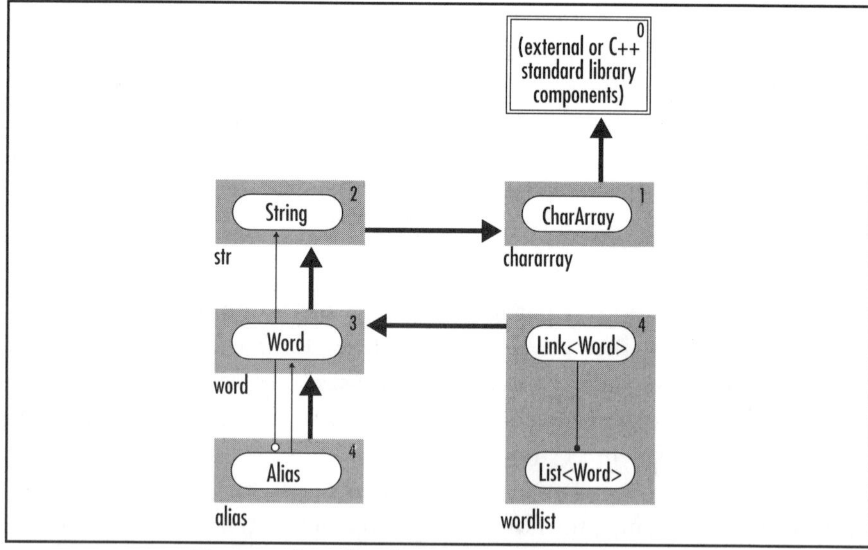

Figure 7. Levelized component/class diagram.

but may depend on the standard C++ library components (which are all assumed to be at level 0) so chararray has a level of 1. A level-1 component (e.g., chararray) that depends only on compiler-supplied libraries is called a "leaf" component. Leaf components are always testable in isolation.

Component str depends only on chararray. The level of str is 2, one more than that of chararray. Component word depends on str (and indirectly on chararray). Since str has a level of 2, word has a level of 3. Since word is at level 3, and the only component on which alias depends directly is word, alias is at level 4. The wordlist component also depends directly on word but does not depend on alias, so wordlist is also at level 4.

In other words, the level of a component is the length of the longest path from that component through the local component dependency graph to the (possibly empty) set of external or compiler-supplied library components.

With a levelized diagram it is easy to tell what components in this system are testable in isolation. In the example of Figure 7, there is only one independently testable component: chararray. By starting at the lowest level (i.e., 1) and testing all components on the current level before moving to the next higher level, we are assured that all the components on which the current component depends have already been tested. In this case, we can test either wordlist or alias last, but the rest of the testing order is implied by the level numbers.

High-quality designs are levelizable.

Notice that the term levelizable applies to *physical*, not logical, entities. While an acyclic logical dependency graph might imply that a testable physical partition exists, the level numbers of (physical) components, along with our physical design rules (see Part 1), imply a viable order for effective testing. Moreover, Figure 7 identifies what subsystems can be reused independently (see Table 2).

Another significant advantage to levelizable designs is that they are more

Table 2. Independently reusable subystems of Figure 7.

To test or reuse	*You also need*
chararray_1	
string_2	chararray_1
word_3	string_2 chararray_1
alias_4	word_3 string_2 chararray_1
wordlist_4	word_3 string_2 chararray_1

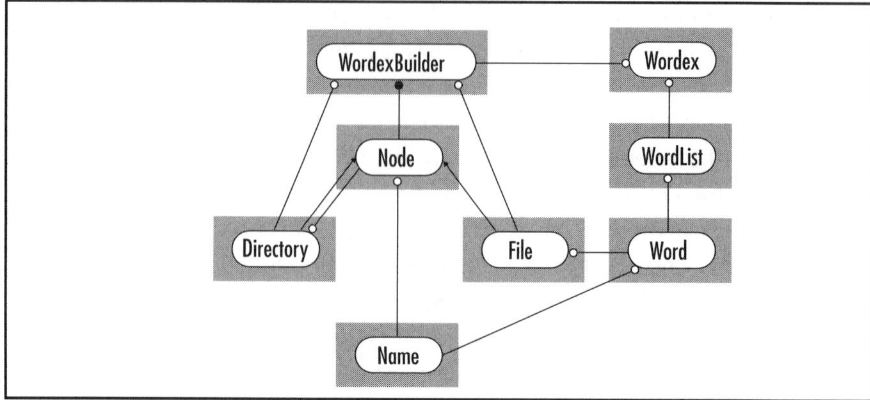

Figure 8. Is this design levelizable?

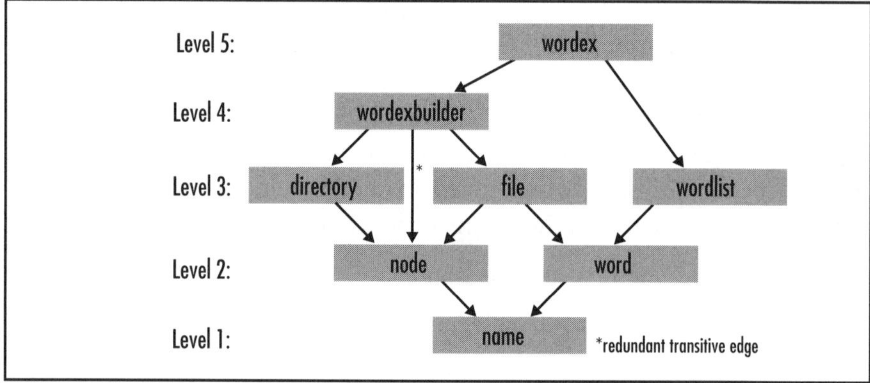

Figure 9. Component (direct) dependency diagram.

easily comprehended incrementally. The process of understanding a levelizable design can proceed in an orderly manner (either top-down or bottom-up).

Not all subsystems formed by hierarchical designs are reusable. But, to be maintainable, each component must have a well-defined interface that can be readily understood, regardless of how general its applicability.

Of course, not all designs are levelizable. Sometimes whether or not a design is levelizable is not immediately obvious from a logical diagram. Consider the diagram of Figure 8. Can you tell from this diagram whether or not the components in this design are levelizable?

The indicated logical relationships in this design do *not* imply cyclic physical dependencies among any of the components. However, the component/class diagram is cluttered and contains more information than is needed to understand the physical structure of the system. If we rearrange the placement of the components and eliminate the logical detail, we obtain the strikingly lucid component dependency diagram of Figure 9.

There is one redundant edge in the diagram of Figure 9. Component wordexbuilder depends directly on components directory, file, and node. As we know, the DependsOn relationship is transitive. Because directory (and file also) depends on node, the dependency of wordexbuilder on node is implied and can be removed without affecting level numbers. The diagram in Figure 9 is clearly acyclic and typical of those for subsystems that address a specific application. At this level of abstraction, the design appears to be sound.

One of the great values of this analysis is that after untangling the component dependency diagram, we were able to make a substantive, qualitative comment about the integrity of the physical design without even the tiniest discussion of the application domain. Simple tools to help automate this process are easy to write, and have proven to be invaluable for large projects.

Hierarchical and Incremental Testing

Components are the fundamental building blocks of a system. Every component is different. Each is an instance of the physical design pattern: *component* Outwardly, they all have the same basic physical structure—i.e., a physical interface (.h file) and a physical implementation (.c file).

In this sense, implementing and testing a software system is like building a house. After the overall architectural design is complete, the bricks (i.e., the components not objects) are put in place one by one. The successful addition of each brick depends not only on its own integrity but also on the integrity of the mortar used to integrate the brick with the lower-level bricks on which this brick depends. It is easy enough to inspect each brick for defects along the way. But once complete, the house is often large and complex, presenting too many barriers to inspect each detail.

> *A component also is analogous to a real-world* instance *with respect to testing.*

Figure 10 illustrates the abstract physical structure of the hierarchical testing strategy. Each component at level 1 can depend on only external components (all of which are at level 0).

Therefore, each component at level 1 can be tested independently of all other (local) components.

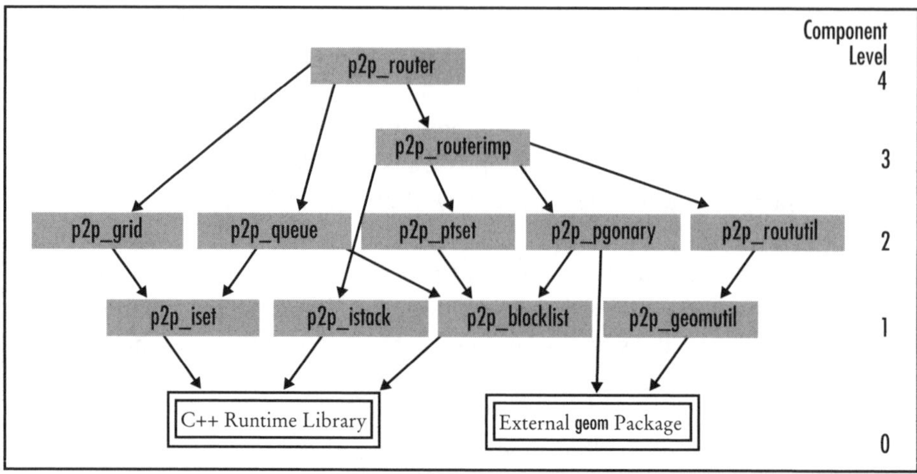

Figure 10. Hierarchical testing strategy.

> *Hierarchical testing refers to the practice of testing individual components at each level of the physical hierarchy.*

As we proceed to higher levels of the physical design hierarchy, the complexity of the subsystems will grow (often exponentially). This explosive growth implies that we will soon reach the point where tests designed to cover the complete behavior of a high-level interface will be too difficult to write or take too long to run.

Our hierarchical approach makes it unnecessary to retest the internal behavior of lower-level components. If instead we attempt to test only the functional value added by a given component, the test complexity for each component is more likely to be kept to a manageable level. The practice of targeting only the new functionality added by a given component is referred to as *incremental testing.*

> *Incremental testing refers to the practice of deliberately testing only the functionality actually implemented within the component under test.*

Because we can assume that the components at lower levels are supplying objects that are working properly, the task of incremental testing is often reduced to testing the way in which these lower level objects combine to form higher level objects.

Exploiting knowledge of the implementation of the component is a genre of testing known as *white-box testing.* White-box testing allows the tester to approach nearly complete internal code coverage with a much smaller test driver by carefully choosing test cases that exercise all of an object's internal functionality.

Unlike the white-box test that verifies that the code works as the developer intended, the *black-box* test verifies that the component satisfies its requirements and complies with its specification. While white-box testing tends to ensure that we have *solved a problem correctly*, black-box testing helps to make sure that we have *solved the correct problem*. Thorough tests of complex components will make effective use of both strategies.

The complexity of an incremental component test should mirror the implementation complexity of the component under test.

One of the appealing properties of incremental testing is that the difficulty of testing any given component is roughly proportional to the functional value added by that component itself rather than to the combined complexity of the lower-level components on which that component depends. Consequently, hierarchical physical implementations of complex subsystems can be both more reliable and less costly to test than non-hierarchical alternatives.

Cumulative Component Dependency

We now formalize our discussion of designing in quality by providing a metric, referred to as the cumulative component dependency (CCD) of a subsystem, that is closely tied to the link-time and disc space costs of incremental regression testing. More generally, the CCD provides a numerical value that indicates the relative costs associated with developing, testing, maintaining, and reusing a given subsystem.

Linking a large program takes a long time. Typically, developers will need to link a single component many times in the process of creating both the component and its test driver. After that, the component will need to be linked to its driver whenever regression tests are run. For small projects, link times are comparable with the compile times of individual components. As projects get larger, the link time grows to be much larger than the time needed to compile even the largest of components.

Most of our development time is spent on low-level components, primarily because there are simply a lot more low-level components than high-level ones. These low-level pieces of the system can be intricate and are sometimes selected for performance tuning. It is to our advantage to streamline the process of developing, testing, and maintaining low-level components.

For the sake of this discussion, let's say that the component dependencies in a physical design formed a perfect binary tree. Just over half of the components would be at level 1 and could be tested in complete isolation. Another quarter would each depend on two leaf components. Only one of the *2Levels-1* components would actually depend on all the rest. Although real designs are not nearly so regular, the advantage of testing a hierarchy of components with acyclic dependencies remains clear.

Consider the costs associated with developing a set of components. For the moment, let's assume that link time is proportional to the number of components being linked together. For instance, if linking one component to a test driver takes 1 CPU second, then linking five components would take roughly 5 CPU seconds. (This assumption is of course only a crude approximation, since link cost will clearly be affected by variation in component sizes and by the structure of the function-call hierarchy.)

In the presence of cyclic dependencies, it may be necessary to link in most or all of the components in order to test or reuse any one of them. The total number of components needed in order to test a particular component incrementally, is called its component dependency (CD). CCD for a subsystem is simply the sum of the component dependencies for each component in the subsystem.

> *Cumulative component dependency is the sum over all components Ci in a subsystem of the number of components needed in order to test each Ci incrementally.*

Suppose our system is very tightly coupled and each component is either directly or indirectly dependent on all the others. If we let *N* represent the number of components in our system, the cost of linking any one of these components to its test driver is proportional to *N*. The link cost alone of building all *N* test drivers for these components is then proportional to *N2*. This fact explains why linking often dominates the cost of running thorough regression tests for large systems.

Now consider what would happen if our dependencies were acyclic and formed a binary tree. Now, not all components have equal link cost. Components at level 1 could be linked to their respective test drivers in unit time (e.g., 1 CPU second). Fully half of the link cost associated with component testing—i.e., that of testing level1 components—could be virtually eliminated. Each component at level 2 would depend on two components at level 1 and comprise a subsystem of size 3 (i.e., would take 3 CPU seconds to link). That is, another quarter of the test cost associated with linking could be reduced

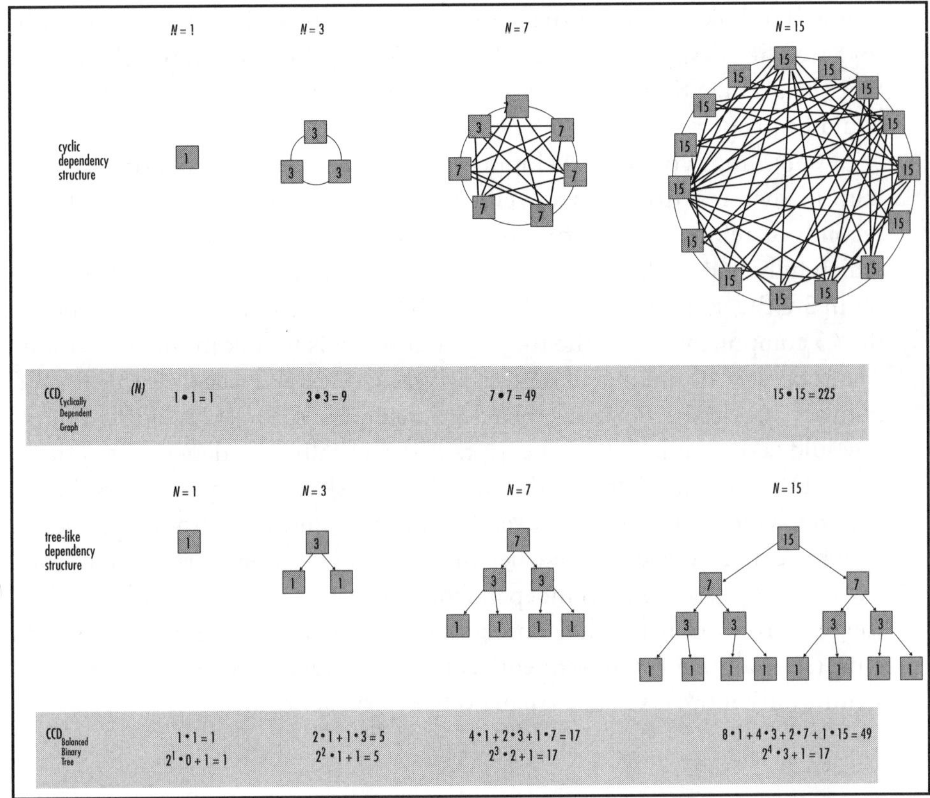

Figure 11. Relative link costs associated with incremental testing.

dramatically (by a factor of *N*/3). Only one component in this hypothetical system (the root) would require the full *N*CPU seconds of link time previously required by each of the *N* components.

Figure 11 compares link-time costs associated with testing cyclic and hierarchical systems with *N*=1,3,7, and 15 components. The number shown corresponding to each component position in the dependency graph indicates the component dependency—i.e., the link cost associated with incrementally testing that component. The CCD for each system is calculated and shown at the bottom of its dependency graph.

> *Insisting on acyclic physical dependencies can dramatically reduce costs associated with developing, maintaining, and resting large systems.*

The benefits of acyclic dependencies in terms of link time, disk space, testability, reusability, and understandability are enormous. For example, the time required to link all N test drivers to a cyclically-dependent design is $O(N^2)$; for a tree-like design the cost is only O $(N\Sigma log(N))$. As a developer, this means that the average time it takes you to link a component with its test driver could be proportional to log(N) instead of N.

Suppose that you are developing a system that has 63 components each with its own test driver. In a cyclic design, each component would take 63 seconds to relink in order to test. Compare this to a hierarchical design in which fully half of the components can be linked in 1 CPU second, a quarter in 3 CPU seconds, an eighth in 7 CPU seconds, and so on. Only one of the 63 components takes the full 63 CPU seconds to link in order to test it. The total cost of linking all 63 test drivers is 321 CPU seconds (5.35 CPU minutes). Compare this with the *632*=3,969 CPU seconds (1.1 CPU hours) it would take to link all 63 test drivers to a cyclically interdependent system.

CCD is also a predictor of the cumulative disk space requirements. Large systems typically implement several main programs. In addition, disk space is an important consideration when incrementally testing a large system concurrently. The size of each independent executable program on disk will be roughly proportional to the number of component to which the main driver must (statically) link. Consequently, cyclicly-dependent systems can require significantly more disk space than do hierarchical designs.

PHYSICAL DESIGN QUALITY

Imagine joining a company that is developing a very large system. You are handed a subsystem of about 150,000 lines of C++ code and you are asked to understand what it does and make suggestions as to how to improve it. Upon examination, you find that the components (for the most part) are consistent with good logical design practices, and are partitioned into discrete physical components. You then discover that most of the components in the system depend (either directly or indirectly) on most of the other components. What do you do? Unfortunately there is no happy ending to this story. The best anyone can do may be to try to fit the entire design into his or her head, and that may take months.

Had the same subsystem been designed with an eye toward minimizing CCD, most if not all—cyclic dependencies would have been eliminated. It would be possible to study pieces of the subsystem in isolation, test, verify, tune, and even replace them, without having to involve the entire subsystem

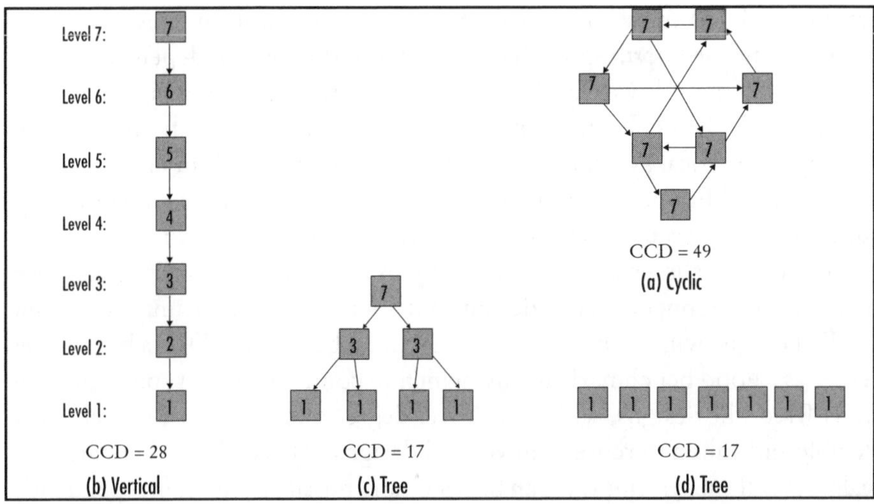

Figure 12. CCD for various component hierarchies of size 7.

either mentally or physically. In other words, actively reducing the intercomponent dependencies, as quantified by CCD, improves understandability and therefore maintainability.

Comprehension is one of several hard-to-quantify yet very real advantages of minimizing intercomponent dependencies; selective reuse is another. Consider the architecture of the subsystem illustrated in Figure 12(a). This system consists of seven components. Each component depends either directly or indirectly on every other component in the system. Each of the components can be tested directly, but none of them can be tested in isolation or reused independently of the rest. It is primarily the ability to understand and reuse a component or subsystem independently that makes hierarchical physical design so important.

If each independent driver is forced to link with the entire system, the amount of disk space required just to store all these independent programs will be quadratic as well. Sophisticated development environments with incremental linkers, fast processors, and vast amounts of disk space can push the envelope of what can be achieved without considering physical design quality. This brute-force approach does nothing to overcome the barriers to independent understanding, testability, and reuse—particularly reuse outside the original environment.

Suppose now that the cyclic dependencies in the design are eliminated, making it levelizable. Levelizability is highly desirable, in all cases, however, some levelizable architectures are more maintainable and reusable than others. Figure 12(b) shows one extreme version of levelization. Designs of this nature are termed *vertical.* Each component in this system depends on all of the components at lower levels. Vertical subsystems exhibit a high degree of coupling, which inhibits independent reuse. Reusing a randomly chosen component in a vertical system of size *N* will on average result in having to link to (*N*- 1)/2 additional components. Design (b) is none-the-less qualitatively superior to (a) because there is an order that enables effective testing.

Figure 12(c) shows a design hierarchy in the form of a binary tree. Over half of the components in this design contribute only a single unit each to the CCD. Designs will not be perfect binary trees, but the CCD of a binary tree serves as a good benchmark against which to compare many typical applications. Tree-like designs, with their lower degree of coupling, are much more flexible and suited to reuse than vertical designs. At each level there are typically several subsystems that can be tested and possibly reused independently of the rest of the system. The link time and disk space requirement for most of the incremental test driver programs will be relatively low.

By making the dependency graph flatter rather than taller, we increase flexibility. The flatter the design, the greater the potential for independent reuse. Flattening the dependencies also helps to decrease the time needed for understanding and maintenance. The flatter the design, the more likely a bug can be tracked to a single, isolated component or a small independent subsystem, and therefore the less disk space will be required by the program to exercise the defect as it is being repaired.

Figure 12(d) shows the other end of the levelization spectrum. This type of design is characterized as *horizontal* because all of the components are entirely independent and decoupled from one another. Components belonging to purely horizontal subsystems may be tested in any order and reused in any combination desired. The disk space requirement for every incremental test driver programs will be quite low. Such dependency characteristics are typical in reusable component libraries but atypical of subsystems in general.

To get the flavor of how we might incrementally improve a design, consider the two systems with similar dependency structures shown in Figure 13. Design A has a cyclic dependency between two of its components. Testing either one of these components requires linking to both of them, along with all of the components on which either one of them depends; this gives each of them an individual component dependency of 7. Notice also that at the right of design A, thvere is a portion of the hierarchy that is purely vertical.

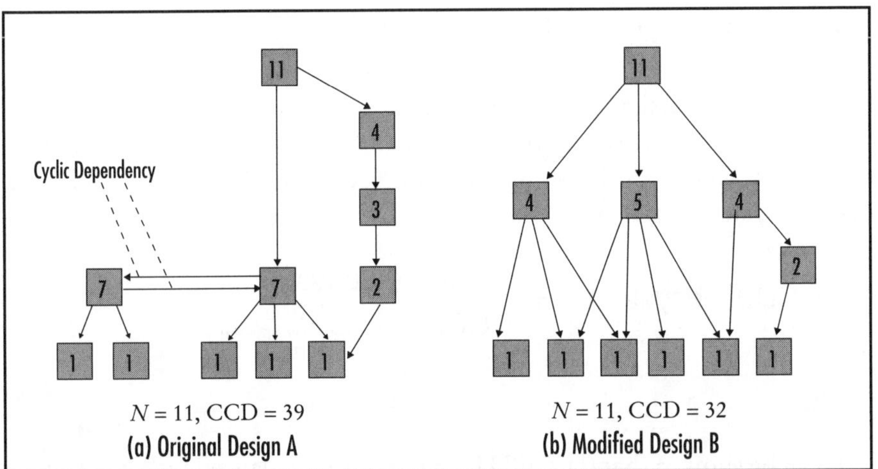

Figure 13. Dependency graphs for two alternative designs of a subsystem.

Minimizing CCD for a given set of components is a design goal.

To improve this design we would first like to try to break the cyclic dependency and then examine the vertical section to see if it can be made less serial. (Methods for reducing physical dependencies are presented in Part 3 of this article.) In this case, it may be possible to break the cycle merely by escalating some code to a higher level and/or factoring out a shared resource. As for the vertical section, it may be that one or more components in the chain can be removed and made leaf components, independent of the rest. The result of making these modifications might look like Design B, shown in Figure 13(b). The CCD of 39 for our original Design A, is much lower than the CCD of 121 for a fully interdependent design. Yet we were still able to reduce the CCD in this nearly hierarchical system from 39 to 32—an improvement of about 18%.

We can make some objective, quantitative statements about the relative maintainability and reusability (hut not necessarily the "goodness") of a design of a given size based on its CCD. Design dependencies form a continuum that ranges from cyclic to vertical to tree-like to horizontal. Even in the presence of cycles, every design can be assigned a CCD. All other things being equal, the lower the CCD, the less expensive (in terms of link time, disk space, and human comprehension) the system will be to develop test, maintain, and reuse.

NORMALIZED CCD (NCCD)

Fully horizontal designs are not an option for most real-world systems. Well-designed systems are usually tree-like in nature. We define NCCD as the ratio of the CCD of a subsystem containing N component to the CCD of a tree-like system of the same size:

$$\text{NCCD9subsystems} = \frac{\text{CCD(subsystem)}}{\text{CCD}_{\substack{\text{Balanced}\\ \text{Binary}\\ \text{Tree}}}(N_{\text{subsystem}})}$$

It can be shown[2] that the CCD for a theoretical balanced binary tree containing *N* components is given by

$$\text{CCD}_{\substack{\text{Balanced}\\ \text{Binary}\\ \text{Tree}}}(11) = (11 + 1) \bullet \log_2(11+1) - 11$$

In other words, the NCCD of a system can be used to characterize the degree of physical coupling within the system relative to a theoretical binary dependency tree of the same size. For example, with N=11 we get

$$\begin{aligned}\text{CCD}_{\substack{\text{Balanced}\\ \text{Binary}\\ \text{Tree}}}(11) &= (11 + 1) \bullet \log_2(11+1) - 11\\ &= 12 \bullet \log_2(12) - 11\\ &= 32.02\end{aligned}$$

Referring back to Figure 13, the NCCD of design B was 32/32.02 = 1 as compared with an NCCD of 39/32.02 = 1.21 for Design A (and 121/32.02 = 3.78 for the completely interdependent implementation).

NCCD is an objective metric that characterizes the physical coupling within a system. NCCD can flag subsystems with unusually high incremental development and maintenance costs. A system with an NCCD of less than one can be thought of as more horizontal or loosely coupled. An NCCD near one suggests a typical tree-like physical architecture. An NCCD of more than one implies a more vertical or tightly coupled design. An NCCD substantially greater than 1 indicates that there is excessive or cyclic physical coupling within the system.

The degree of maintainability in terms of the CCD that we are able to achieve depends on the nature of the subsystem. We will not always achieve perfect tree-like maintainability. For horizontal component libraries, we would expect a much lower NCCD. The NCCD will be higher for tightly interconnected topologies. The precise numerical value of the CCD (or NCCD) for a given system is not important. What is important is actively designing systems to keep the CCD for each subsystem from becoming larger than necessary.

Summary

High-quality, complex subsystems are composed of many components layered atop each other to form an acyclic physical hierarchy. Thorough testing at the system level is not just expensive, but highly unfeasible—if not impossible—particularly for "good" interfaces.

A "good" interface encapsulates the complexity of the implementation behind a simple facade that is easy to understand and use. At the same time, it makes our ability to test the implementation through this interface exceedingly difficult.

Much of the testing strategy in this article is motivated by the success of design for testability (DFT) over a decade ago. But, unlike real-world objects, instances of classes defined within a software system are no different from instances of the same classes defined outside that system. We can exploit this fact to verify portions of the design hierarchy in isolation, thereby reducing part of the risk of integration.

Isolation testing is a cost-effective way of ensuring reliability in complex, low-level components. By pushing the testing to the lowest possible level in the design hierarchy, we ensure that if the component or subsystem is enhanced, ported, or reused in another system, that it will continue to adhere to its specified behavior independently of its clients.

Level numbers characterize components in terms of their physical dependencies on other components within a subsystem. Furthermore, level numbers provide an order in which systems with acyclic component dependency graphs can be tested effectively. Subsystems whose component dependencies form a DAG are said to be *levelizable*. A levelized component dependency diagram makes the physical structure of a system easier to understand and consequently easier to maintain.

Hierarchical testing refers to testing components at each level of the physical hierarchy. Each lower-level component should provide a well-defined interface and implement predictable functionality that can be tested, verified, and reused, independently of components at higher levels.

Incremental testing refers to having individual drivers test only the functionality actually implemented within the component under test; functionality implemented at lower levels of the physical hierarchy is presumed at this point to be internally correct. Consequently, incremental tests mirror the complexity of the implementation of the component under test and not that of the hierarchy of components upon which this component depends. Incremental testing is a form of *white-box* testing, which relies on knowing the implementation of the component in order to improve reliability. *Black-box* testing derives from requirements and specifications, and is independent of implementation. These two forms of testing are complementary, and both contribute to ensuring overall quality.

Testability is a design goal. Cyclic physical dependencies inhibit testing, understanding, and reuse Cumulative component dependency (CCD) provides a crude numerical measure of the overall link-time cost associated with incrementally testing a given subsystem. More generally, CCD is an indicator of the relative maintainability of a given design.

Cyclically dependent designs are not levelizable. Such designs are known to be difficult to maintain and have a correspondingly high CCD. Among designs that are levelizable, the more horizontal the hierarchy the lower the CCD.

Flattening physical dependencies helps to decrease the time needed for understanding, development, and maintenance, while improving the flexibility, testability, and reusability of a system. NCCD helps to categorize the physical structure of arbitrary designs as *cyclic*, *vertical*, *tree-like*, or *horizontal*.

In the final installment of this article we will look at specific (levelization) techniques for eliminating cyclic link-time dependencies. We will also examine specific (insulation) techniques for eliminating unnecessary compile-time dependencies. Finally, we will extend the principles of levelization and insulation to yet larger systems by introducing a macro unit of physical design: the *package*.

REFERENCES

1. Lakos, J. "Large-Scale C++ Software Design," *C++ Report* 8(6), June 1996.

2. Lakos, J. *Large-Scale C++ Software Design*, Addison-Wesley, Reading, MA, 1996, Fig. 4-22, Section 4.12, p. 190.

PART 3: AVOIDING EXCESSIVE COMPILE- AND LINK-TIME DEPENDENCIES

IN THE FIRST ARTICLE[1] of this three-part series, I introduced the notion of physical design (involving files, directories, and libraries) in contrast to logical design (involving classes, functions, and operators) as an essential consideration of large-scale C++ software development.

I introduced the component (a corresponding pair of .h and .c files) as the atomic unit of physical design, and then argued that the component, not the class, is the appropriate fundamental unit of design because it captures a complete abstraction (which may span several logical entities) in a single physical unit that can readily be lifted from one system and reused in another without modification.

Two distinct kinds of physical dependency were discussed, and it was demonstrated that compile-time dependency almost always implies link-time dependency and that the physical dependence relation `DependsOn` among components is transitive.

Inferring physical dependencies among components from logical relationships (such as IsA and Uses) at design time enables us to detect/prevent excessive physical dependencies early in the development process. By following a few common-sense physical design rules, we are also able to extract all actual physical dependencies among the components in a system, just by analyzing the (component `#include` graph (including both .c and .h files).

In Part 2,[2] we continued our discussion of physical design by introducing the notion of physical hierarchy and demonstrating how it enables effective testing, significantly improves maintainability, and allows for independent reuse—all without violating encapsulation.

A "good" interface encapsulates the complexity of the implementation behind a simple façade that is easy to understand and use. At the same time, it makes our ability to test the implementation through this interface exceedingly difficult.

High-quality, complex subsystems are therefore composed of not one but many components layered atop each other to form an acyclic physical hierarchy. Level numbers characterize components in terms of their physical dependencies on other components within a subsystem. Furthermore, level numbers provide an order in which systems with acyclic component dependency graphs can be tested effectively.

Cumulative component dependency (CCD) provides a crude numerical measure of the overall link-time cost associated with incrementally testing a given subsystem. More generally, CCD is an indicator of the relative maintainability of a given design. Normalized CCD (NCCD) helps to categorize the physical structure of arbitrary designs as *cyclic*, *vertical*, *tree-like*, or *horizontal*.

Subsystems whose component dependencies form a directed acyclic graph (DAG) are said to be *levelizable*, are relatively easy to maintain, and allow for selective reuse. Cyclically-dependent designs are not levelizable, are difficult to maintain, and have a correspondingly high CCD.

In this final installment we will explore specific (levelization) techniques for eliminating cyclic link-time dependencies. We will also examine specific (insulation) techniques for eliminating unnecessary compile-time dependencies. Finally, we will extend the principles of levelization and insulation to yet larger systems by introducing a macro unit of physical design: the *package*.

LEVELIZATION

Link-time dependencies within a system (as quantified by CCD) play a central role in establishing the overall physical quality of a system. More conventional aspects of quality, such as understandability, maintainability, testability, and reusability, are all closely tied to the quality of the physical design. If not carefully prevented, cyclic physical dependencies will rob a system of this quality, leaving it inflexible and difficult to manage.

Initial designs are often carefully planned out and should be levelizable. In time, the unanticipated needs of clients can evoke less well-thought-out enhancements that introduce unwanted cyclic dependencies. For example, we sometimes find we have similar objects that, for one reason or another (e.g., performance), coexist in a system but that contain essentially the same information.

Figure 1 shows a simple but illustrative example consisting of two classes, each representing a kind of box. A `Rectangle` is defined by two points that determine its lower-left and upper-right corners. A `Window` is defined by a

```
// rectangle.h
#ifndef INCLUDED-RECTANGLE
#define INCLUDED_RECTANGLE

class Rectangle {
  // ...
  public:
    Rectangle(int x1,
              int y1 ,
              int x2,
              int y2);

  // ...
  int lowerleftX() const;
  // . ..
};

#endif
```

```
// window.h
#ifndef INCLUDED-WINDOW
#define INCLUDED_WINDOW

class Window {
  // ...
  public:
    Window(int xCenter,
           int yCenter,
           int xwidth,
           int height);

  // ...
  int width() const;
  // . ..
};

#endif
```

Figure 1. Two representations of a box.

center point, a width, and a height. These objects have distinct performance characteristics but contain the same logical information.

Each of these objects will be used to facilitate the rendering of very large designs interactively on a graphics terminal; draw speed will be critical. For performance reasons, we do not even consider employing virtual functions and most of the functions are inline.

> *Allowing two components to "know" about each other via* #include *directives implies cyclic physical dependency.*

It turns out that clients will occasionally need to be able to convert between these two types of boxes, perhaps to obtain the performance characteristics of the other. This is one way in which good designs can sometimes start to deteriorate.

Consider the "solution" set forth in Figure 2. We have added to each class a constructor that takes as its only argument a `const` reference to the other class. We can now pass a `Window` object to a function requiring a `Rectangle` and vice versa, the conversion being performed implicitly. How does that sound to you?

If it sounded good to you, you are not alone. But it is not a good solution. For one thing, any speed benefit that might be realized could be lost by having to construct a temporary object of the other type on entry to a function. Since the conversion is implicit and automatic, your clients may not even realize that the extra temporary is being created (and will blame you for your "slow" class).

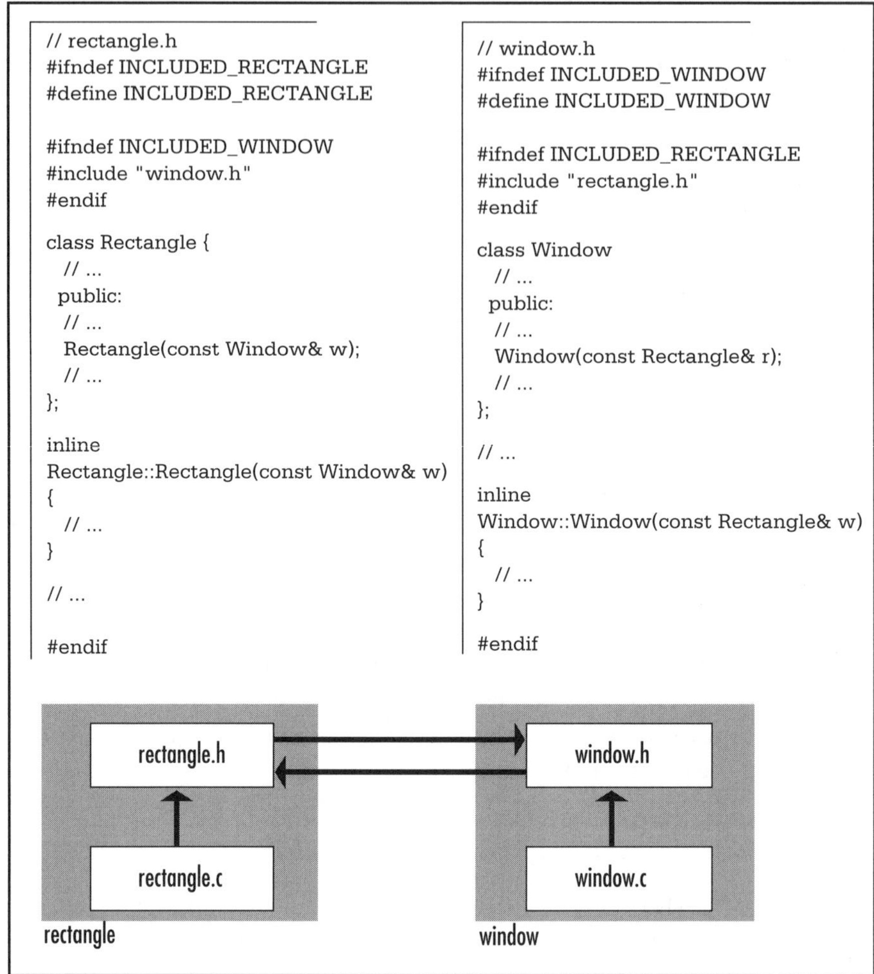
// rectangle.h
#ifndef INCLUDED_RECTANGLE
#define INCLUDED_RECTANGLE
#ifndef INCLUDED_WINDOW
#include "window.h"
#endif
class Rectangle {
// ...
public:
// ...
Rectangle(const Window& w);
// ...
};
inline
Rectangle::Rectangle(const Window& w)
{
// ...
}
// ...
#endif
// window.h
#ifndef INCLUDED_WINDOW
#define INCLUDED_WINDOW
#ifndef INCLUDED_RECTANGLE
#include "rectangle.h"
#endif
class Window
// ...
public:
// ...
Window(const Rectangle& r);
// ...
};
// ...
inline
Window::Window(const Rectangle& w)
{
// ...
}
#endif
rectangle.h
window.h
rectangle.c
window.c
rectangle
window

Figure 2. Two mutually dependent components.

Much more importantly, we have introduced a cyclic physical dependency between the header files of two (previously independent) components. Each of these components now must "know" about the other. It is no longer possible to compile, link, test, or use either one of these components without the other. Most clients will not be concerned about the subtle differences in performance characteristics between these classes and would opt to use either one, but rarely both. This unlevelizable enhancement forces them to take both.

We can move the preprocessor `#include` directives from the `.h` files to the `.c` files (as shown in Figure 3), but this does not eliminate the physical coupling. Both components still depend on each other at compile time, and each

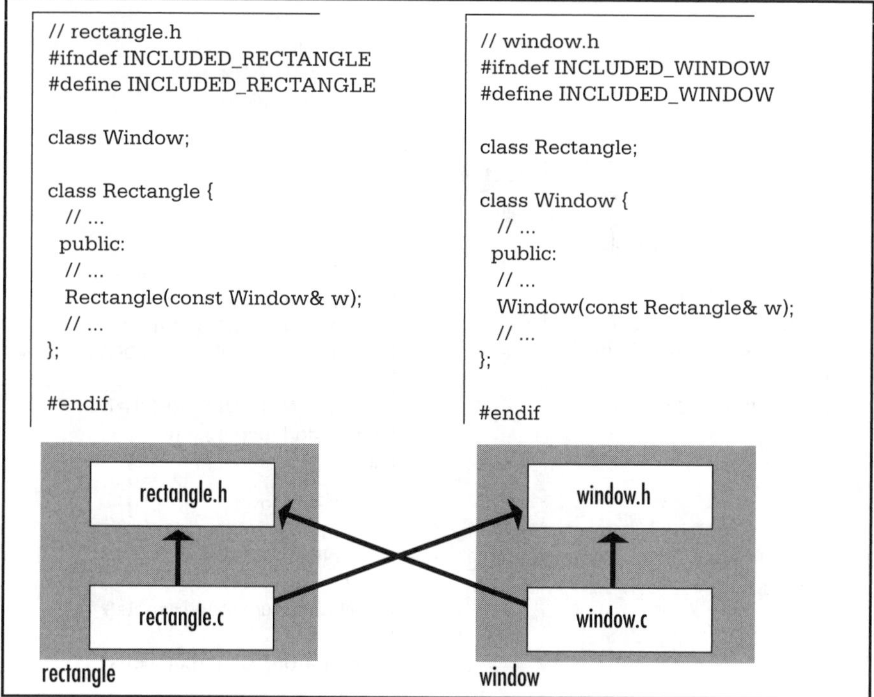
// rectangle.h
#ifndef INCLUDED_RECTANGLE
#define INCLUDED_RECTANGLE
class Window;
class Rectangle {
// ...
public:
// ...
Rectangle(const Window& w);
// ...
};
#endif
// window.h
#ifndef INCLUDED_WINDOW
#define INCLUDED_WINDOW
class Rectangle;
class Window {
// ...
public:
// ...
Window(const Rectangle& w);
// ...
};
#endif
rectangle.h
rectangle.c
rectangle
window.h
window.c
window

Figure 3. Two components still mutually dependent.

will potentially depend on the other at link time. We need to do something a bit more radical.

Suppose that instead of having Rectangle and Window "know" about each other, we decide arbitrarily that rectangles are more basic than windows. We can move both conversions into class Window. Window now Uses Rectangle but not vice versa, as is illustrated in Figure 4.

This solution requires that we change our point of view somewhat, because the Rectangle and Window classes are no longer symmetric. Rectangle lives at level 1, but Window is now defined at level 2. If we want any old box we can reuse Rectangle and not worry about Window or conversions between the classes. If we need a Window, however, we will have to take Rectangle also.

Of course we could have gone the other way and made Window the primitive object. In that case rectangle knows about window but not vice versa. This situation is depicted in Figure 5. Notice that in this example we have elected to move the #include "window.h" directive to the rectangle.c file, which implies that the conversion routines will *not* be inline.

Both solutions imply that only one component can be used independently

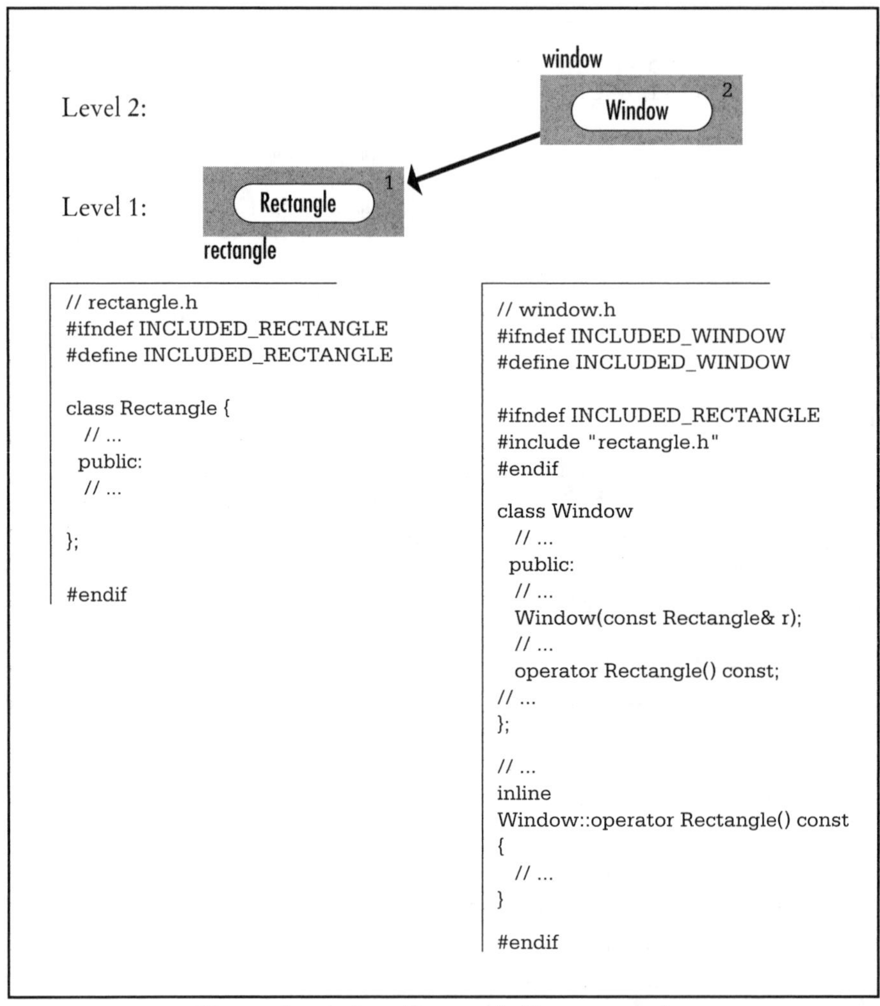
window
Level 2:
Window
2
Level 1:
Rectangle
1
rectangle
// rectangle.h
#ifndef INCLUDED_RECTANGLE
#define INCLUDED_RECTANGLE
class Rectangle {
// ...
public:
// ...
};
#endif
// window.h
#ifndef INCLUDED_WINDOW
#define INCLUDED_WINDOW
#ifndef INCLUDED_RECTANGLE
#include "rectangle.h"
#endif
class Window
// ...
public:
// ...
Window(const Rectangle& r);
// ...
operator Rectangle() const;
// ...
};
// ...
inline
Window::operator Rectangle() const
{
// ...
}
#endif

Figure 4. window DependsOn rectangle.

of the other. Either solution is an improvement over the original cyclically-dependent design, but we can do still better. Many clients who use these components will need one or the other but not both. Of those that do need to use both components, only some will need to convert between them. To maximize independent reusability, we can avoid having either component depend on the other by moving the cycle-inducing functionality to a higher level—a technique referred to as *escalation*.

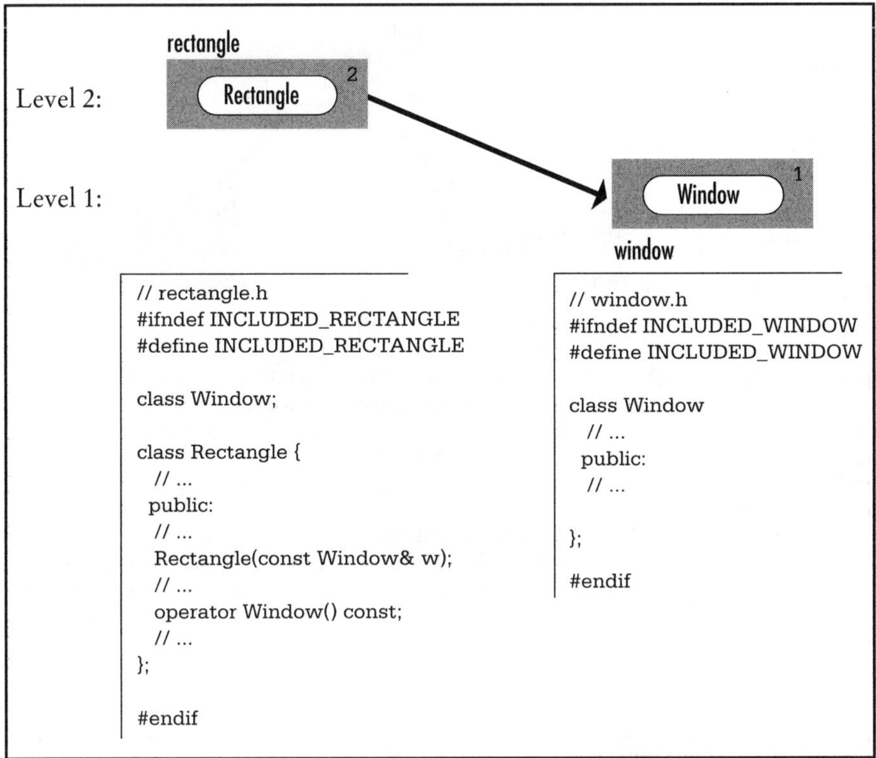
rectangle
Level 2:
Rectangle
2
Level 1:
Window
1
window
// rectangle.h
#ifndef INCLUDED_RECTANGLE
#define INCLUDED_RECTANGLE
class Window;
class Rectangle {
// ...
public:
// ...
Rectangle(const Window& w);
// ...
operator Window() const;
// ...
};
#endif
// window.h
#ifndef INCLUDED_WINDOW
#define INCLUDED_WINDOW
class Window
// ...
public:
// ...
};
#endif

Figure 5. rectangle DependsOn window.

> *If peer components are cyclically-dependent, it may be possible to escalate the interdependent functionality from each of these components to static members in a (potentially new) higher-level component that depends on each of the original components.*

In corporations, if two employees are not able to resolve a dispute, the common practice is to escalate the problem to a higher level. In the case of objects competing for dominance, the same solution is often effective. We can create a utility class called BoxUtil that knows about both Rectangle and Window classes and then place the definition of this class in an entirely separate component, as shown in Figure 6.

The conversion between Rectangle and Window, which used to be implicit, must now be performed explicitly. In return for this "concession" clients interested in Rectangle or Window are free to use either class independently. If a single client happens to use both classes but does not need to convert between

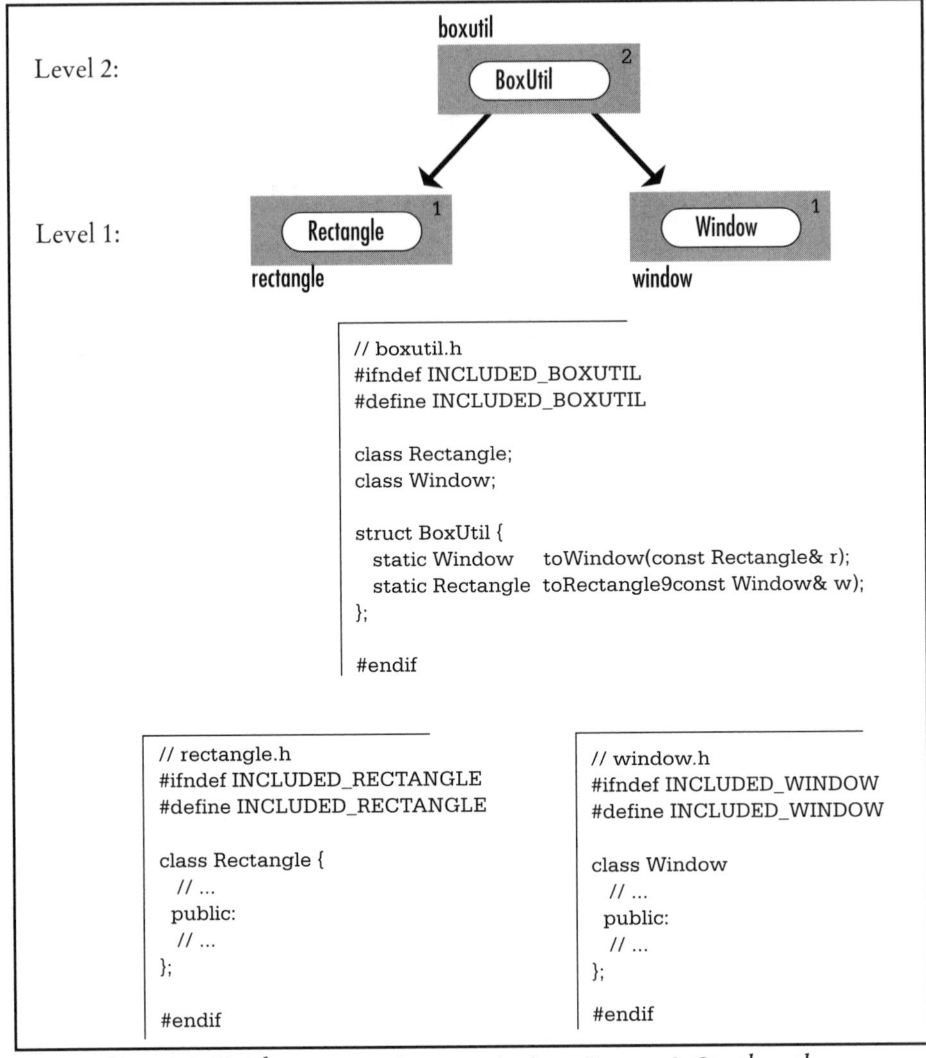

Level 2:
boxutil
BoxUtil
2
Level 1:
Rectangle
1
rectangle
Window
1
window
// boxutil.h
#ifndef INCLUDED_BOXUTIL
#define INCLUDED_BOXUTIL
class Rectangle;
class Window;
struct BoxUtil {
static Window toWindow(const Rectangle& r);
static Rectangle toRectangle9const Window& w);
};
#endif
// rectangle.h
#ifndef INCLUDED_RECTANGLE
#define INCLUDED_RECTANGLE
class Rectangle {
// ...
public:
// ...
};
#endif
// window.h
#ifndef INCLUDED_WINDOW
#define INCLUDED_WINDOW
class Window
// ...
public:
// ...
};
#endif

Figure 6. Neither rectangle *nor* window DependsOn *the other.*

them so be it. If yet other clients require the conversion routines, they are available. By escalating the mutually dependent functionality to a higher level, we have fundamentally improved the physical design quality of this subsystem.

Often, in an effort to make a system usable, developers are tempted to create designs that are not structurally sound. As a second, more involved example of this recurring theme, consider a graphical shape editor whose design

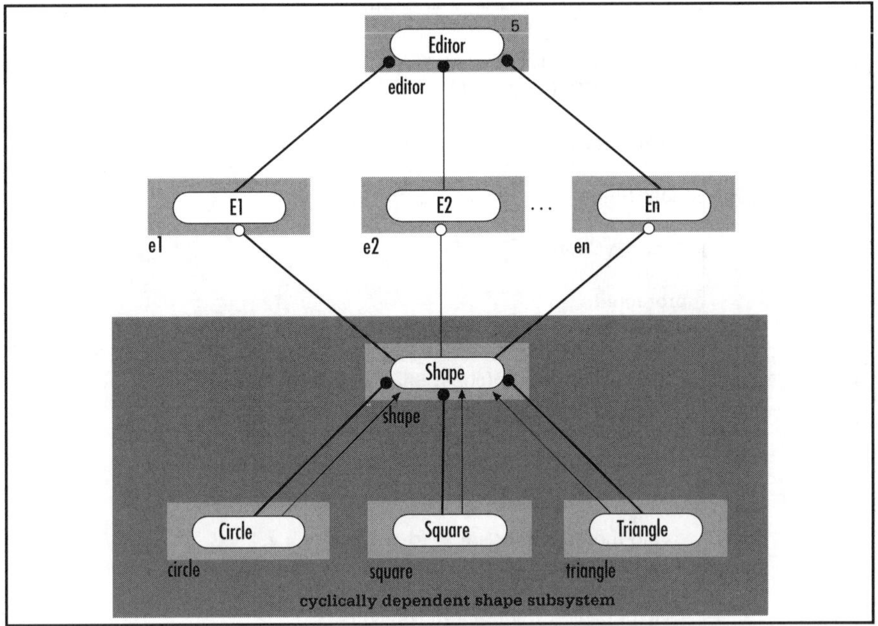

Figure 7. Unlevelizable design of a shape editor.

is depicted abstractly in Figure 7. The Shape class is abstract and defines a protocol that all concrete shapes must implement. Every shape has a location that we will assume for now must be manipulated as quickly as possible (i.e., via inline functions). Since some of the functionality in the Shape class is already implemented, Shape serves not only to define a common interface, but also to factor the common part of the implementation. (Note that we could reduce compile-time coupling between consumers and suppliers of the Shape interface if we relaxed the speed requirement for the moveTo function).

The Shape class could potentially define a large number of pure virtual functions. A sparse representation of the header file for the shape component is presented in Figure 8. Clients of the Shape class will need to be able to create actual shapes, but will not need to interact with the derived class interfaces directly. In order to insulate clients of Shape from concrete classes derived from Shape, the ability to create specific kinds of shapes is incorporated directly into Shape's interface.

To make it easy to add new shapes by name, the Shape class implements the static member function create. This method takes the type name of the Shape (as a const char *) and returns a pointer to a dynamically allocated, newly constructed shape of the appropriate concrete type derived from Shape.

```
// shape.h
#ifndef INCLUDED_SHAPE
#define INCLUDED_SHAPE

class Screen;

class Shape {
  int d_xCoord;
  int d_yCoord;

protected:
  Shape(int x, int y);
  Shape (const Shape& shape);
  Shape& operator=(const Shape& shape);

public:
  static Shape *create(const char *typeName);
  virtual ~Shape();
  // ...
  void moveTo(int x, int y) {d_x = x; d_y = y: }
  // ...
  virtual Shape *clone() const = 0;
  virtual void draw(Screen &s) const = 0;
  // ...
};

#endiif
```

Figure 8. Elided .h file for component shape.

If no shape corresponding to that type name exists, the function returns 0.

The Editor class itself is layered upon a number of custom types (E1,..., En) used solely in the implementation of class Editor. Each of these types uses Shape in its interface in order to perform various abstract operations on shapes (e.g., moveTo, scale, intersect, and so on). Only one of the implementation components, e1, which implements the add command needs to be able to create a shape from a type name. The rest of these components can use Shape's virtual functions to access a particular shape's functionality, and do not need to depend on any concrete shape directly. Does this sound reasonable?

Although this design may seem appealing from a usability standpoint, it has a design flaw that makes it quite a bit more expensive to maintain than it need be. The create member function of Shape uses a constructor of each of the classes derived from Shape, which forces a mutual dependency between Shape and all classes derived from Shape. It is therefore not possible to test a specific kind of shape independently of all the rest, significantly increasing the link time and disk space required during incremental testing. The shape

```
// shapeutil.h
#ifndef INCLUDED_SHAPEUTIL
#define INCLUDED_SHAPEUTIL

class Shape;

struct ShapeUtil {
  static Shape *create(const char *typeName);
};

#endiif
```

Figure 9. Header file for new component shapeutil.

subsystem, which is otherwise horizontal and therefore highly reusable, is turned into an all-or-nothing proposition.

Adding a new kind of shape to this subsystem requires modifying the Shape base class, which could produce errors in functionality pertaining to the other independently derived classes. The high degree of coupling brought on by having a base class "know" about its derived classes implies a considerable increase in maintenance cost and a considerable loss of flexibility and reuse.

The maintenance disadvantage worsens when we consider that only component e1 needs to create each of the Editor's concrete shapes and therefore only e1 needs to depend on all of the individual concrete shape components. Components e2, e3,...en merely use these shapes via the virtual functions of the abstract base class Shape. If we can assume that the functionality of each shape is working properly, then we need test only that the editor component is interacting with the Shape protocol properly. There could be dozens or even hundreds of different kinds of shapes, and it is neither necessary nor practical to test each editor component with every type of shape all the time. Yet, because of the coupling in the shape subsystem, we are forced to link to all shapes whenever incrementally testing any one of the editor implementation components.

In order to improve the maintainability of this system, we need to find a way to repackage the shape subsystem so that it becomes acyclic and therefor levelizable. Suppose we escalate create above the level of its derived classes by introducing a new utility class, ShapeUtil, whose sole purpose is to create shapes. This new class would be placed in its own component and contain the create function from the original shape class, as shown in Figure 9.

By adding a new component and escalating the Uses relationship to a higher level, we have removed the cyclic dependencies among all components in the shape subsystem. The levelized diagram for the new system is shown in Figure 10.

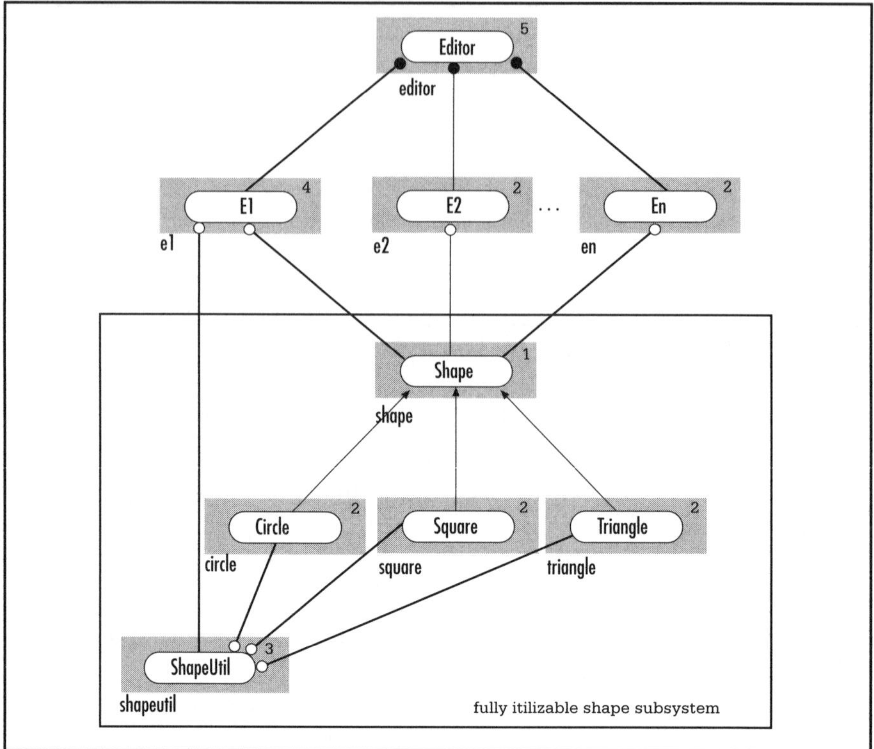

Figure 10. Acyclic design for a shape editor.

It is now possible for each concrete shape to be tested in isolation. Even the partial implementation provided by class Shape can be tested modularly by deriving a concrete "stub" class from Shape in the test driver for the shape component. Each of the concrete shapes can now be reused independently of the rest in any combination. For example, another system is now able to reuse circle and square without having to link in triangle.

It is now also possible to test each of e2,...,en without having to link to every concrete shape. Since these components require only the Shape base class interface, it may be deemed sufficient to test the incremental value added by each of the editor component e2,...,en on only a representative sample of all concrete shapes.

The advantage of this new design over the original is a reduction in coupling that will translate directly into reduced development and maintenance costs while amplifying the potential for reuse. It may be difficult to appreciate the importance of this design approach when the number of implementation components in the editor, and particularly the number of concrete shapes, are small. The real advantage is that this new design scales up much better than the original as more editor commands and new shapes are added.

As an objective, quantitative measure of the improvement levelization brings to this design, let us consider four variants of the editor system. In the "scaled-down" version of this system, Table 1a, both the editor and the number of shapes it operates on are small (three shapes, and three editor-implementation components). Even with the additional component in the new design, the coupling associated with hierarchically testing the shape subsystem as measured by CCD is reduced by a full 25 percent. The coupling associated with incrementally testing the editor subsystem is reduced by 17.4 percent, giving an overall reduction in CCD of 20.5 percent. Table 1b illustrates the effect when the editor subsystem is made large (30 implementation components instead of only 3). Now the reduction in component coupling for the editor subsystem is nearly 46 percent, pushing the overall reduction in CCD to 43.3%.

Cyclic physical dependencies in large, low-level subsystems have the greatest capacity to increase the overall cost of maintaining a system.

Cyclic coupling at lower levels of the physical hierarchy can have a dramatic effect on the cost of maintaining clients. As can be seen in Table 1c, when the shape hierarchy is made large (30 concrete types instead of only 3), the advantage of the new design, as measured by CCD, amounts not only to a reduction in coupling of over 90 percent in the shape subsystem, but also a reduction of over 44 percent in the editor subsystem, for a reduction of close to 85 percent overall. When both the shape subsystem and editor are large, the overall percentage reduction in coupling continues to improve, as shown in Table 1d.

The important lesson to be learned from this analysis is that a high degree of coupling associated with lower-level subsystems not only increases costs for those subsystems, but can also dramatically increase the cost of developing and maintaining clients and subsystems at higher levels. By considering the physical implications of our logical design and proactively engineering our system as a levelizable collection of components, we create a hierarchy of modular abstractions that can be understood, tested, and reused independently of the rest of our design.

Escalating mutual dependencies to a higher level can be used to convert cyclic dependencies into welcome downward dependencies. We have just seen two situations in which this technique can be used to eliminate excessive physical interdependencies. Escalation, however, is only one of several levelization techniques described in my book[3]; the others are listed in Table 2.

Table 1. Relative coupling of cyclic versus acrylic designs.

			With Cycles			Without Cycles			Reduction
			size	*CCd*	*NCCD*	*size*	*CCD*	*NCCD*	*IN CCD*
a)	(Small)	Editor:	4	23		4	19		17.4%
	(Small)	Shape:	4	16	2.10	5	12	1.14	25.1%
		Combined:	8	39	1.90	9	31	1.28	20.5%
b)	(Large)	Editor:	31	185		31	100		45.9%
	(Small)	Shape:	4	16	2.10	5	12	1.14	25.1%
		Combined:	35	201	1.33	36	112	0.90	43.3%
c)	(Small)	Editor:	4	131		4	73		43.3%
	(Large)	Shape:	31	961	8.47	32	93	0.69	90.3%
		Combined	35	1092	7.23	36	166	1.06	84.8%
d)	(Large)	Editor:	31	1022		31	154		84.9%
	(Large)	Shape:	31	961	8.47	32	93	0.69	90.3%
		Combined	62	1983	6.30	63	247	0.77	87.5%

Table 2. Levelization techniques.

Name	*Description*
Escalation	Moving mutually dependent functionality higher in the physical hierarchy.
Demotion	Moving common functionality lower in the physical hierarchy.
Opaque Pointers	Having an object use another in name only.
Dumb Data	Using data that indicates a dependency on a peer object, but only in the context of a separate, higher-level object.
Redundancy	Deliberately avoiding reuse by repeating small amounts of code or data to avoid coupling.
Callbacks	Client-supplied functions that enable lower-level subsystems to perform specific tasks in a more global context.
Manager Class	Establishing a class that owns and coordinates lower-level objects.
Factoring	Moving idependently testable sub-behavior out of the implementation of complex component involved in excessive physical coupling.
Escalating Encapsulation	Moving the point at which implementation details are hidden from clients to a higher level in the physical hierarchy.

Using these techniques to create levelizable designs tends to reduce the large, sometimes even overwhelming, logical design space, and helps to guide developers in the direction of more mainstream, maintainable architectures. Fortunately there is a serendipitous synergy between good logical design and good physical design. Given time, these two design goals will come to reinforce one another.

INSULATION

Avoiding unnecessary compile-time dependencies is another important aspect of good physical design. Excessive compile-time coupling can profoundly impede our ability to maintain a system. Programmatically inaccessible implementation details that reside in the physical interface (i.e.,.h file) of a component cannot, in general, be modified without forcing all clients to recompile. For even moderately large projects, the cost of recompiling the entire system will inhibit any modification of the physical interface of low-level components, limiting our ability to make even local changes to the encapsulated details of their implementations.

Insulation is a physical design issue; its logical analog is commonly referred to as *encapsulation.* For example, consider the header file for the stack component shown in Figure 11. The logical interface of this Stack class fully encapsulates its implementation. Programmatically, there is no way to distinguish this array-based implementation from the linked-list-based implementation with the identical interface shown in Figure 12.

Even though both Stack classes fully encapsulate their implementations, any experienced C++ programmer looking at these header files can immediately determine the general implementation strategy of these components. Each of these stack component headers illustrate the difficulty in concealing proprietary implementations even with encapsulating interfaces. Inline functions can exacerbate the problem by exposing clients to algorithmic details as well.

But the desire to keep component implementations proprietary is not the dominant problem for large projects. A client has a right to expect that the logical interface of a component will not change and, ideally, that changes

```
// stack.h
#ifndef INCLUDED_STACK
#define INCLUDED_STACK

class StackLink;

class Stack {
  StakLink *d_stack_p;

public:
  Stack();
  Stack(const Stack 7stack);
  Stack& operator=(const Stack &stack);
  ~Stack();
  void push(int value);
  int pop();
  int top() const;
  int is Empty() const;
};

#endiif
```

Figure 11. Fully encapsulated array-based Stack implementation.

made to the logical implementation of a component will not affect clients. In reality, however, the C++ compiler depends on all information in a header file, including private data. If a human being can determine the implementation strategy of a component by inspecting its header, then it is likely that clients of the component would be forced to recompile if the implementation strategy of that component changes.

Forcing clients to recompile even when only the implementation of a component changes is not a desirable physical property of a component. The more components that depend on that component, the more undesirable such compile-time coupling can become. Failing to insulate clients from changes to our logical implementation can have a dramatic impact on the cost of developing large projects.

Imagine a system with *N* components in which each component is compile-time dependent on all the rest. That is, compiling a component means including and parsing the definitions from the header files of all *N* components. Instead of being proportional to the size of the component itself, the cost of compiling any single translation unit depends on the size of the entire system! As more headers are read into a translation unit, the compiler's data structures are taxed more and more heavily. That is, doubling the number of lines in-

```
// stack.h
#ifndef INCLUDED_STACK
#define INCLUDED_STACK

class StackLink;

class Stack {
  int *d_stack_p;
  int d_size;
  int d_length;

public;
  Stack();
  Stack(const Stack &stack);
  ~Stack();
  Stack& operator=(const Stack &stack);
  void push(int value);
  int pop();
  int top() const;
  int isEmpty() const;
};

#endiif
```

Figure 12. Fully encapsulated linked-list-based Stack implementation.

Table 3. Empirical cost of compile-time coupling.

System Size: N	*CPU Seconds to parse headers*	
(number of headers)	*100-line headers*	*1000-line headers*
1	0.1	0.4
2	0.1	1.0
4	0.2	3.4
8	0.4	11.0
16	0.8	32.2
32	2.4	137.7
64	8.2	497.5
128	26.5	more than a day
256	98.1	
512	397.6	
1024	more than a day	

cluded in a translation unit more than doubles the time it takes to parse them.

Even for relatively small systems (say, 50,000 lines total) this type of coupling is burdensome at best; for medium and large systems, it is intolerable. A .c file that should take only seconds to compile might now take minutes, and the total compile-time cost of a single uninsulated change would be measured not in CPU seconds but in CPU hours!

To illustrate the severity of the problem, I devised a simple experiment. I mechanically generated a varying number of simple header files, each 100 lines long. All headers were then included in an otherwise empty .c file. I then measured the CPU time needed to compile the .c file. The experiment was repeated using headers 1,000 lines long instead of 100 lines. Table 3 provides the results of running this simple experiment using the CFRONT 3.0 compiler on a SUN SPARC 20 workstation with 32 megabytes of memory.

If, when compiling any single translation unit, the amount of included header file information causes the compiler to exceed available physical memory, virtual memory swapping will completely overwhelm the cost of compilation, as was the case for the last entry in column 2 and the last four entries in column 3 of Table 3. That is, for a given compiler and system configuration, there can be fairly hard limits to the absolute size of any given translation unit. For this particular configuration, 60,000 lines was practical; 100,000 lines was not.

As a concrete example of compile-time coupling, let's consider the system illustrated in Figure 13. This system consists of a base class `Shape`, a number

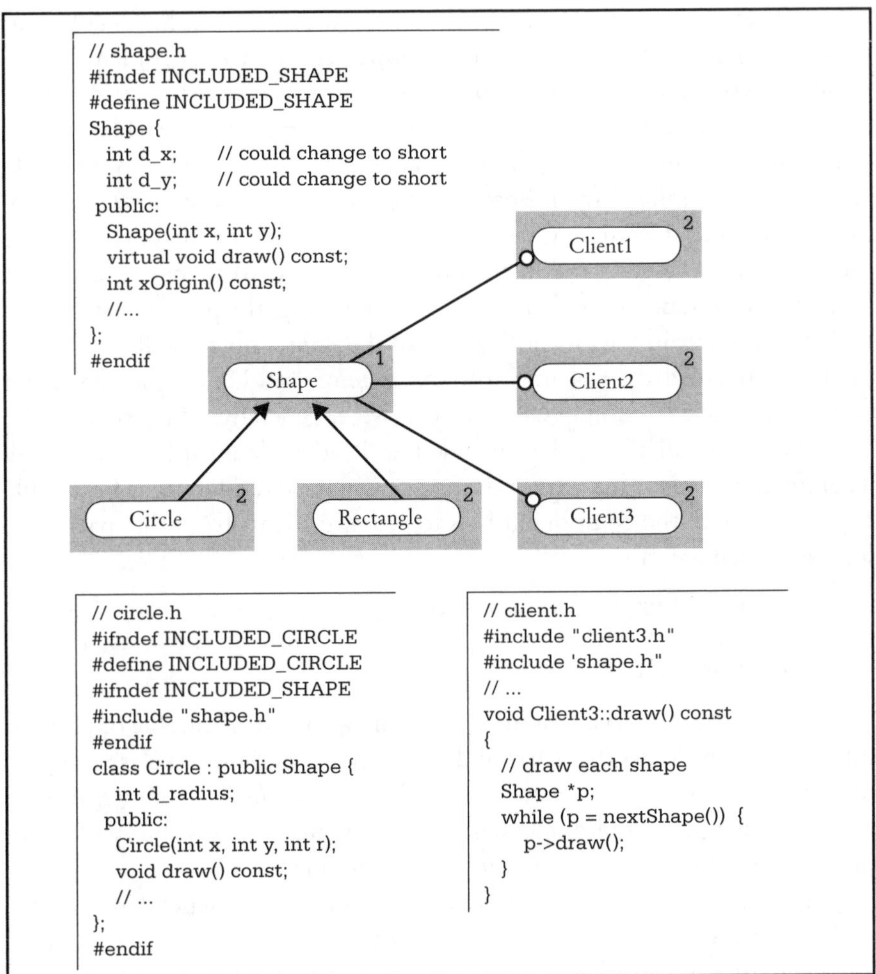

// shape.h
#ifndef INCLUDED_SHAPE
#define INCLUDED_SHAPE
Shape {
int d_x; // could change to short
int d_y; // could change to short
public:
Shape(int x, int y);
virtual void draw() const;
int xOrigin() const;
//...
};
#endif
Client1
2
Shape
1
Client2
2
Circle
2
Rectangle
2
Client3
2
// circle.h
#ifndef INCLUDED_CIRCLE
#define INCLUDED_CIRCLE
#ifndef INCLUDED_SHAPE
#include "shape.h"
#endif
class Circle : public Shape {
int d_radius;
public:
Circle(int x, int y, int r);
void draw() const;
// ...
};
#endif
// client.h
#include "client3.h"
#include 'shape.h"
// ...
void Client3::draw() const
{
// draw each shape
Shape *p;
while (p = nextShape()) {
p->draw();
}
}

Figure 13. Illustration of compile-time coupling.

of specific shapes derived from `Shape`, and a number of clients that depend only on the base class `Shape`. This system has no cyclic physical dependencies and is therefore levelizable.

Originally the author of class `Shape` decided to use integers to represent the coordinates of the origin. Later the author realized that the integer range afforded by a short int was sufficient and that the size of `Shape` instances could be reduced significantly. The fundamental type of a private data member used to store the coordinates is clearly an implementation detail of the `Shape` class. The interface would not change, and it would continue to accept and return normal integers in the valid range. In fact, this detail is entirely encapsulated by the interface of Shape. Yet there is a problem.

Suppose that the author of Shape changes the private coordinate data type from int to short int. Which of the components in Figure 13 would be forced to recompile? Unfortunately, the correct answer is "all of them!" Both Circle and Rectangle inherit from Shape and depend intimately on the internal physical layout of Shape. When any of Shape's data members change, the internal layout of Circle and Rectangle will also have to change accordingly.

Clients of Shape are no better off. For one thing, the position of the virtual table pointer in the physical layout of the Shape object will almost certainly be affected by the change from int to short int. Unless the dependent code is recompiled, it simply will not work. More generally, whenever a header file is modified, all clients that include that header file must be recompiled. Therefore, whenever any part of the implementation resides in the header file of a component, the component fails to *insulate* clients from that part of its logical implementation.

> *A contained implementation detail (type, data, or function) that can be altered, added, or removed without forcing clients to recompile is said to be* insulated.

The term *encapsulation* conjures up an image of a clear bubble of perhaps infinitesimal thickness that surrounds the implementation of a class and protects it only from programmatic access. The term *insulation* connotes instead an opaque barrier of finite thickness that eliminates any possibility of direct interaction with the implementation of a component.

For widely used interfaces, avoiding all compile-time dependency on the underlying implementation details is highly desirable. There are three general techniques for insulating clients from all implementation details:

- Protocol Class
- Fully Insulated Concrete Class
- Insulating Wrapper Component

Here I will describe briefly each of these techniques, and illustrate them by applying each to the example in Figure 13.

PROTOCOL CLASS

Extracting a *protocol* class is a general insulation technique for factoring the interface and implementation of an abstract base class. Not only are clients insulated from changes to the implementation at compile time, but even link-time dependency on a specific implementation is eliminated.

Because **Shape** was already an abstract class, extracting a protocol (as shown in Figure 14) is the natural way to improve insulation without altering its usage model. Performance for all but the origin-related functions will be left unaffected. Clients of **Shape** will continue to use **Shape** as before.

The original **Shape** class, is renamed to **ShapeImp**. Concrete shapes originally derived from **Shape** must now derive from **ShapeImp**. In this way, the partial implementation common to all shapes defined by **ShapeImp** cannot affect clients of **Shape**.

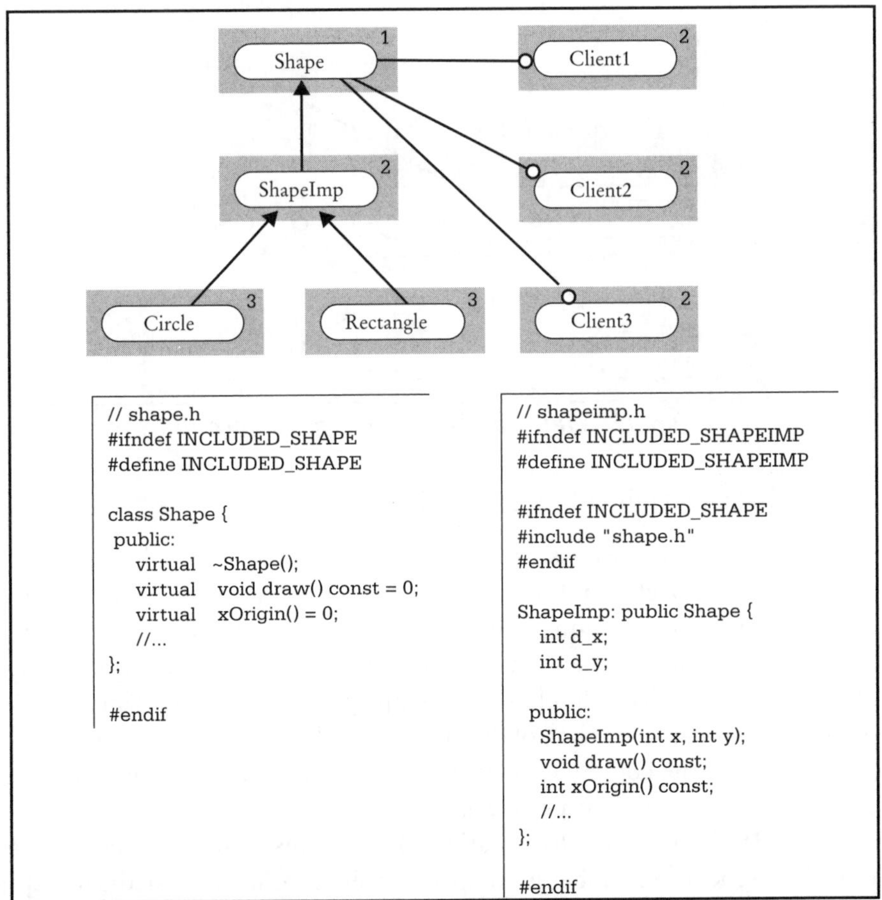
Shape 1
Client1 2
ShapeImp 2
Client2 2
Circle 3
Rectangle 3
Client3 2
// shape.h
#ifndef INCLUDED_SHAPE
#define INCLUDED_SHAPE
class Shape {
public:
virtual ~Shape();
virtual void draw() const = 0;
virtual xOrigin() = 0;
//...
};
#endif
// shapeimp.h
#ifndef INCLUDED_SHAPEIMP
#define INCLUDED_SHAPEIMP
#ifndef INCLUDED_SHAPE
#include "shape.h"
#endif
ShapeImp: public Shape {
int d_x;
int d_y;
public:
ShapeImp(int x, int y);
void draw() const;
int xOrigin() const;
//...
};
#endif

Figure 14. Reducing compile-time coupling with a protocol class.

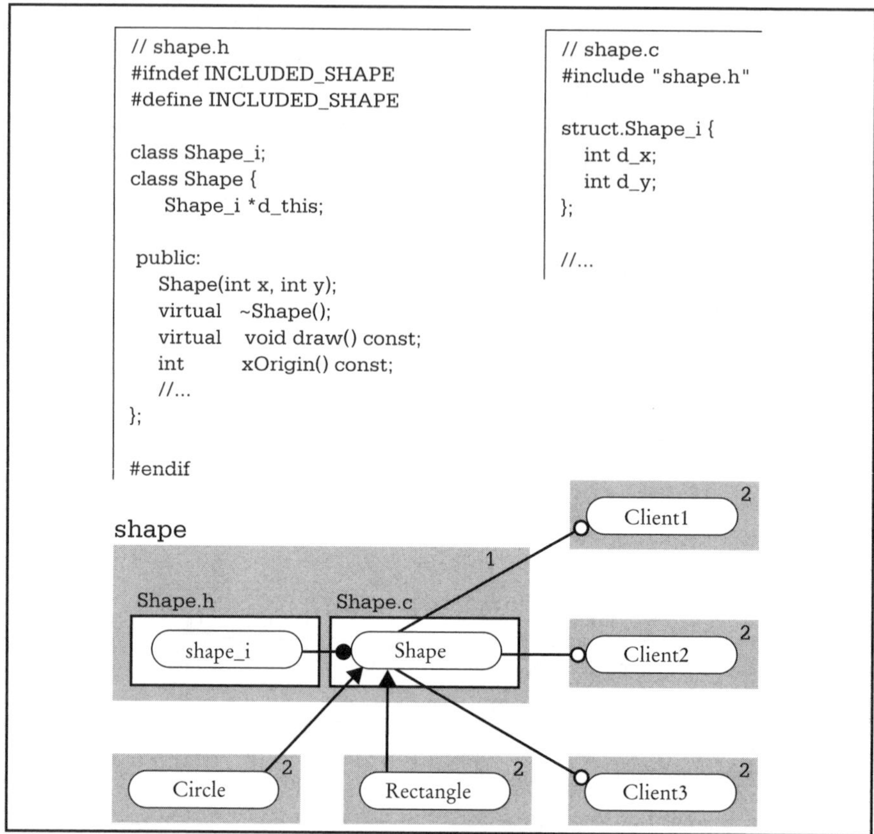
// shape.h
#ifndef INCLUDED_SHAPE
#define INCLUDED_SHAPE
class Shape_i;
class Shape {
Shape_i *d_this;
public:
Shape(int x, int y);
virtual ~Shape();
virtual void draw() const;
int xOrigin() const;
//...
};
#endif
// shape.c
#include "shape.h"
struct.Shape_i {
int d_x;
int d_y;
};
//...
shape
1
Shape.h
Shape.c
shape_i
Shape
Client1
2
Client2
2
Client3
2
Circle
2
Rectangle
2

Figure 15. A fully-insulating concrete Shape *class.*

FULLY INSULATING CONCRETE CLASS

Concrete classes can be constructed as automatic variables and hence have a different usage model than abstract classes. In such cases we may choose to employ an insulation technique that continues to allow the object to be constructed directly by the client. Instead of embedding the instance data directly in the class, we can have the class hold an opaque pointer to a dynamically allocated struct that contains all of the private data. By defining this struct within the .c file of the component, we ensure that no other component can be affected by a change to the private data.

Figure 15 shows an implementation of a fully insulating concrete Shape class. The lone data member is an opaque pointer to the insulated data representation. We must now access the "data members" via d_this:

```
int Shape::xOrigin() const { return d_this->d_x; }
```

What makes this implementation fully insulated is that, to the client, all such implementations look identical. No other component can access the data representation defined in the c.file. Hence we are free to change the implementation without having to change any header files or recompile any other component.

Insulating Wrapper Component

The technique of creating an encapsulating wrapper component allows us to escalate the level of encapsulation, and often to achieve an efficient levelizable design. This technique can be extended, by making the wrapper itself fully insulating as well. Wrappers are typically used to insulate several other components or even an entire subsystem. A wrapper layer requires considerable up-front planning and top-down design. In particular, care must be taken in the design of a multi-component wrapper to avoid the need for long-distance (i.e., intercomponent) friendships.

In the design shown in Figure 16, the shape system is insulated from clients by a separate component that implements a façade through which external clients can manipulate the entire subsystem. In this example, the constructor takes the coordinates of the origin of the new shape as well as an enumerated type, ShapeType, that identifies the kind of shape to construct. Using a character string instead of an enumeration would allow new types to be added without forcing existing clients to recompile. But that interface would circumvent compile-time type checking and therefore is not the kind of coupling insulation seeks to eliminate. If extensibility is a design goal, then extracting a protocol is preferable. A powerful generalization of the protocol class-a design pattern called *Protocol Hierarchy*—is described in detail in appendix A of my book.[3]

Partial Insulation Techniques

A totally insulated implementation is not appropriate for every component. But all other things being equal, it is better to insulate a particular implementation detail from a client than not—even if other details remain uninsulated. Partial insulation techniques can be used to reduce the extent of compile-time coupling without incurring all of the overhead that total insulation could imply. A list of partial insulation strategies is provided in Table 4.

Internal releases are an integral part of any large development project. Rebuilding the entire system to fix critical bugs between releases can be prohibitively expensive. A patch is a local change to a previously released version

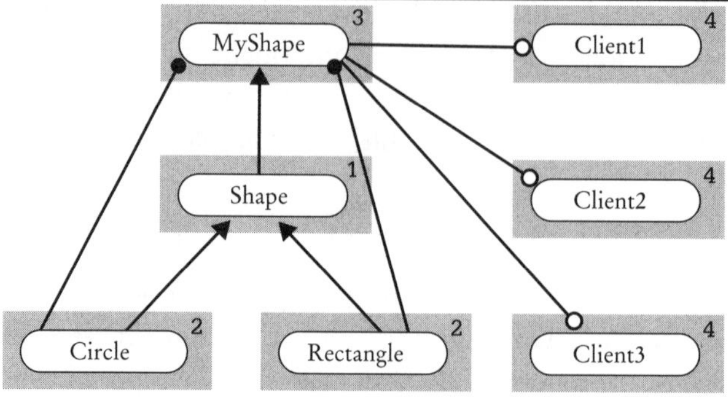

```
// myshape.h
#ifndef INCLUDED_MYSHAPE
#define INCLUDED_MYSHAPE

class Shape {

 class MYShape {
    Shape *d_shape;

  public:
    enum ShapeType (CIRCLE, RECTANGLE);
    MYShape(int x, int y, ShapeType type);
    ~Shape();
    void draw() const;
    int xOrigin() const;
      //...
};

#endif
```

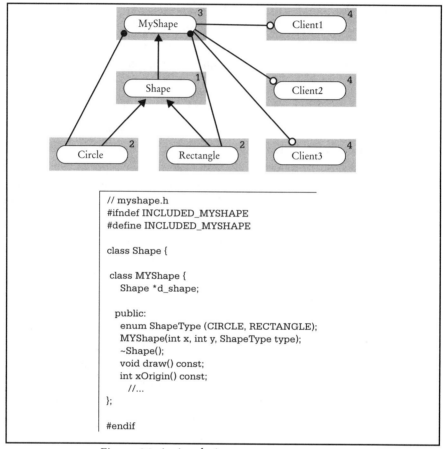

Figure 16. An insulating wrapper component.

of software. When critical bugs are encountered between releases, making a patch is typically less expensive and far less disruptive than rereleasing the entire system. As long as the physical interface of a component is not altered, the modified implementation can often be recompiled and dropped in place without having to recompile other components or worrying about headers becoming out of date. The more insulated the implementation of a component, the more likely it is that it can be repaired locally. Our ability to patch a release is directly related to the degree to which implementation details are insulated from clients throughout the system.

One final testament to the value of insulation is the ability to replace dynamically loaded libraries transparently. If you supply a

Table 4. Partial insulatoin techniques.

Cause of Compile-Time Coupling	*Strategy to Eliminate Compile-Time Coupling*
Private Inheritance	Convert WasA to HoldsA.
Embedded Member data	Convert HasA to HoldsA.
Private Member functions	Make them static at file scope and move them to the .c file.
Protected Member functions	Creating a separate utility component and/or extract a protocol.
Private Member data	Extract a protocol and/or move static data to the .c file at file scope.
Compiler-Generated Functions	Explicitly define these functions.
Include Directives	Remove unnecessary #include directives or replace them with (forward) class declarations.
Default Arguments	Replace valid default values with invalid default values or employ multiple function declarations.
Enumerations	Relocate them to the .c file, replace them with const static class member data, or redistribute them among the classes that use them.

fully insulated library implementation, then you can provide performance enhancements and bug-fixes without impacting your clients at all. Sending them an update does not force them to recompile or even relink. All they do is reconfigure their environment to point to the new dynamically-loaded library and off they go.

Packages

A large project can span many developers, several layers of management and even multiple geographic sites. The physical structure of our system will reflect not only the logical structure of the application but also the organizational structure of the development team that implements it. Large systems require physical organization beyond what can be accomplished by a levelizable hierarchy of individual components alone. In order to encompass more complex functionality, we need to introduce a unit of physical design at a higher level of abstraction.

When designing a system from the highest level, there are almost always large pieces that makes sense to talk about abstractly as individual units. Consider the design of an interpreter for a large language (such as C++) shown in Figure 17. Each of the subsystems described in that design is likely to be too large and complex to fit appropriately into a single component. These larger units (indicated in Figure 17 with a double box) are each implemented as a collection of levelizable components.

The dependencies in Figure 17 between these larger units represent an envelope for the aggregate dependencies among the components that comprise each subsystem. For example, the runtime database is an independent subsystem; it has no dependencies on any external components. Each of the parser, evaluator, and formatter subsystems have components that depend on one or more components in the runtime database, but none of the components in any of these three subsystems depends on any components in the other two parallel subsystems. The top-level interpreter consists of components that depend on components within each of the three parallel subsystems (and perhaps directly on components within the runtime database).

Carefully partitioning a system into large units and then considering the aggregate dependencies among these units is critical when distributing the development effort for projects across multiple individuals, development teams, or geographical sites.

Although the design of Figure 17 would not be considered a "large" project, it could easily be assigned to more than one developer. There is a natural

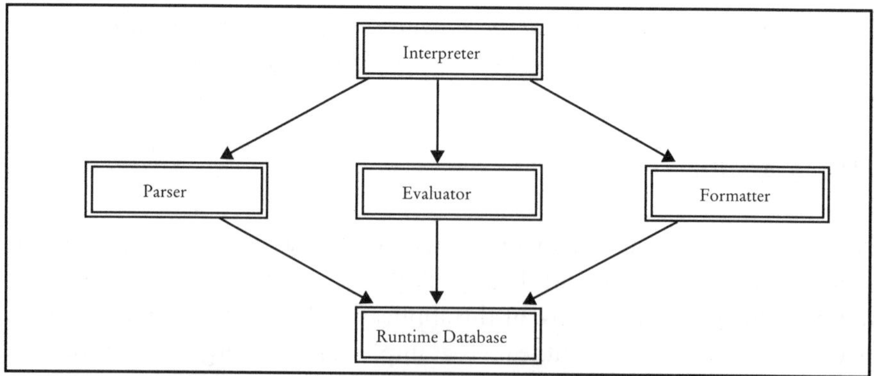

Figure 17. High-level interpreter architecture.

partitioning that would allow several developers to work on this project concurrently. After the runtime database is designed, there would be an opportunity for three concurrent development efforts to begin on the parsing, evaluating, and formatting functionality, respectively. Once these pieces start to fall into place, the implementation and testing of the top-level interpreter can begin.

A package is an acyclic collection of components organized as a physically cohesive unit.

Until now, we have discussed these separate subsystems as conceptual units with no actual physical partitions. The term package refers to an acyclic collection of components that together have a cohesive semantic purpose. Physically, a package consists of a collection of header files along with a single library file containing the information in the corresponding object (.o) files. A package might consist of a loosely coupled collection of low-level, reusable components, such as the standard template library (STL).

A package might also consist of a special-purpose subsystem intended for use by only a single client.

Figure 18 illustrates the way we have all along been treating the dependencies of our subsystem (`pkgb`) on another subsystem (`pkga`). When testing our own package, we assume that components defined outside our package are already tested and known to be internally correct. We therefore can assign to each of these external components a level number of `0` with respect to our local components. Components within our own package that do not depend on any other components local to this package (e.g., i and j) are defined to have a level of 1. Components that depend locally on components at level 1 but no higher (e.g., `k` and `l`) are at level 2.

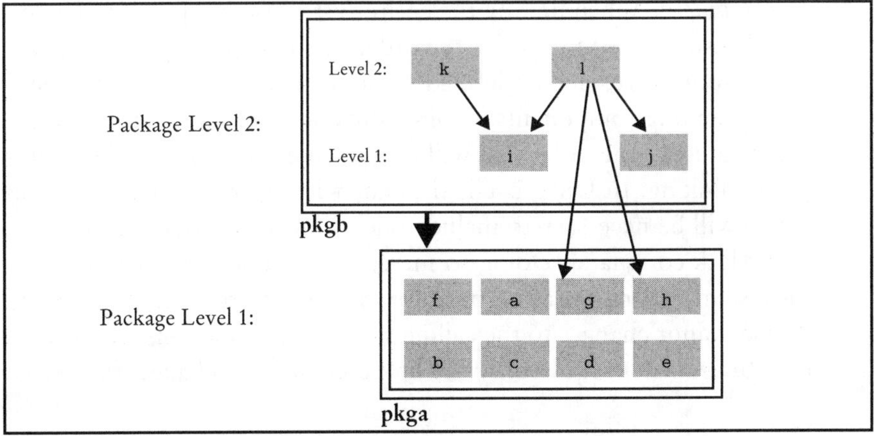

Figure 18. Dependencies on components in other packages.

A package x *DependsOn another package* y *if one or more components in* x *DependsOn one or more components in* y.

Just as relationships between logical constructs defined within components imply physical dependencies, dependencies among packages are implied by the individual dependencies among the components that comprise them. In Figure 18 for example, component i in pkgb DependsOn component a in pkga and component l in pkgb DependsOn components g and h in package pkga. Therefore according to the definition, pkgb DependsOn pkga. And provided pkga does not depend back on pkgb, we can assign level numbers to these packages as a whole, just as we did for the individual components within a package.

Packages provide a powerful mechanism of abstraction for developers and architects alike. Figure 19a shows a collection of 20 components, a through t, grouped into four packages: pkga, pkgb, pkgc, and pkgd. Each package defines a high-level, architectural unit consisting of a cohesive hierarchy of cooperating components, united for a common purpose.

By contrast, Figure 19b shows the identical system represented as an unpackaged, levelizable collection of individual components. The modularity and the abstraction of the high-level architecture is gone; we have lost the semantic value attached to these high-level partitions created during the process of the top-down design.

Avoid cyclic dependencies among packages.

Avoiding cyclic dependencies among packages is critical to the success of large systems for the following reasons:

1. *Development.* When linking the entire system or any portion thereof, it will be necessary to specify the order in which package libraries are called upon to resolve undefined symbols. If the envelope of dependencies among components within individual packages is acyclic, there will be at least one order that will be guaranteed to resolve all symbols during linking. In Unix, cyclic dependencies among packages implies that it will be necessary to include one or more libraries at least twice in the link command. Doing so increases the time necessary to link a subsystem by forcing one or more libraries to be searched multiple times. Worse, minor changes to the calling sequence of functions could cause the library order required by the link command to change, thus caus-

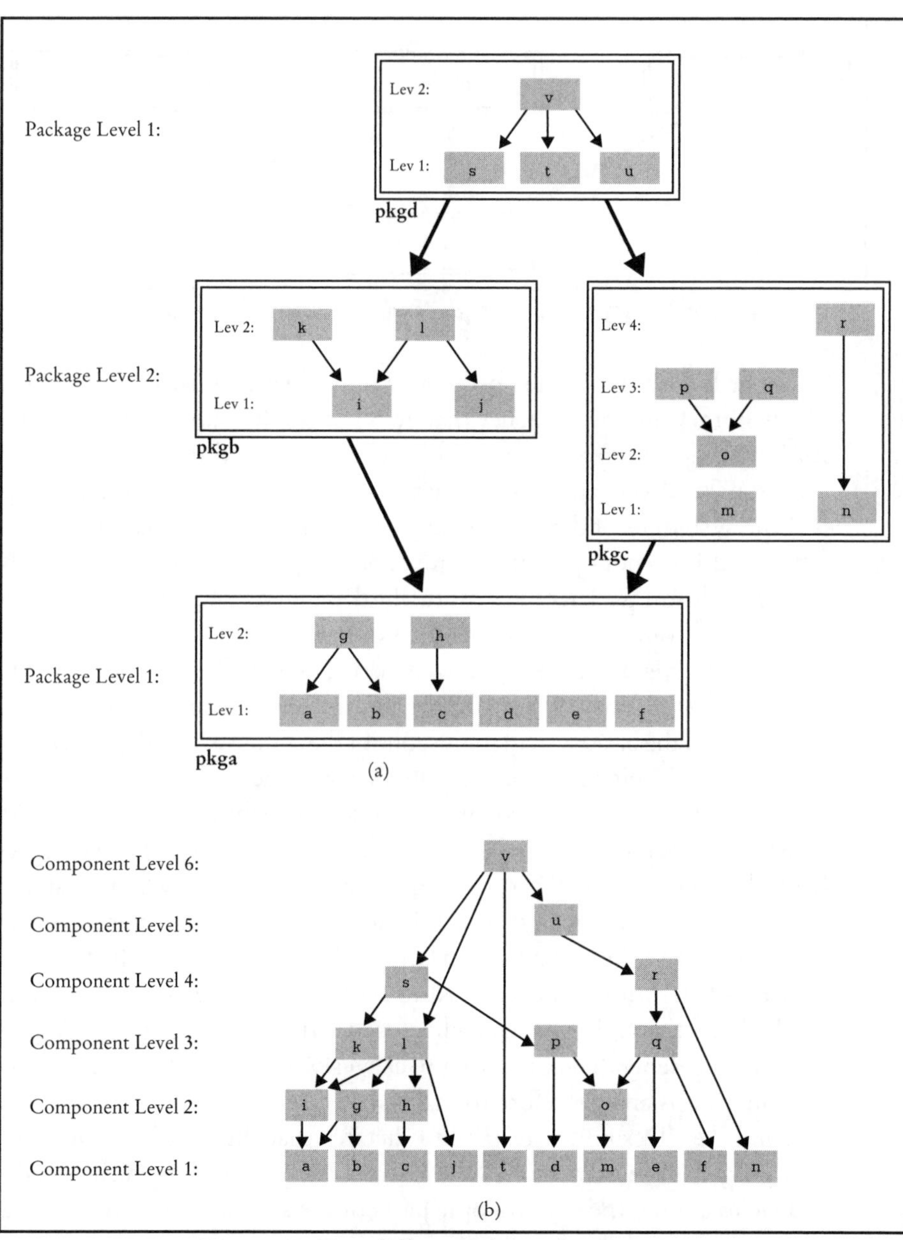

Figure 19. Two different views of a system.
(a) Top-down decomposition of a system into packages of components.
(b) Equivalent unpackaged system.

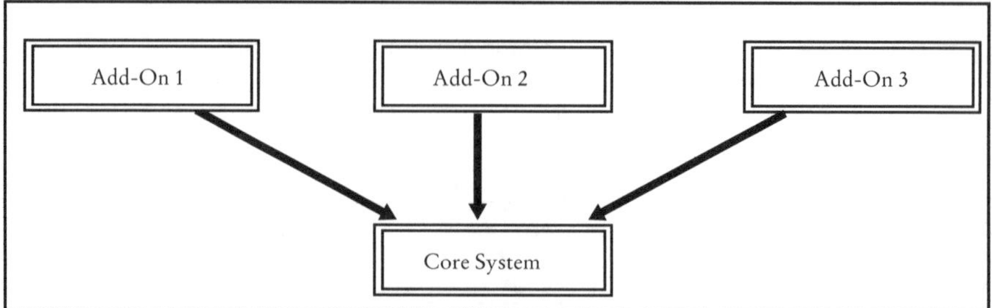

Figure 20. Acyclic package dependencies provide flexibility.

ing the link to fail. It then becomes a nontrivial exercise to determine a new library linking sequence that does not result in undefined symbols.

2. *Marketing.* Often a system will have a basic functionality and several optional add-on packages of functionality, as is illustrated in Figure 20. If the system itself depends on any one of these add-on packages, then that add-on is not optional and must be shipped with the system. If any of the add-on packages are mutually dependent, they cannot be marketed and sold as truly independent options.
3. *Usability.* Even if marketing is not an issue, users will not want to have to link in a huge library or several large libraries just to use some simple functionality of the basic system (or just one of the supposedly independent applications). Minimizing package interdependencies reduce the number of libraries that must be linked into an application, which can in turn help to reduce the ultimate size of the executable image (both in core and on disk).
4. *Production.* To support concurrent development in very large systems, it is effective to have a staged release process. Acyclic hierarchies of packages are collected into even larger architectural units called groups. Group levelization is then used to partition these groups into layers which are then released in levelized order from bottom to top. Allowing cyclic dependencies among packages would impede our ability to form groups and therefore to make staged releases.
5. *Reliability.* Design for testability dictates that there be away to test a large system incrementally and hierarchically. Avoiding cyclic dependencies among the macroscopic parts of the system is merely a natural consequence of this paradigm.

Although we might be serene enough to tolerate cyclic dependencies among a few components within a single package due to carelessness, ignorance, or special circumstance, we must be steadfast in our resolve to avoid cyclic dependencies among packages. The techniques for avoiding cyclic dependencies among packages are similar to those for avoiding cyclic dependencies among components.

Often a package will hold dozens of components. While a typical package might encompass anywhere from 5,000 to 50,000 lines of source. Decomposing large designs into cohesive packages of manageable size greatly simplifies the development process. For developers, comprehending up to a few dozen components and their detailed interdependencies within a package (Figure 19a) is significantly easier than understanding the arbitrary dependencies among hundreds of unpackaged components (Figure 19b).

The partitioning of components into packages is governed by more than just some arbitrary threshold of size or complexity. Although ensuring levelizability among packages is essential, that alone is not sufficient. For example, Figure 21 a illustrates a bottom-up approach to packaging in which we have merely taken the unpackaged design of Figure 2lb and carefully diced it into packages whose aggregate dependencies on other packages forms an acyclic graph. But simply partitioning a sea of levelizable components into an otherwise arbitrary set of levelizable packages does not address an important aspect of design: cohesion. To be effective, a package should consist of components and logical entities that have related semantic characteristics, tight coupling, or otherwise make sense to be packaged together and treated abstractly at a higher level.

Identifying package-sized units of cohesive functionality is a natural consequence of top-down design. As with class dependencies within a single component, component dependencies within a package are often more numerous and intricate than dependencies across package boundaries. Because of their more localized nature, the physical character of dependencies among components within a package often involves more compile-time coupling than their interpackage counterparts. Insulating wrapper components are sometimes used to minimize this coupling across package boundaries.

Insulation at the package level involves reducing the number (and size) of header files that must be exported for clients to use the package. Insulating clients of a package from a particular component contained within the package requires that 1) the component itself is not directly needed by external clients of the package as a whole, 2) all exported components that use this component insulate its definition from external clients, and 3) the individual component is not independently reused by other packages. Whenever we insulate our clients from the underlying complexities of a subsystem, we are likely to have improved both its usability and maintainability.

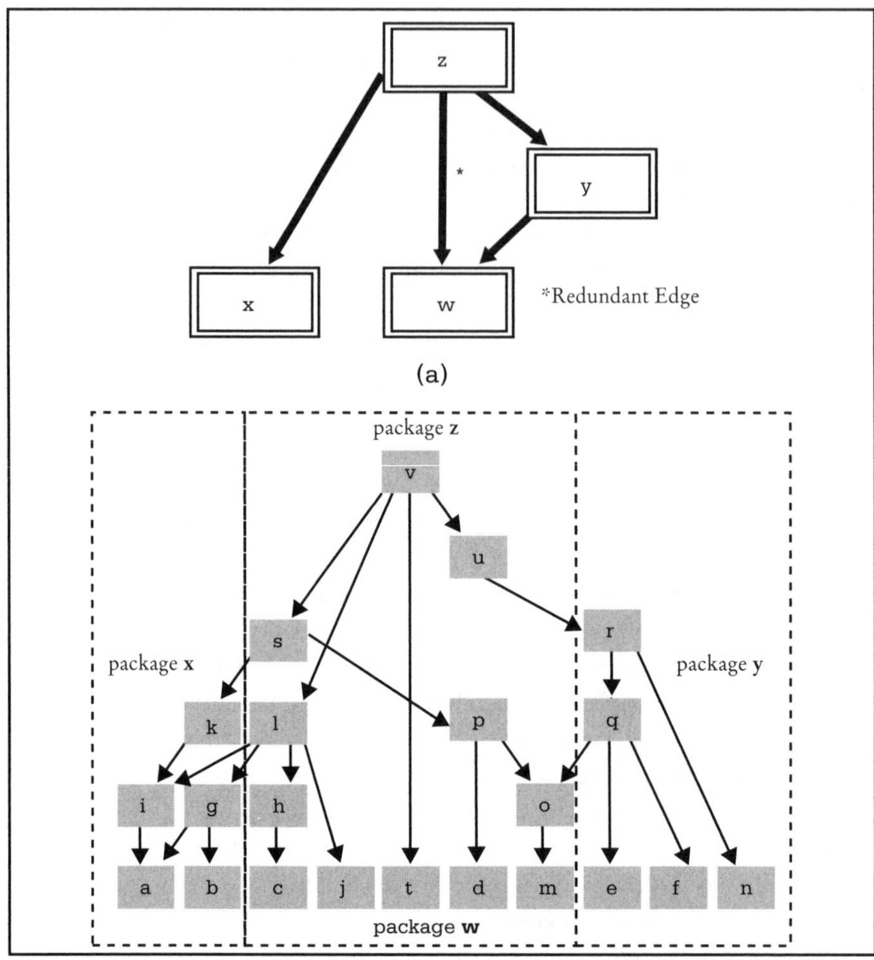

Figure 21. Less useful, physically partitioned system (compare with Figure 19). (a) Abstract package-level dependency diagram. (b) Detailed package/component dependency diagram.

The decision to export a component's header file outside its package will depend on whether it is needed (or useful) for purposes other than creating the .o files that belong to this package. This decision should not be based on a desire to hide programmatically accessible information. Encapsulation is a logical property that must hold in the presence of all header files in order to preserve the integrity of our system and to uniformly enable side-by-side reuse. Note that we are not proposing to withhold header files here for the purpose of encapsulating details, but rather as a means of reducing the clutter that clients must wade through in order to use our package.

Packaging also reflects the development organization. Typically, a package will be owned/authored by a single developer. The impact of change within a package can be well understood by its owner and dealt with both consistently and effectively. Changes across package boundaries affect other developers and perhaps even the entire system. Therefore, highly coupled parts of the system are often better off being part of a single package.

The degree to which parts of the system are likely to be reused as a unit also plays a role in the packaging of components. In the example of Figure 17, the runtime database may be used by a suite of tools, while the three parallel subsystems are used only once.

Even if the runtime database was very small in comparison to these other parts of the system, it could make sense to place this low-level subsystem in its own package to avoid tying its reusable functionality to any of the other less-often-used packages.

An inability to readily identify the physical location of a particular component or class definition can present a barrier to large-scale C++ software development. The technique of propounding a registered package prefix to each global logical or physical name serves not only to partition the global name space, but, more importantly, to identify the physical location of every class and file within the development directory structure of a company or organization. The consistent use of package prefixes has proven effective for developing systems consisting of millions of lines, involving hundreds of developers, and spanning multiple geographic sites.

The C++ namespace construct is not a substitute for registered package prefixes because it does not identify physical location. An organization-wide namespace can, however, be used in conjunction with package prefixes to enable independently developed subsystems to coexist within a single program.

To summarize: a package is an aggregate unit of physical design. Like a component, a package serves as a cohesive unit of related functionality fulfilling a common purpose. Packages serve both as abstractions for architects and as partitions for developers. Package composition is determined by several factors, including semantic cohesion, the nature of physical dependencies, the organization of the development team, and the potential for independent reuse.

CONCLUSION

Developing large systems in C++ that are both reliable and maintainable requires knowledge that cannot be gleaned from smaller development efforts. Naive design techniques invariably lead to quadratic behaviors in compile-time, link-time, and disk-space that simply do not scale well to larger systems.

Logical entities (e.g., classes and functions) are like the flesh and skin of a system. The logical entities that make up large C++ systems are distributed across many physical entities (e.g., files and directories). The physical architecture is the skeleton of the system if it is malformed, there is no cosmetic remedy for alleviating its unpleasant symptoms.

We have demonstrated the value of organizing the physical design of our subsystems as levelizable hierarchies of components in terms of development, testing, maintenance, and reuse. By replacing cyclic physical dependencies with tree-like hierarchies, the average cost of developing a single component for a system with N components drops from O(N) to O(log(N)).

We identified several general techniques for achieving levelizable subsystems and applied one of them, escalation, to two separate examples. We also demonstrated three separate total insulation techniques—*protocol class, fully insulating concrete class, and insulating wrapper component*—for eliminating all compile-time dependencies of our clients on encapsulated implementation details, and identified several partial insulation techniques for incrementally reducing compile-time coupling. Finally we described how subsystems can be organized effectively as an acyclic hierarchy of logically cohesive physical entities called *packages.*

Good physical design does not preclude the practice of good logical design. In fact, good logical and physical design reinforce one another. For example, all 23 patterns in the book, *Design Patterns: Elements of Reusable Object-Oriented Software,*[4] readily lend themselves to acyclic physical implementations. However, both logical and physical issues must be addressed if we are to be effective in developing large, high-quality software systems in C++.

Space limitations for this article precluded discussing several physical design topics related to large-scale C+ software design (such as initialization techniques, object-specific memory management, etc.) as well as many important logical design issues. My book, *Large Scale C++ Software Design*[3] has no such restriction; all of the information contained here, as well as much more, can be found there.

References

1. Lakos, J. "Large-Scale C++ Software Design, Part I," C++ *Report,* June 1996.
2. Lakos, J. "Large-Scale C++ Software Design: Physical Hierarchy, Part 2," C++ *Report,* Sept. 1996.
3. Lakos, J. *Large Scale C++ Software Design,* Addison-Wesley, 1996.
4. Gamma, E. et al., *Design Patterns,* Addison-Wesley, 1995.

TASKMASTER: AN ARCHITECTURE PATTERN FOR GUI APPLICATIONS

ROBERT C. MARTIN,
JAMES W. NEWKIRK, AND BHAMA RAO

From 1993 through 1997 I , and several of the consultants who work for me, had been embroiled in a very large project for Educational Testing Service. (Details of that project are described in the article: A Case Study of Reuse and OOD in C++, *which appeared in Object Magazine in 1996, and in ROAD in 1995. You can get a copy from the publications section of http://www.objectmentor.com.) That project involved the production of many graphical user interface applications. Because there were so many such applications, we developed a framework for the GUIs that rode on top of Borland's OWL framework.*

Our framework employed a very powerful architectural pattern for managing the individual tasks within a GUI. We called that pattern "Taskmaster." Taskmaster mixes the MVC and State patterns in such a way that highly isolated and very flexible finite state machines can control the entire GUI. The pattern turned out to be extremely beneficial for us. This article is our description of that pattern.

TASKMASTER, an architecture pattern for developing complex GUI applications, employs the principles of OOD to guide developers in creating GUI architectures that are flexible, easy to maintain, and reusable. This architecture contains elements of Document/View and Model/View/Controller; thus it builds upon other successful architectures. However, you will also find that with Taskmaster, a number of problems inherent in those architectures have been addressed in a simple, easy-to-implement way.

The requirements for most GUI applications are usually very volatile. Users always want new features and extra ways of looking at and manipulating the data. Thus the software is always changing, sometimes in unexpected ways. For this reason, the software architecture of GUI applications should be very flexible and robust. It must allow changes to be made easily, and it must be highly decoupled so that when those changes are made they have a minimal impact. Otherwise, the changes will cause the software to degrade quickly into an unmaintainable morass.

The Taskmaster architecture pattern helps to prevent this degradation, and provides for high levels of modification, maintenance, and reuse by creating high-level abstractions that provide isolation boundaries between the various functions of the GUI. With this isolation in place, one can easily change the manner in which a particular object is drawn, or the way a certain field is edited, without affecting or recompiling other parts of the system. One can change the interactions that drive the creation and manipulation of objects on the screen without affecting any other parts of the software. One can add new GUI objects without affecting any of the code that manipulates the already existing objects. One can also reuse the screen objects independent of the interactions that create and manipulate them.

ROOTS

The Taskmaster architecture has grown from the work that we at Object Mentor Inc. have done with some significant GUI applications we have been working on for the last several years. These applications are complex drawing tools that allow users to draw a variety of diagrams. The entities in these diagrams are familiar with each other and have well-defined relationships. Thus, there is a great deal of intelligence surrounding the way that they are manipulated and drawn.

The platform for this project is Windows 95, and the development tool is Borland C++ 4.5 using the OWL framework. However, the examples here will all be done using Visual C++ 4.2 and MFC. We can easily change compilers and frameworks, which supports our claim that Taskmaster is an architecture *pattern*, and not a platform specific architecture.

THE PROBLEM

Consider a simple GUI application that allows users to draw a series of lines on a blank canvas. These lines are drawn when the user clicks a mouse button on a point, drags to another point, and then releases the mouse button. During this interaction, the screen shows a "rubber band" line that follows the mouse until the button is released. Once the mouse button is released, the line remains on the screen and is added to a list of lines that the window maintains. We call this part of the application the *task*. We can use this task to draw many lines on the screen.

Now consider what happens when we put another window on top of our window, and then move it away again. The lines that had been covered up need to be redrawn. The window that contains the lines receives a PAINT message. In response to this message it looks through its list of lines and redraws them all.

In simple form, such an application might look like Listings 1 and 2. Here we see some of the code for controlling this simple application living inside the class LineApplicationWindow.

The simplicity and elegance of this program is compelling (see Fig. 1). Everything is straightforward. When the left button goes down (OnLButtonDown), we capture the cursor (so that we know if it leaves our window), and record the point at which the button was clicked. For every mouse move event (OnMouseMove), we erase the current line and redraw it in the new position. (This is done by drawing in XOR mode. If you don't understand this, don't worry about it.) Then we record the new position. When the left button finally comes back up (OnLButtonUp), we create an instance of a

Listing 1. LineApplicationWindow.h.

```
class LineApplicationWindow : public CFrameWnd
{
public:
	LineApplicationWindow(GraphicFactory* aFactory);
	virtual ~LineApplicationWindow();
private:
	CPoint itsSecondPoint;
	CPoint itsFirstPoint;
	GraphicFactory* itsGraphicFactory;
	vector<GraphicObject*> itsObjects;
	CPen* itsBluePen;
	afx_msg void OnMouseMove(UINT nFlags, CPoint point);
	afx_msg void OnLButtonDown(UINT nFlags, CPoint point);
	afx_msg void OnLButtonUp(UINT nFlags, CPoint point);
	afx_msg void OnPaint();
	DECLARE_MESSAGE_MAP()
};
#endif
```

Listing 2. LineApplicationsWindow.cpp.

```
LineApplicationWindow::LineApplicationWindow(GraphicFactory* aFactory)
: itsGraphicFactory(aFactory)
{
    Create (NULL, "Line Application");
    itsBluePen = new CPen(0,1,RGB(255,255,0));
      // when the pen is drawn in XOR mode it will be blue
}
LineApplicationWindow::~LineApplicationWindow()
{
    // delete the object stored in the vector

    vector<GraphicObject*>::iterator index;
    for(index = itsObjects.begin(); index != itsObjects.end(); ++index)
    {
      GraphicObject* anObject = *index;
      delete anObject;
    }
    delete itsBluePen;
}
void LineApplicationWindow::OnPaint()
{
    CClientDC dc(this);

    vector<GraphicObject*>::iterator index;
    for(index = itsObjects.begin(); index != itsObjects.end(); ++index)
    {
      GraphicObject* anObject = *index;
      anObject->Draw(dc);
    }
}
void LineApplicationWindow::OnLButtonUp(UINT nFlags, CPoint point)
{
    if(GetCapture() == this)
    {
      itsSecondPoint = point;
      CClientDC dc(this);
        GraphicObject* anObject = itsGraphicFactory->MakeLine
                                  (itsFirstPoint,itsSecondPoint);
      anObject->Draw(dc);

      itsObjects.push_back(anObject);
      ReleaseCapture();
    }
    return;
}
```

(continued)

Listing 2. (continued)

```
void LineApplicationWindow::OnLButtonDown(UINT nFlags, CPoint point)
{
      SetCapture();
      itsFirstPoint = itsSecondPoint = point;
}
void LineApplicationWindow::OnMouseMove(UINT nFlags, CPoint point)
{
      if(GetCapture() == this)
      {
         CClientDC dc(this);
         // save the current dc parameters that we are changing
         int previousROP = dc.SetROP2(R2_XORPEN);
         CPen* currentPen = dc.SelectObject(itsBluePen);
         // draw the previous line
         dc.MoveTo(itsFirstPoint);
         dc.LineTo(itsSecondPoint);
         // draw the new line
         dc.MoveTo(itsFirstPoint);
         dc.LineTo(point);
         itsSecondPoint = point;
         // reset previous parameters
         dc.SetROP2(previousROP);
         dc.SelectObject(currentPen);
      }
      return;
}
```

GraphicLine from the GraphicFactory and place it in the vector that holds the list of lines. Upon reception of a PAINT event (OnPaint), we simply iterate through the list of GraphicObjects telling each one to draw.

Document/View

The simplicity of this program masks some potential problems. For example, what if we wanted to show two windows; one with the lines drawn as before, and another text window displaying a scrolling list of lines in the following format:

```
Line((0,0),(1,1));
Line((5,2),(8,3));
```

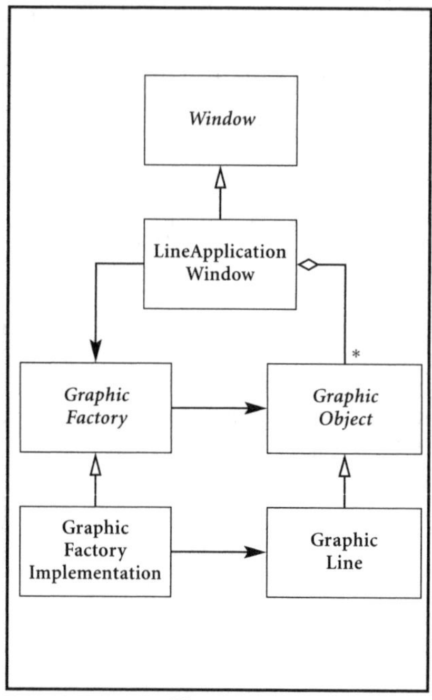

Figure 1.

Each time a new line was added to one window, it would appear on the other. Clearly we are not currently set up to do that.

Or, what if we wanted to store all the created lines into a file and then read them back later? Presumably, we could do this by adding the appropriate Save and Store methods to the LineApplicationWindow class. However, why should those methods be in the same class with the event functions such as OnLButtonDown? We would rather that the code that knows how to read and write lines to a file was reusable separately from the code that knows how to create and display the lines.

This is an instance of a violation of the Open Closed Principle (OCP).[1] By definition, the window class cannot be closed to gross changes in the way that the data is displayed. However, such changes should not affect the way that the data is stored or retrieved. By putting both functions together in the same class, we find that we cannot close data manipulation functions against changes in the way that the data is displayed. By the same token, we cannot close the code that manages the display of the data against changes in the way that the data is stored and manipulated. Clearly some kind of separation of concerns is needed.

It was issues such as these that motivated the Document/View split in many of the current frameworks. These are also the issues that partially motivated the Model/View split in the Model/View/Controller paradigm used in Smalltalk nearly two decades ago.

We need to separate representation and manipulation from creation and display. That is, the mechanisms that store and manipulate the data should be separate from, and reusable independent of the mechanisms that display that data to humans, or present that data to other computers. Figure 2 shows such a split.

Here we see two fundamental splits. First, there is an class named Line; and another similar class named GraphicLine. The Line class is a pure mathematical model of a line segment; it knows nothing about how to display or create a line on a GUI. GraphicLine, on the other hand, contains a Line. It knows nothing about the mathematical model of a line segment, but knows how to draw a line segment on a GUI.

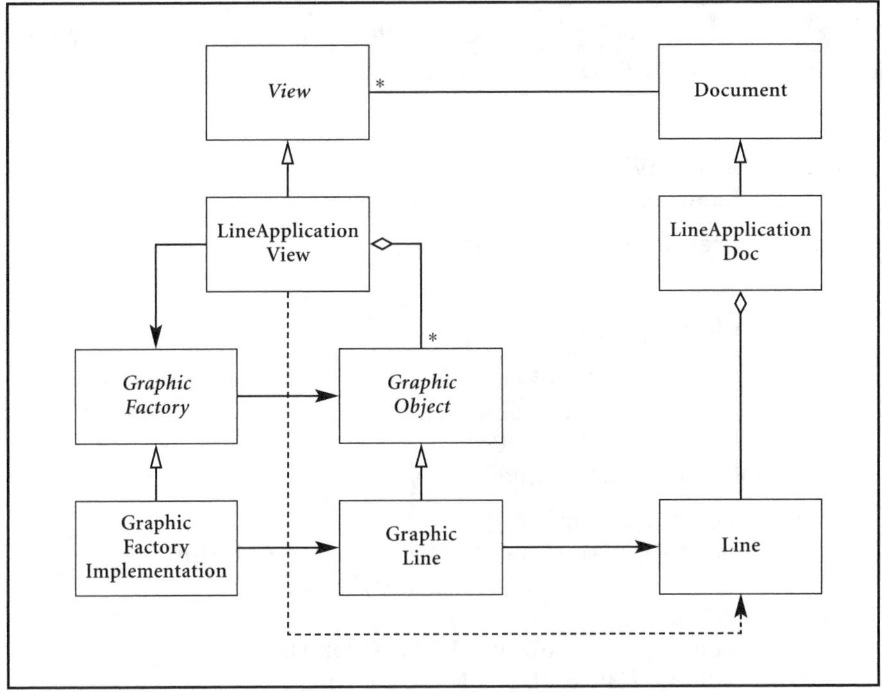

Figure 2. Document/View Solution.

We see a parallel split between LineApplicationDoc and Line ApplicationView. LineApplicationDoc contains a list of Line objects. It knows how to save and restore them to a file, but it knows nothing about how to draw them, or otherwise present them to a user. On the other hand, LineApplicationView contains a list of GraphicObjects and knows how to draw them. It also knows how to interpret the mouse to create Line objects that it passes to the LineApplicationDocument.

An Observer[2] pattern is set up between the LineApplicationView and the LineApplicationDoc. The view observes the document and is informed whenever the document is changed. Thus, when a new Line object is added to the document, the view is notified and the appropriate GraphicObject is added to its list and drawn.

There is a distinct asymmetry in the relationships of this split. LineApplicationView knows about LineApplicationDoc; and Graphic Line knows about Line. However, the reverse is not true. Line ApplicationDoc could be reused with a completely different view; and Line could be reused with a completely different presentation mechanism. Thus, this structure achieves our goal of separating the manipulation of the data from its presentation. We can now present

Listing 3. LineApplicationView.h.

```
class LineApplicationView : public CView
{
public:
      LineApplicationView();
      virtual ~LineApplicationView();

      LineApplicationDoc* GetDocument();

private:

      vector<GraphicObject*> itsObjects;

      CPen*                 itsBluePen;
      CPoint                itsFirstPoint;
      CPoint                itsSecondPoint;
      GraphicFactory*       itsGraphicFactory;

      virtual void OnInitialUpdate();
      virtual void OnUpdate(CView* pSender, LPARAM lHint,
                            CObject* pHint);
      virtual void OnDraw(CDC* aDC);
      afx_msg void OnLButtonDown(UINT, CPoint);
      afx_msg void OnLButtonUp(UINT, CPoint);
      afx_msg void OnMouseMove(UINT, CPoint);
      virtual void DeleteObjects();

DECLARE_DYNCREATE(LineApplicationView)

DECLARE_MESSAGE_MAP()
};
```

the data in many completely different ways, without affecting the code that manipulates that data in any way.

Listings 3–6 show snippets of the code that implements this example. Only the most important bits of code are shown. Notice that in some ways this code is very similar to our first example. The new LineApplicationView class looks very similar to the previous LineApplicationWindow class. However, there are some important differences.

In LineApplicationView::OnLButtonUp, we are creating instances of class Line rather than GraphicLine. Also, rather than adding the instance to our own list, we instruct the document to add it to its list.

In LineApplicationDoc::AddLine we not only add the instance of the Line into the document's list, but we also call the function UpdateAllViews, passing the instance of the Line back in the "hint" parameter. This function will find all

Listing 4. LineApplicationView.cpp.

```
void LineApplicationView::OnDraw(CDC* aDC)
{
    vector<GraphicObject*>::iterator index;
    for(index = itsObjects.begin(); index != itsObjects.end(); ++index)
    {
        GraphicObject* anObject = *index;
        anObject->Draw(*aDC);
    }
}
void LineApplicationView::OnLButtonUp(UINT nFlags, CPoint point)
{
    if(GetCapture() == this)
    {
        itsSecondPoint = point;
        ReleaseCapture();
        LineApplicationDoc* document = GetDocument();
        Line* newLine = new Line(itsFirstPoint, itsSecondPoint);
        document->AddLine(newLine);
    }
    return;
}
void LineApplicationView::OnLButtonDown(UINT nFlags, CPoint point)
{
    SetCapture();
    itsFirstPoint = itsSecondPoint = point;
}
void LineApplicationView::OnUpdate(CView* sender, LPARAM lHint,
                                   CObject* pHint)
{
  if(Line* aLine = dynamic_cast<Line*>(pHint))
  {
    GraphicObject* anObject = itsGraphicFactory->MakeLine(*aLine);
    itsObjects.push_back(anObject);
    CClientDC dc(this);
    OnPrepareDC(&dc);
    anObject->Draw(dc);
  }
  else
  {
    CView::OnUpdate(sender, lHint, pHint);
  }
  return;
}
```

Listing 5. LineApplicationDoc.h.

```
class LineApplicationDoc : public CDocument
{
public:
	LineApplicationDoc();
	virtual ~LineApplicationDoc();
	virtual void AddLine(Line*);
	virtual void GetLines(vector<Line*>& lines) const;
private:
	CObArray itsLines;
	virtual void DeleteContents();
	virtual void Serialize(CArchive& ar);
	void ClearArray();
DECLARE_DYNCREATE(LineApplicationDoc)
DECLARE_MESSAGE_MAP()
};
```

Listing 6. LineApplicationDoc.cpp.

```
void LineApplicationDoc::AddLine(Line* aLine)
{
	itsLines.Add(aLine);
	SetModifiedFlag();
	UpdateAllViews(NULL, 0, aLine);
}
```

the views associated with this document and invoke their OnUpdate functions.

In LineApplicationView::OnUpdate we check to see if the "hint" being passed in is an instance of a Line. And if so, we use the Line to create a GraphicObject, which we then add to the view's list of GraphicObjects. Then we draw the newly created GraphicObject.

By adopting the Document/View architecture we have made it possible to completely replace the way that the Line instances are displayed, without affecting the way that they are stored or "Serialized" (i.e., read and written from files). We have also made it possible to display these lines in many different ways, and in many different windows, within the same application.

Push versus Pull

The Observer relationship between the Line ApplicationView and LineApplicationDoc classes conforms to the *push* model. This means that the data that the observing view is interested in is "pushed" along with the message that notifies the observing view that the document has changed. In our example, the Line instance was "pushed" in the "hint" argument of the OnUpdate function.

The alternative to the "push" model is to use the "pull" model. In the "pull" model, no data is sent in the OnUpdate message. Upon receipt of the OnUpdate message, the views must pull all the data from the document and redisplay it all.

Clearly, the push model is more efficient than the pull model. However, the pull model is more general. When using the push model, the OnUpdate message must contain enough information to tell the view exactly what changed. As the document becomes more complicated, and the kinds of manipulations become more varied, the complexity and amount of information that will have to be pushed to the view will increase.

For example, suppose that we wrote an application in which we could draw lines, circles, and squares. If we used the push model, the OnUpdate method would have to query the "hint" to see what kind of object it was. This could amount to an if/else chain of dynamic casts—a blatant violation of the OPC! Suppose also that we could move, stretch, and delete those lines, circles, and squares. Then, not only would we have to pass the changed object into OnUpdate; but we would also have to tell OnUpdate the kind of change that it had experienced. If deleted, it would have to be erased. If stretched or moved, it would have to be erased and redrawn. If merely added, it would have to be drawn for the first time.

This extra information could be passed as some kind of enum in the second hint field of the OnUpdate method. However, this would turn the OnUpdate method into a horrible stew of nested if/else and switch statements. A better approach would be to use Command objects. Consider Listing 7.

All the views could implement the ViewInterface class by using multiple inheritance. This is a good example of the Interface Segregation Principle (ISP).‹ The interface needed by the ViewCommand class is kept separate from the view class so that the ViewCommand class does not have to depend upon the views.

Now, when a view has decided that a square, circle, or line has been added, removed, moved, or stretched, it can create a derivative of the ViewCom-

Listing 7. Pushing Commands.

```
class ViewInterface
{
public:
	virtual void AddNew(Shape*) = 0;
	virtual void Delete(Shape*) = 0;
	virtual void Replace(Shape* old, Shape* new) = 0;
};
class ViewCommand
{
public:
	virtual void Execute(ViewInterface&) = 0;
};
```

mand class that knows how to manipulate the ViewInterface class appropriately. This command instance can be passed to the document that will then pass it in the "hint" argument of the UpdateAllViews member function. All the views will therefore receive this instance of the ViewCommand in the "hint" argument of their OnUpdate member functions. They will then invoke the Execute function and pass themselves as its argument:

```
void SomeView::OnUpdate(CView* v, LPARAM lp, CObject* hint)
{
   if (ViewCommand* cmd = dynamic_cast<ViewCommand*>(hint))
   {
      cmd->Execute(this);
   }
   else
      CView::OnUpdate(v,lp,hint);    // defer to base class.
}
```

By using this technique, we can add arbitrary complexity to the push model interface without creating a rat's nest of if/else and switch statements in the OnUpdate functions of all the views.

ARCHITECTURE

What is that Command mechanism really doing? It seems to be allowing one part of the view to communicate with another part of the view! Decisions that are made in the interactive part of the view are being communicated to the part of the view that manages what to display. Perhaps another separation is order.

We have identified two different parts of the view object. There is the part that handles the interactions with the mouse and keyboard, and then there is the part that handles display and update. And these two appear to be quite separate. The interaction part sends messages to the document, and the display part receives `OnUpdate` messages from the document.

Whenever there are two aspects to one object, we should consider whether those aspects should be separated into two objects. We can use the Open–Closed Principle (OCP) as a way of determining the value of such a separation: Are there changes that could be made to the interaction part of the view, to which the display part of the view should be closed? Would we want to reuse the display portion of the view with several different variations of the interaction part?

Consider what would happen if we wanted to change the way that users create lines. Rather than having them depress the button at the start point, drag to the end point, and then release the button; we have them press and release the button at the start point, move the mouse to the end point, and then press and release the button again. In the above example, this would cause some rather drastic changes to `OnLButtonUp`, `OnLButtonDown`, and `OnMouseMove`; but would not affect `OnUpdate` at all! It seems likely that different applications that use different styles of interactions will want to reuse the `OnUpdate` function, and all the other aspects of object display.

Model/View/Controller

This was the issue that drove the View/Controller split in the MVC paradigm. Indeed there are many different interaction schemes that could be used to create and manipulate objects. These interaction schemes need not be tightly coupled to the display mechanism. Thus, in those instances where we expect the interactions to change frequently, or where we expect many different applications to display the same data but manipulate it differently, separating the interaction from the view is probably a good idea.

In MVC the object that controls the interaction is called the controller. The controller is responsible for intercepting all the events from the user interface and interpreting them into commands that manipulate the model.

Tasks

In the Taskmaster architecture (see Fig. 3), things are a bit different. All the events coming in from the user interface are received by the `View`. However,

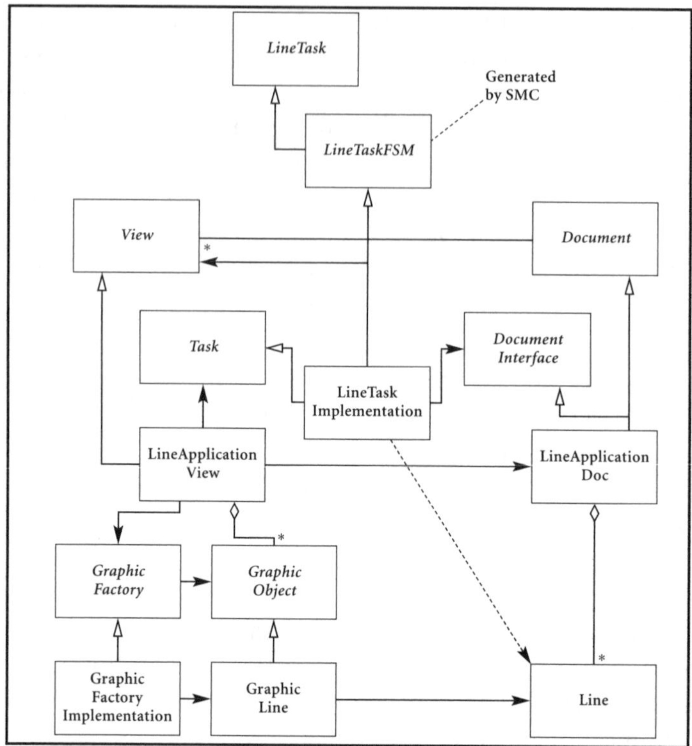

Figure 3. Taskmaster.

those events are then delegated to an object that is derived from the Task interface. Each derivative of Task encapsulates an interaction with the user and eventually communicates with the document. The appropriate derivative of Task is selected by a menu command or a click on a palette item, etc.

Figure 3 is quite similar to the Document/View model shown in Figure 2, but it has some extra classes and interfaces. We see that the LineApplicationView is associated with the Task class. It is through this association that the user interface events received by the View are delegated to the Task. LineImplementationTask is the object that encapsulates the interaction. We will discuss it in more detail later. For the moment, simply understand that this object interacts with the user and knows when a Line object has been created.

LineTaskImplementation is associated with an abstract class called DocumentInterface. This is another instance of the Interface Segregation Principle (ISP). This class contains nothing but the pure virtual function AddLine(Line*);. Notice that LineApplicationDoc inherits from DocumentInterface. This is the pathway by which the LineTaskImplementation communicates with the LineApplicationDoc without having to depend upon it. Thus the LineApplicationDoc class can be freely modified without affecting any of the derivatives of Task.

LineTaskImplementation also has an association with View. This is needed since the task must call member functions of View to run the interaction. One example of this is the View::Setcapture method that must be managed by the interaction.

Finite State Machines

In Taskmaster, we consider all Task derivatives to be finite state machines. The events that drive the FSM are the mouse and keyboard events that the View delegates to the Task. Indeed, the Task class consists of little more than a set of pure virtual functions representing these events.

There are numerous ways of implementing finite state machines. One can use nested switch-case statements, or some kind of table driven approach. My favorite scheme in C++ was documented in a wonderful article› from the *C++ Report*'s antiquity (when it was a 24-page nonglossy newsletter.)

This style of FSM is more generically documented as the State pattern in the book *Design Patterns*.[2] The particular variation of this that we use in Taskmaster is a pattern called Three Level FSM.[5] This pattern is convenient because it yields well to automatic code generation. We use a tool called SMC* to generate all our finite state machine code.

The finite state machine for adding a line is shown in Figure 4. The operation of this state machine is quite simple. It starts its life in the Start state. When the task is associated with the view, it is sent the Do event that kicks everything off.

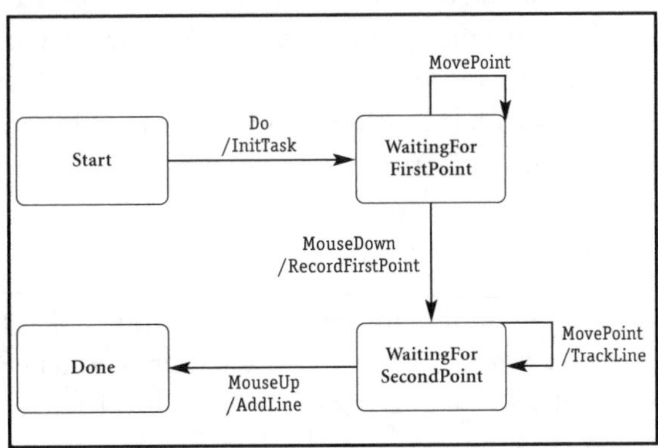

Figure 4. LineTaskFSM.

Table 1 describes the rest of the operation of this simple FSM. You read it as follows: "If we are in the Start state, and we receive the Do event, then we go to the WaitingForFirstPoint state and call the InitTask function."

* SMC is freely available in the public domain. You can get it from the freeware section of our Web site: http://www.oma.com.

Table 1. Line Task State Transition Table.

Current State	*Event*	*Next State*	*Action*
Start	Do	WaitingForFirstPoint	InitTask
WaitingForFirstPoint ondPoint	MouseDown RecordFirstPoint		WaitingForSec-
WaitingForFirstPoint	MovePoint	WaitingForFirstPoint	
WaitingForSecondPoint AddLine		MouseUp	Done
WaitingForSecondPoint WaitingForSecondPoint		MovePoint TrackLine	

Referring back to Figure 3, we have created a class named **LineTask**. This class has four pure virtual functions, one for each of the actions of the finite state machine. We call this class the context of the FSM. One of the classes generated by SMC is named **LineTaskFSM**. This class inherits from **LineTask**; allowing it to invoke the action functions declared there. Finally, we implement the action function in a class named **LineTaskImplementation**. This class inherits from **LineTaskFSM** in order to implement the pure virtual action functions. It also inherits from **Task** so that it can receive the events from the view. This is, once again, an example of the ISP. We don't want the view to know anything about the details of the task, so the view communicates with the task through an abstract base class. This lets us change the task without affecting the view.

TASK ISOLATION

Our example application has only one task. However, a real application would have dozens or hundreds, and each would be isolated from the associated view and document classes. The tasks can be changed without affecting any other part of the system. Indeed, the interactions can be reused in other applications that have different document and view classes. Also, the document and view classes can be reused in systems that have different interactions.

TASK SWITCHING

In a more elaborate application, tasks will be short-lived entities. They will be associated with a view as a result of some kind of command; perhaps a menu choice, a keyboard shortcut, or a click in the appropriate button of a palette or toolbar. Once associated with the view, the task will continue to collect events and communicate with the document class until its life cycle ends. This may be as a result of completing its job, or because it was somehow canceled. Then another task will replace it.

Thus, the current task within a view represents the global state of that view. It defines how the view will react to events. In order to implement this, a suite of other interfaces is required within `Task`. These interfaces provide for task cancellation, task restart, backstepping, pausing, etc. The exact complement of interfaces will depend upon the GUI and application domains.

TASKMASTER IN (SOME) DETAIL

Listings 8–13 show portions of the Taskmaster implementation of our sample application. The bulk of the document and view classes have not changed, so they are not shown here. What is shown is the structure surrounding the tasks. Notice how all of the interaction code from the first two examples has been moved into the class `Line TaskImplementation`.

Notice that we are still using the push model here. Notice also that all the comments that we made about Command objects still apply, except that now they can be created by the individual tasks rather than in the view.

BUT IT'S NOT SIMPLE ANYMORE!

True. The additional decoupling and isolation has increased the complexity of the structure several fold. A simple glance at Figures 1–3 will serve to convince you of that. Also consider that the total line count of example 1 is only 396 lines; whereas example 2 has grown to 1263 and example 3 to 1985 (a good year). So we have multiplied the number of lines of code (including comments) by nearly a factor of five!

Why incur this extra expense? For small applications you probably wouldn't. But when the applications get large, that factor of five will decrease to nearly 1:1. In other words, Taskmaster represents a superstructure upon which large applications can be built and maintained. As more and more functionality gets added into that superstructure, the additional complexity of Taskmaster will dwindle in significance. The ability of such programs to be easily changed, maintained, and reused will offset the extra complexity even more. Remember, it takes complexity to manage complexity.

Listing 8. LineTask.h.

```
class LineTask
{
public:
	LineTask();
	virtual ~LineTask();
	virtual void InitTask() = 0;
	virtual void RecordFirstPoint() = 0;
	virtual void AddLine() = 0;
	virtual void TrackLine() = 0;
};
```

Listing 9. LineTask.sm (the Input to SMC).

```
FSMName  LineTaskFSM
Context  LineTask
Initial  Start
Header   linetask.h
{
Start
{
	Do WaitingForFirstPoint InitTask
}
WaitingForFirstPoint
{
	MouseDown WaitingForSecondPoint RecordFirstPoint
	MovePoint  WaitingForFirstPoint {}
}
WaitingForSecondPoint
{
	MouseUp Done AddLine
	MovePoint WaitingForSecondPoint TrackLine
}
Done
{}
}
```

Listing 10. Task.h.

```
class Task
{
public:
	Task();
	virtual ~Task();
	virtual void Start() = 0;
	virtual void LeftMouseUp(UINT nFlags, const CPoint& point) = 0;
	virtual void LeftMouseDown(UINT nFlags, const CPoint& point) = 0;
	virtual void MouseMove(UINT nFlags, const CPoint& point) = 0;
};
```

Listing 11. DocumentationInterface.h.

```
class DocumentInterface
{
public:
	DocumentInterface();
	virtual ~DocumentInterface();
	virtual void AddLine(Line*) = 0;
};
```

Conclusion

We have had a great deal of success with the Taskmaster architecture. We have used it in more than a dozen GUI applications of significant size; and have found that the reduced coupling between tasks, views, and documents allows us the ability to make many changes to the software without incurring massive recompiles. This is a large benefit when working on a 70,000-line application. We have also been able to put much of the Taskmaster software into DLLs and then reuse it in different applications.

Taskmaster is not for everyone, or for every application. But in those cases where the applications are large, variable, and present a potential for reuse, Taskmaster is an option to consider.

References

1. Martin, R. C. "The Open–Closed Principle," *C++ Report,* Jan. 1996.
2. Gamma, *et al. Design Patterns*, Addison Wesley, 1995.

3. Martin, R. C. "The Interface Segregation Principle," *C++ Report*, Aug. 1996.

4. Hüneke, I. "Finite State Machines: A Model of Behavior for C++" *C++ Report*, Jan. 1991.

5. Coplien, J. O., and D. Schmidt. *Pattern Languages of Program Design*, Addison Wesley, 1985.

Listing 12. LineTaskImplementation.h.

```
class LineTaskImplementation : public LineTaskFSM,public Task
{
public:
      LineTaskImplementation(CView* theView,
                                    DocumentInterface* theDoc);
      virtual ~LineTaskImplementation();
      // member function defined in task
      virtual void Start();
      virtual void LeftMouseUp(UINT nFlags, const CPoint& point);
      virtual void LeftMouseDown(UINT nFlags, const CPoint& point);
      virtual void MouseMove(UINT nFlags, const CPoint& point);
      // member functions defined in the actions of the FSM
      virtual void InitTask();
      virtual void RecordFirstPoint();
      virtual void AddLine();
      virtual void TrackLine();
private:
      CPen*    itsBluePen;
      CPoint   itsFirstPoint;
      CPoint   itsSecondPoint;
      CPoint   itsTemporaryPoint;
      GraphicFactory*  itsGraphicFactory;
      // for update purposes
      CView*   itsView;
      DocumentInterface*      itsDocument;
};
```

Listing 13. LinetaskImplementaion.cpp.

```
void LineTaskImplementation::Start()
{
      Do();
}
void LineTaskImplementation::LeftMouseUp(UINT nFlags, const
                                          CPoint& point)
{
      itsTemporaryPoint = point;
      MouseUp();
}
void LineTaskImplementation::LeftMouseDown(UINT nFlags,
                                          const CPoint& point)
{
  itsTemporaryPoint = point;
  MouseDown();
}
void LineTaskImplementation::MouseMove(UINT nFlags,
                                      const CPoint& point)
{
  itsTemporaryPoint = point;
  MovePoint();
}
void LineTaskImplementation::AddLine()
{
      if(itsView->GetCapture() == itsView)
      {
         itsSecondPoint = itsTemporaryPoint;

         // release the mouse
         ReleaseCapture();
         Line* newLine = new Line(itsFirstPoint, itsSecondPoint);
         itsDocument->AddLine(newLine);
      }
      return;
}
void LineTaskImplementation::RecordFirstPoint()
{
      itsView->SetCapture();
      itsFirstPoint = itsSecondPoint = itsTemporaryPoint;
}
```

(continued)

Listing 13. (Continued)

```
void LineTaskImplementation::
TrackLine()
{
      if(itsView->GetCapture() == itsView)
      {
         CClientDC dc(itsView);
         itsView-> OnPrepareDC(&dc);
         // save the current dc parameters that we are changing
         int previousROP = dc.SetROP2(R2_XORPEN);
         CPen* currentPen = dc.SelectObject(itsBluePen);
         // draw the previous line
         dc.MoveTo(itsFirstPoint);
         dc.LineTo(itsSecondPoint);
         // draw the new line
         dc.MoveTo(itsFirstPoint);
         dc.LineTo(itsTemporaryPoint);
         itsSecondPoint = itsTemporaryPoint;
         // reset previous parameters
         dc.SetROP2(previousROP);
         dc.SelectObject(currentPen);
      }
      return;
}
void LineTaskImplementation::InitTask()
{}
```

MONOSTATE CLASSES: THE POWER OF ONE

STEVE BALL AND JOHN CRAWFORD

This marks the point in time where I became the Editor of the C++ Report*. The "Monostate" article was one of the first that I selected for publication.*

I was especially happy about this article. Prior to this the only documented pattern for maintaining a single instance in memory was Singleton from the Design Patterns *book. Singleton, while a great pattern, has a number of flaws. Monostate solves many of these flaws in an extremely elegant way.*

HOW CAN YOU ensure that all objects of a class share the same state? Why, indeed, would you want to? Surely the point of multiple instantiations is to produce objects that differ in state even while they share the same behavior?

Indeed, which problems are solved more easily by using objects that share the same state and *differ* in behavior? Moreover, how can you leverage C++'s inheritance and template mechanisms to facilitate the solution of these problems?

We'll see that such problems are more common than one might think. A number of them are presented here—you may find the problems surprisingly familiar. Their solution is presented in the form of a design pattern for the construction and implementation of state-sharing objects. It's a pattern that seems made to be implemented in C++, and which offers mechanisms that fit snugly with the contours of the solution.

A SAMPLE SCENARIO

We're designing a simulation of an ecosystem to study the effects of industrial pollution. Among the classes identified by our analysis are those representing such environmental factors as sunlight intensity and oxygen level. These classes have two conspicuous features:

- Their instantiated state must be *unique* within the system—although the sunlight intensity and oxygen level will fluctuate, it's inconceivable that for either environmental factor we could have instantiations that represent independent and different states; contrast this with the ordinary class objects that populate the system—for example, the Pollutant and Rainforest class objects, which will exist in multiple differing states.
- They're *pervasive*—they will impact on, or be affected by almost every other object in the system, and any change in the state of their instantiations must be immediately available to those other objects.

A CONVENTIONAL SOLUTION

One acceptable solution (though imperfect, as we'll see) is simply to have a global variable of class type for each of these unique objects. Their properties would neatly match the special nature of the items they represented—globals are unique objects, their value is readily accessible from anywhere in the system, and a change in their state is instantly propagated.

Past experience with global variables would cause many of us to regard this approach with suspicion because of their inability to resist modification by other objects in the system. Ironically, it is this property that makes them suitable as a solution in this scenario, and another problem altogether that makes them undesirable.

The problem lies not in their global accessibility,* but in devising a suitable implementation for the class of which the global objects are instantiations.

The opacity of code that relies heavily on global variables is familiar to many of us. This tends to be less of a costly maintenance problem with C++ code than with C, because global variables may be encapsulated. Notwithstanding this maintenance liability, it is frequently outweighed (even in C code) by the cost to clarity of constructing variables in a high-level function and passing them down the function call hierarchy. Often such use of globals is clearer than the alternatives; consider cin and cout.

The real problem then is this: The class is unable to protect itself against having more than one current instantiation. There is nothing to prevent a second object of the same type from being constructed. After all, the class name must be available at global scope and its constructor must be publicly accessible for the first object to be constructed. The potential for constructing multiple instantiations of such a class opens the way for violation of two essential principles:

- The existence of more than one object of the type should be considered logically meaningless. That is, the simulation model goes astray at the point that a second `Atmosphere` object comes into being, departing from the analog of the material world. We have all seen wayward data abstractions like these and know that no good comes of them.
- The implementation of the class should be able to rely upon there being only one object of its type, otherwise there can be no guarantee against misbehavior in the code that implements the class. For example, one could imagine a class acquiring (and locking) a resource in the constructor in such a way that a second attempted construction would cause the program to hang indefinitely.

What is required, it would seem, is a way to guarantee, both to the implementer of the class and to its consumers, that at most one object of the type will exist and, by implication, that whenever references are made to an object of the class they are always made to the same object.

The Conventional Solution Elaborated

The perception that global objects would do the trick if only we could control their propensity to multiply leads us down the road of epicyclic elaboration.[1] This is the same road taken by early astronomers who sought to retain Ptolemy's geocentric paradigm (which attempted to represent planetary motion in terms of uniform circular motions) in the face of evidence of its inability to reconcile new observational data. Additional mechanisms were elaborated to force the paradigm into conformity. "Kludge" is the less complimentary term that programmers give to epicyclic elaboration.

If we choose to follow this rocky road a little further, we find we need to decorate our global objects with an embellishment that forces their constructors to become private (or protected) and inaccessible. The corollary is that we need to nominate a function as a friend (or incorporate a member function to eliminate the requirement for explicit friendship) to return a reference or pointer to a single static hidden global variable.

Given the spate of recent discussion about the Singleton pattern, you'll have already identified that pattern as a traveler on this road.[2-5] The Singleton "ensure[s] a class only has one instance, and provide[s] a global point of access to it."[2]

However, there are burdens to be borne with this approach. The chief three are:

- The programmer is obliged to use counter-intuitive syntax to access the objects, `Singleton::Instance().mem_func()`.
- As a corollary of the previous requirement, the programmer faces further obfuscation in having to interact with a "global" object that is never given a name—the object is anonymous and is only referred to by name within the (hidden) implementation of the access function. We shouldn't underestimate the reluctance of programmers to use a programming feature or library component they feel they do not understand and perhaps, as a consequence, wonder if they can trust.
- The amenability of the class to inheritance is impeded. Proposals to enable subclassing of a Singleton class in C++ produce invasive mechanisms that are a considerable departure from the simplicity and cleanliness of C++'s native inheritance mechanism. (These subclassing mechanisms will be investigated when we discuss Monostate inheritance later.)

For these reasons we might consider moving the stricture on instantiation from compile-time access to runtime checking—have the constructor for the class count the number of instances that exist, and respond appropriately, aborting the construction if necessary.[3] This has the advantage over private constructors that no special syntax is required to construct or access the global variable.

Unfortunately, one is left to choose between the usual options available for failed constructors. Commonly, these are either to place the constructed object in a state that indicates its failed construction (as in `ofstream` construction) or to throw an exception forcing an exit from the scope that contains the unconstructable object.

The former option creates the requirements for tests that make no sense in the problem domain: "You mean I have to test whether the `Atmosphere` object was constructed successfully? If it had failed, wouldn't we all be dead?"

The latter approach is favored by Meyers as being more straightforward. However it must also be seen as both punitive and unfair. If consumers should not construct a second instance of the class (and are punished for doing so), why are they given the means to do so?

Taking a Different Road

A solution that attempts to control the number of instantiations in the constructor is destined to fail, by definition. One can punish those who attempt one too many constructions, but one has already lost the battle—the constructor has been invoked, the one-object limit is no longer inviolate, and reparative action must be taken as a second object now exists. This approach merely creates new problems in an attempt to solve an old one.

If we accept that we cannot satisfactorily limit construction (or may not want to), then we must also accept that multiple objects of the class will exist concurrently. How then can we meet our requirements for a class to represent sunlight intensity within our ecosystem simulation? How can we allow unlimited instantiations without violating either the semantic requirement for a guaranteed uniqueness of state or the practical requirement for the implementation code being able to rely on there being ever only one object of that class?

What is needed is some way of guaranteeing that a fresh instantiation does not result in a fresh state.

The Monostate Pattern

The pattern that we propose is nonpunitive. This is in keeping with the philosophical fundaments of the C++ language. C++ deliberately abjures attempts to eliminate programmer error by imposing arbitrary constraints.[6,7]

The Monostate pattern represents a class that can be instantiated any number of times, but whose every instance shares a single state. By imposing no restrictions on construction, it overcomes the problems introduced in attempting to enforce such a limitation, but does so in a way that provides the crucial protection needed by consumers of the class and by its implementer too. It guarantees that:

- Although there may be more than one object of the class, all objects share the same state.

- The implementation may rely upon there only ever being a unique state for all objects of the class.

THE SPECIAL CHARACTER OF A MONOSTATE CLASS

To create a Monostate class, we simply make all its data members static:

```
class Sunlight
{
   public:
      int lumens() const;       // accessors
      int UVlevel() const;
      void lumens( int );       // mutators
      void UVlevel( int );
   private:
      static int _lumens;
      static int _UVlevel;
};
```

You'll note that the class has no constructor or destructor—the question of their addition will be addressed later.

Since the totally static character of its member variables restricts this class to a unique state, it's natural to think of it as having but a single instantiation. Not so—*there is no restriction on the number of instantiations* of a Monostate class. This ability of a Monostate class object to endlessly clone itself gives it unique properties:

- Any number of functions can have their own local Monostate class object—but *all instantiations share an identical state*. (Different instances can even be given different identifiers, each acting as an alias for the same object, in the way that a reference is an alternative name for a single object.)
- A change in the state of one instance instantly propagates to every other instance.
- In a Monostate-based hierarchy, a change in the state of any derived object will instantly change the state not only every object of that (derived) class, *but also of every object of every class in that hierarchy*.
- The size of each object is always one byte, no matter how many data members it has. C++ adds a padding byte to an otherwise vacant struc-

ture to ensure that address arithmetic will work with Monostate objects.

- No matter where its storage is allocated—automatically, globally, statically, on the heap (or even as a temporary)—its state actually always resides in the same place.
- The object state is persistent between instantiations, and is even maintained during the periods when no object of the class exists. This attribute alone opens the door to surprising efficiency gains—for example, the construction of a local server object can appear to supply an instantaneous network connection when the actual connection was established only once, in the initial construction.

At a stroke, it eliminates the difficulties that arise with the other solutions we have examined:

- Being locally instantiated, a Monostate class object has none of the problems of unrestricted global access.
- As a plain vanilla-flavored object, its consumer deals with it using a familiar syntax.
- Since it allows as many instantiations as the consumer requires, there is no need to invoke a procedure to check the number of instances.
- Explicit local instantiation signals intended use of its member functions; unlike a Singleton object, a scope is introduced that encloses all operations on the object. This overcomes a type of problem experienced by Singleton objects that is typified by the quest for a means of acquiring locks on their operations.[8,9] (The utilization of constructors and destructors is discussed in a later section.)
- By far most the most significant difficulty overcome by the Monostate class, as well as the most significant opportunity offered, is that of subclassing. A Monostate class may participate freely in an inheritance hierarchy without requiring Monostate-specific coding in the implementation of either base or derived classes and without obliging the user of derived classes to cope with unconventional syntax. Dependency between base and derived classes is no greater than between any two conventional classes. As shown below, the breadth of opportunity opened to developers by subclassing Monostate classes is startling—objects from anywhere in a class hierarchy that share a common Monostate ancestor share part of their state with each other. Modifications to any family member instantly affect all other members.

We can characterize the essential difference between the Monostate pattern and those solutions which limit construction by using the analogy of road construction—the Monostate lays all its roads so that they lead to Rome, while other road-layers place covered pits at the end of all roads that don't end up there. It seems an undesirable and self-defeating practice to threaten your customers with penalties for using your class.

MONOSTATE CLASSES AT WORK

PROVIDING STATE AND BEHAVIOR SPECIALIZATION VIA INHERITANCE

How can we provide specialized forms of a Monostate class object where the core state is shared with the original object and further enhanced? Suppose, for example, that in our ecosystem simulation, we have a Monostate AmbientTemperature class and we wish also to represent that temperature as modified by Stiple's wind-chill factor. We derive an EffectiveTemperature Monostate class:

```
class AmbientTemperature
{
    public:
        int fahrenheit() const;
        int celsius() const;
        void fahrenheit( int );
        void celsius( int );
    private:
        static int _degreesKelvin;
};

class EffectiveTemperature: public AmbientTemperature
{
    public:
        int windVelocity() const;
        void windVelocity( int );
    private:
        static int _windVelocity;
    };
```

The effect will be that any change in the state of AmbientTemperature objects will be matched in the state of EffectiveTemperature objects, and vice versa.

This, of course, is exactly what we would want. Given that all *x*Temperature objects must necessarily operate with identical values for _degreesKelvin (for the moment, we ignore the possibility of local variations in temperature), we want both base and derived class objects to march in lockstep. Moreover, if we derive another class from AmbientTemperature, say ShadeTemperature, a change in _degreesKelvin in ShadeTemperature objects will propagate through the hierarchy to EffectiveTemperature objects.

Inheritance for Monostate classes is a type of inheritance that's usually not encountered in C++ programming—it is inheritance of *object state* as much as inheritance of class behavior. As such, is a form of *delegation*.[7,10] The base class AmbientTemperature acts as a *prototype* to which the subclasses/objects have delegated the storage and management of a portion of their state, while at the same time they extend and specialize the inherited state of the base class/object.

The unusual outcome of inheritance in a Monostate class hierarchy underscores the sharp difference between the Monostate pattern and the Singleton pattern (or its instance-counting variant), in which inheritance may defeat the utility of the pattern rather than enhance it, and raises problems to be overcome rather than offering a welcome extension of the pattern's benefits.[2]

The nub of the subclassing problem faced by the Singleton class is that if derivation is freely permitted, as for "normal" classes, the essential nature of the Singleton is lost, since the mechanism disallowing multiple instances applies only to base class objects and is not itself inherited.

Three approaches have been proposed to deal with this problem:

1. Simply outlaw derivation by declaring Singleton base class constructors private.
2. Declare these same constructors protected to permit inheritance but risk losing the behavior, since objects of the base class may be constructed freely (each with a potentially differing state) by perversely constructing them during the base class initialization of a (conceivably empty) derived class.
3. Retain private constructors, but at the same time nominate as friends those classes that may derive from the base class. This is merely a constrained variation on the first approach that introduces a dependency between the base and derived classes, but still allows objects to be multiply instantiated into differing states.

In the first option, you're cutting off your nose to spite your face, and in other two options, you're confronted with the unattractive prospect of having noses sprout all over your face!

For the Singleton class, then, inheritance is futile—it strips Singleton of its essence. The best that can be done is to provide a pseudo-inheritance mechanism that is obliged to subvert the typical mode of C++ inheritance in an attempt to mimic subclassing.[2] This mechanism is implemented using a combination of the second option, protected constructors in the base class, and an implication of the base's `Instance()` function in the knowledge of its (at least, immediate) descendants. In the case of more than one derived class, the type returned by that function is determined by runtime means—the Singleton cataloguers suggest registration by name string or the use of environment variables.

Further problems arise in choosing the access level of the constructors of the *derived* classes; the choices are:

1. *private or protected*: in this case, the base class (or its `Instance()` function) needs to be given explicit friendship to be able to dynamically allocate an object of the derived type; the relationship between the base and derived classes has progressed from dependency to co-dependency, and further derivation is prohibited without further friendship.
2. *public*: The singleton behavior of the class is lost; a global point of access is provided to one class instance through the `Instance()` function, but other instances may be freely constructed.

Monostate subclassing, which fully embraces the familiar C++ mode of inheritance, has to grapple with none of these problems. Its efficacy can be seen when we consider its use in a quite different scenario.

SECOND SCENARIO SHOWING STATE SPECIALIZATION

Monostate inheritance enables us to model a hardware device that functions in three separate guises. An MC146818 (there's one inside every PC) can be used as a real-time clock, as a store for CMOS settings, and as a programmable frequency interrupt generator. For practical purposes, each can be considered and used as a separate device in its own right. To model these devices, it would seem sensible to create three separate types, each with a discrete set of methods. From the design viewpoint, there is no reason to derive these types from a common base—after all, a clock has nothing in common with a frequency generator.

However, there are real implementation benefits to be gained from grouping the three types in a hierarchy that has as its base a Monostate class representing the underlying hardware device. Since each instantiation will share the state of this device, a change in the state of one specialized device should be reflected in a change in the state of each of its siblings, making this a good candidate for private inheritance. Note how different this use of inheritance is from the standard model where a change in the *behavior* (not the *state*) of a base object is mirrored in a derived object; here, a change in the state of a sibling (or, in a more extended hierarchy, a child, a cousin, an aunt, or a nephew) will effect a modification in an object's own state.

To illustrate, we take a minimal definition of a class representing the hardware device:

```
class MC146818
{
   public:
      MC146818();

      enum registerEnum{ REGISTER_A, REGISTER_B, REGISTER_C
};

         unsigned char readRegister ( registerEnum ) const;
         void writeRegister ( registerEnum, unsigned char );

      private:
         static const int baseAddr = 0x70;

         static bool   updateInProgress;
         static int    interruptType;

         static volatile unsigned char *_registerA;
         static volatile unsigned char *_registerB;
         static volatile unsigned char *_registerC;
   };
```

The implementation of the class initializes _registerA, _registerB, and _registerC with literal pointer values into the PC BIOS interface area. The other members, updateInProgress and interrupt Type, that indicate the current internal state of the device are assigned values to match the initial power-up state of the device (termination code returns the state of the device to its initial power-up state, of course).

Note that the registers in the PC BIOS interface area are pointed to by pointers to volatile storage. Because the state of the device reflected in the status registers may change at any time, the compiler needs to be warned not to perform any optimizations that eliminate memory fetches. The other data members reflect the attributes of the current state that have been set by operations on the device that may not be determined by querying the hardware.

The other classes representing the functions of the device may be derived (privately) from this base class:

```
class Clock : private MC146818
{
   public:
      Clock &operator =( time_t );
      operator time_t() const;
};

   class CMOSSettings : private MC146818
   {
      public:
         unsigned char operator[]( int byteNo ) const;
         void setByte( int byteNo, unsigned char );
   };

   class interruptGenerator: private MC146818
   {
      public:
         typedef void (*handler)();
         handler setHandler( handler );
         void frequency( time_t startTime, time_t period );
   };
```

None of the derived classes writes to or reads from the device directly. As all interaction with the device occurs via the supplied member functions of the base class, the Monostate MC146818 object is able to keep track of the internal state of the hardware device, even though it exists as a base object inside every object of Clock, CMOSSettings and interruptGenerator type.

This is the true power of the Monostate object—all objects derived from the same Monostate class share the same state *even though they may be of different types.*

In this example, changes to the state of the device that any CMOSSettings object needs to make in order to change the CMOS settings are recorded in the base MC146818 object so that when any Clock object (there may more than one—pick one, any one, don't tell me which) needs to examine the time, the current state of the device is known.

PROVIDING DIFFERENTIATED STATES VIA TEMPLATES

Although all instantiations of a Monostate class are essentially aliases for a single object, we are not prevented from using the class as a source of multiple state-differentiated objects. Suppose we wish to allow for the possibility that someone may have two (or more) MC146818 devices. The classes may simply be templated on the basis of the unique interface address that identifies them:

```
template<int baseAddr> class _MC146818 { ... };

template<int baseAddr> class _Clock
   : private _MC146818<baseAddr> { ... };

typedef _Clock<0x70>        PrimaryClock;
typedef _Clock<0x170>       SecondaryClock;

typedef PrimaryClock Clock;    // equivalent to previous example
```

If we're concerned that this mechanism opens the floodgates to a too loosely bounded spate of template instantiations and we'd like to keep them within stricter bounds, all we need to do is to parameterize the template over our own defined enumeration rather than over an inbuilt data type:

```
enum MC146818Id { PRIMARY_MC146818,
SECONDARY_MC146818 };
template<MC146818Id id> class _MC146818 { ... };
```

Although an unlimited number of instantiations of each parameterized class is allowed (each sharing the single state of their particular device), no further _MC146818 types can be created.

Providing Type Specialization via Templates and Inheritance

We saw above with our EffectiveTemperature derived class that Monostate class inheritance provides us with specialized *objects* as well as specialized types. This is in contrast to conventional derived classes that provide only specialized types from which state-differentiated objects can be instantiated. If we do want to achieve the effect of conventional type specialization with Monostate classes, we need to involve templates in the inheritance hierarchy. Suppose that, in our ecosystem simulation, we have a LightLevel Monostate class, and we wish to specialize it into distinct SunlightLevel and MoonlightLevel classes whose instantiations will be state-differentiated. We turn the LightLevel class into a template, and derive from that:

```
enum light { SUN, MOON };

template <light> class LightLevel
{
      public:
         int lumens() const;
         void lumens( int );
      private:
         static int _lumens;
};

class SunlightLevel : public LightLevel<SUN>
{
public:
         int             UVcontent() const;
         void UVcontent( int);
private:
         static int _UVcontent;
};

class MoonlightLevel : public LightLevel<MOON>
{
public:
      int       phase() const;
      void phase( int );
private:
      static int _phase;
};
```

Each derived template class now has its own independent instantiation of the base class, but we've been able in its construction to benefit from the reuse of code as well as to express the intended structural relationship between the classes in the hierarchy.

Earlier, in our ecosystem scenario, we chose to overlook the possibility of local variations in temperature. Here now, we have a mechanism for representing such variations of the primary abstraction.

It's also worth noting that, despite templates and inheritance being sometimes cast in rival roles.[11,12] here the two mechanisms work together in a strange harmony, helping each other accomplish goals that in this case they are powerless to achieve on their own.

Loose Ends

Canonical Form

Since the construction of the static member variables of a locally instantiated Monostate object will have taken place before the instantiation of the object itself, a constructor can have no part in the object's initialization. It demonstrates this fact at compile-time by rejecting any attempt to provide it with a member initialization list. A constructor may, however, find a use as a mutator and also, as will be seen, as a means of signaling a local instantiation.

Similarly, although a Monostate class may provide a destructor, it cannot tidy its static member variables off the scene. They will continue to exist. The problems encountered in implementing Singleton destructors are largely irrelevant for Monostate destructors.[9] (The next section will present a means of effecting specialized initialization and termination for Monostate objects.)

Since any two objects of the same Monostate class share the same state, the usual semantics of copy construction and assignment cannot apply, nor is it easy to anticipate what function these operations might perform. At the same time, there's no harm in including a copy constructor and an assignment operator for the sake of completeness. Nor is there any extra expense involved since they may simply be defined to have empty function bodies.

Initialization

Occasionally it is not sufficient to initialize the Monostate class by merely assigning suitable values to its data members. Where this is the case, code such as the following may be added to the module that defines the Monostate class in order to initialize the class in a more computational manner, or to perform more elaborate tidy-up and termination:

```
static struct Janitor
{
   Janitor() { setup(); }
   ~Janitor() { tidyup(); }
} janitor;

static void setup() { /* initialization code */ }
static void tidyup() { /* termination code */ }
```

Some linkers, for example that are used by IBM's AIX C++ compiler, will link into every executable all modules in used libraries that contain static variables of inbuilt types initialized by function call or static objects with constructors. This can be a problem resulting in potentially enormous initialization overhead and executable-size blow-out. There are more sophisticated alternatives. The so-called Schwarz counter, used to initialize objects `cin` and `cout`, is one.[13]

The nature of Monostate classes implies that initialization of the Monostate objects is always performed irrespective of whether the objects are ever used. Paying for potentially unused objects may be seen as spendthrift. The same charge, of course, can be laid against `cin` and `cout`, and a similar defense offered. It's in the nature of such objects that they're essential to the operation of the system in which they appear and the inclusion of the pertinent header expresses a firm intention to use them. In fact, the initialization price is lower than the cost that the consumer pays to access Singleton objects, where their initialization flag has to be checked on every occasion.[2]

Member Functions

Should member functions of Monostate classes be static or nonstatic? Consider how the Monostate object appears to consumers: as an ordinary object—even though a fresh instantiation borrows from an established state and current instantiations may be modified by operations on other objects of the same or derived classes, the consumer should not be required to deal with the object in any special way. The provision of static member functions dissolves the transparency of the Monostate's special attributes. There are other reasons also:

- static functions may not be defined `virtual` so derived classes may not override them polymorphically
- nonstatic functions ensure that all member functions are invoked in the scope of a locally instantiated object; static functions would subvert any quasi-initialization or serialization mechanisms installed in the constructor and destructor
- where initial construction is deferred until the time of the first local instantiation, static functions permit indirect access to the object's data members at a time when construction has not yet occurred.

Multithreading Behavior

Monostate objects exhibit none of the alarming behavior observed with Singleton objects in a multithreaded environment since their true construction has already occurred before the execution of main() and the first opportunity to create additional threads.[8] The problems arise with Singletons because access to them is provided not by name (as for Monostates) but via the non-atomic Instance() function. Schmidt deals with the Singleton problems by elaborating a further Double-Check pattern whose intent is to "allow atomic initialization, regardless of initialization order." The nature of Monostate classes ensures atomic initialization, so that no special treatment is required to enable their use in multiple threads.

At the same time, Monostate objects do show interesting behavior of their own when instantiated in multiple threads. Because each instantiation is an alter ego of the one object, a Monostate object in one thread can act as a monitor *of itself* in another thread. The Monostate object in this case would be made const to reflect its role as spectator only.

The Final Loose End?

The astute reader will have perceived a gaping hole in the Monostate scheme for ensuring that all objects of a class share a single state: there could be more than one program running using the same class, each with its own Monostate object, and—how repugnant—with potentially differing states!

True enthusiasts of the "One Class, One State" credo can enlist the help of shared memory (or DLLs) to ensure that all objects of a class share a single state despite the temporal transiencies of ephemeral programs. Of course, the Monostate attribute of persisting between instantiations (including those times when there are no programs running that use the Monostate class) is as much broadened as the issue of when real construction and destruction occurs. It is left to the same astute readers to propose their own solutions.

Where to Use It

At the beginning of this article, we asked for a means of ensuring that all objects of a class share the same state. We went on to present scenarios where such a Monostate class was the most desirable solution to a problem. It is time now to express the nature of that class using elements of a design pattern, and, where appropriate, to show how this pattern differs substantially from the superficially similar Singleton pattern.

INTENT

Ensure all objects of a class to share a single state, and allow those objects to be locally instantiated. Contrast this with the intent of the Singleton class, which is to "ensure a class has only one instance, and provide a global point of access to it."

MOTIVATION

It's important for objects of some classes to share a single state. (The Singleton pattern states: "It's important for some classes to have exactly one instance.") Where the motivation for the Singleton leads its designers to duplicate in the solution domain the single instance in the problem domain, we contend that this design decision takes a too literal approach. The intent and motivation are better achieved by focusing on the single *state*, rather than the single *instance*.

Examples given for the Singleton class can also serve for the Monostate's motivation: a single printer in a system, and a single file system and a single window manager. Indeed, a Monostate object can substitute for a Singleton in most applications.

A further motivation for the Monostate pattern is to express relationships between objects that partially share state and functionality, by taking advantage of inheritance hierarchies. One example is a single hardware device that may be accessed in a variety of guises; another is the representation of an ecosystem's ambient temperature both as the actual bulb temperature and as modified by a wind-chill factor.

APPLICABILITY

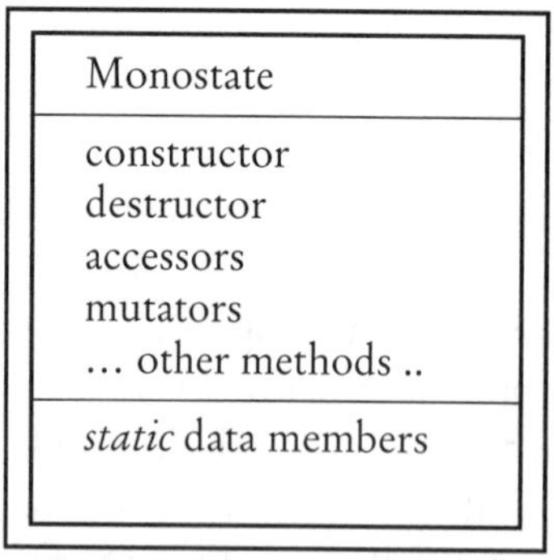

Monostate
constructor destructor accessors mutators ... other methods ..
static data members

Figure 1. Monostate pattern structure

Use the Monostate pattern when:

- a number of objects must share a single state
- changes in that state must be automatically propagated to all objects
- the single state should be extensible by subclassing, and that subclassing should be carried out without modification of the base class.
- instances of a Monostate object should have the same "look and feel" as normal objects.

Structure

See Figure 1.

Participants

The Monostate functions as a normal C++ class, allowing its clients to instantiate an unlimited number of objects while ensuring that state changes in any one instance are instantly propagated to all others. Contrast this with the Singleton that is obliged to define "an Instance operation that lets its clients access its unique instance"—producing an idiosyncratic species of class, and leaving its users to deal with it via an unnatural syntax.

Collaborations

Clients access a Monostate instance as they access instances of any other class—via its name and public members. By contrast, clients of a Singleton instance are obliged to access it "solely through Singleton's Instance operation."

Consequences

The Monostate pattern has several benefits. In summary, they are:

1. multiple local instantiations but always with only a single state
2. persistent object state in the absence of any instantiations
3. familiar syntax
4. specialization of object state and behavior via standard C++ inheritance mechanisms
5. controlled replication of a Monostate class via standard C++ template mechanisms allowing differentiation of state while retaining behavior

However, there are drawbacks to the Monostate pattern, which include:

1. The sharing that is occurring may be overly subtle since all instances of a Monostate class may appear to be unique.
2. The subtlety of sharing can lead to aliasing problems, e.g., calling mutators on one instance of a Monostate object will update all instances. This can cause subtle bugs if programmers don't understand that all the instances are aliases.

IMPLEMENTATION

Major implementation issues that have been discussed are:

1. *Ensuring a unique state for all objects.* The crucial step is to declare all data members to be static.
2. *Mandating local instantiation.* Here, the crucial requirement is that *no* member functions be declared static.
3. *Subclassing a Monostate class.* Implementation of an inheritance hierarchy takes place as for any "ordinary" class and requires no supplementary coding. The effect, however, is to create not simply specialized types but specialized objects.
4. *Templating Monostate classes and hierarchies.* Templating a single Monostate class will replicate behavior while allowing state differentiation; if it is parameterized over an enumeration, the number of templated classes can be held within defined bounds. Templating the base class in a Monostate hierarchy will express the structural relationship of the derived types and achieve code reuse while allowing state differentiation, as in the familiar use of inheritance.

PARADOXICAL AND POWERFUL

Monostate classes have an aura of the paradoxical. They allow local global variables; they produce dynamic static objects; they can have multiple singular instantiations; those instantiations can exist simultaneously in widely separated locations; derivation of the class produces not just specialized classes but specialized objects. The novelty of these paradoxes points out the uniqueness of the Monostate pattern.

Its practical application is seen most powerfully when Monostate class objects participate in a hierarchy. Where we have within a system a number of discrete objects that share a portion of their state and which require changes in that state to be instantly propagated to other family members, we have the fullest expression of the Monostate pattern. To implement that pattern, the C++ Monostate class presented here offers a mechanism whose simplicity, cleanliness and paradoxicality mask its power.

REFERENCES

1. Polanyi, M. "The Stability of Beliefs," *The British Journal for the Philosophy of Science III* (II):217–232, Nov. 1952.
2. Gamma, E., *et al. Design Patterns*, Addison-Wesley, Reading, MA, 1995.

3. Meyers, S. "Bounding Object Instantiations, Part 1" C++ *Report* 7(3):18-22, Mar./Apr. 1995.
4. Meyers, S. "Bounding object instantiations, Part 2" C++ *Report* 7(5):8–12, Jun. 1995.
5 White, R. G. "Advantages and Disadvantages of Unique Representation Patterns," C++ *Report* 8(8), Sep. 1996.
6. Stroustrup, B. *The C++ Programming Language*, 2nd ed., Addison-Wesley, Reading, MA, 1991.
7. Stroustrup, B. *The Design and Evolution of* C++, Addison-Wesley, Reading, MA, 1994.
8. Schmidt, D. "The Double-Checked Locking Optimization Pattern," *Pattern Languages of Program Design*, Vol. 3, (Martin, Buschmann, and Riehle, Eds.), Addison-Wesley, Reading, MA, 1997.
9. Vlissides, J. "To Kill a Singleton,"C++ *Report* 8(6):10–19, Jun. 1996.
10. Wegner, P. "Concepts and Paradigms of Object-Oriented Programming," *OOPS Messenger* 1(1):7–87, Jun. 1990.
11. Carroll, M. "Tradeoffs of Runtime Parameterization," C++ *Report* 7(9):20–27, Nov./Dec. 1995
12. Crawford, J. "Response to 'Tradeoffs of Runtime Parameterisation,'" C++ *Report* 7(9):26, Nov./Dec. 1995.
13. Stroustrup, B., and M. A. Ellis, *The Annotated* C++ *Reference Manual*, Addison-Wesley, Reading, MA, 1990.

APPLYING THE ABC METRIC TO C, C++, AND JAVA

JERRY FITZPATRICK

I first met Jerry Fitzpatrick in the late '70s. He and I used to play Dungeons and Dragons together. Later we worked for several years on the software and hardware of one of the original voice messaging products. Indeed, he and I held the patent pending for those annoying machines that answer nearly all business main numbers now. (Unfortunately, and unbeknownst to us, our company dropped the patent application after deciding it was not a lucrative business to be in. The current patent holder filed three months after we did...)

I like metrics. But I don't like the kind that simply counts methods, or semicolons. I like a little more thought put into the metrics. (See "Object Oriented Design Quality Metrics" in the publications section of http://www.objectmentor.com). When Jerry submitted this article to me, I thought: "Now these are interesting metrics."

METRICS ARE BECOMING increasingly important in software design and analysis. Experience shows that even simple metrics, when properly applied, provide valuable insights into the software development process.

The ABC metric provides a measure of software size. A size measure does not provide sufficient design guidance by itself, but it has several uses and is an underpinning for more advanced measures.

I developed the ABC metric to overcome the disadvantages of lines of code and similar measures. Before examining the benefits of the ABC metric, let's review some other software size measures.

SIZE MEASURES

There are many potential ways that software size can be measured. Regardless of how measurements are made, an ideal metric should be:

- measurable
- accountable
- precise
- independent of the measurer

One of the earliest methods to measure software size was developed in 1975 by the late Maurice Halstead of Purdue University.[1]Using an approach dubbed "software science," Halstead reasoned that the syntactic components (tokens) of every computer program fall into two distinct categories: operators and operands.

An operator is a token—like plus, equals, or function call. An operand is any token that is not an operator. By counting the amount of unique operators, operands, and their combined total, software science formulas provide numeric values for program length, volume, and level.

Although software science appears scholarly and intriguing, its conclusions have been widely disputed. Consequently, token counting has not been widely adopted. Halstead's contribution is nevertheless important because he applied analytical techniques to the then young field of software development.

The oldest and most popular way to measure a program's size is by the lines of code (LOC). Two reasons LOC is popular are that it is easy to calculate, and most developers have an intuition as to what defines a line of code. But the LOC metric has never been formalized by any standards organization, and there are several variations in the methods used for counting. However, in the core analysis, a line of code is considered to be a nonblank, noncomment line of program code.

Although program size is often quoted in LOC, this system of measurement has many shortcomings. To begin with, the LOC measure has no theoretical foundation, as there is no clear relationship between lines of code and program operation.

Also, LOC is a very unreliable measure. Consider the code fragments shown in Figures 1(a) and (b).

Although these routines are functionally and semantically identical, their LOC value varies by a value of three! This example demonstrates that the LOC count is dependent on the programming style. This dependency implies

```
bool SearchList(char *cmd, char **list, unsigned n) {

   // search entire list for command string
   for(unsigned i=0; i < n; i++)
   if (stricmp(cmd,list[i]) == 0) return true;
   return false;
}
```

Figure 1(a). A Concise Style (LOC=5).

```
bool SearchList(
      char *cmd,                    // command string
      char **list,                  // list/array of strings
      unsigned n)                   // max. no. of elements
{
   unsigned i;

   // search entire list for command string

   for(i=0; i < n; i++)        // for each element
   {
      if (stricmp(cmd,list[i]) == 0) // matched?
      {
         return true;          // found match
      }
   }

   return false;             // no match
}
```

Figure 1(b). A Verbose Style (LOC=15).

that LOC may provide inconsistent results between projects and programmers. This inconsistency may mean that our previously mentioned "developer's intuition" regarding lines of code is not the best method of measurement.

A different type of size metric that has become increasingly popular is called "function points" (FP). LOC and the software science formulations are *code metrics*, unlike FP, which is a *design metric.*

Function points were introduced in a paper published in 1979 by Alan Albrecht, then of IBM. FP is based on the concept that the workings of a computer program are determined by the data generated and retained by that program. The number of function points in an application is the weighted sum of the program inputs, outputs, files, and inquiries.

Contrary to the terminology, function point calculations do not directly involve program functions (routines); nor do they relate to the specific functionality of the program. Instead, the term *function* is intended to denote the program's capability for transmuting data and user input and output.

The FP metric was developed with data-processing systems in mind, but it has recently been applied to more diverse systems. The International Function Point Users Group (IFPUG) has provided standardization and popularized the technique.

It is important to understand that FP provides a high-level program size measurement. Its primary advantage is that a program's size can be estimated from specifications before it is written. FP is not an appropriate measure for small modules, such as individual files or routines, and applying it at this level often leads to counter-intuitive results.

The ABC metric was developed to overcome the disadvantages of LOC and token-counting techniques. However, since it is a code metric, it supplements, rather than replaces, measures such as FP.

ABC CALCULATIONS

Imperative programming languages like C, PASCAL, and other common languages, use data storage (variables) to perform useful work. Such languages have only three fundamental operations: storage, tests (conditions), and branching.

A raw ABC value is a vector that has three components:

- *Assignment*—an explicit transfer of data into a variable
- *Branch*—an explicit forward program branch out of scope
- *Condition*—a logical/boolean test

Each component identifies the number of fundamental operations. Data storage usually takes the form of assignment—the A in ABC. Branching, (the B in ABC), usually takes the form of function calls. Finally, conditions, (the C in ABC), are provided by **IF**, **ELSE**, and other constructs. The complete definitions for each component of the ABC metric follow.

There are many other aspects of a program that could be factored into a size measure. For example, you could consider variable declarations, arithmetic operators, and so on. Many of these factors are important to program complexity, but not always to program size.

Metric design is somewhat like language design, as it requires reasoning, experimentation, and a number of tradeoffs. Although it is not entirely possible to distinguish between size and complexity, my goal for the ABC metric was only to isolate the most fundamental components of size.

ABC values are written as an ordered triplet of integers. For example, a C subroutine may have an ABC value of

```
<7,12,2>
```

where 7 is the assignment count, 12 is the branch count, and 2 is the condition count. To standardize this subroutine, the counts are always written in the order A, B, and C, and are enclosed by angle brackets.

To simplify code comparisons, it is necessary to use a scalar size measure. However, because each component of an ABC vector is a distinct entity, it is not feasible to add them together to form a single value.

Instead, I have assumed that the components are orthogonal and have comparable scales. On this basis, a single ABC size value may be obtained by finding the magnitude of the ABC vector using the following formula:

```
|ABC| = sqrt((A*A) + (B*B) + (C*C))
```

Using this example as a standard, the subroutine mentioned in the previous paragraph would have an ABC magnitude value of 14.0.

Further research might show that the scales are *not* comparable and that a weighted sum, or other calculation, will provide better results. For now, however, I am recommending the magnitude calculation.

An ABC magnitude value is always rounded to the nearest tenth and is reported using one digit following the decimal point. Also, ABC magnitudes should not be presented without the accompanying ABC vector.

Because of semantic differences between programming languages, the specific rules for counting ABC values must be interpreted within the context of that language. Instead of covering more background theory, let's look at the ABC rules for C, C++, and Java, which have been formulated to provide comparisons between the languages.

1. Add one to the assignment count for each occurrence of an assignment operator (excluding constant declarations):

   ```
   = *= /= %= += -= <<= >>= &= |= ^=
   ```

2. Add one to the assignment count for each occurrence of an increment or decrement operator (prefix or postfix):

   ```
   ++ --
   ```

3. Add one to the branch count for each function call.
4. Add one to the branch count for the "goto" statement, which has a target at a deeper level of nesting than the level currently in use.
5. Add one to the condition count for each use of a conditional operator:

   ```
   == != <= >= < >
   ```

6. Add one to the condition count for each use of the following keywords:

   ```
   else case default ?
   ```

7. Add one to the condition count for each unary conditional expression.

Figure 2. ABC Counting Rules for C.

C RULES AND EXAMPLES

Let's begin by examining the counting rules for C (see Fig. 2), the predecessor of C++ and Java. Note that although the counting rules may be used as stated, there may be alternative rules that achieve the same values.

In many ways, the C language is more simple than the C++ or Java languages. Although a few comments are in order, the seven counting rules are self-explanatory.

Rule 1 specifically excludes constant declarations such as:

```
const double PI = 3.14159;
```

The reason for this exclusion is that PI is not a variable and only variable assignments, (i.e., data storage), are counted. Although the syntax is almost identical to a normal assignment, the expression joins the symbol "PI" and the value 3.14159.

Rule 2 adds increment and decrement operations to the A count because they implicitly perform an assignment. For example, the expression

```
x++;
```

is equivalent to

```
x = x + 1;
```

In the same way, Rule 6 states that a ternary expression such as:

```
x = (a == 3) ? a : b;
```

is equivalent to:

```
if (a == 3)
   x = a;
   else
   x = b;
```

Usually, according to the ABC definitions, only explicit assignments are counted. But by treating these equivalent but semantically different expressions in the same way, the ABC count provides a greater consistency between programming styles and languages.

Function calls increment the branch count, but function returns are not counted, as their direction is considered to be backward, not forward.

Rule 4 is that certain goto statements are also branches. These are tricky to determine automatically. Fortunately, there usually aren't many gotos in a well-structured program.

Lastly, the unary conditional expression in Rule 7 is an implicit condition that uses no relational operators. In the construct

```
if (x || y)
printf("test failure\n");7
```

there are two unary conditions since both **x** and **y** are tested as conditional expressions.

Listing 1 shows the ABC count for a small C subroutine. The annotations to the left of each line of source code show where each component of the ABC count is generated. The ABC vector for this routine is <5,6,3> and has a magnitude of 8.4.

A more complicated C routine is shown in Listing 2. In this example the ABC vector is <7,12,14> and it has a magnitude of 19.7. Notice that it becomes much easier to make a mistake when performing an ABC count for larger routines.

There are no symbolic constants in this routine because it has been run through the C preprocessor to expand macro definitions. To ensure accuracy, the ABC counting rules should only be applied to C code that has been preprocessed. We will examine the reasons for this in the C++ example later.

Listing 1. C Subroutine ABC=<5,6,3> [8.4].

```
          static ushort CalculatePageSize(void)
          {
            const ushort MAX_NVRAM_PAGE_SIZE = 256;
            utiny save;
            ushort i, n;

[b]         outportb(0x800,1);
[aca]       for(i=1; i < MAX_NVRAM_PAGE_SIZE; i*=2)
            {
[a]             n = i + 5;
[ab]            save = inportb(0x800+n);

[b]             outNVRAM(0x800+n,0x55);

[bc]            if (inportb(0x800+n) != 0x55)
                {
[b]                 outNVRAM (0x800+n,save);
                    break;
                }
[b]             outNVRAM (0x800+n,save);
            }

[c]         if (i == 1)
[a]           i = 0;

          return i;
          }
```

C++ RULES AND EXAMPLE

The ABC counting rules for C++ (see Fig. 3) are similar to the counting rules for C. However, there are some important differences.

As with C, constant declarations are not counted. Similarly, default parameter assignments such as:

```
class Point
{
   Point(int x=0, int y=0);
   ...
};
```

are not counted.

The try and catch keywords for C++ exception-handling are additional conditionals not found in C.

Listing 2. More Complex C Subroutine ABC=<7,12,14> [19.7].

```
        void UpdateSchedule(ADI_EVENT *evt)
        {
            EVENT tempevt;
[a]         char am=0;

[bc]        if (!Lock(evt->file,evt->data.rec))
            {
[b]             DisplayMessage(errorMessage[2],0x71);
                return;
            }

[b]         ReadLog(&tempevt,evt->file,evt->data.rec);
[bc]        if (memcmp(&tempevt,&evt->data,sizeof (tempevt)))
            {
[bc]            if (memcmp(tempevt.src,evt->
                            data.src,sizeof(tempevt.src)) ==0 &&
[bc]               memcmp(tempevt. house,evt->data.house,
                            sizeof(tempevt.house))== 0)
                {
[b]                memcpy(&evt->data,&tempevt,sizeof(evt->data));
                }
[c]             else
                {
[b]                     UnLock(evt->file,evt->data.rec);
[b]                     DisplayMessage(errorMessage[5],0x71);
[a]                     updateFlag = 1;
                }
            }

[aa]        evt->data.adistate[0] = evt->adiStatus++;

            switch(evt->adiStatus)
            {
[c]         case 0x11:
[b]             memcpy(evt->data.src,device.utility,sizeof
                          (evt->data.src));\
            break;

[c]         case 0x23:
[cc]            if (device.mode == 19 || device.channel == 2)
                {
[b]                     memcpy(evt->data.src,device.utility,sizeof
                                  (evt->data.src));
```

(continued)

Listing 2. (continued)

```
                }
            break;

[c]         default:
[c]             if (device.mode == 2)
                {
[b]                     memcpy(evt->data.src,device.utility,sizeof
                                (evt->data.src));
[a]                     evt->data.adistate[0] = 0;
                }
            break;
            }

[a]         am = evt->data.amarc[0];
[accc]      evt->data.amarc[0] = (am >= 0 && am <= 0xF) ? ‘ ’ : ‘C’;
           }
```

Branches occur not only for free function calls, but also for class method calls (see Rule 4). The new and delete operators are counted as function calls (see Rule 6) mainly because they are equivalent to the function calls malloc and free.

You may wonder why operators aren't counted as branches, since their operation is often identical to a function call. For example, the statement

```
x = y + 6;
```

whose ABC=<1,0,0> could be rewritten as:

```
x = Add(y,6);
```

whose ABC=<1,1,0>.

It is important that the rules for counting are made in the context of the language and not the underlying implementation. The definition of an ABC branch is an explicit forward program branch out of scope. In the original expression, we do not know, and should not consider, the implementation of the addition operator. Even though we may know that the expression is merely "syntactic sugar," the operation is still not considered to be an ABC branch. Figure 3 lists the ABC counting rules for C++.

Unlike C and Java, C++ has a special initialization syntax that can be more efficient than traditional assignment. However, initialization still amounts to data storage, so nonconstant initializations are counted as an ABC assignment.

1. Add one to the assignment count for each occurrence of an assignment operator. Be sure to exclude constant declarations and default parameter assignments.

   ```
   =  *=  /=  %=  +=  -=  <<=  >>=  &=  |=  ^=
   ```

2. Add one to the assignment count for each occurrence of an increment or decrement operator (prefix or postfix).

   ```
   ++  --
   ```

3. Add one to the assignment count for each variable and nonconstant class member initialization.
4. Add one to the branch count for each function or class method call.
5. Add one to the branch count for "goto" statement whose target is at a deeper level of nesting than the current level.
6. Add one to the branch count for each occurrence of the new and delete operators.
7. Add one to the condition count for each use of a conditional operator.

   ```
   ==  !=  <=  >=  <  >
   ```

8. Add one to the condition count for each use of the following keywords:

   ```
   else  case default try   catch      ?
   ```

9. Add one to the condition count for each unary conditional expression.

Figure 3. ABC Counting Rules for C++.

Each of the two C++ constructors shown below have the same ABC vector: <2,0,0>.

```
List::List(void)
{
    itsData = 0;
    itsElements = 0;
}
List::List(void) : itsData(0), itsElements(0);
{
}
```

Listing 3 demonstrates how the ABC metric is applied to a simple C++ class method. The ABC vector for this method is <5,13,1> and the magnitude is 14.0.

Listing 3. C++ Class Method ABC=<5,13,1> [14.0].

```
        void UartStream::Transmit(unsigned char *data)
        {
[aa]        unsigned char i(0), n = data[1] + 3;

[ab]        data[n-1] = Checksum(n-1,data);
[b]         memcpy(itsLastMessage,data,n);
[b]         WaitReceiveFifoEmpty();

[b]         disable();
[b]         SetParityEven();

[b]         SendByte(data[0]);
[b]         SendByte(data[1]);
[b]         SendByte(data[2]);

[b]         WaitTransmitRegisterEmpty();

[b]         SetParityOdd();
[b]         enable();

[aca]       for(i=3; i < n; i++)
[b]         SendByte(data[i]);

[b]         delay(itsXmtDelay);
        }
```

As in previous C examples, this C++ code has been preprocessed. Preprocessing is necessary because macros and preprocessor directives may hide elements of the program that are needed for an accurate ABC count. Consider the following program:

```
#include <stdio.h>

#define EQUALS =
#define LT       <
#define GT     >
#define INC(x)++(x)
#define DEC(x)   —(x)

void main()
{
    int y;
```

```
        for(y EQUALS 0; y LT 10; INC(y))
            printf("%u  %u\n", y, y*y);
}
```

Although this is a bit unusual, it is not uncommon for beginning C/C++ developers to create macros reminiscent of another language they may be more familiar with.

Determining the ABC count by hand for this unprocessed program is not very difficult, but it could be easy to make a mistake. However, because the semantics are nonstandard, an automated program could not parse this code directly.

The use of preprocessor directives is another problem. Debug statements may not always be removed from released code. One way to elude a debug statement is the use of comments, such as:

```
for(i=0; i < n; i++)
{
    outportb(0x378,data[i]);
    // delay(100);    // slow it down (debug)
}
```

Yet another way is to use a preprocessor directive in this manner:

```
for(i=0; i < n; i++)
{
    outportb(0x378,data[i]);

#if 0
    delay(100);       // slow it down (debug)
#endif
}
```

Without preprocessing, it's difficult for an ABC counting program to ignore these unused sections of code. Although preprocessing is a nuisance in measuring C and C++ programs, it is not needed in Java programs.

Java Rules and Example

Java does not use header files or a preprocessor like C and C++. This simplifies the language in many ways, but trades off some expressive power by doing so. However, it does make ABC counting easier.

1. Add one to the assignment count for each occurrence of an assignment operator, excluding constant declarations.

   = *= /= %= += -= <<= >>= &= |= ^= >>>=

2. Add one to the assignment count for each occurrence of an increment or decrement operator (prefix or postfix).

   ++ --

3. Add one to the branch count for each function or class method call.
4. Add one to the branch count for each occurrence of the new operator.
5. Add one to the condition count for each use of a conditional operator:

   == != <= >= < >

6. Add one to the condition count for each use of the following keywords:

   else case default try catch ?

7. Add one to the condition count for each unary conditional expression.

Figure 4. ABC Counting Rules for Java.

Figure 4 shows the ABC counting rules for Java. The rules are similar to, and simpler than, the counting rules for C++.

Java has one extra assignment operator that C++ doesn't: the ">>>=" operator. The ">>>=" operator performs an unsigned right shift and assignment, whereas the ">>=" operator performs a signed shift and assignment.

As in C and C++, constant assignments are not counted. However, constant expressions are identified by the **final** modifier rather than the **const** modifier.

Finally, gotos are not implemented in Java. (This provides one less branch counting rule for the ABC metric.) Java reserves goto as a keyword to provide better error-checking at compile time.

Listing 4 shows a simple Java class. When compiled, the class forms a complete application that displays the contents of a file in hexadecimal and ASCII form.

Notice that the constants FIELD_WIDTH and HEXADECIMAL have been excluded from the count. Also notice that the statement

```
s = Integer.toHexString(tmp).toUpperCase();
```

counts as two branches since two class methods are called.

Listing 4. Java Class ABC=<13,15,11> [22.7].

```
          public class dump
          {
            public static void main(String av[])
            {
               final short FIELD_WIDTH = 16;
               final short HEXADECIMAL = 16;

               FileInputStream infile;
[ab]           byte data[] = new byte[FIELD_WIDTH];
[a]            int total=0;

[c]            try
               {
                      int actual;
[ab]                  infile = new FileInputStream(av[0]);
[bc]                  while (infile.available() > 0)
                      {
[a]                         String ascii="";
                            int i;
[ab]                        actual = infile.read(data);
[a]                         total += actual;
[aca]                       for(i=0; i < actual; i++)
                            {
                                  String s;
                                  int tmp;
[a]                               tmp = (int)data[i] & 0xff;
[abb]                             s = Integer. toHexString
                                      (tmp).toUpperCase();

[cc]                              if (data[i] > 31 && data[i] < 128)
[a]                                  ascii += (char)data[i];
[c]                               else
[a]                                  ascii += ".";

[c]                               if (tmp < HEXADECIMAL)
[b]                                  System.out. print("0");
[b]                               System.out. print(s + " ");

[c]                               if (i == ((FIELD_WIDTH/2)-1))
[b]                                  System.out. print(" ");
                            }
```

(Continued

Listing 4. (Continued)

```
[c]                     if (i < FIELD_ WIDTH/2)
[b]                         System.out. print(" ");
[ca]                    for(; i < FIELD_ WIDTH; i++)
[b]                         System.out. print("  ");

[b]                     System.out. print("  " + ascii);
[b]                     System.out. println();
                    }
                }
[c]             catch(IOException ioe)
                {
[bb]                System.out. println(ioe.toString());
                }
            }
        }
```

Because there is only one method (main) in the dump class, the ABC vector is applicable to the entire class. If more than one method were implemented, the ABC vector for the class would be equal to the sum of the vectors of each method.

APPLICATIONS OF THE ABC METRIC

My original interest in source code metrics was to gain a better understanding of modules and their relationships. It is almost impossible to compare the amount of code in two modules without an accurate size measure.

Existing size measures did not seem to me to capture the essence of software size reliably or practically. Because the ABC metric provides useful, style-independent measurements, I'm advocating that it be used in place of LOC for both private and published studies. In most cases, the ABC magnitude is best for estimations.

One application of the metric is for estimating project schedules. The first step is to estimate the number of ABCs in the completed project. This number is divided by the average number of ABCs the developers can produce per day. The resulting estimate is the number of days to complete the project.

As with LOC usage, the overall project estimate is the most subjective step and is therefore easily misjudged. Practice makes perfect, however, and this technique should still provide reasonable time estimates for small projects. Better yet, the progress of development may be tracked by monitoring the ABC counts on a daily or weekly basis.

Software reliability is often quoted in terms of bugs/LOC, and could be easily replaced by bugs/ABC. Of course, either kind of macroscopic measurement implies that all parts of the code have an equal potential for bugs—a notion not clearly collaborated by any studies.

As we've seen, the LOC metric is made unreliable by its dependency on a specific style. As a result, project estimates and reliability figures are apt to be inaccurate from project to project. By using ABC magnitudes instead of LOC values, the accuracy of these figures should improve considerably.

More importantly, the actual productivity (in ABC/day or similar) can be accurately compared between developers, products, and businesses. Because syntax of the languages is similar, the ABC counts for C, C++, and Java should allow direct comparisons of programs written in any of these languages.

There are other potential applications of the ABC metric that may be more interesting to you.

It is commonly accepted that cohesion is a desirable attribute of subroutines. It is usually assumed that the larger a subroutine is, the less likely it is to be cohesive. This seems to make sense, but the exact relationship is not clear. However, by analyzing a large number of programs, it may be possible to statistically identify modules that lack cohesion (requiring rework).

An accurate size measure also provides a vehicle for source code visualization. Using size and other relevant code measures, an application could be viewed graphically to enhance the understanding of the architecture and topology. This could provide insights into pathological designs, potential malfunctions, and maintenance concerns.

Although there are many potential applications of the ABC metric, you should remember that it does not provide architecture or complexity information. The metric does not directly utilize comments, macros, data flow, or other aspects of programs. It simply provides a low level, style-independent measure of program size.

Benefits of the ABC Metric

The ABC metric has several properties that make it more useful and reliable than LOC. First, the metric is based on the idea that a program performs "useful work" for which data storage, tests, and branching are the base of operations. This concept is easily understood by anyone who has written a program using an imperative programming language.

Because ABC counting is based on these basic operations, the metric is virtually independent of a programming style. This is an important attribute since styles vary enormously in languages such as C and C++.

Another valuable property of the ABC metric is its linearity. ABC measurements can be given for any module (i.e., any section of code having the same scope), whether it is a subroutine, package, class method, and so on.

The ABC vector for any module is the sum of the vectors of all its submodules. For example, the ABC vector of a C++ class implementation is the sum of the vectors of each of the class methods.

This linearity makes it easy to compare the sizes of routines, files, and classes with complete accuracy. In essence, the topology of the program can be clearly mapped.

Although ABC vectors are linear, ABC magnitudes are not. This nonlinearity, coupled with the assumption that the component scales are comparable, is the primary reason that ABC magnitudes should not be reported without the original vectors. A change in the way ABC magnitudes are reported will not undermine published research.

It may also be possible to gain more insight into the nature of an application by retaining the ABC counts in vector form. Tom DeMarco[3] has categorized programs as being "data strong" or "function strong." Viewed this way, programs in which assignment statements are dominant could be considered "data strong." Programs in which branches dominate could be considered "function strong."

Although DeMarco does not make this distinction, programs in which conditionals are dominant could be considered "logic strong." Accordingly, the ABC metric can provide additional information about the driving principles behind the application.

Currently, there are no guidelines for establishing how much larger one component should be to be considered dominant. Additional research should provide some interesting ratios.

Another interesting property of the ABC metric is that it is zero-based. Consider the following C++ destructor:

```
AbstractPoint::~AbstractPoint(void)
{
   // does nothing
}
```

The LOC value for this destructor is three (3), which suggests the code is actually performing some action. On the other hand, the ABC vector and magnitude are both zero, signifying that the destructor does not contribute directly to program size. However, this does not imply that the destructor is not needed.

Perhaps the most important aspect of the ABC metric is that it seems to judge a program's size the way that most developers do. For research purposes, a set of C++ class methods was ranked by eighteen developers who had little familiarity with LOC and no familiarity with ABC. Their rankings showed a significantly higher correlation to ABC magnitudes than to LOC.*

The result is not too surprising, since LOC is merely a convenient measure, and not a well-constructed one. No one is fooled into thinking that there is a greater amount of source code if it is spread out over several lines. Likewise, developers do not normally estimate size by assessing the number of operators and operands, as software science would suggest.

Conclusion

The ABC metric overcomes many of the limitations of the LOC metric. It has a theoretical foundation, is style independent, and has useful mathematical properties. Furthermore, the ABC counting rules for C, C++, and Java are defined to allow accurate cross-language comparisons, thereby enhancing the applicability of the metric.

Preliminary research suggests that the ABC metric provides program size measurements similar to those given by professional developers.

Because of its consistency, the ABC metric should allow better estimates of project development time and program reliability. Specifically, it should

---

* Currently unpublished research conducted by the author during December 1996. Details are expected to be published later this year after additional studies have been completed.

provide more accurate comparisons of projects created by different individuals and businesses.

Although the ABC is a promising metric, further research is needed to assess its viability for larger programs. The metric must compared to LOC and other measures to determine the extent of its benefits. The relationship between the ABC components should be better explored. Finally, the hypothesis regarding size and cohesion should be confirmed, and the relationship between the two must be defined.

Because ABC counting is too tedious to perform by hand, I am developing programs for Windows 95/NT that will automate the process. When completed, you'll be able to download them from the Website http://www.redmtn.com. I encourage you to try ABC instead of LOC. I'd be interested in your results, ideas, and comments.

REFERENCES

1. Halstead, M.H. *Elements of Software Science,* Elsevier North Holland, 1977.
2. Fenton, N. *Software Metrics*, Chapman & Hall, 1991.
3. DeMarco, T. *Controlling Software Projects*, Prentice-Hall, 1982.
4. Shepperd, M. *Software Engineering Metrics*, Volume I, McGraw-Hill, 1993.
5. Kitchenham, B., *et al. IEEE Transactions on Software Engineering*, "Towards a Framework for Software Measurement Validation," (21)12, Dec. 1995.

Patterns for Mapping OO Applications to Relational Databases

Alberto Antenangeli

This is one of those classic articles that makes an editor smile. It was so nicely put together and so well thought through, and so very timely.

In this article, Alberto discusses several ways to use a relational database to represent an object-oriented data model. There are a whole bunch of reasons why you would not want to do this. Chief among them is that object-oriented models are not *data models at all, rather they are models of the partitioning of behavior into different classes. Also, relational databases have their own constraints and rules. Their structure is best designed in the context of those rules, and in the context of the many applications, that* will *access the database.*

Still, there are times when the best solution is simply to write your objects out to a relational database. And if you find yourself in that position, Alberto's article should prove very valuable.

As object-oriented languages become more widely used, many people are faced with the integration between those languages and relational databases. The OO and the relational paradigms are excessively different, and it seems almost impossible to reconcile them in a reasonable way.

There is a good reason for that: The two paradigms have roots in different sets of principles, and they were created with different purposes in mind.

This problem is not as serious as it seems to be at first glance. We describe different approaches to help people tackle this problem in an orderly manner. We also discuss the tradeoff associated with each approach.

RELATIONAL VERSUS OO: THE FUNDAMENTAL DIFFERENCES

In the OO world, the word is to hide the structure of the data, and expose only functionality. OO designers expose an object to the world in terms of the services it provides. The object's data is hidden to the external world, and only interfaces to functions that manipulate that data are exposed.

This approach reduces dependency, since the behavior of the object becomes independent from how information is structured. Changes in the object's internal structure do not affect the object's interface and, consequently, the clients of that object are not affected by those changes.

In the relational world, what you want is exactly the opposite: you want to expose data that satisfy relationships and match search conditions dynamically. Business is modeled through entities that have relationships with each other. We typically have many applications accessing portions of the same database through different views. There is much dependency between how data is structured and how applications access the data.

There are some techniques that provide some level of encapsulation to relational databases. One of them is to create views of the data, and let applications query the views instead of querying the tables directly. Another approach is to use stored procedures to access data. Although those techniques do provide some level of encapsulation, the granularity is still too coarse.

Therefore, the question still remains: How can we reconcile both paradigms?

The answer is simple: We don't have to. The real problem is that people don't try to make the best use of what OO and the relational model have to offer. Instead, they try to implement an OO functionality on top of a relational database, and they end up with the worst of each model. One thing to always keep in mind is that a relational database was not designed to be an object-oriented database.

Finally, the question is: how can we make the two models get along? Let's look at the problem from a different perspective. Instead of trying to implement an OO database on top of a relational database, let's think of the relational database as the place where you store the state of an object. Nothing more than this. Therefore, our problem becomes: how can we map the state of objects to a relational database?

How to Approach the Development

Whenever you need to define a mapping between A and B, you can take one of two paths: from A to B or from B to A. Although this might seem very obvious, you should keep in mind that sometimes things become evident only after someone has formalized them. So let's apply the A & B principle to our mapping problem.

You can map the OO and the relational world following two different paths:

1. From the object hierarchy to the relational model.
2. From the relational model to the object hierarchy.

Both approaches have advantages. Mapping from your class hierarchy to the relational model is useful when you are starting a new system from scratch, and all applications that will access the relational database will share the part of the design that accesses the database. However, the resulting database schema will probably reflect the needs of those applications, and not the business you are trying to model. If you later decide, for example, to use a report generator in conjunction with that database, you might find out that, although the database schema seems to be perfect for your application, it is not very meaningful for the report generator.

Mapping from the database schema to the class hierarchy is particularly useful when your application has to operate with an existing database that cannot be modified because other applications are already accessing it. However, this approach usually imposes restrictions in the (OO) design of your application: When following this path, the relational model gives you a starting point for your OO design, and what is good for the relational side might not be good for the OO side.

Before we explore both paths in detail, let's ask ourselves the question: Which path is the best? As expected, the answer is: It depends on the situation. There is a tradeoff for each path. Bottom line, you typically end up doing a combination of both approaches.

Path 1: Mapping Classes to Tables

In this part of the article we focus on one aspect of this problem: How inheritance can be mapped to a relational database. Of course, this is only one aspect of OO design: We can also have containment, use, etc. However, mapping those aspects to a relational database is somewhat intuitive, and by far less complex than mapping inheritance.

Roughly speaking, there are two major components in the design of a relational database: tables and relationships. A class hierarchy, therefore, has to be mapped to tables that have some sort of relationship with other tables.

There are three basic strategies for this mapping:

- Map each class to one table.
- One table holds it all.
- Map only the most derived classes.

As expected, each strategy has advantages and disadvantages. We will explain in detail how they work, and the tradeoff associated with each one.

We will use a simple class hierarchy as an example, as depicted in Figure 1. This is not a sophisticated design, but it has all the basic elements we need for our discussion.

We will assume that the Social Security Number (SSN) uniquely identifies an employee. As you can see, we are already imposing some policy on our OO

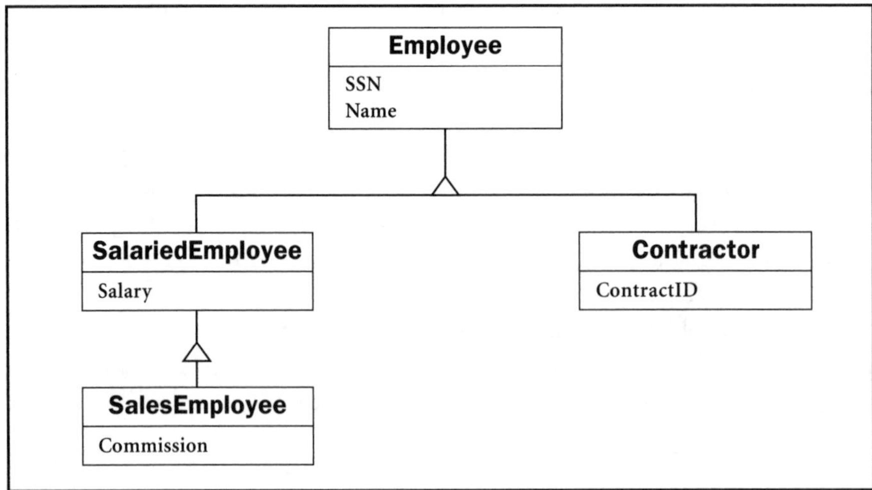

Figure 1. A simple class hierarchy.

design: There ought to be some member data in some classes that can work as a unique identifier. Those member data will be used as primary keys on the database side. We can't totally abstract ourselves from the fact that state will be persisted into and retrieved from a relational database!

Let's start with the simpler case: Each class maps to a different table. We have four classes, we have four tables. Figure 2 is what the tables look like.

This mapping strategy looks simple and straightforward. Each class has its own table, and we use the SSN as the primary key whenever we need to find information. This approach is also very efficient in terms of disk usage, since there is no redundant information besides the primary key.

Another advantage of this approach is that changes in one class affect only the table to which the class maps. For example, if we decide to add a hiringDate member data to the Employee class, only the Employee table is affected. What's more, when classes are added to the hierarchy, the existing tables are not affected. For example, if we add an HourlyEmployee class to our hierarchy, the existing tables are not affected. As we will see later, there are other mapping strategies to which this does not apply.

The tradeoff? Performance will not be good. Keeping different classes in different tables implies doing joins whenever information has to be retrieved. The deeper the class hierarchy, the worse the performance, since more tables will be involved in the join process. Another problem is that you cannot insert, delete, or update a derived class with only one SQL statement, because the class is spread in different tables. For some applications where performance is critical, this might be a serious problem, so watch out!

However, keep in mind that this approach is very easy to implement, since each class should only know how to hit the database given its primary key. This

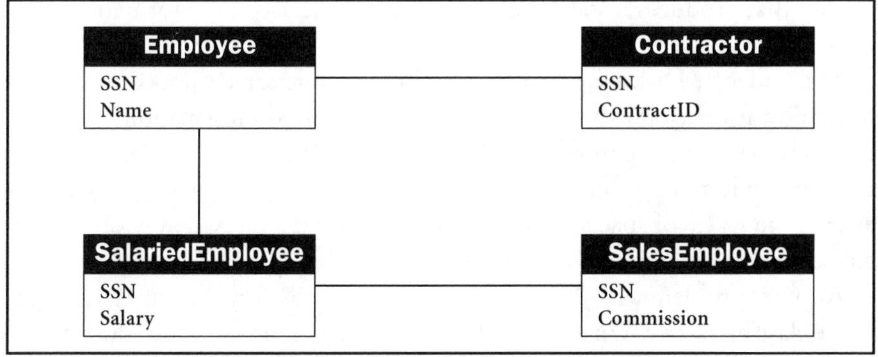

Figure 2.

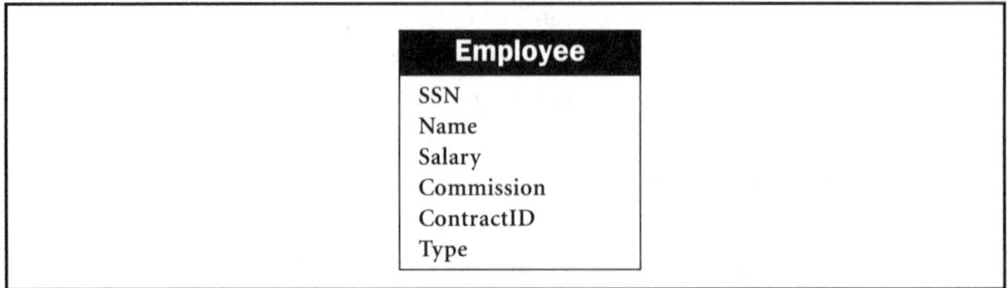

Figure 3.

approach might turn out to be useful for shallow class hierarchies.

There is one tricky point about this approach: derived classes are associated with more than one table; therefore, whenever a derived class accesses the database, it should do it in the context of a transaction in order to guarantee the referential integrity. One thing to bear in mind for this case is the use of server-side triggers. Many relational databases allow you to define triggers that are automatically called in the context of some operations. For example, if you define a trigger for the delete operation, whenever a row (or a set of rows) is deleted, that trigger is automatically called. You can use this feature to cascade the delete operation to the other tables. Let the server do the work for you!

Let's now turn the world upside down, and do exactly the opposite: let's map the entire class hierarchy to a single table. In our example, we would have a single table Employee, as we show in Figure 3.

The big advantage of this model is performance: one hit in the database is enough to perform any operation (select, insert, delete, or update). It also somewhat conforms with the idea of polymorphism, since from that single table we can produce instances of any derived classes. It would be easy to implement a factory that produces instances of the correct class based on information from the table.

The tradeoff? Disk usage. Every row in that table carries not only state information for the class it represents, but also unused information related to other classes that are part of the inheritance tree. If the derived classes do not differ much in terms of member data, then this model should work fine. Otherwise, the waste of space makes its use prohibitive. The two previous strategies are a good example of trading performance for space.

Another problem with this model is that the table is very sensitive to changes in the class hierarchy. When derived classes with member data are added to the model, then the table has to be expanded to accommodate the new information.

SalariedEmployee
SSN
Name
Salary

SalesEmployee
SSN
Name
Salary
Commission

Contractor
SSN
Name
ContractID

Figure 4.

One last thing to discuss: flags. Since we are putting all classes in the same table, we also need to know what kind of employee each row represents. That is why we have a new column, Type, which does not map to any member data of our original hierarchy.

The last approach we will analyze is the mapping of the classes that are instantiated by your application into separate tables. In our example, we would have the tables in Figure 4. Since our application instantiates SalariedEmployee, SalesEmployee and Contractor, we have the three corresponding tables. As you can see, fields like SSN, Name, and Salary show up in more than one table.

This approach frequently offers good performance, since one database hit is enough to perform any operation. This approach is also good in terms of disk usage, since the tables hold only the information that is necessary.

The tradeoff? This model is also sensitive in terms of changes in the base class. Those changes have to be consistently replicated in all mapped tables. This model also does not fit well in terms of polymorphism, since there is no single table that holds all employees, but they are scattered in different tables. This might have performance implications when you don't know exactly what kind of employee you want to retrieve: You might need to query different tables to find the information you want.

The mapping can become potentially confusing when multiple inheritance is used. You would have to be very careful when mapping the common base class.

Which One Should I Use?

So far, we have analyzed three different approaches, and all of them have their advantages and disadvantages. Which approach should be used? There is no right answer to this question. The bottom line is that you usually will employ a combination of the different techniques, and the decision will be based on how many instances of each class you expect to have, and the implications in terms of performance and disk usage.

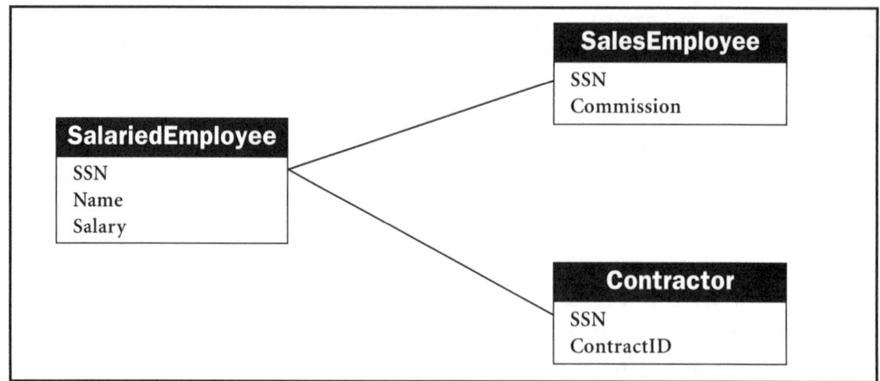

Figure 5.

Let's consider an example of how the different techniques can be combined. Suppose that 90% of the employees in our system are salaried employees. In this case, the mapping in Figure 5 probably makes a lot of sense.

In this case, we have a SalariedEmployee table that holds both the Employee base class, and also SalariedEmployee. We use the SSN key to access information about SalesEmployee and Contractor, which have their own tables. Because we know that most of the time we will be manipulating instances of SalariedEmployee, in practical terms, this mapping offers good performance and good disk usage.

PATH 2: MAPPING VIEWS OF DATA TO CLASSES

So far, we have analyzed the case where the OO design is done first, without taking the database design into account. We have also discussed some techniques to design a database to reflect the existing OO design. However, there is one important issue that we have not taken into account: we are assuming that we can decide what the database schema will look like. Is that a fair assumption?

If we stop for a moment to analyze typical database systems, we will soon conclude that in most cases they are centered in the database, with many client applications orbiting around them. Seldom do we find a database system where one single client application accesses the database.

Well designed databases are created having the business in mind, not a particular application. In other words, well designed databases reflect the way the enterprise conducts business, and they are not likely to change (unless the busi-

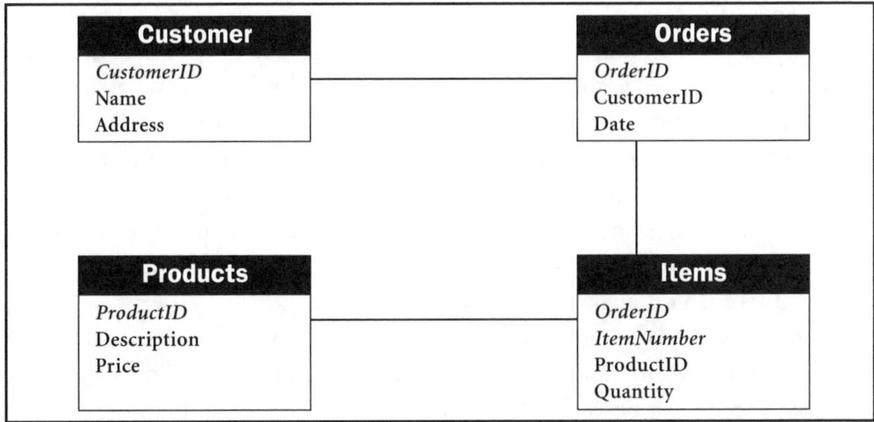

Figure 6.

ness itself changes). Modeling a database with a particular application in mind may lead to instability when other applications join the system. For example, go back and look at the databases we have designed for the OO to relational mapping. Would they make sense if you were trying to use a report builder? Maybe so, but maybe not… Let's see why.

Suppose we have chosen to map the classes that are instantiated in our hierarchy into separate tables, because our application "knows" the type of employee it accesses, and performance and space are an issue. Suppose also that we have added information about the sex of the employee to our tables. Sometime later comes the requirement to print a report that shows the average age, grouped by sex, for all employees who work for our company. What could have been done easily in a simple query (`SELECT AVG (…) FROM… GROUP BY Sex`), now becomes a very complicated problem, since there is no easy and efficient way to express that query in SQL. On the other hand, had we chosen to map all classes to a single table, the problem wouldn't have existed at all.

Having said that, we can assume that the database schema is the most stable part of our system. That assumption gives us two choices: we design our client OO application either ignoring the underlying database, or taking it into account. If we decide for the former, then we will probably need to write a mapping layer on the client side to isolate the application design from the database design. Although we can be very inventive, sometimes this "glue" layer leads to bad performance.

Our second choice is to take the existing database design into account. Let's start from a simple (but representative) database (see Fig. 6).

We have customers placing orders. Orders have several items, and each item consists of a product and the quantity. Products have descriptions and prices.

Now let's assume we are writing the order entry application. What are good candidate abstractions for our application? Well, the database design gives us a hint! The good candidates are Customers, Orders, Items, and Products.

Formalizing the concept: The database defines the classes that are in the root of a class hierarchy. Those classes abstract the concept of information that can be mapped to the database, i.e., whose state can be stored to, and retrieved from, a database.

We say "root of a class hierarchy" because from the mapped classes you have to inherit and specialize application-specific classes. The internal data structure of a class should not be visible to the user of that class. If all that our class has is a set of mutators and accessor functions, this class is closer to a structure than to any other thing.

However, there are some interesting corollaries to this concept. The first one is related to code generation: one can write a tool that, based on schema information from the database, generates those base classes from which application classes will derive, as well as code to the interface instances of those classes with the database. This represents big savings when a large number of tables are involved in the application.

Another interesting consequence of this approach is that the base classes can also map the relationships that exist among the database tables if foreign and primary key information was included as part of the database design. In the above example, we can see that the Customers and Orders have a relationship based on ClientID. This sort of relationship can be captured in the mapped classes. One-to-one relationships look like pointers. One-to-many relationships look like collections.

Is the world as simple and as beautiful as this example? Of course not. To assume that mapping one table to one class addresses all design problems of our application is to overly simplify the OO design. However, we should keep in mind that not only can we map tables to classes, but also to views, or queries to classes. For example, for an application that prints orders, it might make sense to directly map a join between the Items and the Products table to one class, instead of hitting the database two times (once for the Items, and again to get the product description and price).

WHERE DO YOU WANT TO GO TODAY?

I hope I've given you some practical ideas on the subject of mapping the relational and the object-oriented worlds. As I mentioned, there is no magic recipe to solve this problem, nothing replaces good and meticulous analysis!

Which path should you use? It depends on several issues. How much can you influence the design of your database? How many different applications will access the database? How complex is the application you are designing? What are the performance requirements? I would venture to say that, typically, you will end up using a combination of all the paths and techniques described here.

One topic that is not covered in this article is how you actually implement the database access. There are several techniques that can be employed. One of them is a factory-like approach: all database access goes to a class that knows how to "manufacture" instances of mapped classes based on database information. Another approach is to separate the mapped data from the database access itself using a variant of the Memento design pattern. Yet another approach is to have only one class that holds the mapped information and "knows" how to talk to a database.

Which approach is the best? As expected, they all have advantages, disadvantages, and tradeoffs, and they should be analyzed in light of the application you are developing. Hopefully you will see this discussion in a forthcoming article!

DESIGNING EXCEPTION-SAFE GENERIC CONTAINERS

HERB SUTTER

In late 1995, the participants of comp.lang.c++ decided that the noise had simply gotten too loud to bear. So we formed comp.lang.c++.moderated. This turned out to be a remarkably successful newsgroup, and it still flourishes today.

One of the moderators of the new newsgroup was Herb Sutter. Herb's postings were always sharp and accurate, and I admired his knowledge and writing skill. When I became editor of the C++ Report, *I invited Herb to become a columnist. He writes Sutter's Mill to this day. This was one of the best moves I made for the magazine. Herb's articles have been top-notch, highly technical and poignant.*

This article, and the sequel immediately following it, scared (and continues to scare) the willies out of me. It shows how very very difficult the proper use of exceptions is. It also shows that by following a suite of very strict rules, one can indeed make exception safe code.

EXCEPTION SUPPORT AND generic programming are two of C++'s most powerful features. Yet both require exceptional care, and writing an efficient reusable generic container is nearly as difficult as writing exception-safe code.

This article tackles both of these major features at once, by examining how to write exception-safe (works properly in the presence of exceptions) and exception-neutral (propagates all exceptions to the caller) generic containers. That's easy enough to say, but it's no mean feat. If you have any doubts on that score, see Tom

Cargill's excellent article, "Exception Handling: A False Sense of Security."[1]

This article begins where Cargill's left off, namely by presenting an exception-neutral version of the Stack template he critiques. In the next article, we'll significantly improve the Stack container by reducing the requirements on T, the contained type, and show advanced techniques for managing resources exception-safely. Along the way we'll find the answers to questions like the following:

- What are the different "levels" of exception safety?
- Can or should generic containers be fully exception-neutral?
- Are the standard library containers exception-safe or exception-neutral?
- Does exception safety affect the design of your container's public interface?
- Should generic containers use exception specifications?

THE Stack<> CONTAINER

Here is the declaration of the Stack template, substantially the same as in Cargill's article. Our mission: to make Stack exception-neutral. That is, Stack objects should always be in a correct and consistent state regardless of any exceptions that might be thrown in the course of executing Stack's member functions, and if any exceptions are thrown they should be propagated seamlessly through to the caller, who can deal with them as he pleases since he knows the context of T and we don't:

```
template <class T> class Stack {
public:
   Stack();
   ~Stack();
   Stack(const Stack&);
   Stack& operator=(const Stack&);

   size_t Size() const;
   void  Push(const T&);
   T     Pop();                          // if empty, throws exception

private:
   T*    v_;                    // ptr to a memory area big
   size_t vsize_;               //  enough for 'vsize_' T's
   size_t vused_;               // # of T's actually in use
};
```

Before reading on, stop and think about this class and consider: What are the exception-safety issues? How can this class be made exception-neutral, so that any exceptions are propagated to the caller without causing integrity problems in the Stack object?

Default Construction

Right away, we can see that Stack is going to have to manage dynamic memory resources. Clearly, one key is going to be avoiding leaks even in the presence of exceptions thrown by T operations and standard memory allocations. For now, we'll manage these memory resources within each Stack member function. In the next article, we'll improve on this by using a private base class to encapsulate resource ownership.

First, consider one possible default constructor:

```
template<class T>
Stack<T>::Stack()
   : v_(0),
     vsize_(10),
     vused_(0)              // nothing used yet
{
   v_ = new T[vsize_];      // initial allocation
}
```

Is this constructor exception-safe? To find out, consider what might throw. In short, the answer is: "Any function." So the first step is to analyze this code and determine what functions will actually be called, including both free functions and constructors, destructors, operators, and other member functions.

This Stack constructor first sets vsize_ to 10, then attempts to allocate some initial memory using "new T[vsize_]." The latter first tries to call operator new[] (either the default operator new[] or one provided by T) to allocate the memory, then tries to call T::T() vsize_ times. There are two operations that might fail. First, the memory allocation itself, in which case operator new[] will throw a bad_alloc exception. Second, T's default constructor, which might throw anything at all, in which case any objects that were constructed are destroyed and the allocated memory is automatically guaranteed to be deallocated via operator delete[].

Hence the above function is fully exception-safe, and we can move on to the next ...

... what? Why is it exception-safe, you ask? All right, let's examine it in a little more detail:

1. We're exception-neutral. We don't catch anything, so if the new throws then the exception is correctly propagated up to our caller as required.
2. We don't leak. If the operator new[] allocation call exited by throwing a bad_alloc exception, then no memory was allocated to begin with so there can't be a leak. If one of the T constructors threw, then any T objects that were fully constructed were properly destroyed and finally operator delete[] was automatically called to release the memory. That makes us leak proof, as advertised.*
3. We're in a consistent state whether any part of the new throws or not. Now, you might think that if the new throws, then vsize_ has already been set to 10 when in fact nothing was successfully allocated. Isn't that inconsistent? Not really, because it's true, yet irrelevant. Remember, if the new throws, we propagate the exception out of our own constructor, right? And, by definition, "exiting a constructor by means of an exception" means our Stack proto-object never actually got to become a completely constructed object at all, its lifetime never started, and hence its state is meaningless since the object never existed. It doesn't matter what the memory that briefly held vsize_ was set to, any more than it matters what the memory was set to after we leave an object's destructor. All that's left is raw memory, smoke, and ashes.

All right, I admit it... I put the "new" in the constructor body purely to open the door for this #3 discussion. What I'd actually prefer to write is

```
template<class T>
Stack<T>::Stack()
: v_(new T[10]),        // default allocation
vsize_(10),
vused_(0)    // nothing used yet
{}
```

Both versions are practically equivalent. I prefer the latter because it follows the usual good practice of initializing members in initializer lists whenever possible.

* I'm ignoring for now the possibility that one of the T destructor calls might throw during the cleanup, which would call terminate() and simply kill the program altogether leaving events well out of your control anyway. See the forthcoming follow-up article for more information on "Destructors That Throw and Why They're Evil."

Destruction

The destructor looks a lot easier, once we make a (greatly) simplifying assumption:

```
template<class T>
Stack<T>::~Stack() {
  delete[] v_;          // this can't throw
}
```

Why can't the delete[] call throw? Recall that this invokes T::~T() for each object in the array, then calls operator delete[] to deallocate the memory. Now, we know that the deallocation by operator delete[] may never throw, since its signature is always one of the following:

```
void operator delete[](void*) throw();
void operator delete[](void*, size_t) throw();
```

Hence the only thing that could possibly throw is one of the T::~T() calls, and we're arbitrarily going to have Stack require that T::~T() may not throw. Why? To make a long story short, we just can't implement the Stack destructor with complete exception safety if T::~T() can throw, that's why. However, requiring that T::~T() may not throw isn't particularly onerous, since there are plenty of other reasons why destructors should never be allowed to throw at all.† Any T::~T() that can throw is likely to cause you all sorts of other problems sooner or later anyway and you can't even reliably new[] or delete[] an array of them. More on that next time.

Copy Construction and Copy Assignment

The next few functions will use a common helper function, NewCopy, to manage allocating and growing memory. NewCopy takes a pointer to (src) and size of (srcsize) an existing T buffer, and returns a pointer to a new and possibly larger copy of the buffer, passing ownership of the new buffer to the caller. If exceptions are encountered, NewCopy correctly releases all temporary re-

† Frankly, you won't go far wrong if you just habitually write "throw()" after the declaration of every destructor you ever write. Even if exception specifications cause expensive checks under your current compiler, at least write all your destructors as though they were specified as "throw()"... that is, never allow exceptions to leave destructors.

sources and propagates the exception in such a way that nothing is leaked:

```
template<class T>
T* NewCopy( const T* src,
        size_t  srcsize,
        size_t  destsize ) {
  assert( destsize >= srcsize );
  T* dest = new T[destsize];

  try {
    copy( src, src+srcsize, dest );
  } catch(...) {
    delete[] dest;  // this can't throw
    throw;                    // rethrow original exception
  }
  return dest;
}
```

Let's analyze this one step at a time:

1. In the new statement, the allocation might throw bad_alloc or the T::T()'s may throw anything. In either case, nothing is allocated and we simply allow the exception to propagate. This is leak-free and exception-neutral.
2. Next, we assign all the existing values using T::operator=(). If any of the assignments fail, we catch the exception, free the allocated memory, and rethrow the original exception. This is again both leak-free and exception-neutral.
3. If the allocation and copy both succeeded, then we return the pointer to the new buffer and relinquish ownership (that is, the caller is responsible for the buffer from here on out). The return simply copies the pointer value, which cannot throw.

With NewCopy() in hand, the Stack copy constructor is easy to write:

```
template<class T>
Stack<T>::Stack( const Stack<T>& other )
  : v_(NewCopy( other.v_,
                other.vsize_,
                other.vsize_ )),
    vsize_(other.vsize_),
    vused_(other.vused_)
{ }
```

The only possible exception is from NewCopy(), which manages its own resources. Next, we tackle copy assignment:

```
template<class T>
Stack<T>&
Stack<T>::operator=( const Stack<T>& other ) {
   if( this != &other ) {
      T* v_new = NewCopy( other.v_,
                          other.vsize_,
                          other.vsize_ );
      delete[] v_;            // this can't throw
      v_ = v_new;             // take ownership
      vsize_ = other.vsize_;
      vused_ = other.vused_;
   }
   return *this;       // safe, no copy involved
}
```

Again, after the routine weak guard against self-assignment, only the NewCopy() might throw, and if it does we correctly propagate that exception without affecting the Stack object's state. To the caller, if the assignment throws the state is unchanged, and if it doesn't throw the assignment and all of its side effects are successful and complete.

Size(), Push(), and Pop()

The easiest of all Stack's members to implement safely is Size(), since all it does is copy a built-in that can never throw:

```
template<class T>
size_t Stack<T>::Size() const {
   return vused_;      // safe, built-ins don't throw
}
```

However, with Push() we need to apply our now-usual duty of care:

```
template<class T>
void Stack<T>::Push( const T& t ) {
   if( vused_ == vsize_ )       // grow if necessary
   {                            // by some grow factor
```

```
        size_t vsize_new = (vsize_+1)*2;
        T* v_new = NewCopy( v_, vsize_, vsize_new );
        delete[] v_;      // this can't throw
        v_ = v_new;       // take ownership
        vsize_ = vsize_new;
    }

    v_[vused_] = t;
    ++vused_;
}
```

If we have no more space, we first pick a new size for the buffer and make a larger copy using NewCopy(). Again, if NewCopy() throws, our own Stack's state is unchanged and the exception propagates through cleanly. Deleting the original buffer and taking ownership of the new one involves only operations that are known not to throw, so the if block is exception-safe.

After any required grow operation, we attempt to copy the new value before incrementing our vused_ count. This way, if the assignment throws, the increment is not performed and our Stack's state is unchanged. If the assignment succeeds, the Stack's state is changed to recognize the presence of the new value, and all is well.

Only one function left... that wasn't so hard, was it? Well, don't get too happy just yet, because it turns out that Pop() is the most problematic of these functions to write with complete exception safety. Our initial attempt might look something like this:

```
template<class T>
T Stack<T>::Pop() {
    if( vused_ == 0) {
        throw "pop from empty stack";
    } else {
        T result = v_[vused_-1];
        --vused_;
        return result;
    }
}
```

If the stack is empty, we throw an appropriate exception. Otherwise, we create a copy of the T object to be returned, update our state, and return the T object. If the initial copy from v_[vused_-1] fails, the exception is propagated and the state of the Stack is unchanged, which is what we want. If the initial copy succeeds, our state is updated and the Stack is in its new consistent state, which is also what we want. So this works, right?

Well, kind of. There is a subtle flaw here that's completely outside the purview of Stack::Pop(). Consider the following client code:

```
int i(s.Pop());
int j;
j = s.Pop();
```

Note that above we talked about "the initial copy" (from v_[vused_-1]). That's because there is another copy[Δ] to worry about in either of the above cases, namely the copy of the returned temporary into the destination. If that copy construction or copy assignment fails, then the Stack has completed its side effect (the top element has been popped off) but the popped value is now lost forever because it never reached its destination (oops). This is bad news. In effect, it means that any version of Pop() that is written to return a temporary like this cannot be made completely exception-safe, because even though the function's implementation itself may look technically exception-safe, it forces clients of Stack to write exception-unsafe code.

The bottom line—and it's significant—is this: Exception safety affects your class's design! In other words, you must design for exception safety from the outset, and exception safety is never "just an implementation detail." One alternative, in fact the minimum possible change,[ß] is to respecify Pop() as follows:

```
template<class T>
void Stack<T>::Pop( T& result ) {
    if( vused_ == 0) {
        throw "pop from empty stack";
    } else {
        result = v_[vused_-1];
        --vused_;
    }
}
```

Δ Actually, "zero or more copies" since the compiler is free to optimize away the second copy, perform only a single additional second copy, or insert arbitrarily many more copies in between, whatever it's in the mood to do. Bottom line, you have to assume that at least one more copy can be done here to get the temporary return value into the target of the assignment or initialization.

ß The minimum possible acceptable change, that is. You could always simply change the original version to return T& instead of T (this would be a reference to the popped T object, since for the time being the popped object happens to still physically exist in your internal representation) and then the caller could still write exception-safe code. But this business of returning references to "I no longer consider it there" resources is just purely evil. If you change your implementation in the future, this may no longer be possible! Don't go there.

This ensures that the Stack's state is not changed unless the copy arrives safely in the caller's hands. Another option (and a preferable one in my opinion) is to separate the functions of "querying the topmost value" and "popping the topmost value off the stack." We do this by having one function for each:

```
template<class T>
T& Stack<T>::Top() {
   if( vused_ == 0) {
      throw "empty stack";
   } else {
      return v_[vused_-1];
   }
}

template<class T>
void Stack<T>::Pop() {
   if( vused_ == 0) {
      throw "pop from empty stack";
   } else {
      --vused_;
   }
}
```

Incidentally, have you ever grumbled at the way the standard library containers' pop functions (e.g., list::pop_back(), stack::pop(), etc.) don't return the popped value? Well, here's one reason why: to avoid weakening exception safety.

In fact, you've probably noticed that the above separated Top() and Pop() now match the signatures top() and pop() members of the standard library's stack<> adapter. That's no coincidence! We're actually only two public member functions away from the stack<> adapter's full public interface, namely:

```
template<class T>
const T& Stack<T>::Top() const {
   if( vused_ == 0) {
      throw "empty stack";
   } else {
      return v_[vused_-1];
   }
}
```

to provide Top() for const Stack objects, and:

```
template<class T>
bool Stack<T>::Empty() const {
   return( vused_ == 0 );
}
```

Of course, the standard stack<> is actually a container adapter that's implemented in terms of another container, but the public interface is the same and the rest is just an implementation detail.

Levels of Safety

Just as there's more than one way to skin a cat (somehow I have a feeling I'm going to get enraged email from animal lovers), there's more than one way to write exception-safe code. In fact, there are two main alternatives we can choose from when it comes to guaranteeing exception safety:

1. *Basic Guarantee:* "Even in the presence of T or other exceptions, Stack objects don't leak resources." Note that this also implies the container will be destructible and usable even if an exception is thrown while performing some container operation. However, if an exception is thrown, the container will be in a consistent, but not necessarily predictable state. Containers that support the basic guarantee can work safely in most settings.
2. *Strong Guarantee:* "If an operation terminates because of an exception, program state will remain unchanged." This always implies commit-or-rollback semantics, including that no references or iterators into the container be invalidated if an operation fails. For example, if a Stack client calls Top() and then attempts a Push(), that fails because of an exception, then the state of the Stack object must be unchanged and the reference returned from the prior call to Top() must still be valid. For more information on these guarantees, see Dave Abrahams' documentation of the SGI exception-safe standard library adaptation at http://www.ipmce.su/~fbp/ stl/eh_contract.html.

Probably the most interesting point here is that when you implement the basic guarantee, the strong guarantee often comes along for free. For example, in our Stack implementation, almost everything we did was needed to satisfy just the basic guarantee... and we got the strong guarantee with little or no extra work. Not half bad, considering all the trouble we went to.

Points to Ponder

Note that we've been able to implement `Stack` to be not only exception-safe but fully exception-neutral, yet we've used only a single try/catch. As we'll see in the next issue, using the private base class technique can get rid of even this try block. Writing a fully exception-safe and exception-neutral generic container without using "`try`" or "`catch`"... heck, that's kind of cool!

As originally defined, `Stack` requires its instantiation type to have:

- default constructor (to construct the `v_` buffers)
- copy constructor (if `Pop()` returns by value)
- nonthrowing destructor (to be able to guarantee exception safety)
- copy assignment (to set the values in `v_`)

In a future article, we'll also see how to reduce even these requirements without compromising exception safety, and along the way we'll get an even more detailed look at the standard operation of the statement "`delete[] x;`."

Reference

1. Cargill, T. "Exception Handling: A False Sense of Security," *C++ Report*, 9(6), Nov./Dec. 1994, available online at http://www.awl.com/cp/mec++-cargill.html.

More Exception-Safe Generic Containers

Previously,[1] we considered a basic Stack template originally analyzed by Cargill in "Exception Handling: A False Sense of Security,"[2] and demonstrated how to write a container that is both exception-safe (works properly in the presence of exceptions) and exception-neutral (propagates all exceptions to the caller). This time we'll delve deeper into the same example, and write two new and improved versions of `Stack`. Not only is it possible to write exception-safe generic containers, but between the last article and this one we'll have demonstrated no fewer than three different solutions to the exception-safe `Stack` problem.

We'll also answer several more interesting questions:

- How can we use more advanced techniques to simplify the way we manage resources, and get rid of the last try/catch in the bargain?
- How can we improve Stack by reducing the requirements on T, the contained type?
- Should generic containers use exception specifications?
- What do "new[]" and "delete[]" really do?

The answer to the last may be quite different than you expect. Writing exception-safe containers in C++ isn't rocket science; it just requires significant care and a good understanding of how the language works. In particular, it helps to develop a habit of eyeing with mild suspicion anything that might turn out to be a function call—including user-defined operators, user-defined conversions, and silent temporary objects, among the more subtle culprits—since any function call might throw.*

An Improved Stack

One way to greatly simplify an exception-safe container like Stack is to use better encapsulation. Specifically, we'd like to encapsulate the basic memory management work. Most of the care we had to take while writing our original exception-safe Stack was needed just to get the basic memory allocation right, so let's introduce a simple helper class to put all of that work in one place:

```
template <class T> class StackImpl {
/*????*/:
   StackImpl(size_t size=0)
      : v_( static_cast<T*>
            ( size == 0
               ? 0
               : ::operator new(sizeof(T)*size) ) ),
         vsize_(size),
         vused_(0)
   { }

   ~StackImpl() {
```

* Except for functions declared with an exception specification of "throw()", or certain functions in the standard library that are documented to never throw.

```
        destroy( v_, v_+vused_ );   // this can't throw
        ::operator delete( v_ );
    }

    void Swap(StackImpl& other) throw() {
        swap(v_, other.v_);
        swap(vsize_, other.vsize_);
        swap(vused_, other.vused_);
    }

    T*     v_;            // ptr to a memory area big
    size_t vsize_;        // enough for 'vsize_' T's
    size_t vused_;        // # of T's actually in use
};
```

There's nothing magical going on here: StackImpl is responsible for simple raw memory management and final cleanup, so that any class using it won't have to worry about those details. We won't spend much time analyzing why this class is fully exception-safe and exception-neutral; the reasons are pretty much the same as those we dissected in detail last time.

Note that StackImpl has all of the original Stack's data members, so that we've essentially moved the original Stack's representation entirely into StackImpl. StackImpl also has a helper function named Swap(), which exchanges the guts of our StackImpl object with those of another StackImpl.

Before reading on, stop and think about this class and consider: What access specifier would you write in place of the comment "/*????*/"? How might you use a class like this to simplify Stack? (Hint: the name StackImpl itself hints at some kind of "implemented-in-terms-of" relationship, and there are two main ways to write that kind of relationship in C++.)

TECHNIQUE 1: PRIVATE BASE CLASS

The missing /*????*/ access specifier must be either "protected" or "public." (If it were private, no one could use the class.) First, consider what happens if we make it "protected."

Using "protected" means that StackImpl is intended to be used as a private base class. So Stack will be "implemented in terms of" StackImpl, which is what private inheritance means, and we have a clear division of responsibilities: the StackImpl base class will take care of managing the memory buffer and destroying all remaining T objects during Stack destruction, while the Stack derived class

Some Standard Helper Functions

The Stack and StackImpl presented in this article use three helper functions from the standard library: construct(), destroy(), and swap(). In simplified form, here's what these functions look like:

```
// construct() constructs a new object in
// a given location using an initial value
//
template <class T1, class T2>
void construct( T1* p, const T2& value ) {
  new (p) T1(value);
}
```

This is called "placement new," and instead of allocating memory for the new object it puts it into the memory pointed at by p. Any object new'd in this way should generally be destroyed by calling its destructor explicitly (as in the following two functions), rather than using "delete".

```
// destroy() destroys an object or a range of objects
//
template <class T>
void destroy( T* p ) {
  p->~T();
}

template <class FwdIter>
void destroy( FwdIter first, FwdIter last ) {
  while( first != last ) {
      destroy( first );
      ++first;
  }
}

// swap() just exchanges two values
//
template <class T>
void swap( T& a, T& b ) {
  T temp(a); a = b; b = temp;
}
```

Of these, destroy(iter,iter) is the most interesting. We'll return to it a little later in the main article; it illustrates more than you might think!

To find out more about these standard functions, take a few minutes to examine how they're written in the standard library implementation you're using. It's a very worthwhile and enlightening exercise.

will take care of constructing all T objects within the raw memory. The raw memory management takes place pretty much entirely outside Stack itself, since, for example, the initial allocation must fully succeed before any Stack constructor can be called. So far, so good.

Using the private base class method, our Stack class will look something like this (the code is shown inlined for brevity):

```
template <class T>
class Stack : private StackImpl<T> {
public:
   Stack(size_t size=0) : StackImpl<T>(size) { }
```

Stack's default constructor simply calls the default constructor of StackImpl, which sets the stack's state to empty and optionally performs an initial allocation. The only operation here which might throw is the 'new' done in StackImpl's constructor, and that's unimportant when considering Stack's own exception safety; if it does happen, we won't enter the Stack constructor and there will never have been a Stack object at all, so any initial allocation failures in the base class don't affect Stack. (See the previous article for additional comments about exiting constructors via an exception.)

Note that we slightly changed Stack's original constructor interface to allow a starting 'hint' at the amount of memory to allocate. We'll make use of this in a minute when we write the Push() function.

We don't need to provide a Stack destructor. The default compiler-generated Stack destructor is fine, since it just calls the StackImpl destructor to destroy any objects that were constructed and actually free the memory.

```
Stack(const Stack& other)
   : StackImpl<T>(other.vused_)
{
   while( vused_ < other.vused_ ) {
      construct( v_+vused_, other.v_[vused_] );
      ++vused_;
   }
};
```

Copy construction now becomes efficient and elegant. The worst that can happen here is that a T constructor could fail, in which case the StackImpl destructor will correctly destroy exactly as many objects as were successfully created, and then deallocate the raw memory. One big benefit derived from

StackImpl is that we can add as many more constructors as we want without putting cleanup code inside each one.

```
Stack& operator=(const Stack& other) {
   Stack temp(other);          // does all the work
   Swap( temp );     // this can't throw
   return *this;
}
```

Copy assignment is even more elegant, if a little subtle: we construct a temporary object from other, then call Swap() to swap our own guts with temp's, and finally when temp goes out of scope and destroys itself, it automatically cleans up our old guts in the process, leaving us with the new state. Also, when operator= is made exception-safe like this, a side effect is that it usually also automatically handles self-assignment (e.g., Stack s; s =s s;) correctly without further work. (Since self-assignment is exceedingly rare, I omitted the traditional "if(this != &other)" test which has its own subtle problems. (See Guru of the Week #11 at www.cntc.com/resources/gotw011.html for all the gory details.)

Note that since all the real work is done while constructing temp, any exceptions that might be thrown (either by memory allocation or T copy construction) can't affect the state of our object. Also, there won't be any memory leaks or other problems from the temp object because the Stack copy constructor is already fully exception-neutral. Once all the work is done, we simply swap our object's internal representation with temp's, which cannot throw (because Swap() has a "throw()" exception specification, and because it does nothing but copy built-ins), and we're done.

Note how much more elegant this is than the exception-safe copy assignment we implemented last time! This version also requires much less care to ensure that it's been made properly exception-safe.

```
size_t Count() const {
   return vused_;
}
```

Yes, Count() is still the easiest member function to write.

```
void Push( const T& t ) {
   if( vused_ == vsize_ ) { // grow if necessary
      Stack temp( (vsize_+1)*2 );
      while( temp.Count() < vused_ ) {
         temp.Push( v_[temp.Count()] );
      }
```

```
        temp.Push( t );
        Swap( temp );
    }
    else {
        construct( v_+vused_, t );
        ++vused_;
    }
}
```

First, consider the simple 'else' case: if we already have room for the new object, we attempt to construct it. If the construction succeeds, we update our vused_ count. This is safe and straightforward.

Otherwise, like last time, if we don't have enough room for the new element, we trigger a reallocation. In this case, we simply construct a temporary Stack object, push the new element onto that, and finally swap out our original guts to it to ensure they're disposed of in a tidy fashion.

But is this exception-safe? Yes. Consider:

1. If the construction of temp fails, our state is unchanged and no resources have been leaked, so that's fine.
2. If any part of the loading of temp's contents (including the new object's copy construction) fails by throwing an exception, temp is properly cleaned up when its destructor is called as temp goes out of scope.
3. In no case do we alter our state until all the work has already been completed successfully.

Note that this provides the strong commit-or-rollback guarantee, because the Swap() is performed only if the entire reallocate-and-push operation succeeds. If we were supporting iterators into this container, for instance, they would never be invalidated (by a possible internal grow operation) if the insertion is not completely successful:

```
T& Top() {
    if( vused_ == 0) {
        throw "empty stack";
    }
    return v_[vused_-1];
}
```

The Top() function hasn't changed at all.

```
    void Pop() {
        if( vused_ == 0) {
            throw "pop from empty stack";
        } else {
            —vused_;
            destroy( v_+vused_ );
        }
    }
};
```

Neither has Pop(), except for the new call to destroy().

In summary, Push() has been simplified, but the biggest benefit of encapsulating the resource ownership in a separate class was seen in Stack's constructor and destructor. Thanks to StackImpl, we could now go on to write as many more constructors as we like without having to worry about cleanup code, whereas last time each constructor would have had to know about the cleanup itself.

You may also have noticed that even the lone try/catch we had to include in the first version of this class has now been eliminated—that is, we've written a fully exception-safe and exception-neutral generic container without writing a single "try"! (Who says writing exception-safe code is trying?)

Technique 2: Private Matter

Next, consider what happens if StackImpl's missing /*????*/ access specifier is "public."

Using "public" hints that StackImpl is intended to be used as a struct by some external client, since its data members are public. So again Stack will be "implemented in terms of" StackImpl, only this time using a "has-a" containment relationship instead of private inheritance. We still have the same clear division of responsibilities: the StackImpl object will take care of managing the memory buffer and destroying all T objects remaining during Stack destruction, and the containing Stack will take care of constructing T objects within the raw memory. Because subobjects are created before a class's constructor body is entered, the raw memory management still takes place pretty much entirely outside Stack, since, for example, the initial allocation must fully succeed before any Stack constructor body can be entered.

This implementation of Stack is only slightly different from the above. For example, Count() returns impl_.vused_ instead of just an inherited vused_. See Listing 1 for the complete code.

WHICH TECHNIQUE IS BETTER?

So, how do you choose between using StackImpl as a private base class or as a member object? After all, both give essentially the same effect and nicely separate the two concerns of memory management and object construction/destruction.

When deciding between private inheritance and containment, my rule of thumb is to always prefer the latter and use inheritance only when absolutely necessary. Both techniques mean "is implemented in terms of," and containment forces a better separation of concerns since the using class is a normal client with access to only the used class's public interface. Use private inheritance instead of containment only when absolutely necessary, which means when either:

- you need access to the class's protected members;

or

- you need to override a virtual function.††

RELAXING THE REQUIREMENTS ON T

When writing a templated class, particularly something as potentially widely useful as a generic container, always ask yourself one crucial question: How reusable is my class? That is, what constraints have I put upon users of the class, and do those constraints unduly limit what those users might reasonably want to do with my class?

These Stack templates have two major differences from the one in the last article. We've discussed one already: they decouple memory management from contained object construction and destruction, which is nice but doesn't really affect users. However, there is another important difference: the new Stacks construct and destroy individual objects in-place as needed, instead of creating default T objects in the entire buffer and then assigning them as needed.

This second difference turns out to have significant benefits: efficiency, and reducing the requirements on T, the contained type. Our original Stack from last time required T to provide four operations:

†† Admittedly, in this case it's tempting to use private inheritance anyway for syntactic convenience so that we wouldn't have to write "impl_." in so many places.

- default constructor (to construct the v_ buffers)
- copy constructor (if Pop() returns by value)
- nonthrowing destructor (to guarantee exception safety)
- copy assignment (to set the values in v_)

Now, however, no default construction is needed since the only T construction that's ever performed is copy construction. Furthermore, no copy assignment is needed since T objects are never assigned within Stack or StackImpl. On the other hand, now we always need a copy constructor. This means that the new Stacks require only two things of T:

- copy constructor
- nonthrowing destructor (to guarantee exception safety)

How does this measure up to our original question about usability? While it's true that many classes have both default constructors and copy assignment operators, many useful classes do not. (In fact, some objects simply cannot be assigned to, such as objects that contain reference members, since references cannot be reseated.) Now, even these can be put into Stacks, whereas in the original version they could not. That's definitely a big advantage over the original version, and one that quite a few users are likely to appreciate as the Stack class gets reused over time.

Should Stack Provide Exception Specifications?

In short: No, because we the authors of Stack don't know enough, and we still probably wouldn't want to even if we did. The same is true in principle for any generic container.

First, consider what we as the authors of Stack do know about T, the contained type: the answer is, precious little. In particular, we don't know in advance which T operations might throw or what they might throw. We could always get a little fascist about it and start dictating additional requirements on T, which would certainly let us know more about T and maybe add some useful exception specifications to Stack's member functions. However, doing that would run completely counter to the goal of making Stack widely reusable, and so it's really out of the question.

Next, you might notice that some container operations (e.g., Count()) simply return a scalar and are known not to throw. Isn't it possible to declare these as "throw()"? Yes, but there are two good reasons why you probably wouldn't:

1. Writing "throw()" limits you in the future if you want to change the underlying implementation to a form which could throw. Loosening an exception specification always runs some risk of breaking existing clients (since the new revision of the class breaks an old promise), and so your class will be inherently more resistant to change and therefore more brittle. (Writing "throw()" on virtual functions can also make classes less extensible, since it greatly restricts people who might want to derive from your classes. It can make sense, but such a decision requires careful thought.)
2. Exception specifications can incur a performance overhead whether an exception is thrown or not, although many compilers are getting better at minimizing this. For widely-used operations and general-purpose containers, it may be better not to use exception specifications to avoid this overhead.

DESTRUCTORS THAT THROW AND WHY THEY'RE EVIL

This brings us to our last topic, namely the innocent-looking "delete[] p;". What does it really do? And how safe is it?

First, recall our standard destroy() helper function (see the accompanying sidebar, "Some Standard Helper Functions"):

```
template <class FwdIter>
void destroy( FwdIter first, FwdIter last ) {
   while( first != last ) {
      destroy( first ); // calls "*first"'s dtor
      ++first;
   }
}
```

This was safe in our example above because we required that T destructors never throw. But what if a contained object's destructor were allowed to throw? Well, consider what happens if destroy() is passed a range of five objects: If the first destructor throws, then as it is written now destroy() will exit and the other four objects will never be destroyed! This is obviously not a good thing.

"Ah," you might interrupt, "but can't we clearly get around that by writing destroy() to work properly in the face of T's whose destructors are allowed

Exception Safety and the Standard Library

Are the standard library containers exception-safe and exception-neutral? The short answer is: Yes.[#] All standard containers must implement the basic guarantee: they are always destructible, and they are always in a consistent (if not predictable) state even in the presence of exceptions. To make this possible, certain important functions are required not to throw—including `swap()` and `allocator::deallocate()`, the importance of which were illustrated by our example above and the discussion of ::`operator delete()` last time, respectively.

However, only the list container must implement the strong guarantee: it always has commit-or-rollback semantics, so that either an operation (e.g., an insert) succeeds completely or else it does not change the program state at all. "No change" also means that failed operations do not affect the validity of any iterators that happened to be already pointing into the list.

The other containers are not required to implement the strong guarantee with its commit-and-rollback semantics for all operations. For example, in the presence of exceptions a map or vector will not have predictable contents after certain operations, even though it is still in a usable state. Why does `list` get preferred treatment? One reason is that `list` is one of those cases where, if you implement the basic guarantee, the strong guarantee comes along for free. Another is for efficiency reasons, since, for example, some vector operations cannot provide strong commit-or-rollback semantics without incurring some extra overhead.

What does this mean for you? Well, if you write a class that has a container member other than list, you are responsible for doing the extra work to ensure that your own class's state is predictable if exceptions occur. Fortunately, this "extra work" is pretty simple, although it can degrade performance more than if the strong guarantees had been implemented in the containers themselves: whenever you want to change the container, take a copy of the container, perform the change on the copy, and use `swap()` to switch over to using that new version after the change has succeeded.

Note that vendors can still provide the strong guarantee for other standard library containers (or selected operations thereof) if they want to, even though the standard doesn't force them to. For example, Silicon Graphics's (SGI's) adapted implementation already goes farther than what the draft standard requires, and provides the strong guarantee for all container operations where it does not hurt efficiency.

[#] Here we're focusing our attention on the containers and iterators portion of the standard library. Other parts of the library, such as iostreams and facets, are specified to be strongly exception-safe.

to throw?" Well, that's not as clear as you might think. For example, you'd probably start writing something like this:

```
template <class FwdIter>
void destroy( FwdIter first, FwdIter last ) {
   while( first != last ) {
      try {
         destroy( first );
      } catch(...) {
         /* what goes here? */
      }
      ++first;
   }
}
```

The tricky part is the "what goes here?" There are really only three choices: either the catch body rethrows the exception, or it converts the exception by throwing something else, or it throws nothing and continues the loop.

1. If the catch body rethrows the exception, then the destroy() function nicely meets the requirement of being exception-neutral, since it does indeed allow any T exceptions to propagate out normally. However, it still doesn't meet the safety requirement that no resources be leaked if exceptions occur. Since destroy() has no way of signaling how many objects were not successfully destroyed, those objects can never be properly destroyed and so any resources associated with them will be unavoidably leaked. Definitely not good.
2. If the catch body converts the exception by throwing something else, we've clearly failed to meet both the neutrality and the safety requirements. Enough said.
3. If the catch body does not throw or rethrow anything, then the destroy() function nicely meets the safety requirement that no resources be leaked if an exception is thrown.[Δ] However, obviously it fails to meet the neutrality requirement that T exceptions be allowed to pass through, since exceptions are absorbed and ignored (as far as the caller is concerned, even if the catch body does attempt to do some sort of logging).

Δ True, if a T destructor could throw in a way that its resources might not be completely released, then there could still be a leak. However, this isn't destroy()'s problem—this just means that T itself is not exception-safe, but destroy() is still properly leak-free in that it doesn't fail to release any resources that it should (namely the T objects themselves).

Listing 1.

```
template <class T>
class Stack {
public:
   Stack(size_t size=0) : impl_(size) { }

   Stack(const Stack& other) : impl_(other.impl_.vused_)
   {
      while( impl_.vused_ < other.impl_.vused_ ) {
         construct( impl_.v_+impl_.vused_,
         other.impl_.v_[impl_.vused_] );++impl_.vused_;
      }
   };

   Stack& operator=(const Stack& other) {
      Stack temp(other);
      impl_.Swap(temp.impl_);  // this can't throw
      return *this;
   }

   size_t Count() const {
      return impl_.vused_;
   }

   void Push( const T& t ) {
      if( impl_.vused_ == impl_.vsize_ ) {
         Stack temp( (impl_.vsize_+1)*2 );
         while( temp.Count() < impl_.vused_ ) {
            temp.Push( impl_.v_[temp.Count()] );
         }
         temp.Push( t );
         impl_.Swap( temp.impl_ );
      }
      else {
         construct( v_+vused_, t );
         ++vused_;
      }
   }

   T& Top() {
      if( impl_.vused_ == 0) {
         throw "empty stack";
```

(continued)

Listing 1. (continued)

```
        }
        return impl_.v_[impl_.vused_-1];
    }

    void Pop() {
        if( impl_.vused_ == 0) {
            throw "pop from empty stack";
        } else {
            —impl_.vused_;
            destroy( impl_.v_+impl_.vused_ );
        }
    }

private:
    StackImpl<T> impl_; // private implementation
    };
```

I've heard people suggest that the function should catch the exception and "save" it while continuing to destroy everything else, then rethrow it at the end. That, too, isn't a solution; for example, it can't correctly deal with multiple exceptions should multiple T destructors throw (even if you save them all until the end, you can only end by throwing one of them, and the others are silently absorbed). You might be thinking of other alternatives, but trust me, they all boil down to writing code like this somewhere, because you have a set of objects and they all need to be destroyed. Someone, somewhere, is going to end up writing nonexception-neutral code (at best) if T destructors are ever allowed to throw.

Which brings us to the innocent-looking "new[]" and "delete[]". The issue with both of these is that they have fundamentally the same problem we just described for destroy()! For example, consider the following code:

```
T* p = new T[10];
delete[] p;
```

Looks like normal harmless C++, doesn't it? But have you ever wondered what new[] and delete[] do if a T destructor throws? Even if you have wondered, you can't know the answer for the simple reason that there isn't one: the draft standard says you get undefined behavior if a T destructor throws anywhere in this code, which means that any code that allocates or deallocates an array of objects whose destructors could throw can result in undefined behavior. This may raise some eyebrows, so let's see why this is so:

First, consider what happens if the constructions all succeed, and then during the delete[] operation the fifth T destructor throws. Then delete[] has the same catch-22 problem outlined above for destroy(): it can't allow the exception to propagate, because then the remaining T objects would be irretrievably undestroyable, but it also can't translate or absorb the exception since then it wouldn't be exception-neutral.

Second, consider what happens if the fifth constructor throws. Then the fourth object's destructor is invoked, then the third's, and so on until all the T objects that were successfully constructed have again been destroyed, and the memory is safely deallocated. But what if things don't go so smoothly? In particular, what if after the fifth constructor throws, the fourth object's destructor throws? And, if that's ignored, the third's? You can see where this is going.

If destructors may throw, then neither new[] nor delete[] can be made exception-safe and exception-neutral.

The bottom line is simply this: Don't *ever* write destructors that can allow an exception to escape.[ß] If you do write a class with such a destructor, you will not be able to safely even new[] or delete[] an array of those objects. All destructors should always be implemented as though they had an exception specification of "throw();". That is, no exceptions must ever be allowed to propagate.

Granted, some may feel that this state of affairs is a little unfortunate, since one of the original reasons for having exceptions was to allow both constructors and destructors to report failures (since they have no return values). This isn't quite true, since the intent was mainly for constructor failures (after all, destructors are supposed to destroy, so the scope for failure is definitely smaller). The good news is that exceptions are still perfectly useful for reporting construction failures, including array and array-new[] construction failures, since there they can work predictably even if a construction does throw.

Safe Exceptions

The advice "be aware, drive with care" certainly applies to writing exception-

[ß] As of the London meeting, the draft makes the blanket statement: "No destructor operation defined in the C++ Standard Library will throw an exception." Not only do all of the satndard classes have this property, but, in particular, it is illegal to instatiate a standard container with a type whose destructor does throw.

safe code for containers and other objects. To do it successfully, you do have to meet a sometimes significant extra duty of care, but don't get unduly frightened by exceptions. Apply the guidelines outlined above—that is, isolate your resource management, use the "update a temporary and swap" idiom, and never write classes whose destructors can allow exceptions to escape—and you'll be well on your way to safe and happy production code that is both exception-safe and exception-neutral. The advantages can be both concrete and well worth the trouble for your library and your library's users.

ACKNOWLEDGMENTS

Thanks to Dave Abrahams and Greg Colvin for their comments. Dave and Greg are, with Matt Austern, the authors of the two complete committee proposals for adding these exception safety guarantees into the standard library. A compromise between these two similar proposals was accepted at the London meeting in July 1997 (see accompanying sidebar, "Exception Safety and the Standard Library").

REFERENCES

1. Sutter, H. "Designing Exception-Safe Generic Containers," *C++ Report*, Sept. 1997.
2. Cargill T. "Exception Handling: A False Sense of Security," *C++ Report*, Nov./Dec. 1994, also available at http://www.awl.com/cp/mec++-cargill.html.

The Anatomy of the Assignment Operator

Richard Gillam

Another terrific addition to the editorial staff of the C++ Report, *Rich Gillam writes the Java Liason column. In that column he compares and contrasts the various features of Java and C++.*

In this duet, Rich talks about the C++ assignment operator. Again, like Herb, he is concerned with exceptions. And there are some strong similarities between the articles. Still, Rich has a different perspective that anyone writing C++ code need to understand.

My team recently hired someone. Normally, this wouldn't be such a big deal, but we've been looking for someone for a year and a half. In that time, we interviewed at least a dozen candidates and phone-screened at least a couple of dozen more. Practically every candidate we talked to had at least two years of C++ experience, rated himself a 7 or 8 on a scale of 10 in C++ skills, and had one or two lucrative offers on the table. Unfortunately, we would have rated almost all of them somewhere between a 4 and a 6. In my opinion, this shows that working with C++ for a long time doesn't guarantee that you really understand the language.

During our search, I developed a stock interview question that's proven to be a pretty good gauge of C++ knowledge. No one has yet been able to just rip out the correct answer, but we had several, including the guy we hired, who understood the important issues and were able to get the question right with prompting. As a public service, I'd like to share my stock question and its answer with you, exploring the various programming issues it presents. The question is as follows:

> Consider the following class definition:
>
> ```
> class TFoo : public TSuperFoo {
>     TBar*  fBar1;
>     TBar*  fBar2;
> // various method definitions go here...
> };
> ```
>
> You have a class, TFoo, descending from a class, TSuperFoo, which has two data members, both of which are pointers to objects of class TBar. For the purpose of this exercise, consider both pointers to have owning semantics and TBar to be a monomorphic class. Write the assignment operator for this class.

This seems like a simple enough exercise, but it gets at some interesting issues. It's a good way to test a programmer's grasp of C++ syntax and style, but more importantly, it tests the programmer's knowledge of C++ memory management and exception handling.

For the impatient among you, let's cut right to the chase; one correct answer to this question would look something like this:

```
TFoo& TFoo::operator=(const TFoo& that)
{
    if (this != &that) {
        TBar*  bar1 = 0;
        TBar*  bar2 = 0;

        try {
            bar1 = new TBar(*that.fBar1);
            bar2 = new TBar(*that.fBar2);
        }
        catch (...) {
            delete bar1;
            delete bar2;
            throw;
        }
        TSuperFoo::operator=(that);
        delete fBar1;
        fBar1 = bar1;
```

```
        delete fBar2;
        fBar2 = bar2;
    }
    return *this;
}
```

Yes, it's a lot of code. Yes, it's ugly. But all the code you see here is necessary. We'll go through it piece by piece and see why.*

"But I Never Have to Write an Assignment Operator!"

The first reaction I usually get from people is something along the lines of "But I never have to write assignment operators." You should. If you've ever created a new class, you've needed to write an assignment operator.

Let's examine why this is so. In C++, there are three things every object is expected to be able to do: An object should be able to initialize itself to a default state, it should be able to initialize itself from another instance of the same class, and it should be able to assume the semantic state of another instance of the same class. In C++, these operations are expressed with the default constructor (e.g., TFoo::TFoo()), the copy constructor: (TFoo::TFoo(const TFoo&)), and the assignment operator: (TFoo& TFoo::operator= (const TFoo&)).

These three functions are special in C++: If you don't provide them yourself, C++ provides them for you, and automatically makes them public. Among other things, this means you have to define these operations even if you *don't want* a client to be able to copy or default-construct a particular class. If you don't want a class to be copied, for example, you have to define an empty copy constructor and assignment operator yourself, and make them private or protected.

Furthermore, the compiler isn't guaranteed to create versions of these functions that do exactly what you want them to do. For copying and assignment, for example, the automatically generated code will do a *shallow member-wise copy*. If your class has pointer members, this is practically never what you want,

---

* The more advanced programmers reading this will probably be able to come up with one or two better ways of doing this than this particular example. Stick with me; I'll get to them. I present this example as a good general solution to the problem that works with almost all C++ compilers.

and even when you don't have pointer members, this isn't always the right behavior. It's definitely not what we want in our example.

Even when the default versions of the special functions do what you want them to, it's still generally a good policy to always spell things out explicitly by writing them yourself. It avoids ambiguity, and it forces you to think more about what's going on inside your class. Always give any new class a default constructor, a copy constructor, and an assignment operator.

COPY VERSUS ASSIGN

Another misconception I see often is a fuzzy idea of the difference between the copy constructor and the assignment operator. They're not the same thing, although they're similar. Let's take a moment to look at the difference.

The copy constructor and assignment operator do similar things. They both copy state from one object to another, leaving them with equivalent semantic state. In other words, both objects will behave the same way and return the same results when their methods are called. If they have public data members (generally a bad idea), they have the same values. This doesn't necessarily mean that the objects are identical: some purely internal data members (such as caches) might not be copied, or data members pointing to other objects might end up pointing to different objects that are themselves semantically equivalent, rather than pointing to the same objects.

The difference between the copy constructor and assignment operator is that the copy constructor is a *constructor*— a function whose job it is to turn raw storage into an object of a specific class. An assignment operator, on the other hand, copies state between two *existing objects*. In other words, an assignment operator has to take into account the current state of the object when copying the other object's state into it. The copy constructor is creating a new object from raw storage and knows it's writing over garbage. For many classes, the current state of the object doesn't matter and both functions do the same thing. But for some classes (including the one in our example), the current state does matter, and the assignment operator is more complicated.

DEFINING THE FUNCTION

WHAT PARAMETERS DOES THE FUNCTION TAKE?

C++ requires that an assignment operator take one parameter: the thing on the right-hand side of the = sign. This can be of any type, but the assignment operator that C++ automatically generates for you (and therefore, the one we're interested in here) is the one where you have the same type of object on both sides of the = sign. That means the parameter is either an instance of or a reference to an instance of the same class as the object on the left-hand side. You'll pretty much always want to use a reference rather than a full-blown instance of the class (i.e., pass by reference instead of pass by value). This is because passing an object by value requires creating a new instance of the class with the same state as the object passed as a parameter: in other words, its copy constructor must be called. This isn't necessary, and it wastes time. The parameter can be either a `const` or a non-`const` reference, but since it would be terrible form for the assignment operator to have side effects on the object on the right-hand side, you should use a `const` reference.

WHAT DOES THE FUNCTION RETURN?

An assignment operator can return anything it wants, but the built-in C and C++ assignment operators return a reference to the left-hand operand. This allows you to chain assignments together like so:

```
x = y = z = 3;
```

Unless you have a *really good reason*, you want to follow this convention. This way, your assignment operator works the same way the built-in ones do, which is what your clients probably expect. Therefore, the outer shell of a properly-written assignment operator would look like this:

```
TFoo& TFoo::operator=(const TFoo& that)
{
    // copy the state...
    return *this;
}
```

VIRTUAL OR NONVIRTUAL?

I had one applicant suggest that operator= should be a virtual function. Let's take a look at this issue. Many C++ programmers are trained to make everything virtual; in fact, some older frameworks do just that. In the specific example of the assignment operator, however, it's not a good idea. An override of a virtual function has to take the same parameters as the function it's overriding. Therefore, TFoo's operator= function would have to be declared as

```
virtual TSuperFoo& TFoo::operator=(TSuperFoo& that);
```

You could declare the function this way and still have it return "this," of course, because a reference to a TFoo *is* a reference to a TSuperFoo. However we have no way of knowing whether "that" is a reference to a TFoo or a reference to some other derivative of TSuperFoo. If it's not a TFoo, you have several problems. First, you'd have to check "that"'s class, which can be expensive. If it isn't a TFoo, you obviously wouldn't want to try to carry out the assignment, but then you'd have to define some kind of error-handling protocol to handle this situation. Better to just make operator= take the right type and let the compiler check the classes of your operands for you at compile time.

Of course, as soon as each class has operands with different types, the functions have different signatures and the operator= function is no longer being overridden. So it doesn't make sense to make operator= virtual.

OWNING AND ALIASING POINTERS

OK, now that we've got the preliminaries out of the way, we can get into the actual nitty-gritty of having our assignment operator actually perform an assignment. Let's refresh our memory of what the object we're working on looks like:

```
class TFoo : public TSuperFoo {
    TBar*  fBar1;
    TBar*  fBar2;
    // method definitions...
};
```

It seems the obvious way to do the assignment would be

```
    TFoo& TFoo::operator=(const TFoo& that)
    {
```

```
        fBar1 = that.fBar1;
        fBar2 = that.fBar2;
        return *this;
    }
```

Unfortunately, that's the wrong answer here. Remember, in the original question I said that fBar1 and fBar2 are *owning* pointers. To understand why the previous example won't do what we want, we need to take a look at the unique problems of C++ memory management.

Because of its evolution from C, C++ is much closer to the hardware than most other object-oriented languages. One of the chief consequences of this is that you have to do your own memory management. Every "new" that happens during a program's execution must be balanced by one and only one "delete." You don't want objects you've allocated to clutter up memory after you're done with them, you don't want to try to delete an object more than once, and you don't want to access an object after you've deleted it. Double-deleting an object can corrupt the memory manager's free list, leading to crashes down the road; reading through a pointer to a deleted object (a "dangling pointer") can lead to wrong results; and writing through a dangling pointer can corrupt other objects or cause crashes. Failing to delete an object you're done with (a "memory leak") is less obviously malignant, but can seriously degrade performance and eventually cause crashes when the system runs out of memory.

In a system of any complexity, sticking to this "one delete for every new" rule can be quite difficult, so a strict protocol for managing memory is necessary. The basic rule we follow at Taligent is that for every object in the runtime environment, there is one and only one pointer to it through which the object can be deleted. This pointer is an "owning pointer," and the object or function containing that pointer is the object's "owner." All other pointers to the object are called "aliasing pointers." The owner of the object expects to delete the object; objects with aliasing pointers don't.

So when we say that TFoo's two TBar pointers are owning pointers, we're saying that TFoo expects to delete those TBars. In other words, its destructor looks like this:

```
TFoo::~TFoo()
{
    delete fBar1;
    delete fBar2;
}
```

You can see that if more than one TFoo object points to a given TBar, then as soon as one of those TFoos is deleted (taking the TBars down with it), the other TFoos are hosed. The next time any one of them tried to access one of its TBar objects, it'd be reading or writing through a dangling pointer, with potentially disastrous consequences. Therefore, every TFoo must have its own unique TBar objects, which means our assignment operator must create new copies of the source object's TBars for the destination object to point to.

In some cases, of course, it's overkill to make a copy of an object, because the current owner of the object is just going to delete that object after passing its content on to another object. In other words, one object is *transferring ownership* of an object to another object. This happens quite frequently. A simple factory method starts out with ownership of the object it creates, but when it returns its value, it passes ownership of that object to the caller. Its return value is an owning pointer. At other times, a function returns a pointer to an object, but intends that the caller merely use it for a short time to perform some operation. Ownership is not transferred; the return value is an aliasing pointer.

When you have functions that return pointers or have pointer parameters, you must make it explicit whether the function transfers ownership, and you must then make sure that code calling the function upholds these semantics. C++ doesn't do any of this for you. Sometimes you can do this through the parameter types (references are virtually always aliases, and const pointers are always aliases), and sometimes you have to do it with naming conventions (at Taligent, for example, we use "adopt," "orphan," and "create" in the names of functions that transfer ownership).

In the case of the assignment operator, our parameter is a const reference to another TFoo. That alone signifies that we are not taking ownership of its internal state (there are some very rare, but important, exceptions to this rule—we'll look at one later). Since TFoo's pointers are defined as owning pointers, however, we have to reconcile the difference in semantics by making new copies of the objects the other TFoo points to.

memcpy() IS EVIL!

So we have to copy the TBars in our assignment operator. I've seen a lot of interesting attempts to do this. The most frightening was

```
TFoo& TFoo::operator=(const TFoo& that)
```

```
{
    memcpy(&fBar1, &that.fBar1, sizeof(fBar1));
    memcpy(&fBar2, &that.fBar2, sizeof(fBar2));
    return *this;
}
```

I really hope this guy was just nervous. This code just copies the *pointer values* from one TFoo to the other. In other words, it's an ugly way of doing

```
fBar1 = that.fBar1;
fBar2 = that.fBar2;
```

Closer to the mark, but ever scarier in terms of its results, is

```
memcpy(fBar1, that.fBar1, sizeof(TBar));
memcpy(fBar2, that.fBar2, sizeof(TBar));
```

This would copy the data members of "that"'s TBars into "this"'s TBars, so "this" and "that" retain their own separate TBar objects. So we're doing well so far. The problem is that it bypasses the assignment operator and copy constructor for TBar, so if TBar has any owning pointers of its own, you have the same problem. You'll also have problems if TBar owns locks or system resources that need to be properly cleaned up or duplicated when you change the internal state of the object. And, of course, if any of these pointers is NULL, you'll probably crash.

Finally, I had one applicant propose

```
fBar1 = new TBar;
memcpy(fBar1, that.fBar1, sizeof(TBar));
fBar2 = new TBar;
memcpy(fBar2, that.fBar2, sizeof(TBar));
```

This is kind of a cheap way of initializing brand-new TBars from existing ones, or copy constructing them without using the copy constructor. It suffers from all of the same limitations as the previous example, plus an additional one we'll get to in a moment.

Keep in mind one thing: memcpy() is *evil!* It's a C construct you should never use in C++. memcpy() operates on bits and bytes, not on objects. At best, it just looks ugly and forces you to be concerned with things you shouldn't need to worry about—like the size of TBar. At worst, it fails to take into account what's actually being stored in the objects you're copying, leading to erroneous results, or even uglier code that takes the special cases into account. Never use memcpy() in C++ code. There are always better, more object-oriented ways to do the same thing.

So what's the right answer? Since the TFoo expects to delete the TBars it points to, we have to create new ones for it to point to. We can create duplicates of the other TFoo's TBars by using TBar's copy constructor (remember from our introduction that every object has a copy constructor), so the correct solution (so far) would look like this:

```
TFoo& TFoo::operator=(const TFoo& that)
{
   fBar1 = new TBar(*that.fBar1);
   fBar2 = new TBar(*that.fBar2);
   return *this;
}
```

PLUGGING THE LEAKS

Of course, there's still a glaring error here: Remember that fBar1 and fBar2 are owning pointers. This means that TFoo is responsible for deleting them. Here, we've copied right over the top of these pointers without taking into account their former values. This'd be OK if we were writing a copy constructor, where we're guaranteed that fBar1 and fBar2 contain garbage, but it's not OK for an assignment operator. In the assignment operator, fBar1 and fBar2 are both valid pointers to TBar objects. If you just write over them, you now have two TBar objects in memory that *nobody* points to anymore (or at least, no one who points to them expects to have to delete them). This is a memory leak. Memory leaks won't cause your program to crash or produce wrong results, at least not right away. Instead, depending on how numerous and bad they are, they'll slowly degrade your program's performance. If you run the program long enough, you'll run out of memory and it *will* crash.

So we have to delete the objects that we currently own before we can create new ones:

```
TFoo& TFoo::operator=(const TFoo& that)
{
     delete fBar1;
     fBar1 = new TBar(*that.fBar1);
```

```
        delete fBar2;
        fBar2 = new TBar(*that.fBar2);
        return *this;
    }
```

ASSIGNING YOURSELF

Now we're beginning to get to something reasonable. But we're not quite there yet. Consider the following expression:

```
foo1 = foo1;
```

This might seem like a silly example, but it does happen. Consider a setter function on some object where the variable being set is a TFoo and the other value is passed in. A caller knows he wants to set that variable to "x". The caller shouldn't have to check to see whether the value of that variable is already "x". If it is "x" and the caller doesn't check for this, look at what happens in our code: "this" and "that" refer to the same object, so by the time we get down to "fBar1 =new TBar(*that.fBar1)", that.fBar1 is gone. "delete fBar1" also deleted that.fBar1. The call to TBar's copy constructor will either crash because it's trying to access a deleted object, or it'll get away with that, create a brand-new TBar, and initialize it with the contents of raw memory. What's worse, most of the time the data that had been in those two objects won't have been overwritten yet, so it'll probably work right 90% of the time and randomly fail the other 10%. This kind of bug is notoriously hard to track down.

There are many ways of coding around this, but the obvious answer is the best: just check at the top of the function to see whether you're assigning to yourself, and drop out if you are. So our operator now looks like

```
TFoo& TFoo::operator=(const TFoo& that)
{
    if (this != &that) {
        delete fBar1;
        fBar1 = new TBar(*that.fBar1);
        delete fBar2;
        fBar2 = new TBar(*that.fBar2);
    }
    return *this;
}
```

HONORING YOUR ANCESTRY

We've also forgotten another important detail. Remember the first line of our sample class definition:

```
class TFoo : public TSuperFoo {
```

TFoo is not a root class; it has a base class. This means we also have to copy over the base class's data members. If we were writing a copy constructor, we wouldn't generally have to worry about this, because the compiler will make sure our base class members are initialized before our constructor is called. But the compiler doesn't do anything like this for us with assignment operators; we have to do it.

The easiest way to do this is to call our superclass's assignment operator ourselves. That gives us

```
TFoo& TFoo::operator=(const TFoo& that)
{
    if (this != &that) {
        TSuperFoo::operator=(that);
        delete fBar1;
        fBar1 = new TBar(*that.fBar1);
        delete fBar2;
        fBar2 = new TBar(*that.fBar2);
    }
    return *this;
}
```

CLEANING UP AFTER YOURSELF

We're still not really out of the woods here. The code above will work great unless we encounter an error while trying to create one of our TBar objects. If we get an exception while creating a TBar object, the data member we're setting retains its old value, which now points to a deleted object. If we continue to use this TFoo, we'll probably eventually crash because of the dangling pointer. If we delete the TFoo in response to the exception, we'll probably blow sky high trying to double-delete the TBar.

You need to make sure that the creation of a new object succeeds before you do anything to the variable you're assigning to. This way, if creation fails, you're still pointing to a perfectly good TBar—the assignment operation simply didn't have an effect. In fact, since we have two TBars, we should new up *both* of them before carrying out the assignment. In fact, we should wait to call our inherited function until we've successfully created the TBars, too. This will ensure that the TFoo is always in an internally consistent state; either the whole assignment happened or none of it did:

```
TFoo& TFoo::operator=(const TFoo& that)
{
   if (this != &that) {
      TBar* bar1;
      TBar* bar2;

      bar1 = new TBar(*that.fBar1);
      bar2 = new TBar(*that.fBar2);

      TSuperFoo::operator=(that);
      delete fBar1;
      fBar1 = bar1;
      delete fBar2;
      fBar2 = bar2;
   }
   return *this;
}
```

But there's a problem with this solution: Consider what happens if creation of bar1 succeeds and creation of bar2 fails. You'll exit with the actual object untouched, but what happens to the TBar pointed to by bar1? That's right; it leaks. To avoid this, you actually have to catch and rethrow the exception and delete bar1 if it's been created. To tell if you've created bar1, you need to set it to NULL first, so this all gets rather complicated:

```
TFoo& TFoo::operator=(const TFoo& that)
{
   if (this != &that) {
      TBar*  bar1 = 0;
      TBar*  bar2 = 0;

      try {
         bar1 = new TBar(*that.fBar1);
         bar2 = new TBar(*that.fBar2);
      }
```

```
        catch (...) {
            delete bar1;
            delete bar2;
            throw;
        }

            TSuperFoo::operator=(that);
            delete fBar1;
            fBar1 = bar1;
            delete fBar2;
            fBar2 = bar2;
        }
        return *this;
    }
```

Delegating Our Work

Of course, we're not really handling the exception here; we're just catching it to enable us to clean up properly. The try/catch block is a really ugly construct to have to use in this way. It'd be really nice if we could lose it.

One of the niceties of C++ exception handling is that destructors for any stack-based objects are guaranteed to be called even if the function that declares them exits prematurely with an exception or a return statement. We can take advantage of this behavior by having an object whose destructor deletes the object that would otherwise leak.

The new ANSI C++ standard provides us with just such an object: It's called auto_ptr. Using auto_ptr, we can write

```
TFoo& TFoo::operator=(const TFoo& that)
{
    if (this != &that) {
        auto_ptr<TBar>        bar1 = new TBar(*that.fBar1);
        auto_ptr<TBar>        bar2 = new TBar(*that.fBar2);

        TSuperFoo::operator=(that);
        delete fBar1;
        fBar1 = bar1.release();
        delete fBar2;
        fBar2 = bar2.release();
    }
    return *this;
}
```

The release() function gets rid of the auto_ptr's reference to the object so that it won't delete the object in its destructor. So, the auto_ptr will only delete the object it points to if we exit the function with an exception before getting to the release() call. Which is correct; the only things in this function that can fail are the constructor calls.

Taking Full Advantage

You've probably already guessed this part: We can actually utilize auto_ptr more fully than this. auto_ptr actually implements owning pointer semantics for us; if you assign to an auto_ptr, it deletes the object it points to before taking on the new pointer. Also, if an auto_ptr goes out of scope, it automatically deletes the object it points to. So if we relaxed the rules of our exercise to allow us to redefine the class, we could redefine the class using auto_ptr:

```
class TFoo : public TSuperFoo {
    auto_ptr<TBar>  fBar1;
    auto_ptr<TBar>  fBar2;
    // method definitions...
};
```

Functions accessing the objects pointed to by fBar1 and fBar2 would look exactly the same as they did when fBar1 and fBar2 were regular pointers; auto_ptr defines its * and -> operators to do the same thing as those for a regular pointer.

And now we can take full advantage of auto_ptr in our assignment operator:

```
TFoo& TFoo::operator=(const TFoo& that)
{
    if (this != &that) {
        auto_ptr<TBar> bar1 = new TBar(*that.fBar1);
        auto_ptr<TBar> bar2 = new TBar(*that.fBar2);
        TSuperFoo::operator=(that);
        fBar1 = bar1;
        fBar2 = bar2;
    }
    return *this;
}
```

Note that auto_ptr doesn't automatically take care of duplicating "that"'s data members; we have to do that ourselves. Instead, auto_ptr's assignment operator passes ownership from one auto_ptr to the other, leaving the auto_ptr on the right-hand side set to NULL (this is the big exception to the rule I mentioned earlier, about assignments not affecting the right-hand operand). In the expression "fBar1 = bar1", this is exactly what we want. This way, when we exit the function at the "return," bar1 won't try to delete the new TBar it was originally handed.

The other beauty of auto_ptr is its documentary value; if a pointer is declared as an auto_ptr, you know it's an owning pointer. If you consistently use auto_ptrs for all owning pointers and regular pointers only for aliasing pointers, the meanings of pointers are no longer ambiguous and you don't have to worry as much about naming conventions and documentation.

Of course, auto_ptr isn't yet available on all C++ compilers; if you're concerned about portability, don't use it. Do the assignment the first way I described, or make your own auto_ptr-like class. If your compiler does provide auto_ptr, and you're not worried about portability, it's definitely the way to go.

THE REAL ANSWER

Actually, I lied at the beginning of this article. There is an infinitely better solution to the problem as I stated it than the one we just worked our way to.

To see what I'm getting at, consider two points:

- If any other objects contain aliasing pointers to TFoo's TBar objects, they will be invalid after you assign to the TFoo.
- Every object in a well-designed C++ system has a default constructor, a copy constructor, and an assignment operator.

That's right; you can perform the whole assignment just by calling *TBar*'s assignment operator. That solution looks like this:

```
TFoo& TFoo::operator=(const TFoo& that)
{
    TSuperFoo::operator=(that);
    *fBar1 = *(that.fBar1);
    *fBar2 = *(that.fBar2);
    return *this;
}
```

This is *so* much easier. So why didn't I start with this at the outset? There are several reasons:

- Going with the longer solution was a good way to explore many of the details of C++ memory management.
- The shorter solution won't work if NULL is a valid value for fBar1 and fBar2. In this case, you'd have to use a hybrid solution: follow the longer example when you're copying an object into a null pointer, and the shorter example when you're copying an object into an object. (I'll leave this example as an exercise for the reader.)
- The shorter solution won't work if we want to transactionize the whole assignment. In other words, if we have a situation where both assignments have to complete successfully for our object to be in a consistent state, we can't use the simple solution because there's no way to roll back our changes to fBar1 if assigning to fBar2 throws an exception. You'd have to use the longer example. However, if the two data members are unrelated, or you know their assignment operators can't throw an exception, this solution is perfectly adequate.
- The shorter solution won't work if TBar is a polymorphic class. Let's take a closer look at this situation.

Handling Polymorphism

I stated in the original problem that you could assume, for the purposes of the exercise, that TBar was a monomorphic class— that is, that TBar has no subclasses. If TBar is a polymorphic class—that is, if we know it has or can have subclasses—then the shorter solution won't work.

Let's pretend for a moment that TBar is an abstract class and that it has two concrete subclasses, TDerivedBar1 and TDerived Bar2 (yeah, I know I'm really creative with these names). All we have in our short example are pointers to TBar. Each assignment above will call *TBar's* operator= function, *not* the operator= function of TDerivedBar1 or TDerivedBar2 (remember, operator=() isn't virtual). This means that any data members defined by the TDerivedBar classes won't be copied. This is called *slicing*, it's something you have to watch out for in C++. You must always pay special attention to whether a class is polymorphic or monomorphic. Polymorphism imposes special restrictions on what you can do with your objects, and the compiler doesn't enforce these restrictions.

Of course, we could theoretically get around these problems by making TBar's operator= function virtual. If this->fBar1 is an instance of TDerived-

Bar1, you'll call TDerivedBar1::operator=() instead of TBar::operator=(). But if it's a TDerivedBar2, you're in trouble. TDerivedBar1 isn't going to know what to do with TDerivedBar2's members; it has nowhere to put them. You really want it to look like the object pointed to by this->fBar1 has morphed from a TDerivedBar2 to a TDerivedBar1. There's only one way to do this, and that's to delete the TDerivedBar2 and new up a brand-new TDerivedBar1.

So our longer solution, where we delete the old objects and replace them with newly-created objects (either directly or with auto_ptr), is closer to the mark. But it won't work as written, either. Consider the line

```
fBar1 = new TBar(*that.fBar1);
```

If TBar is an abstract class, this will generate a compile-time error, because you're trying to create an instance of a class that can't be instantiated. If TBar is a concrete, but polymorphic, class, it'll compile, but you'll get slicing again: the "new" expression will only return an instance of TBar, even if the original object was a TDerivedBar1. At best this isn't a real copy and at worst it has incomplete and inconsistent state.

The C++ language doesn't provide a built-in way around this problem, unfortunately—if you need to copy an object polymorphically, you have to do it yourself. The typical way to do this is to define a virtual function called clone() and have every class that inherits clone() override it to call its own copy constructor.

```
class TBar {
    ...
    virtual TBar* clone() const = 0;
    ...
};

TDerivedBar1::clone() const
{
    return new TDerivedBar1(*this);
}

TDerivedBar2::clone() const
{
    return new TDerivedBar2(*this);
}
```

Once you've given all the classes in question a clone() method, you can go back and rewrite TFoo's assignment operator properly:

```
TFoo& TFoo::operator=(const TFoo& that)
{
    if (this != &that) {
        auto_ptr<TBar> bar1 = that.fBar1->clone();
        auto_ptr<TBar> bar2 = that.fBar2->clone();
        TSuperFoo::operator=(that);
        fBar1 = bar1;
        fBar2 = bar2;
    }
    return *this;
}
```

CONCLUSION

Well, there you have it: a whirlwind tour of some of the finer points of C++ memory management, as seen through the lens of a simple assignment operator. C++ is a monster of a language, and writing good code in it takes some practice and concentration. I hope these pointers help illuminate some of the more esoteric but important areas of C++ programming for you and help you to write better code.

THE ASSIGNMENT OPERATOR REVISITED

IF YOU THINK YOU KNOW it all in the C++ world, it must mean you're not talking to your colleagues very much. If I had any pretensions to knowing it all when I wrote my assignment-operator article,[1] they didn't last long afterward.

The assignment-operator article drew a huge response, with a lot of people sending me corrections and disagreements of various kinds. The issues have been mounting, so I thought a follow-up article discussing the issues would be appropriate.

THE BIG MISTAKE

One I heard about almost instantly from several people (and that I'm really glad I heard about before delivering a talk on this subject at C++ World) was a serious mistake. When I first came up with this article, I wrote "the big right answer" as follows:

```
TFoo&TFoo::operator=(const TFoo& that)
{
   if (this != &that) {
      TSuperFoo::operator=(that);
      TBar*  bar1 = 0;
      TBar*  bar2 = 0;

      try {
         bar1= new TBar(*that.fBar1);
         bar2= new TBar(*that.fBar2);
      }
      catch (...) {
         delete bar1;
         delete bar2;
         throw;
      }

      delete fBar1;
      fBar1 = bar1;
      delete fBar2;
      fBar2 = bar2;
   }
   return *this;
}
```

This was wrong, and it was caught in the review process. The problem here is that if you're trying to transactionize the assignment, so that either all of it happens or none of it happens, this breaks that. If an exception occurs trying to new up bar1 or bar2, the TFoo part of the object won't have changed, but the TSuperFoo part will have. The call to TSuperFoo::operator=() can't go at the top of the function.

As I said, this was caught during the review process. So when the article appeared in print, the example looked like this:

```
TFoo&TFoo::operator=(const TFoo& that)
{
   if (this != &that) {
      TBar*  bar1 = 0;
      TBar*  bar2 = 0;

      try {
         bar1= new TBar(*that.fBar1);
         bar2= new TBar(*that.fBar2);
      }
      catch (...) {
         delete bar1;
         delete bar2;
         throw;
      }

      TSuperFoo::operator=(that);
      delete fBar1;
      fBar1 = bar1;
      delete fBar2;
      fBar2 = bar2;
   }
   return *this;
}
```

Unfortunately, that's wrong too. The problem is we're still in trouble if TSuperFoo's assignment operator can also throw an exception, a reasonable thing to expect. If we succeed in creating our TBar objects, but TSuperFoo::operator=() fails to create whatever it needs to (presumably it's also transactionized), the object will correctly be left untouched, but we'll leak the new TBars we will have created. So the *right* answer (he said sheepishly) is this:

```
TFoo&TFoo::operator=(const TFoo& that)
{
   if (this != &that) {
      TBar*  bar1 = 0;
      TBar*  bar2 = 0;

      try {
         bar1= new TBar(*that.fBar1);
         bar2= new TBar(*that.fBar2);
         TSuperFoo::operator=(that);
```

```
        }
        catch (...) {
            delete bar1;
            delete bar2;
            throw;
        }

        delete fBar1;
        fBar1 = bar1;
        delete fBar2;
        fBar2 = bar2;
    }
    return *this;
}
```

The call to TSuperFoo::operator=() has to go inside the try. Notice that it comes *after* we create the new TBars. We want to make sure creating the TBars has succeeded before we call TSuperFoo::operator=(), because TSuperFoo::operator=() might succeed in changing the object, and we only want to change the object if we can carry out the whole assignment operation.

One interesting consequence of this is that you can imagine a class with a fairly deep inheritance chain where every class up the chain has other objects it owns. You'd call an assignment operator low in the chain: It would create the objects it needs before calling its parent, which would create the objects it needs and call *its* parent, and so on up the chain. Eventually, all of the new objects would have been created and would be pointed to by temporary variables on the stack. Then, at the root level, the assignment would finally begin to be carried out, with objects being deleted and the object's data members being changed as each function returned. So the allocations happen in one order and the assignments and deletions happen in reverse order, which feels awkward at first glance, but gets the job done. It also means that there has to be enough free memory to hold two instances of every subobject, but there really isn't a safe way around allocating the extra memory.

By the way, I've also had several people question my assumption that the delete operations won't throw exceptions. Technically they're right, but I'd strongly counsel against letting this happen. I think it's wise to declare "Destructors will not throw exceptions, nor will they allow exceptions thrown by functions they call to propagate out of them" to be a program invariant. The reason for this is that destructors are called in the course of *handling* exceptions. If exception-handling code can throw more exceptions, it's extremely difficult, if not downright impossible, for a programmer to properly clean up after himself, and extremely difficult for the program to completely recover from the error condition and go on. Therefore, throwing or propagating exceptions from within destructors is not a good idea.

The Magic Three

In my previous article, I singled out C++'s "magic three" functions—the default constructor, copy constructor and default assignment operator—and claimed that one should always define them. This raised a few hackles.

First, several people correctly pointed out that the default constructor is only defined by the compiler when you don't create *any other* constructors. This is indeed true; I left this fact out for simplicity. In retrospect, I shouldn't have.

Several people took exception to my statement that every class should define the "magic three." They were disturbed by the suggestion that every object should have a default constructor. They're right. There are probably more objects for which it *isn't* appropriate to have a default constructor than there are for which it is. Often, you can't initialize an object to a meaningful state without some data being supplied from outside, or you can only do it by adding special-case code just to support a default constructor you don't really need.

Occasionally, you even have a default constructor forced on you. Taligent's CommonPoint system did this: Its serialization facilities required a default constructor to work right—one of the bigger architectural gaffes in that system, in my opinion (of course, now I'll get angry letters from ex-Taligent employees explaining why it had to be that way).

The intended message of my original article didn't come through strongly enough: You should always *declare* the magic three functions. This way, you make an explicit statement that you are not accepting the default implementations of these functions. If a default constructor isn't appropriate for your class, don't write one just for the sake of writing one; declare it private and give it an empty implementation. But be sure you declare it. The same holds true for the copy constructor and assignment operator.

A number of people also suggested an improvement to my original advice: "If you don't want it, declare it private and give it an empty implementation." You actually don't have to give an unwanted function an implementation at all. You can declare the function private and not define it. The declaration will suppress the compiler-generated version of the function, but not defining it saves you from having to supply dummy code that doesn't actually do anything and will never be called. Further, while declaring the function private will prevent outside classes from calling it, it won't prevent *the same class* from calling it. If you don't supply an implementation, the class will get a link error if it calls its own unwanted magic functions. This is somewhat nonintuitive to debug, but it's better than having the compiler silently let the caller get away with calling a function nobody's supposed to call.

I also had people take rather violent exception to my suggestion that one should always define the copy constructor and assignment operator, even when they really do what you want them to do. These critics pointed out that it's a lot of wasted boilerplate code, which is ugly and a pain to maintain. Further, it's possible for the compiler to perform optimizations on the default functions that it might not be able (or willing) to perform on user-written code. Most importantly, if you add or delete members from the class, the default copy constructor and assignment operator pick up the changes automatically. If you define these functions yourself, you have to remember to maintain them when the class definition changes, or you'll have compiler errors or runtime bugs.

This critique is all very true, but I'll stand by my original advice just the same. Boilerplate copy constructors and assignment operators are ugly code and a hassle to maintain, but being in the habit of always writing the copy constructor and assignment operator also puts you in the habit of thinking about just what the correct copy behavior is for all the members of your class. If all the members are integers, this probably isn't a big deal, but if they're pointers, it's a very big deal. Getting into the habit of accepting the defaults without taking the time to think about it can also lead to bugs down the road if you mistakenly accept the default when it *doesn't* do the right thing.

Of course, if you do accept the Language's defaults, you have to rely on comments to explain that you know about the default and are failing to define these functions *on purpose.* I'm always a little uncomfortable with relying on documentation for things like that.

VIRTUAL ASSIGNMENT

Finally, several people (including my own manager here at IBM) disputed my advice to make the assignment operator of a class nonvirtual. Let's take a closer look at this issue.

Consider the following simple example:

```
X* x;
```

```
void setX(const X& newX) {
    *x = newX;
}
```

This will work as intended, but only if X is a monomorphic class. But suppose X is polymorphic. Pretend it has an inheritance hierarchy like this:

```
 X
/ \
Y Z
```

That is…

```
class X {
    // ...
}

class Y : public X {
    // ...
}

class Z : public X {
    // ...
}
```

Now, if either x or newX points to an object of class Y or Z, we'll slice. Only the members defined in X will get copied. If X is an instance of Y or Z , the members defined by Y or Z won't be updated with new values. If newX is an instance of Y or Z, the members defined by Y or Z won't get copied into x. Bad news.

The problem here, of course, is that we're calling x's assignment operator even when x isn't an instance of X. The obvious solution, therefore, would be to make X's assignment operator virtual; then the correct assignment operator would be called. If we do this, the assignment operators would look like this:

```
X& X::operator=(const X& that) {
    // copy X's members...
    return *this;
}

X& Y::operator=(const X& that) {
    Y& y = dynamic_cast<Y&>(that);
    X::operator=(that);
    // copy Y's members using y
```

```
        return *this;
    }

    X& Z::operator=(const X& that) {
        Z& z = dynamic_cast<Z&>(that);
        X::operator=(that);
        // copy Z's members using z
        return *this;
    }
```

Now, if x and newX are actually both instances of Y, Y's assignment operator will get called and everything will work properly. Big improvement, right?

Well, consider the situation where x is a Y and newX is a Z. In this case, the dynamic_cast will fail, throwing a bad_cast exception. Now we have a problem.

The bad_cast exception is good, in a way, because it traps the mismatched classes and causes an error, rather than just slicing silently. However, we now have an error condition we have to handle.

Remember that after an assignment succeeds, the objects on either side of the equal sign are to be computationally equivalent. That is, all of their visible state and their behavior should be the same. This implies that they should be the same class. What you really want is for x to appear as though it has morphed from whatever class it was to the same class newX is. X, Y, and Z's assignment operators can't do this; there's no way to morph an existing object from one class to another (well, there kind of is, but we'll get to it later). Instead, setX() has to deal with the following:

```
    void setX(const X& newX) {
        try {
            *x = newX;
        }
        catch (bad_cast&) {
            X* temp = newX.clone();
            delete x;
            x = temp;
        }
    }
```

Remember clone(), the polymorphic copy constructor? If you need polymorphic copy on a group of related classes, define a virtual function called clone() such that every class in the tree overrides it to call its own copy constructor. You can't just call x's copy constructor for the same reason you can't just call x's assignment operator.

Another alternative is that setX() doesn't handle this condition, but some other function up the call chain will have to, probably by doing the same thing we're doing here: deleting the old X and creating a new one of the right class. (There might be other meaningful ways of handling the exception, but they'd be more application-specific.)

The other possibility is that nothing handles the exception. We could just declare "assignment operators shall always be called with like classes on either side of the equal sign" as a program invariant. In other words, we declare heterogeneous assignment to be a condition that Should Never Happen.

Violations of program invariants ("Should Never Happen" conditions) are programmer errors; they're things you're assuming you'll never run into at runtime. An exception shouldn't be thrown for a violated invariant; because you're not expecting it to happen at runtime, you don't want to waste time writing lots of extra code to handle it. The program is just malformed. And if you throw an exception that no handler catches, your program terminates. Quietly. With no error messages.

If your program's going to terminate, you want it to terminate loudly, proclaiming to the world that Something Went Wrong. The way to do this is with the assert() macro. Pass an expression to assert() that you expect to always evaluate to true. If it evaluates to false, it prints an error message that usually contains the text of the offending expression and the line number of the assert, and then the program terminates. (You can also cause asserts to be compiled out in production versions of your program, which will cause them to fail silently instead.)

This way, instead of the dynamic cast you can do a static cast and precede it with an assert:

```
X& Y::operator=(const X& that) {
    assert(typeid(that) == typeid(*this));
    Y& y = static_cast<Y&>(that);
    X::operator=(that);
    // copy Y's members using y
    return *this;
}
```

By the way, my original attempt at this was

```
assert(typeid(that) == typeid(Y));
```

You don't want to do it this way, because then when Y::operator=() calls X::operator=(), X::operator=() will choke because "that" isn't an instance of X.

You're not concerned that "that" is some particular static type; you're concerned that "this" and "that" are the *same* type, whatever that type is.

Using the assert is one way around the heterogeneous-assignment problem, and it has a lot to recommend it in situations where you really know that this invariant can hold.

But let's go back to the previous answer for a minute and assume we're going to catch the exception and finagle the assignment in setX(). To refresh our memory, setX() now looks like this:

```
void setX(const X& newX) {
    try {
        *x = newX;
    }
    catch (bad_cast&) {
        X* temp = newX.clone();
        delete x;
        x = temp;
    }
}
```

Let's consider our possibilities here, ignoring Z for a moment. If x and newX are both instances of X or both instances of Y, we're cool. If x is an instance of Y and newX is an instance of X, we're also cool. Y::operator=() will throw a bad_cast exception, and we'll catch it, delete x, and new up a fresh new Y to assign to x.

But what if x is an instance of X and newX is an instance of Y? In this case we'll end up in X's assignment operator, and the dynamic cast will *succeed.* Y is a subclass of X, so dynamically casting a reference to a Y to a reference to an X is legal. Every Y is also an X. But because we're in X's assignment operator, we'll only copy over the members of newX that were defined in X. It's our old friend slicing again.

To avoid this, we would have to manually check for like classes in each assignment operator and throw the bad_cast ourselves, rather than relying on dynamic_cast to do it for us.

Instead, my original solution to this problem was to avoid using the assignment operator in the first place:

```
void setX(const X& newX) {
    X* temp = newX.clone();
    delete x;
    x = temp;
}
```

I still like this. It's simple and clear, and it works correctly with no extra hassles even when x and newX are instances of different classes. The other solution, using try/catch blocks, has an advantage in situations where the cost of deleting and newing the destination object is large and relatively rare. (The try costs nothing in most modern compilers, so you in effect fast-path the case of like classes; however, an actual throw can be quite expensive, so you achieve this fast-path effect at the expense of the different-classes case.)

If the fast-path option makes sense for your application, I'd suggest avoiding the exception and doing it yourself like this:

```
void setX(const X& newX) {
   if (typeid(*x) == typeid(newX))
      x = newX;
   else {
      X* temp = newX.clone();
      delete x;
      x = temp;
   }
}
```

Now, if you avoid using the assignment operator in situations where slicing may be a problem, you are still left with the question of whether it makes more sense to make the assignment operator virtual or nonvirtual. I tend to come down on the side of making the assignment operator virtual with an assert to check for the different-classes condition (because there's no way to handle that in the assignment operator itself, and therefore the calling function already must be aware of the possibility of polymorphism and must know how to handle it).

However, there's another problem here. I remembered Taligent's coding guidelines discouraging virtual assignment operators, so I went back to see why. I wish I had done that before. It turns out Taligent's guidelines weren't hard and fast on the subject. Instead they point out that defining

```
virtual A& B::operator=(const A& that);
```

won't keep the compiler from defining

```
B& B::operator=(const B& that);
```

In other words, an override of an inherited assignment operator doesn't suppress the compiler-generated default assignment operator. You still have to do that manually by declaring it private and not giving it an implementation.

And actually, this won't even work because C++'s overload resolution rules will cause the suppressed version to win in some types of calls. For instance, consider a class like this:

```
class Y : public X {
   public:
      virtual X& operator=(const X& that);
      // other method definitions...
   private:
      Y& operator=(const Y& that);
}
```

Now consider this code snippet:

```
Y someY(/*arguments*/);
// do something with someY
Y someOtherY(/*arguments*/);
someY = someOtherY;
```

Because both someY and someOtherY are instances of Y, the overload-resolution rules will declare the nonvirtual version of operator=() to be the "winner," instead of the inherited virtual operator=(). Because the nonvirtual operator=() is private, you'll get an access-violation error at compile time.

Instead, you'd have to define the default assignment operator to call the virtual one. In every class that inherits the virtual one. Of course, this means defining it as nonvirtual. To see why, imagine if Y in the above example had a subclass called Z. If Y's operator=() was virtual, Z would have to override it, as well as X's operator=(), and then it would have to replace its own default assignment operator. Cutting any corners here risks creating situations where the "winning" function, according to the overload-resolution rules, is a function that is not accessible or isn't implemented. Clearly, this gets ridiculous quickly as the inheritance hierarchy gets deeper.

One side effect in either case is that you have to define an override of the virtual operator=() even when you don't strictly need one; otherwise, the "default" one will hide the virtual one.

So there you go. A truly foolproof method of handling polymorphism in assignment operators involves declaring *both* a virtual and a nonvirtual assignment operator in every class (except the root class of each inheritance hierarchy), with the nonvirtual calling the virtual and the virtual asserting that both objects involved are the same class. Any time a calling function couldn't guarantee the invariant would hold, it would have to avoid using the assignment operator and manually delete the object referenced by the target variable and new up a new one of the proper type.

Beautiful, huh?

Other Ways of Morphing

Before I wrap this up, one more thing: I alluded earlier to the idea that there are ways of making an object look like it has morphed from one class to another. There are two ways to do this, neither of which is really all that much of a winner.

One option is *not* to change the class of the object on the left-hand side. It's perfectly reasonable to define assignment operators that take different types on the left- and right-hand sides. The operator in this case performs some kind of meaningful conversion of the incoming data as part of the assignment process. The result isn't really a copy, but it may produce completely appropriate results. This solution is definitely the right way to go for some classes in some applications, but it's not a general solution. Be sure to consider whether it's appropriate for your classes before going to all the trouble.

The other option is to fake inheritance using containment. In this case, the objects on the left- and right-hand sides of the equal sign *are* the same class, but they behave like members of different classes because they own objects of different classes. The simplest version of this idea is a smart pointer that knows about polymorphism for a certain group of classes and does the right thing. All you're really doing here is encapsulating in this object's assignment operator the delete/new code you'd otherwise have to put in client code, but hiding junk like this in a smart-pointer class is often a useful and effective way to go. (This is the essence of the State pattern, by the way.)

Conclusion

I don't know about you, but there's something really scary to me about a language where copying state from one object to another is this complicated. By now, I suspect at least one or two dozen programmers have contributed something new to this discussion. If it takes this many programmers to write a simple assignment operator, think how complicated writing code that actually does something meaningful must be!

The devil truly is in the details, especially in C++ programming.

I'm sure there are still other issues, both with the original article and this one, that I've missed. I've learned a lot about this, and I'm interested in continuing to learn. Keep those cards and letters coming!

REFERENCE

1. Gillam, R. "The Anatomy of the Assignment Operator," *C++ Report,* 9(10):14–23, Nov./Dec. 1997.

THREAD-SPECIFIC STORAGE FOR C/C++

DOUGLAS C. SCHMIDT, NAT PRYCE, AND TIMOTHY H. HARRISON

Doug Schmidt (http://www.cs.wustl.edu/~schmidt) was editor of the C++ Report *between Stan Lippman and myself. He is in charge of, and is the chief proponent of, a suite of open source distributed processing tools called ACE and TAO. ACE is a low-level framework for distributed processing, and TAO is one of the best ORBs out there, open source or otherwise.*

As part of his researches into distributed processing, Doug and his compadres discover many interesting patterns and techniques. Fortunately for us, they published many of them in the pages of the C++ Report.

In this article, Doug, Nat, and Timothy describe a technique that is valuable in a multithreaded environment when you have objects that are logically global, but physically specific to certain threads.

IN THEORY, multithreading an application can improve performance (by executing multiple instruction streams simultaneously), and simplify program structure (by allowing each thread to execute synchronously, rather than reactively or asynchronously). In practice, multithreaded applications often perform no better, or even perform worse than single-threaded applications due to the overhead of acquiring and releasing locks. In addition, multithreaded applications are hard to program due to the complex concurrency control protocols required to avoid race conditions and deadlocks.

This article describes the Thread-Specific Storage pattern, which alleviates several problems with multithreading performance and programming complexity. The Thread-Specific Storage pattern improves performance and simplifies multithreaded applications by allowing multiple threads to use one logically global access point to retrieve thread-specific data without incurring locking overhead for each access.

INTENT

Allows multiple threads to use one logically global access point to retrieve thread-specific data without incurring locking overhead for each access.

MOTIVATION

CONTEXT AND FORCES

The Thread-Specific Storage pattern should be applied to multithreaded applications that frequently access objects that are *logically* global, but *physically* specific to each thread. For instance, operating systems like UNIX and Win32 report error information to applications using errno. When an error occurs in a system call, the OS sets errno to report the problem and returns a documented failure status. When the application detects the failure status it checks errno to determine what type of error occurred.

For instance, consider the following typical C code fragment that receives buffers from a nonblocking TCP socket:

```
// One global errno per-process.
extern int errno;

void *worker (SOCKET socket)
{
   // Read from the network connection and process the data
   // until the connection is closed.

   for (;;) {
      char buffer[BUFSIZ];
      int result = recv (socket, buffer, BUFSIZ, 0);

      // Check to see if the recv() call failed.
      if (result == -1) {
         if (errno != EWOULDBLOCK)
```

```
            // Record error result in thread-specific data.
            printf ("recv failed, errno = %d", errno);
        } else
          // Perform the work on success.
          process_buffer (buffer);
    }
}
```

If recv returns -1 the code checks that errno != EWOULDBLOCK and prints an error message if this is not the case (e.g., if errno == EINTR), otherwise it processes the buffer it receives.

Common Traps and Pitfalls

Although the "global error variable" approach shown above works reasonably* well for single-threaded applications, subtle problems occur in multithreaded applications. In particular, race conditions in preemptively multithreaded systems can cause an errno value set by a method in one thread to be interpreted erroneously by applications in other threads. Thus, if multiple threads execute the worker function simultaneously, it is possible that the global version of errno will be set incorrectly due to race conditions.

For example, two threads (T1 and T2) can perform recv calls on the socket in Figure 1. In this example, T1's recv returns -1 and sets errno to EWOULDBLOCK, which indicates that no data is queued on the socket at the moment. Before it can check for this case, however, the T1 thread is preempted and T2 runs. Assuming T2 gets interrupted, it sets errno to EINTR. If T2 is then preempted immediately, T1 will falsely assume its recv call was interrupted and perform the wrong action. Thus, this program is erroneous and nonportable since its behavior depends on the order in which the threads execute.

The underlying problem here is that setting and testing the global errno value occurs in two steps: 1) the recv call sets the value, and 2) the application tests the value. Therefore, the "obvious" solution of wrapping a mutex around errno will not solve the race condition because the set/test involves multiple operations (i.e., it is not atomic).

One way to solve this problem is to create a more sophisticated locking protocol. For instance, the recv call could acquire an errno_mutex internally, which

* The sidebars discuss the tradeoffs of reporting errors using alternative techniques (such as exceptions and passing an explicit error parameter to each call).

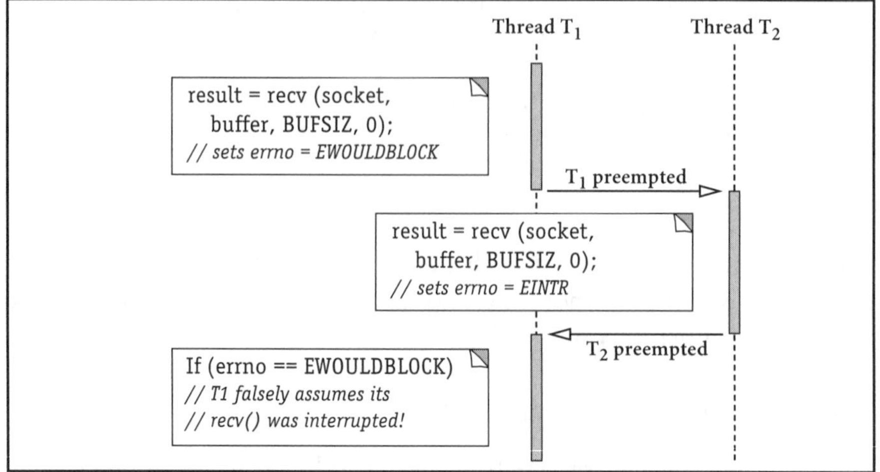

Figure 1. Race conditions in Multithreaded Programs.

must be released by the application once the value of errno is tested after recv returns. However, this solution is undesirable since applications can forget to release the lock, thereby causing starvation and deadlock. Moreover, if applications must check the error status after every library call, the additional locking overhead will degrade performance significantly, even when multiple threads are not used.

SOLUTION: THREAD-SPECIFIC STORAGE

A common solution to the traps and pitfalls described here is to use the *Thread-Specific Storage* pattern. This pattern resolves the following forces:

- *Effificiency*: Thread-specific storage allows sequential methods within a thread to access thread-specific objects atomically without incurring locking overhead for each access.
- *Simplify application programming*: Thread-specific storage is simple for application programmers to use because system developers can make the use of thread-specific storage completely transparent at the source-code level via data abstraction or macros.
- *Highly portable*: Thread-specific storage is available on most multi-threaded OS platforms and can be implemented conveniently on platforms (such as VxWorks) that lack it.

Therefore, regardless of whether an application runs in a single thread or multiple threads, there should be no additional overhead incurred, and no changes to the code required to use the Thread-Specific Storage pattern. For example, the following code illustrates how errno is defined on Solaris 2.x:

```
  // A thread-specific errno definition (typically defined in
<sys/errno.h>).
  #if defined (_REENTRANT)
  // The _errno() function returns the thread-specific value of errno.

  #define errno (*_errno())
  #else
  // Non-MT behavior is unchanged.
  extern int errno;
  #endif /* REENTRANT */

  void *worker (SOCKET socket)
  {
    // Exactly the same implementation shown above.
  }
```

When the _REENTRANT flag is enabled, the errno symbol is defined as a macro that invokes a helper function called _errno, which returns a pointer to the thread-specific value of errno. This pointer is dereferenced by the macro so that it can appear on either the left or right side of an assignment operator.

Applicability

Use the Thread-Specific Storage pattern when an application has the following characteristics:

1. It was originally written assuming a single thread of control and it is being ported to a multithreaded environment *without* changing existing APIs; or
2. It contains multiple preemptive threads of control that can execute concurrently in an arbitrary scheduling order, and
3. Each thread of control invokes sequences of methods that share data common only to that thread, and
4. The data shared by objects within each thread must be accessed through a globally visible access point that is "logically" shared with other threads, but "physically" unique for each thread; and

5. The data is passed implicitly between methods rather than being passed explicitly via parameters.[†]

Understanding the characteristics described above is crucial to using (or not using) the Thread-Specific Storage pattern. For example, the UNIX errno variable is an example of data that is 1) logically global, but physically thread-specific, and 2) passed implicitly between methods.

Do *not* use the Thread-Specific Storage pattern when an application has the following characteristics:

1. Multiple threads are collaborating on a single task that requires concurrent access to shared data. For instance, a multithreaded application may perform reads and writes concurrently on an in-memory database. In this case, threads must share records and tables that are not thread-specific. If thread-specific storage was used to store the database, the threads could not share the data. Thus, access to the database records must be controlled with synchronization primitives (e.g., mutexes) so that the threads can collaborate on the shared data.
2. It is more intuitive and efficient to maintain both a physical *and* logical separation of data. For instance, it may be possible to have threads access data visible only within each thread by passing the data explicitly as parameters to all methods. In this case, the Thread-Specific Storage pattern may be unnecessary.

STRUCTURE AND PARTICIPANTS

Figure 2 illustrates the structure of the following participants in the Thread-Specific Storage pattern:

APPLICATION THREADS

- Application threads use TS Object Proxies to access TS Objects residing in thread-specific storage. As shown in the section titled "Variations," an implementation of the Thread-Specific Storage pattern can use *smart pointers* to hide the TS Object Proxy so that applications appear to access the TS Object directly.

† This situation is common when porting single-threaded APIs to multithreaded systems.

Thread-Specific (TS) Object Proxy (errno macro)

- The TS Object Proxy defines the interface of a TS Object. It is responsible for providing access to a unique object for each application thread via the getspecific and setspecific methods. For instance, in the error handling example from the "Motivation" section, the errno TS Object is an int.

  A TS Object Proxy instance is responsible for a type of object, i.e., it mediates access to a thread-specific TS Object for every thread that accesses the proxy. For example, multiple threads may use the same TS Object Proxy to access thread-specific errno values. The key value stored by the proxy is assigned by the TS Object Collection when the proxy is created and is passed to the collection by the getspecific and setspecific methods.

  The purpose of TS Object Proxies is to hide keys and TS Object Collections. Without the proxies, the Application Threads would have to obtain the collections and use keys explicitly. As shown in the "Variations" section, most of the details of thread-specific storage can be completely hidden via smart pointers for the TS Object Proxy.

Thread-Specific (TS) Object (*_errno() value)

- A TS Object is a particular thread's instance of a thread-specific object. For instance, a thread-specific errno is an object of type int. It is managed by the TS Object Collection and accessed only through a TS Object Proxy.

Thread-Specific (TS) Object Collection

- In complex multithreaded applications, a thread's errno value may be one of many types of data residing in thread-specific storage. Thus, for a thread to retrieve its thread-specific error data it must use a key. This key must be associated with errno to allow a thread to access the correct entry in the TS Object Collection.

  The TS Object Collection contains a set of all thread-specific objects associated with a particular thread, i.e., every thread has a unique TS Object Collection. The TS Object Collection maps keys to thread-specific TS Objects. A TS Object Proxy uses the key to retrieve a specific TS Object from the TS Object Collection via the get_object(key) and set_object(key) methods.

COLLABORATIONS

The interaction diagram in Figure 3 illustrates the following collaborations between participants in the Thread-Specific Storage pattern:

- *Locate the TS Object Collection*: Methods in each Application Thread invoke the getspecific and setspecific methods on the TS Object Proxy to access the TS Object Collection, which is stored inside the thread or in a global structure indexed by the thread ID.[Δ]
- *Acquire the TS Object from thread-specific storage*: Once the TS Object Collection has been located, the TS Object Proxy uses its key to retrieve the correct TS Object from the collection.
- *Set/get TS Object state*: At this point, the application thread operates on the TS Object using ordinary C++ method calls. No locking is necessary since the object is referenced by a pointer that is accessed only within the calling thread.

CONSEQUENCES

BENEFITS

There are several benefits of using the Thread-Specific Storage pattern, including:

Efficiency. The Thread-Specific Storage pattern can be implemented so that no locking is needed to thread specific data. For instance, by placing errno into thread-specific storage, each thread can reliably set and test the completion status of methods within that thread without using complex synchronization protocols. This eliminates locking overhead for data shared within a thread, which is faster than acquiring and releasing a mutex.[1]

Ease of use. Thread-specific storage is simple for application programmers to use because system developers can make the use of thread-specific storage completely transparent at the source-code level via data abstraction or macros.

Δ Every thread in a process contains a unique identifying value called a "thread ID," which is similar to the notion of a process ID.

Liabilities

There are also the following liabilities to using the Thread-Specific Storage pattern:

It encourages the use of (thread-safe) global variables. Many applications do not require multiple threads to access thread-specific data via a common access point. When this is the case, the data should be stored so that only the thread owning the data can access it. For example, consider a network server that uses a pool of worker threads to handle incoming requests from clients. These threads may log the number and type of services performed. This logging mechanism could be accessed as a global Logger object utilizing Thread-Specific Storage. A simpler approach, however, would represent each worker thread as an Active Object[2] with an instance of the Logger stored internally. In this case, no overhead is required to access the Logger, as long as it is passed as a parameter to all functions in the Active Object.

It hides the structure of the system. The use of thread-specific storage hides the relationships between objects in an application, potentially making the application harder to understand. Explicitly representing relationships between objects can eliminate the need for thread-specific storage in some cases (see sidebar "Explicit Contexts for Intercomponent Communication").

Implementation

The Thread-Specific Storage pattern can be implemented in various ways. This section explains each step required to implement the pattern. The steps are summarized as follows:

1. *Implement the TS Object Collections*: If the OS does not provide an implementation of thread-specific storage, it can be implemented using whatever mechanisms are available to maintain the consistency of the data structures in the TS Object Collections.
2. *Encapsulate details of thread-specific storage*: As shown in the "Sample Code" section, interfaces to thread-specific storage are typically weakly-typed and error-prone. Thus, once an implementation of thread-specific storage is available, use C++ programming language features (such as templates and overloading) to hide the low-level details of thread-specific storage behind OO APIs.

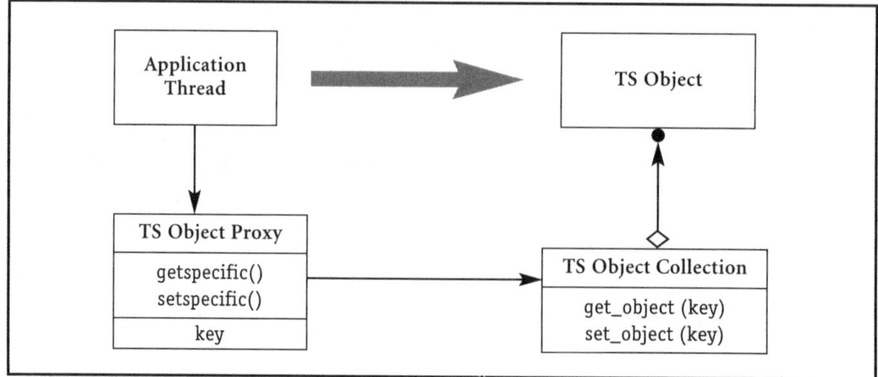

Figure 2. Structure of participants in the Thread-Specific Storage Pattern.

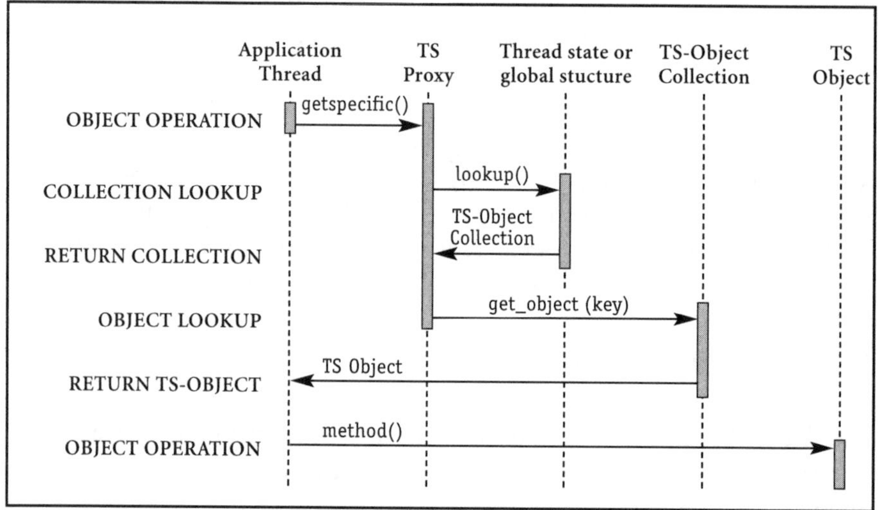

Figure 3. Interactions among participants in the Thread-Specific Storage Pattern.

The remainder of this section describes how to implement the low-level thread-specific storage APIs. The "Sample Code" section provides complete sample code and the "Variations" section examines several ways to encapsulate low-level thread-specific storage APIs with C++ wrappers.

IMPLEMENT THE TS OBJECT COLLECTIONS

The TS Object Collection shown in Figure 2 contains all TS Objects belonging to a particular thread. This collection can be implemented using a table of point-

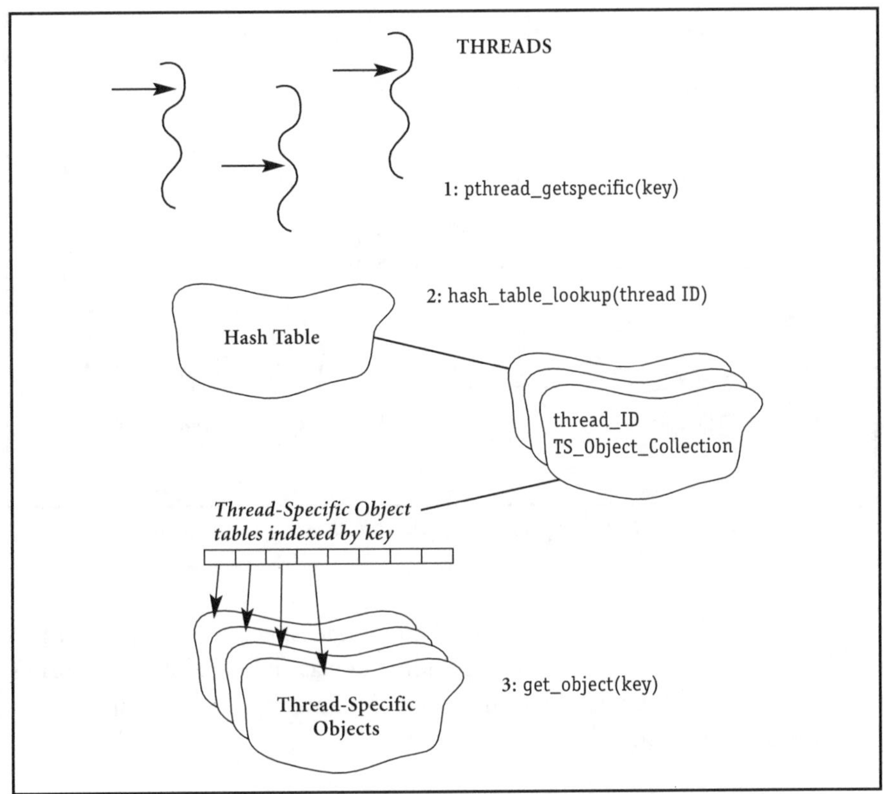

Figure 4. External implementation of Thread-Specific Storage.

ers to **TS Objects** indexed by **keys**. A thread must locate its **TS Object Collection** before accessing thread-specific objects by their **keys**. Therefore, the first design challenge is determining how to locate and store **TS Object Collections**.

TS Object Collections can be stored either 1) externally to all threads, or 2) internally to each thread. Each approach is described and evaluated here:

1. *External to all threads*: This approach defines a global mapping of each thread's ID to its **TS Object Collection** table (see Fig. 4). Locating the right collection may require the use of a reader/writer lock to prevent race conditions. Once the collection is located, however, no additional locking is required, since only one thread can be active within a **TS Object Collection**.
2. *Internal to each thread*: This approach requires each thread in a process to store a **TS Object Collection** with its other internal state (such as a runtime thread stack, program counter, general-purpose registers, and

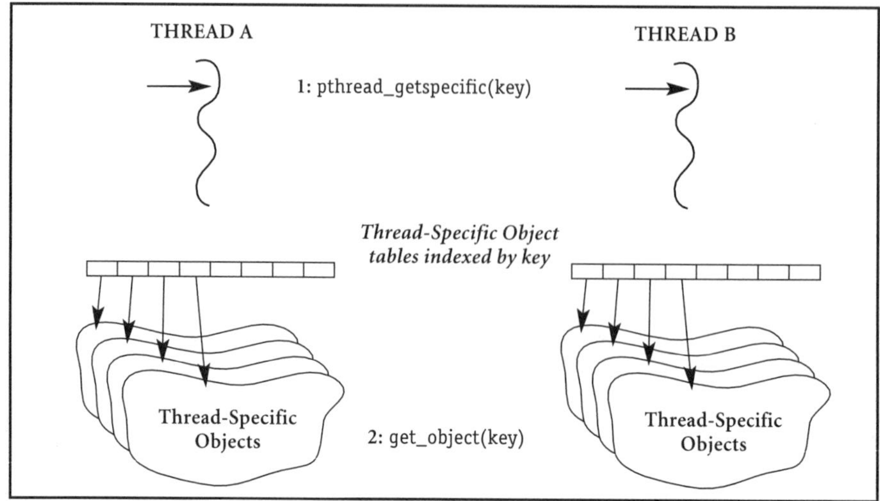

Figure 5. Internal implementation of Thread-Specific Storage.

thread ID). When a thread accesses a thread-specific object, the object is retrieved by using the corresponding **key** as an index into the thread's internal **TS Object Collection** (see Fig. 5). This approach requires no additional locking.

Choosing between the external and internal implementation schemes requires developers to resolve the following tradeoffs:

Fixed- versus variable-sized TS Object Collections. For both the external and internal implementations, the **TS Object Collection** can be stored as a fixed-size array if the range of thread-specific keys is relatively small. For instance, the POSIX Pthread standard defines a minimum number of keys, **_POSIX_THREAD_KEYS_MAX**, that must be supported by conforming implementations. If the size is fixed (e.g., to 128 keys, which is the POSIX default), the lookup time can be **O (1)** by simply indexing into the **TS Object Collection** array using the object's key (see Fig. 5).

The range of thread-specific keys can be large, however. For instance, Solaris threads have no predefined limit on the number of keys. Therefore, Solaris uses a variable-sized data structure, which can increase the time required to manage the **TS Object Collection**.

Fixed- versus variable-sized mapping of thread IDs to TS Object Collections. Thread IDs can range from very small to very large values. This presents no problem for internal implementations since the thread ID is implicitly associated with the corresponding TS Object Collection contained in the thread's state.

For external implementations, however, it may be impractical to have a fixed-size array with an entry for every possible thread ID value. Instead, it is more space-efficient to have threads use a dynamic data structure to map thread IDs to TS Object Collections. One approach is to use a hash function on the thread ID to obtain an offset into a hash table bucket containing a chain of tuples that map each thread ID to its corresponding TS Object Collection (see Fig. 4).

Global versus local TS Object Collections. The internal approach stores the TS Object Collections *locally* with the thread, whereas the external approach stores them *globally*. Depending on the implementation of the external table, the global location can allow threads to access other threads' TS Object Collections. Although this seems to defeat the whole purpose of *thread-specific* storage, it is useful if the thread-specific storage implementation provides automatic garbage collection by recycling unused keys. This feature is particularly important for implementations that limit the number of keys to a small value (e.g., Windows NT has a limit of 64 keys per process).

However, using an external table increases the access time for every thread-specific object, since synchronization mechanisms (such as reader/writer locks) are required to avoid race conditions if a globally accessible table is modified (e.g., when creating new keys). On the other hand, keeping the TS Object Collection locally in the state of each thread requires more storage per-thread, though no less *total* memory consumption.

Sample Code

Implementing the POSIX Pthreads Thread-Specific Storage API

The following code shows how thread-specific storage can be implemented when TS Objects are stored "internally" to each thread using a fixed-sized array of keys. This example is adapted from a publicly available implementation[3] of POSIX Pthreads.[4]

The thread_state structure shown below contains the state of a thread:

```
struct thread_state
{
  // The thread-specific error number.
  int errno_;

  // Thread-specific data values.
  void *key_[_POSIX_THREAD_KEYS_MAX];

  // ... Other thread state.
};
```

In addition to errno and the array of thread-specific storage pointers, this structure also includes a pointer to the thread's stack and space to store data (e.g., the program counter) that is saved/restored during a context switch.

For a particular thread-specific object, the same key value is used to set and get thread-specific values for all threads. For instance, if Logger objects are being registered to keep track of thread-specific logging attributes, the thread-specific Logger proxy will be assigned some key value N. All threads will use this value N to access their thread-specific logging object. A count of the total number of keys currently in use can be stored globally to all threads, as follows:

```
typedef int pthread_key_t;
// All threads share the same key counter.
static pthread_key_t total_keys_ = 0;
```

The total_keys_ count is automatically incremented every time a new thread-specific key is required, as shown in the pthread_ key_create function below:

```
// Create a new global key and specify a "destructor" function callback.
int
pthread_key_create (pthread_key_t *key,
                    void (*thread_exit_hook) (void *))
{
  if (total_keys_ >= _POSIX_THREAD_KEYS_MAX) {
    // pthread_self() refers to the context of the
    // currently active thread.
    pthread_self ()->errno_ = ENOMEM;
    return -1;
  }
```

```
    thread_exit_hook_[total_keys_] = thread_exit_hook;
    *key = total_keys_++;
    return 0;
}
```

The pthread_key_create function allocates a new key value that uniquely identifies a thread-specific data object. It also allows an application to associate a thread_exit_hook with a key. This hook is a pointer to a function that is called automatically when 1) a thread exits, and 2) there is a thread-specific object registered for a key. An array of function pointers to "thread exit hooks" can be stored globally, as follows:

```
// Exit hooks to clean up thread-specific keys.
static void
(*thread_exit_hook_[_POSIX_THREAD_KEYS_MAX]) (void);
```

The pthread_exit function below shows how thread exit hook functions are called in the implementation of pthread_exit:

```
// Terminate the thread and call thread exit hooks.
void pthread_exit (void *status)
{
    // ...
    for (i = 0; i < total_keys; i++)
        if (pthread_self ()->key_[i]
                && thread_exit_hook_[i])
            // Indirect pointer to function call.
            (*thread_exit_hook_[i])
                (pthread_self ()->key_[i]);
    // ...
}
```

Applications can register different functions for each thread-specific data object, but for each object the same function is called for each thread. Registering dynamically allocated thread-specific objects is a common use case. Therefore, thread exit hooks typically look like the following:

```
static void
cleanup_tss_Logger (void *ptr)
{

    // This cast is necessary to invoke the destructor (if it exists).
    delete (Logger *) ptr;
}
```

This function deallocates a dynamically allocated Logger object.

The pthread_setspecific function binds *a value* to the given key for the calling thread:

```
// Associate a value with a data key for the calling thread.
int pthread_setspecific (int key,void *value)
{
   if (key < 0 || key >= total_keys) {
      pthread_self ()->errno_ = EINVAL;
      return -1;
   }

   pthread_self ()->key_[key] = value;
   return 0;
}
```

Likewise, pthread_getspecific stores into value the data bound to the given key for the calling thread:

```
// Retrieve a value from a data key for the calling thread.
int pthread_getspecific (int key,void **value)
{
   if (key < 0 || key >= total_keys) {
      pthread_self ()->errno_ = EINVAL;
      return -1;
   }

   *value = pthread_self ()->key_[key];
   return 0;
}
```

Because data are stored internally in the state of each thread, neither of these functions requires any additional locks to access thread-specific data.

USING THREAD-SPECIFIC STORAGE IN APPLICATIONS

The example below illustrates how to use the thread-specific storage APIs from the POSIX Pthread specification in a C function that can be called from more than one thread *without* having to call an initialization function explicitly:

```
// Local to the implementation.
static pthread_mutex_t keylock =
   PTHREAD_MUTEX_INITIALIZER;
static pthread_key_t key;
```

```
static int once = 0;
void *func (void)
{
   void *ptr = 0;

   // Use the Double-Checked Locking pattern (described further
   // below) to serialize key creation without forcing each access
   // to be locked.

   if (once == 0) {
      pthread_mutex_lock (&keylock);

      if (once == 0) {
         // Register the free(3C) function to deallocation
         // TSS memory when the thread goes out of scope.
         pthread_key_create (&key, free);
         once = 1;
      }
      pthread_mutex_unlock (&keylock);
   }

   pthread_getspecific (key, (void **) &ptr);

   if (ptr == 0) {
         ptr = malloc (SIZE);
         pthread_setspecific (key, ptr);
   }

   return ptr;
}
```

EVALUATION

The solution above directly invokes the thread-specific library functions (such as pthread_getspecific and pthread_setspecific) in application code. However, these APIs, which are written in C, have the following limitations:

- *Nonportable*: The interfaces of POSIX Pthreads, Solaris threads, and Win32 threads are very similar. However, the semantics of Win32 threads are subtly different, since they do not provide a reliable means of cleaning up objects allocated in thread-specific storage when a thread exits. Moreover, there is no API to delete a key in Solaris threads. This makes it hard to write portable code between UNIX and Win32 platforms.

- *Hard to use*: Even with error checking omitted, the locking operations shown by the func example in the section called "Using Thread-Specific Storage in Applications" are complex and nonintuitive. This code is a C implementation of the Double-Checked Locking pattern.[5] It's instructive to compare this C implementation to the C++ version in the section called "The C++ Delegation Operator" to observe the greater simplicity, clarity, and type-safety resulting from the use of C++ wrappers.
- *Nontype-safe*: The POSIX Pthreads, Solaris, and Win32 thread-specific storage interfaces store pointers to thread-specific objects as void *s. Although this approach is flexible, it's easy to make mistakes since void *s eliminate type-safety.

VARIATIONS

The "Sample Code" section demonstrated how to implement and use the Thread-Specific Storage pattern via POSIX pthread interfaces. However, the resulting solution was nonportable, hard to use, and not type-safe. To overcome these limitations, additional classes and C++ wrappers can be developed to program thread-specific storage robustly in a type-safe manner.

This section illustrates how to encapsulate low-level thread-specific storage mechanisms provided by Solaris threads, POSIX Pthreads, or Win32 threads using C++ wrappers. The "Hard-coded C++ Wrapper" section describes how to encapsulate the POSIX Pthread library interfaces with hard-coded C++ wrappers and the "C++ Template Wrapper" section describes a more general solution using C++ template wrappers. The example used for each alternative approach is a variant of the Logger abstraction described in the "Liabilities" section.

HARD-CODED C++ WRAPPER

One way to make all instances of a class be thread-specific is to use thread-specific library routines directly. The steps required to implement this approach are described below. Error checking has been minimized to save space.

Define the Thread-Specific State Information. The first step is to determine the object's state information that must be stored or retrieved in thread-specific storage. For instance, a Logger might have the following state:

```
class Logger_State
{
public:
   int errno_;
   // Error number.

   int line_num_;
   // Line where the error occurred.

   // ...
};
```

Each thread will have its own copy of this state information.

Define an External Class Interface. The next step is to define an external class interface that is used by all application threads. The external class interface of the Logger below looks just like an ordinary nonthread-specific C++ class:

```
class Logger
{
public:
   // Set/get the error number.
   int errno (void);
   void errno (int);

   // Set/get the line number.
   int line_num (void);
   void line_num (int);

   // ...
};
```

Define a Thread-Specific Helper Method. This step uses the thread-specific storage functions provided by the thread library to define a helper method that returns a pointer to the appropriate thread-specific storage. Typically, this helper method performs the following steps:

1. *Key initialization*: Initialize a key for each thread-specific object and use this key to get/set a thread-specific pointer to dynamically allocated memory containing an instance of the internal structure. The code could be implemented as follows:

```
class Logger
{
public:
   // ... Same as above ...
```

```
protected:
   Logger_State *get_tss_state (void);

   // Key for the thread-specific error data.
   pthread_key_t key_;

   // "First time in" flag.
   int once_;
};

Logger_State *Logger::get_tss_state (void)
{
   // Check to see if this is the first time in and if so, allocate the
   // key (this code doesn't protect against multithreaded
   // race conditions...).
   if (once_ == 0) {
      pthread_key_create (this->key_, free);
      once_ = 1;
   }

   Logger_State *state_ptr;

   // Get the state data from thread-specific storage. Note that no
   // locks are required...
   pthread_getspecific (this->key_,(void **) &state_ptr);

   if (state_ptr == 0) {
      state_ptr = new Logger_State;
      pthread_setspecific (this->key_,(void *) state_ptr);
   }

   // Return the pointer to thread-specific storage.
   return state_ptr;
};
```

2. *Obtain a pointer to the thread-specific object*: Every method in the external interface will call the get_tss_state helper method to obtain a pointer to the Logger_State object that resides in thread-specific storage, as follows:

```
int Logger::errno (void)
{
   return this->get_tss_state ()->errno_;
}
```

3. *Perform normal operations*: Once the external interface method has the pointer, the application can perform operations on the thread-specific object as if it were an ordinary (i.e., nonthread-specific) C++ object:

```
Logger logger;
int main (void)
{
   if (recv (...) == -1
         && logger->errno () == EWOULDBLOCK)
      // ...
};
```

Evaluation of the Hard-coded Wrapper. The advantage of using a hard-coded wrapper is that it shields applications from the knowledge of the thread-specific library functions. The disadvantage of this approach is that it does not promote reusability, portability, or flexibility. In particular, for every thread-specific class, the developer needs to reimplement the thread-specific helper method within the class.

Moreover, if the application is ported to a platform with a different thread-specific storage API, the code internal to each thread-specific class must be altered to use the new thread library. In addition, making changes directly to the thread-specific class makes it hard to change the threading policies. For instance, changing a thread-specific class to a global class would require intrusive changes to the code, which reduces flexibility and reusability. In particular, each access to state internal to the object would require changes to the helper method that retrieves the state from thread-specific storage.

C++ Template Wrapper

A more reusable, portable, and flexible approach is to implement a TS Object Proxy template that is responsible for all thread-specific methods. This approach allows classes to be decoupled from the knowledge of how thread-specific storage is implemented. This solution improves the reusability, portability, and flexibility of the code by defining a proxy class called TSS. As shown below, this class is a template that is parameterized by the class whose objects reside in thread-specific storage:

```
// TS Proxy template
template <class TYPE>
class TSS
{
```

```
public:
    // Constructor.
    TSS (void);

    // Destructor
    ~TSS (void);

    // Use the C++ "smart pointer" operator to
    // access the thread-specific TYPE object.
    TYPE *operator-> ();

private:
    // Key for the thread-specific error data.
    pthread_key_t key_;

    // "First time in" flag.
    int once_;

    // Avoid race conditions during initialization.
    Thread_Mutex keylock_;

    // Cleanup hook that deletes dynamically allocated memory.
    static void cleanup_hook (void *ptr);
};
```

The methods in this class are described as follows. As before, error checking has been minimized to save space.

The C++ Delegation Operator. Applications can invoke methods on a TSS proxy as if they were calling the target class by overloading the C++ delegation operator (operator->). The operator used in this implementation controls all access to the thread-specific object of class TYPE. The operator-> method receives special treatment from the C++ compiler. As described in the "Use Case" section, it first obtains a pointer to the appropriate TYPE from thread-specific storage, and then redelegates the original method invoked on it.

Most of the work in the TSS class is performed in the operator-> method shown here:

```
template <class TYPE> TYPE *
TSS<TYPE>::operator-> ()
{
    TYPE *tss_data = 0;
```

```
    // Use the Double-Checked Locking pattern to
    // avoid locking except during initialization.

    // First check.
    if (this->once_ == 0) {
      // Ensure that we are serialized (constructor
      // of Guard acquires the lock).

      Guard <Thread_Mutex> guard (this->keylock_);

      // Double check
      if (this->once_ == 0) {
        pthread_key_create (&this->key_,&this->cleanup_hook);

        // *Must* come last so that other threads
        // don't use the key until it's created.
        this->once_ = 1;
      }
      // Guard destructor releases the lock.
    }

    // Get the data from thread-specific storage.
    // Note that no locks are required here...
    pthread_getspecific (this->key_,(void **) &tss_data);

    // Check to see if this is the first time in for this thread.
    if (tss_data == 0) {
      // Allocate memory off the heap and store it in a pointer
      // in thread-specific storage (on the stack...).
      tss_data = new TYPE;

      // Store the dynamically allocated pointer in
      // thread-specific storage.
      pthread_setspecific (this->key_,(void *) tss_data);
    }

    return tss_data;
  }
```

The TSS template is a proxy that transparently transforms ordinary C++ classes into type-safe, thread-specific classes. It combines the operator-> method with other C++ features like templates, inlining, and overloading. It also utilizes patterns like Double-Checked Locking Optimization[5] and Proxy.[6,7]

The Double-Checked Locking Optimization pattern is used in operator-> to test the once_ flag twice in the code. Although multiple threads could access the same instance of TSS simultaneously, only one thread can validly create a key (i.e., via pthread_key_create). All threads will then use this key to access a thread-specific object of the parameterized class TYPE. Therefore, operator-> uses a Thread_Mutex keylock_ to ensure that only one thread executes pthread_key_create.

The first thread that acquires keylock_ sets once_ to 1 and all subsequent threads that call operator-> will find once_ != 0 and therefore skip the initialization step. The second test of once_ handles the case where multiple threads executing in parallel queue up at keylock_ before the first thread has set once_ to 1. In this case, when the other queued threads finally obtain the mutex keylock_, they will find once_ equal to 1 and will not execute pthread_key_create.

Once the key_ is created, no further locking is necessary to access the thread-specific data. This is because the pthread_{getspecific, setspecific} functions retrieve the TS Object of class TYPE from the state of the calling thread. No additional locks are needed since this thread state is independent from other threads.

In addition to reducing locking overhead, the implementation of class TSS shown here shields application code from knowing that objects are specific to the calling thread. To accomplish this, the implementation uses C++ features such as templates, operator overloading, and the delegation operator (i.e., operator->).

The Constructor and Destructor. The constructor for the TSS class is minimal; it simply initializes the local instance variables:

```
template <class TYPE>
TSS<TYPE>::TSS (void): once_ (0), key_ (0) {}
```

Note that we do not allocate the TSS key or a new TYPE instance in the constructor. There are several reasons for this design:

- *Thread-specific storage semantics*: The thread that initially creates the TSS object (e.g., the main thread) is often not the only one to use this object (e.g., the worker threads). Therefore, there is no benefit from preinitializing a new TYPE in the constructor since this instance will only be accessible by the main thread.
- *Deferred initialization*: On some OS platforms, TSS keys are a limited resource. For instance, Windows NT only allows a total of 64 TSS keys per process. Therefore, keys should not be allocated until absolutely necessary. Instead, the initialization is deferred until the first time the operator-> method is called.

The destructor for TSS presents us with several tricky design issues. The obvious solution is to release the TSS key allocated in operator->. However, there are several problems with this approach:

- *Lack of features*: Win32 and POSIX pthreads define a function that releases a TSS key. However, Solaris threads do not. Therefore, writing a portable wrapper is difficult.
- *Race conditions*: The primary reason that Solaris threads do not provide a function to release the TSS key is that it is costly to implement. The problem is that each thread maintains the objects referenced by that key separately. Only when all these threads have exited and the memory has been reclaimed is it safe to release the key.

As a result of the problems mentioned here, our destructor is a no-op:

```
template <class TYPE>
TSS<TYPE>::~TSS (void)
{
}
```

The cleanup_hook is a static method that casts its ptr argument to the appropriate TYPE * before deleting it:

```
template <class TYPE> void
TSS<TYPE>::cleanup_hook (void *ptr)
{
   // This cast is necessary to invoke the destructor (if it exists).
   delete (TYPE *) ptr;
}
```

This ensures that the destructor of each thread-specific object is called when a thread exits.

Use case. The following is a C++ template wrapper-based solution for our continuing example of a thread-specific Logger accessed by multiple worker threads:

```
// This is the "logically" global, but "physically" thread-specific
// logger object, using the TSS template wrapper.
static TSS<Logger> logger;
```

```
// A typical worker function.
static void *worker (void *arg)
{
  // Network connection stream.
  SOCK_Stream *stream =
    static_cast <SOCK_Stream *> arg;

  // Read from the network connection and process the data
  //  until the connection is closed.

  for (;;) {
    char buffer[BUFSIZ];
    int result = stream->recv (buffer, BUFSIZ);

    // Check to see if the recv() call failed.
    if (result == -1) {
      if (logger->errno () != EWOULDBLOCK)
        // Record error result.
        logger->log ("recv failed, errno = %d",logger->errno ());

    } else
      // Perform the work on success.
      process_buffer (buffer);
  }
}
```

Consider the call to logger->errno above. The C++ compiler replaces this call with two method calls. The first is a call to TSS::operator->, which returns a Logger instance residing in thread-specific storage. The compiler then generates a second method call to the errno method of the logger object returned by the previous call. In this case, TSS behaves as a proxy allowing an application to access and manipulate the thread-specific error value as if it were an ordinary C++ object.[ß]

The Logger example above is a good example of how using a logically global access point is advantageous. Since the worker function is global, it is not straightforward for threads to manage both a physical *and* logical separation of Logger objects. Instead, a thread-specific Logger allows multiple threads to use a single logical access point to manipulate physically separate TSS objects.

ß Note that C++ operator-> does not work for built-in types like int since there are no methods that can be delegated to, which is why we cannot use int in place of the Logger class used above.

Evaluation. The TSS proxy design based on the C++ operator-> has the following benefits:

- *Maximizes code reuse:* By decoupling thread-specific methods from application-specific classes (i.e., the formal parameter class TYPE). It is not necessary to rewrite the subtle thread-specific key creation and allocation logic.
- *Increases portability*: Porting an application to another thread library (such as the TLS interfaces in Win32) only requires changing the TSS class, not any applications using the class.
- *Greater flexibility and transparency*: Changing a class to/from a thread-specific class simply requires changing how an object of the class is defined. This can be decided at compile time, as follows:

```
#if defined (_REENTRANT)
static TSS<Logger> logger;
#else
// Non-MT behavior is unchanged.
Logger logger;
#endif /* REENTRANT */
```

Note that the use case for logger remains unchanged regardless of whether the thread-specific or nonthread-specific form of Logger is used.

Known Uses

The following are known uses of the Thread-Specific Storage pattern:

- The errno mechanism implemented on OS platforms that support the POSIX and Solaris threading APIs are widely-used examples of the Thread-Specific Storage pattern.[1] In addition, the C runtime library provided with Win32 supports thread-specific errno. The Win32 GetLastError/SetLastError functions also implement the Thread-Specific Storage pattern.
- In the Win32 operating system, windows are owned by threads.[8] Each thread that owns a window has a private message queue where the OS enqueues user-interface events. API calls that retrieve the next message waiting to be processed, dequeue the next message on the calling thread's message queue, which resides in thread-specific storage.

- OpenGL[9] is a C API for rendering 3D graphics. The program renders graphics in terms of polygons that are described by making repeated calls to the glVertex function to pass each vertex of the polygon to the library. State variables, set before the vertices are passed to the library, determine precisely what OpenGL draws as it receives the vertices. This state is stored as encapsulated global variables within the OpenGL library or on the graphics card itself. On the Win32 platform, the OpenGL library maintains a unique set of state variables in thread-specific storage for each thread using the library.
- Thread-specific storage is used within the ACE network programming toolkit[10], to implement its error handling scheme, which is similar to the Logger approach described in the "Use case" section. In addition, ACE implements the type-safe thread-specific storage template wrappers described in the "C++ Template Wrapper" section.

RELATED PATTERNS

Objects implemented with thread-specific storage are often used as per-thread Singletons[7], e.g., errno is a per-thread Singleton. Not all uses of thread-specific storage are Singletons, however, since a thread can have multiple instances of a type allocated from thread-specific storage. For instance, each Task object implemented in ACE[10], stores a cleanup hook in thread-specific storage.

The TSS template class shown in the "Sample Code" section serves as a Proxy[6,7] that shields the libraries, frameworks, and applications from the implementation of thread-specific storage provided by OS thread libraries.

The Double-Checked Locking Optimization pattern[5] is commonly used by applications that utilize the Thread-Specific Storage pattern to avoid constraining the order of initialization for thread-specific storage keys.

CONCLUSION

Multithreading an existing application often adds significant complexity to the software due to the additional concurrency control protocols needed to prevent race conditions and deadlocks.[11] The Thread-Specific Storage pattern alleviates some synchronization overhead and programming complexity by allowing multiple threads to use one logically global access point to retrieve thread-specific data without incurring locking costs for each access.

Application threads use **TS Object Proxies** to access **TS Objects**. The proxies delegate to **TS Object Collections** to retrieve the objects corresponding to each application thread. This ensures that different application threads do not share the same **TS Object**. The "C++ Template Wrapper" section showed how the **TS Object Proxy** participant of the Thread-Specific Storage pattern can be implemented to ensure that threads only access their own data through strongly-typed C++ class interfaces. When combined with other patterns (such as Proxy, Singleton, and Double-Checked Locking) and C++ language features (such as templates and operator overloading), the **TS Proxy** can be implemented so that objects using the Thread-Specific Storage pattern can be treated like conventional objects.

Acknowledgments

Thanks to Peter Sommerlad and Hans Rohnert for their insightful comments on earlier versions of this paper. Doug Schmidt's and Tim Harrison's research is supported in part by a grant from Siemens AG. Nat Pryce's research is funded by British Telecom, plc.

References

1. Eykholt, J., *et al.* "Beyond Multiprocessing…Multithreading the SunOS Kernel," in *Proceedings of the Summer USENIX Conference*, San Antonio, TX, Jun. 1992.
2. Lavender, R. G., and D. C. Schmidt. "Active Object: An Object Behavioral Pattern for Concurrent Programming," *Pattern Languages of Program Design*, J. O. Coplien, J. Vlissides, and N. Kerth, Eds., Addison-Wesley, Reading, MA, 1996.
3. Mueller, F. "A Library Implementation of POSIX Threads Under UNIX," *Proceedings of the Winter USENIX Conference*, pp. 29–42, San Diego, CA, Jan. 1993.
4. IEEE. *Threads Extension for Portable Operating Systems (Draft 10)*, Feb. 1996.
5. Schmidt, D. C., and T. Harrison. "Double-Checked Locking—An Object Behavioral Pattern for Initializing and Accessing Thread-Safe Objects Efficiently," *Pattern Languages of Program Design,* R. Martin, F. Buschmann, and D. Riehle, Eds., Addison-Wesley, Reading, MA, 1997.
6. Buschmann, F., *et al. Pattern-Oriented Software Architecture—A System of Patterns*, Wiley, New York, 1996.
7. Gamma, E., *et al. Design Patterns: Elements of Reusable Object-Oriented Software*, Addison-Wesley, Reading, MA, 1995.

8. Petzold, C. *Programming Windows 95*, Microsoft Press, Redmond, WA, 1995.

9. Neider, J., T. Davis, and M. Woo. *OpenGL Programming Guide: The Official Guide to Learning OpenGL, Release 1*, Addison-Wesley, Reading, MA, 1993.

10. Schmidt, D. C. "ACE: An Object-Oriented Framework for Developing Distributed Applications," *Proceedings of the 6th USENIX C++ Technical Conference*, USENIX Association, Cambridge, MA, Apr. 1994.

11. Ousterhout, J. "Why Threads Are a Bad Idea (For Most Purposes)," *USENIX Winter Technical Conference*, USENIX, San Diego, CA, Jan. 1996.

12. Mueller, H. "Patterns for Handling Exception Handling Successfully," *C++ Report*, Jan. 1996.

13. Pryce, N. "Type-Safe Session: An Object-Structural Pattern," *Submitted to the 2nd European Pattern Languages of Programming Conference*, Jul. 1997.

14. Gosling, J., and F. Yellin. *The Java Application Programming Interface Vol. 2: Window Toolkit and Applets*, Addison-Wesley, Reading, MA, 1996.

Alternative Solutions

In practice, thread-specific storage is typically used to resolve the following two use cases for object-oriented software:

1. To communicate information (e.g., error information) implicitly between modules.
2. To adapt legacy single-threaded software written in a procedural style to modern multithreaded operating systems and programming languages.

It is often a good idea, however, to avoid thread-specific storage for use case #1 because it can increase coupling between modules and reduce reusability. In the case of error handling, for instance, thread-specific storage can often be avoided by using exceptions, as described in the "Exception Handling" section.

The use of thread-specific storage for use case #2 cannot be avoided except through redesign. When designing new software, however, thread-specific storage can often be avoided by using exception handling, explicit intercomponent communication contexts, or reified threads, as described in the following section.

Exception Handling An elegant way of reporting errors between modules is to use exception handling. Many modern languages, such as C++ and Java, use exception handling as an error reporting mechanism. It is also used in some operating systems, such as Win32. For example, the following code illustrates a hypothetical OS whose system calls throw exceptions:

```
void *worker (SOCKET socket)
{
  // Read from the network connection and process the data
  //  until the connection is closed.
  for (;;) {
    char buffer[BUFSIZ];

    try {
      // Assume that recv() throws exceptions.
      recv (socket, buffer, BUFSIZ, 0);
      // Perform the work on success.
      process_buffer (buffer);
    } catch (EWOULDBLOCK) {
      continue;
    } catch (OS_Exception error) {
        // Record error result in thread-specific data.
        printf ("recv failed, error = %s",error.reason);
    }
  }
```

There are several benefits to using exception handling:

- *It is extensible*: Modern OO languages facilitate the extension of exception handling policies and mechanisms via features (such as using inheritance to define a

(continued)

Alternative Solutions (continued)

hierarchy of exception classes) that have minimal intrusion on existing interfaces and usage.

- *It decouples error handling from normal processing cleanly*: For example, error handling information is not passed explicitly to an operation. Moreover, an application cannot accidentally "ignore" an exception by failing to check function return values.
- *It can be type-safe*: In strongly typed languages, such as C++ and Java, exceptions are thrown and caught in a strongly-typed manner to enhance the organization and correctness of error handling code. In contrast to checking a thread-specific error value explicitly, the compiler ensures that the correct handler is executed for each type of exception.

However, there are several drawbacks to the use of exception handling:

- *It is not universally available*: Not all languages provide exception handling and many C++ compilers do not implement exceptions. Likewise, when an OS provides exception handling services, they must be supported by language extensions, thereby reducing the portability of the code.
- *It complicates the use of multiple languages*: Since languages implement exceptions in different ways, or do not implement exceptions at all, it can be hard to integrate components written in different languages when they throw exceptions. In contrast, reporting error information using integer values or structures provides a universal solution.
- *It complicates resource management*: Such as by increasing the number of exit paths from a block of C++ code.[12] If garbage collection is not supported by the language or programming environment, care must be taken to ensure that dynamically allocated objects are deleted when an exception is thrown.
- *It is potentially time and/or space inefficient*: Poor implementations of exception handling incur time and/or space overhead even when exceptions are not thrown.[12] This overhead can be particularly problematic for embedded systems that must be small and efficient.

The drawbacks of exception handling are particularly problematic for system-level frameworks (such as kernel-level device drivers or low-level communication subsystems) that must run portably on many platforms. For these types of systems, a more portable, efficient, and thread-safe way to handle errors is to define an error handler abstraction that maintains information about the success or failure of operations explicitly.

Explicit Contexts for Intercomponent Communication Thread-specific storage is usually used to store per-thread state to allow software components in libraries and frameworks to communicate efficiently. For example, `errno` is used to pass error values from a called component to the caller. Likewise, OpenGL API functions are called to pass information to the OpenGL library, stored in thread-specific state. The use of thread-specific storage can be avoided by explicitly representing the information passed between components as an object.

If the type of information that must be stored by the component for its users is known in advance, the object can be created by the calling thread and passed to the component as an extra argument to its operations. Otherwise, the component must create an object to hold context information in response to a request from the calling thread. The component returns an identifier for the object to the thread before the thread can make use of the component. These types of objects are often called *context objects*; context objects

Alternative Solutions (continued)

that are created on demand by a software component are often called *sessions*.

A simple example of how a context object can be created by a calling thread is illustrated by the following error handling scheme, which passes an explicit parameter to every operation:

```
void *worker (SOCKET socket)
{
    // Read from the network connection and process the data
    // until the connection is closed.

    for (;;) {
        char buffer[BUFSIZ];
        int result;
        int errno;

        // Pass the errno context object explicitly.
        result = recv (socket, buffer, BUFSIZ, 0, &errno);

        // Check to see if the recv() call failed.
        if (result == -1) {
            if (errno != EWOULDBLOCK)
                printf ("recv failed, errno = %d", errno);
        } else
            // Perform the work on success.
            process_buffer (buffer);
    }
```

Context objects created by components can be implemented by using the Type-Safe Session pattern.[13] In this pattern, the context object stores the state required by the component and provides an abstract interface that can be invoked polymorphically. The component returns a pointer to the abstract interface to the calling thread that subsequently invokes operations of the interface to use the component.

An example of how Type-Safe Sessions are used is illustrated by the difference between OpenGL and the interface provided by the Java AWT library[14] for rendering graphics onto devices such as windows, printers or bitmaps. In the AWT, a program draws onto a device by requesting a `Graphics Context` from the device. The `GraphicsContext` encapsulates the state required to render onto a device and provides an interface through which the program can set state variables and invoke drawing operations. Multiple `GraphicsContext` objects can be created dynamically, thereby removing any need to hold thread-specific state.

The benefits of using context objects compared with thread-local storage and exception handling are the following:

- *It is more portable*: It does not require language features that may not be supported universally;
- *It is more efficient*: The thread can store and access the context object directly, without having to perform a look-up in the thread-specific storage table. It does not require the compiler to build additional data structures to handle exceptions.
- *It is thread-safe*: The context object or session handle can be stored on the thread's stack, which is trivially thread-safe.

(continued)

Alternative Solutions (continued)

There are several drawbacks with using context objects created by the calling thread, however:

- *It is obtrusive*: The context object must be passed to every operation and must be explicitly checked after each operation. This clutters the program logic and may require changes to existing component interfaces to add an error handler parameter.
- *Increased overhead per invocation*: Additional overhead will occur for each invocation since an additional parameter must be added to every method call, regardless of whether the object is required. Although this is acceptable in some cases, the overhead may be noticeable for methods that are executed very frequently. In contrast, an error handling scheme based on thread-specific storage need not be used unless an error occurs.

Compared to creating context objects in the calling thread, using sessions created by the component has the following benefits:

- *It is less obtrusive*: A thread does not have to explicitly pass the context object to the component as an argument to its operations. The compiler arranges for a pointer to a context object to be passed to its operations as the hidden `this` pointer.
- *It automates initialization and shutdown*: A thread cannot start using a session until it has acquired one from a component. Components can therefore ensure that operations are never called when they are in inconsistent states. In contrast, if a component uses hidden state, a caller must explicitly initialize the library before invoking operations and shut down the component when it has finished. Forgetting to do so can cause obscure errors or waste resources.
- *Structure is explicit*: The relationships between different modules of code is explicitly represented as objects, which makes it easier to understand the behavior of the system.

Creating context objects within the component has the following drawback compared to creating them upon the caller's stack:

- *Allocation overhead*: The component must allocate the session object on the heap or from some encapsulated cache. usually this will be less efficient than allocating the object on the stack.

Objectified Threads In an object-oriented language, an application can explicitly represent threads as objects. Thread classes can be defined by deriving from an abstract base class that encapsulates any state required to run as a concurrent thread and invokes an instance method as the entry point into the thread. The thread entry method would be defined as a pure virtual function in the base class and defined in derived classes. Any required thread-specific state (such as session contexts) can be defined as object instance variables, making it available to any method of the thread class. Concurrent access to these variables can be prevented through the use of language-level access control mechanisms rather than explicit synchronization objects.

The following illustrates this approach using a variant of the ACE `Task`[10], which can be used to associate a thread of control with an object.

```
class Task
{
```

Alternative Solutions (continued)

```
public:
   // Create a thread that calls the svc() hook.
   int activate (void);

   // The thread entry point.
   virtual void svc (void) = 0;

private:
   // ...
};

class Animation_Thread : public Task
{
public:
   Animation_Thread (Graphics_Context *gc)
      : device_ (gc) {}

   virtual void svc (void)
   {
      device_->clear ();
      // ... perform animation loop...
   }

private:
   Graphics_Context *device_;
};
```

The use of objectified threads has the following advantages:

- *It is more efficient*: A thread does not need to perform a look-up in a hidden data structure to access thread-specific state.
- *It is not obtrusive*: When using an objectified thread, a pointer to the current object is passed as an extra argument to each function call. Unlike the explicit session context, the argument is hidden in the source code and managed automatically by the compiler, keeping the source code uncluttered.

The use of objectified threads has the following disadvantages:

- *Thread-specific storage is not easily accessible*: Instance variables cannot be accessed except by class methods. This makes it nonintuitive to use instance variables to communicate between reusable libraries and threads. However, using thread-specific storage in this way increases coupling between components. In general, exceptions provide a more decoupled way of reporting errors between modules, though they have their own traps and pitfalls in languages like C++.[12]
- *Overhead*: The extra, hidden parameter passed to every operation will cause some overhead. This may be noticeable in functions that are executed very frequently.

Making the World Safe for Exceptions

Matthew H. Austern

Matt Austern is one of the authors of the ISO/ANSI C++ Standard, is one of the principal authors of Silicon Graphics version of the Standard Template Library, is the author of the best book on the STL (namely: Generic Programming and the STL, *Addison Wesley, 1999), and is just plain all around a pretty good guy.*

This article fits in nicely with the articles by Gillam and Sutter earlier in the book. Again, we explore the problems of exception safety. You may be saying to yourself that enough is enough. However, where exceptions are concerned, you cannot be too careful. Exceptions introduce a complexity that is similar to the complexity introduced by multi-threading. There are problems of concurrent update, data consistency, and guarding.

Anyway, when Matt writes something, it's a good idea to read it. You can't help but learn something new.

The C++ language has exceptions. It also has a standard library. How do those two features interact? At present, unfortunately, the answer is simple: badly. Many parts of the C++ standard library call user code, and the draft C++ standard* says that a program has undefined behavior "if any of these functions or operations throws an exception, unless specifically allowed in the applicable *Required Behavior* paragraph."

This isn't just legalese, it has real meaning for ordinary programs. Suppose,

* See §17.3.3.6. The second committee draft of the C++ standard is available from www.setech.com/x3.html.

for example, that your program contains a vector<T>. What happens if, when you are inserting another element into the vector, T's constructor happens to throw an exception? According to the draft C++ standard, you can't make any assumptions at all about what will happen: Your program might work, or it might crash with no possibility of recovery. And, in fact, a crash is exactly what you ought to expect if you are using a typical library implementation.

What this means is that, if exception-safety is important for your application, you can't instantiate vector<> with any type that might throw an exception. Since vector<> itself can throw exceptions (it throws bad_alloc if it runs out of memory when trying to expand its size), your program can't even contain a vector<vector<int> >.

This is clearly unsatisfactory. The C++ standardization committee is aware of this problem, and will probably fix it before the standard becomes final. Even aside from what the standard says, though, customers will almost certainly demand exception-safe library implementations and library vendors will have to respond to that demand.

What does a library vendor have to do to make an implementation exception-safe?

WHAT IS EXCEPTION SAFETY?

By now, the reason that exception-safety is an issue is well known: Exceptions subvert the ordinary flow of control. A function f() can't assume that it will be allowed to proceed to completion, because it might receive an exception from any of the functions that it itself calls. Unless f() is written specifically with exceptions in mind, this interruption could be disastrous: f() might leave data structures in some inconsistent intermediate state, or it might not release all of the resources that it obtains.

The general techniques for dealing with exceptions are also well-known. Ideally, we could just make sure that data structures are never in an inconsistent state at any point in f()'s execution. If every intermediate state is also an acceptable final state, then it is harmless for f() to be interrupted at any point.

It isn't always possible to achieve this ideal; when it isn't, C++ provides two different mechanisms for cleanup after an exception is thrown. First, cleanup code can appear explicitly in a catch clause; and second, cleanup code can appear in destructors (see Listing 1). A local automatic object will be destroyed at the end of its scope, regardless of whether its scope is left normally or by means of an exception. This is called "stack unwinding."

Listing 1. Two Mechanisms for Ensuring Cleanup after an Exception is Thrown.

```
void f()
{
aType X;  // X's destructor will be executed when f() is
// exited, even if it exits through an
// exception.
    ...
    try {
    ...
    }
    catch(...) {
    ...        // Cleanup code.
    throw;  // Propagate the exception to f()'s caller.
    }
}
```

(If a destructor throws an exception during stack unwinding, then the program will fail disastrously.† For this reason, among others, destructors should never throw exceptions.)

Note that, in both cases, the exception is allowed to pass through to f()'s caller. If f() is a library function, this is absolutely necessary—if it did anything else, then it would be imposing a specific error-recovery policy on every application that used the library.

Although techniques of dealing with exceptions are well known, there is much less agreement about what it means for a function f() to deal with an exception properly. "Exception safety" means different things to different people, and before we can discuss how to make f() exception-safe—that is, before we can discuss what sort of cleanup f() should do—we have to define our terms. Here are several levels of guarantees about exceptions that a function f() might make:

Level 0. If an exception is thrown from within f(), then there are no guarantees at all about the data structures that f() tried to modify. Parts of them might be lost, and parts might be corrupted. Any attempt to access any of those data structures might cause the program to crash.

Level 1. If an exception is thrown from within f(), then some of the data structures that f() tried to modify might be lost and some might be left in an inconsistent state; it might not be possible to inspect or modify any of those data structures safely. However, all data structures are guaranteed to be

† See §15.5.1 of the draft standard.

destructible. Even if no other operations on them are safe, it is at least possible to call their destructors.

Level 2. Very much like Level 1, but with one additional guarantee: An exception will not cause any resource leaks. All objects in the data structures that f() modifies will have their destructors called, either when f() handles the exception or when those data structures' destructors are called.

Level 3. If an exception is thrown within f(), then it is guaranteed that f() leaves all data structures in some consistent state—not necessarily the state they were in before f() was entered, and not necessarily the state they would have been in if f() had terminated normally, but some state in which all of the data structures' invariants are satisfied. All operations on those data structures, not just their destructors, have well-defined behavior. An exception in f() won't cause the program to leak memory, and the program won't crash just because it tries to inspect a data structure that f() modified.

Level 4. Full commit-or-rollback capability. If an exception is thrown from within f(), then it is guaranteed that the state of the program is exactly the same as if f() had never been executed. All data structures are restored to the state they were in before f() was entered.

Level 4 clearly deserves the term "exception-safe," and, equally clearly, Level 0 does not. What about the intermediate levels?

Level 1 is the minimum level that could possibly be called "exception-safe": The guarantee of destructibility is crucial. Consider, for example, the fragment in Listing 2. What happens if X::f() does not guarantee destructibility? That is, how can g() cope with the situation where it is impossible to call x's destructor safely? There isn't really any good answer to that question, since X::~X() will be called automatically when x goes out of scope. The only real option is for g() to call abort(): g() can't return, and it also can't allow the exception to propagate. Either of those would result in x going out of scope. Without the guarantee of destructibility, it simply isn't possible to recover from exceptions.

If "resource leaks" (resources that are allocated and never reclaimed) aren't a concern, it usually isn't very difficult to guarantee destructibility: Whenever a function catches an exception, it simply throws away any data structures it has touched.

Unfortunately, this simple exception policy is usually inadequate. First, it is unsuitable for long-running programs. If resources are allocated and never reclaimed—if memory is never freed, for example, or if open files are never closed—then eventually the program will run out of resources. Second, C++

Listing 2. An Example of Why the Guarantee of Destructibility Is Important. What Happens When x Goes Out of Scope?

```
class X {
    X();
    ~X();
    void f();
};
```

```
void g() {
    X x;
    try {
        x.f();
    }
    catch(...) {
        // What goes here?
    }
}
```

programs often rely on destructors for cleanup: If destructors aren't executed, then the program's behavior might be incorrect. Third, this strategy is unsuitable for a library: Even if a library doesn't provide commit-or-rollback capability, it shouldn't prevent users from implementing commit-or-rollback themselves. A library should not dictate the error-recovery policy of every application that uses it.

For a library, then, "exception-safety" ought to mean, at a minimum, the guarantee of Level 2. In practice, however, it is usually just as easy to implement Level 3: If it is possible to guarantee that a data structure is destructible, and that all of its resources will be reclaimed, then it is also usually possible to guarantee that the data structure is in some stable state. Level 4 is obviously desirable whenever possible, but it isn't always a realistic option.[1]

Immediately, though, we run into a another problem. In Listing 1, we made an assumption: We assumed that we knew which functions `f()` called, and which of them could throw exceptions. What if we didn't know that?

The problem is that the C++ library consists of *generic* components. Almost every type used by the library is a template parameter; every constructor, every destructor, every `operator++` or `operator*`, could potentially be user-supplied code.

For generic programming, exception-safety takes the form of a sort of contract: Generic classes and functions make certain guarantees about exception-safety, but those guarantees only apply if their template arguments satisfy certain restrictions. The fundamental issue of exception-safety in generic programming is to specify those guarantees and restrictions precisely.

The remainder of this article is devoted to an analysis of one specific library component: `vector<T>`. This analysis is necessarily quite lengthy—like the devil, exception-safety is in the details.

Vectors and Exceptions

The simplest container class in the C++ standard library, and also the most important, is vector<T>. A vector stores its elements in a contiguous block of memory, so accessing elements within a vector is just pointer arithmetic. (In most implementations, in fact, vector<T>'s iterators are nothing but pointers.)

The only slight complication is that the length of a vector is dynamic: elements can be inserted and erased. A vector<T> with N elements stores its elements in a block of memory whose size is larger than N * sizeof(T). That is, a vector reserves some extra space at the end for future expansion; only when this space is exhausted need the vector perform the slow operation of reallocating its storage and copying the elements from the old memory block to the new. A vector<T>, then, manages a single block of memory that is divided into two parts: the vector's elements, and the uninitialized memory that lies beyond the elements.

In most implementations, including the free SGI STL[Δ] (which I am using as the basis for this analysis), vector<T> has three data members, each of type T*: start, finish, and end_of_storage. Start points to the beginning of the vector's storage—that is, to the first element—and finish points immediately beyond the last element. Finally, end_of_storage points immediately beyond the end of the vector's storage.

The library distinguishes between a vector's *size* (the number of elements in the vector) and its *capacity* (the number of elements that it could contain without needing to reallocate its storage). The size of a vector is finish - start, and its capacity is end_of_storage - start. The elements of the vector are contained in the range [start, finish); in fact, the member functions begin() and end() just return the start and finish pointers.

These three pointers must satisfy the following class invariants:

1. start <= finish <= end_of_storage.
2. Every pointer in the range [start, finish) points to a fully constructed object of type T.
3. Pointers in the range [finish, end_of_storage) do not point to objects of type T, but to uninitialized memory.

Making sure that vector is exception-safe means making sure that these class invariants are always maintained, even in the presence of exceptions. It is nec-

Δ The SGI STL is available from http://www.sgi.com/Technology/STL.

essary to consider vector's constructors, its destructor, and all of its non-const member functions.

Constructors

Vector<T> has four constructors: a default constructor, a copy constructor, a constructor that creates a vector of a given size, and a constructor that creates a vector from a range of pointers.

If an exception is thrown from within one of vector's constructors, then the vector will never come into existence; vector's class invariants are therefore not an issue. Resource leaks, however, are. If there is an exception, we have to ensure that any elements that have been constructed get destroyed and that the memory block allocated by the vector is deallocated.

The default constructor, simply consists of pointer assignments. It involves no function calls, so exceptions aren't an issue:

```
1: vector<T>::vector() : start(0), finish(0), end_of_storage(0) {}
```

The other three constructors, in Listings 3 through 5, differ only in details. They all follow the same pattern: Allocate a block of memory just large enough to hold all of the vector's elements, set start to point to the beginning of that block, construct the elements in that block using placement new, and finally set finish and end_of_storage to point to the end of the block.

If the initial allocation fails—that is, if data_allocator::allocate() throws an exception—then no cleanup is necessary. At that point in the constructors' execution, no resources have yet been allocated. The difficulty is in the construction of the vector's elements: One of the elements' constructors might throw an exception after some of the elements have already been successfully constructed. To prevent a resource leak, the vector's constructor must catch that exception and destroy all of the fully constructed elements.

None of vector's constructors, however, call placement new directly: They call uninitialized_copy or uninitialized_fill_n. If the constructor in Listing 4, for example, puts a try block around line 4, it will be able to detect that an exception was thrown from somewhere within uninitialized_fill_n. That information isn't any use, though. It has no way of determining which element's constructor threw the exception, or how many elements had been constructed successfully.

The obvious solution is to change the semantics of uninitialized_ copy, uninitialized_fill, and uninitialized_fill_n. If those three specialized algorithms can provide commit-or-rollback semantics—that is, if they can guarantee that they

Listing 3. Vector's Copy Constructor.

```
vector<T>::vector(const vector& x) {
    start = data_allocator::allocate(x.end() - x.begin());
    finish = uninitialized_copy(x.begin(), x.end(), start);
    end_of_storage = finish;
}
```

Listing 4. One of vector's Constructors. Creates a Vector of Size *n*.

```
vector<T>::vector(size_type n,
        const value_type& value = value_type()) {
    start = data_allocator::allocate(n);
    uninitialized_fill_n(start, n, value);
    finish = start + n;
    end_of_storage = finish;
}
```

Listing 5. One of vector's Constructors. Initializes a Vector from a Range of Elements.

```
vector<T>:: vector(const_iterator first, const_iterator last) {
    size_type n = 0;
    distance(first, last, n);
    start = data_allocator::allocate(n);
    finish = uninitialized_copy(first, last, start);
    end_of_storage = finish;
}
```

will create either all of the requested elements, or none of them—then making vector's constructors exception-safe becomes trivial. All that is necessary, if one of vector's constructors catches an exception, is to deallocate the vector's memory block, and then rethrow the exception.

Fortunately, this is not only possible but easy. The only operation in uninitialized_copy that can possibly fail is the copy constructor; if an element's copy constructor throws an exception, then uninitialized_copy must destroy all of the elements it had constructed up to that point. Listing 6 is an implementation of uninitialized_copy that does this. (Note that this imposes a requirement on uninitialized_copy's template parameter Forward Iterator: iterator operations, such as increment and dereference, cannot throw exceptions. This assumption is valid for our purposes, since vector never calls uninitialized_copy with any argument type other than pointers.)

Listing 6. An Exception-Safe Implementation of uninitialized_copy.

```
template <class InputIterator, class ForwardIterator>
ForwardIterator uninitialized_copy(InputIterator first,
InputIterator last,
ForwardIterator result) {
    ForwardIterator cur = result;
    try {
        for ( ; first != last; ++first, ++cur)
            construct(&*cur, *first);
        return cur;
    }
    catch(...) {
        destroy(result, cur);
        throw;
    }
}
```

Listing 7. An Exception-Safe Implementation of vector's Copy Constructor.

```
vector<T>::vector(const vector& x) {
    start = data_allocator::allocate(x.end() - x.begin());
    try {
        finish = uninitialized_copy(x.begin(), x.end(), start);
        end_of_storage = finish;
    }
    catch(...) {
        data_allocator:: deallocate(start, x.end() - x.begin());
        throw;
    }
}
```

Listing 7 shows an exception-safe version of vector's copy constructor; the generalization to the other constructors is straightforward.

The Destructor

Vector<T>::~vector(), shown here, does two things: It destroys all of the vector's elements, and it deallocates the vector's memory block. Both operations involve calling user code:

```
vector<T>::~vector() {
    destroy(start, finish);
```

```
    data_allocator::deallocate(start, end_of_storage - start);
}
```

Destroying the elements means calling T::~T(), and deleting the memory block means calling a member function of the (potentially user-provided) allocator. Without further restrictions, then, there could be an exception thrown from within vector<T>::~vector(). This is clearly undesirable. Destructors should not throw exceptions.

There is no good way to handle an exception thrown from T::~T() or data_allocator::deallocate(): any recovery from failure would have to involve calling precisely those functions themselves. Indeed, the catch clauses of vector's constructors (Listings 6 and 7) do call those functions. We have therefore arrived at our first restriction on vector's template arguments: T's destructor, and the allocator's deallocation function, may not throw exceptions.

BASIC ACCESSORS

Vector, like all other STL-compliant containers, has several low-level member functions that return basic information about the container—its size, for example, or the value of the *ith* element. All of vector's basic accessors are inline.

There is no need to consider the const basic accessors, since exception-safety for an object X is only an issue when X is being modified. At first glance, the non-const basic accessors (see Listing 8), also appear to be irrelevant, since they do not appear to modify the vector in any way.

That appearance, though, is misleading. The reason that the accessors in Listing 8 are non-const in the first place is that, by providing mutable references

Listing 8. Basic Non-const Accessor Functions.

```
template <class T> class vector {
    ...
public:
    iterator begin() { return start; }
    iterator end() { return finish; }
    reference operator[](size_type n) { return *(begin() + n); }
    reference front() { return *begin(); }
    reference back() { return *(end() - 1); }
    reverse_iterator rbegin() { return reverse_iterator(end()); }
    reverse_iterator rend() { return reverse_iterator(begin()); }
    ...
};
```

to the vector's elements, they allow the user to modify the vector. They thus present a very real problem for exception-safety.

Suppose, for example, that x is of type T and V is of type vector<T>. Then the statement V[0] = x; invokes T's assignment operator. If T is itself a data structure (one obvious example is vector<vector<int> >) then this assignment might throw an exception.

Note that this exception is not thrown from within one of vector's member functions, but in user code; the exception is thrown after vector's member function has already returned. The vector therefore has no way of preventing this exception from corrupting V[0]; in fact, it doesn't even have any way of detecting that the exception was ever thrown. And if the exception renders this element nondestructible, then the vector itself is also nondestructible. A vector's destructor, after all, must invoke the elements' destructors.

This problem is more general than assignment: V[0] returns a mutable reference, so the user may invoke any of T's member functions. If any of them throws an exception and corrupts V[0], then the same reasoning applies. We have thus arrived at an important principle: It is impossible for an object that provides mutable references to its elements to be any more exception-safe than its elements are.

All STL-compliant sequences, including vector, provide mutable references. If vector<T> is to have Level 3 exception-safety, then it must, in turn, require T to have Level 3 exception-safety.

Inserting Elements

The size of a vector is not fixed at the time of the vector's construction: Elements can be inserted into a vector, increasing its size, or erased from it, decreasing its size. There are four member functions for adding elements to a vector: push_back, which appends a single element to the end of the vector, a two-argument version of insert, which inserts a single element at an arbitrary position in the vector, and two three-argument versions, each of which inserts multiple elements at an arbitrary position. One of the three-argument versions inserts n copies of a single value x, and the other inserts values from a range [first, last).

The implementation of the two-argument insert is shown in Listing 9, and the implementation of one of the three-argument inserts is shown in Listing 10. (The two three-argument inserts are almost identical, so there is no reason to show both implementations.)

The overall strategies of the member functions in Listings 9 and 10 are very

Listing 9. The Version of Insert That Inserts a Single Element into a Vector.

```
vector<T>::iterator
vector<T>::insert(iterator position, const T& x = T()) {
   size_type n = position - begin();
   if (finish != end_of_storage && position == end()) {
      construct(finish, x);
      ++finish;
   }
   else
      insert_aux(position, x);
   return begin() + n;
}

void vector<T>::insert_aux (iterator position, const T& x) {
   if (finish != end_of_storage) {
      construct(finish, *(finish - 1));
      T x_copy = x;
      copy_backward (position, finish - 1, finish);
      *position = x_copy;
      ++finish;
   }
   else {
      const size_type old_size = size();
      const size_type len = old_size != 0 ? 2 * old_size : 1;
      const iterator tmp = data_allocator::
      allocate(len);
      uninitialized_copy (begin(), position, tmp);
      construct(tmp + (position - begin()), x);
      uninitialized_copy (position, end(),
         tmp + (position - begin()) + 1);
      destroy(begin(), end());
      deallocate();
      end_of_storage = tmp + len;
      finish = tmp + old_size + 1;
      start = tmp;
   }
}
```

similar. If there is enough space in the vector's memory block for the new elements (that is, if fewer than end_of_storage - finish elements are being inserted), then shift the vector's existing elements towards the end to make room for the new element. Otherwise allocate a new memory block; copy the old elements into it, leaving room for the new elements; and deallocate the old block. Finally, put the new elements into the location that has been reserved for them.

This procedure contains three operations that can potentially fail and throw exceptions: assignment, copy construction, and memory allocation.

The simplest place to insert an element in a vector is at the end. Accordingly, Listing 9 begins, in line 4 of insert(), with a test. If the element is to be inserted at the end, and if no reallocation is required, then line 5 constructs the element, and line 6 increments the finish pointer, so as to preserve the class invariant that all constructed elements are contained in the range [start, finish). Line 5 might fail (T's copy constructor could throw an exception), but this would be harmless: at this point insert has not modified the vector in any other way. No cleanup is necessary, and we can just let the exception propagate to insert's caller.

More complicated insertions are delegated to insert_aux (see Listing 9). This function has two clauses, depending on whether or not the vector's memory block must be reallocated. The first clause, lines 3–7, is the case of no reallocation. Line 3 constructs the new element; an exception in this line is possible, but harmless. Lines 4–5 shift the vector's elements towards the end, to make room for the new element, and line 6 assigns the new value into its designated slot.

Lines 4–6 use T's copy constructor and assignment operator. An exception in any of these three lines requires attention, because finish is not incremented until line 7; we must preserve the class invariant that the range [finish, end_of_storage) consists entirely of uninitialized storage. Fortunately, however, addressing this issue is extremely simple: if line 7 is moved so that it immediately follows line 3, then this invariant will be preserved automatically. The vector's elements will not necessarily have the same values as they did before the attempted insertion, but the vector will be in a consistent state. This suffices for Level 3 exception-safety.

The second clause, lines 10–21 of Listing 9, performs reallocation. No action is required if allocation of the new memory block (line 12) throws an exception. Lines 13–15, however, which copy elements from the old block to the new, do require cleanup action. If any of them throws an exception, then the new memory block must be deallocated; furthermore, if line 14 throws an exception then the elements constructed in line 13 must be destroyed, and if line 15 throws an exception then the elements constructed in both lines 13 and 14 must be destroyed. (Note that we have already required uninitialized_copy to construct either all or none of the requested elements.) Finally, since lines 17–21 consist entirely of deallocation and pointer manipulation, none of them can throw exceptions.

Inserting multiple elements requires more bookkeeping, but is otherwise very similar.

Listing 10. The Version of Insert That Inserts *n* Copies of an Element into a vector.

```
1:  void vector<T>::insert (iterator position,
2:      size_type n, const T& x) {
3:      if (n == 0) return;
4:      if (end_of_storage - finish >= n) {
5:          if (end() - position > n) {
6:              uninitialized_copy (end() - n, end(), end());
7:              copy_backward (position, end() - n, end());
8:              fill(position, position + n, x);
9:          }
10:         else {
11:             uninitialized_copy (position, end(), position + n);
12:             fill(position, end(), x);
13:             uninitialized_fill_n (end(), n - (end() - position), x);
14:         }
15:         finish += n;
16:     }
17:     else {
18:         const size_type old_size = size();
19:         const size_type len = old_size + max(old_size, n);
20:         const iterator tmp = data_allocator::allocate(len);
21:         uninitialized_copy (begin(), position, tmp);
22:         uninitialized_fill_n(tmp + (position - begin()), n, x);
23:         uninitialized_copy (position, end(),
24:                 tmp + (position - begin() + n));
25:         destroy(begin(), end());
26:         deallocate();
27:         end_of_storage = tmp + len;
28:         finish = tmp + old_size + n;
29:         start = tmp;
30:     }
31: }
```

The first clause in Listing 10 (line 3) is trivial. The second clause, lines 6–8, applies if no reallocation is necessary, and if all assignments of **x** are to previously initialized elements. As before, because of the cleanup requirement, it is harmless for the **uninitialized_copy** in line 6 to throw an exception. And again, as before, an exception from line 7 or 8 is dangerous only because **finish** has not yet been incremented. The easiest solution is again to increment **finish** immediately after line 6 instead of waiting until line 15.

The third clause (lines 11–13 of Listing 10) is slightly more complicated than the second, but, again, the main worry is preserving the invariant that all constructed elements are in the range [start, finish). If we define m as n - (finish - position), then the new elements are constructed in two steps: the first step copies old elements into the range [finish + m, finish + n), and the second fills the range [finish, finish + m) with the value x. The easiest way to maintain this invariant is to exchange the order of the operations in lines 13 and 11 (this is necessary, because otherwise the constructed elements would not be contiguous), incrementing finish once by m after the elements in [finish, finish + m) are constructed and again by n - m after the elements in [finish + m, finish + n) are constructed.

The fourth clause (lines 18–29 of Listing 10) performs reallocation; it is essentially the same as the reallocation clause shown in Listing 9, and it may be dealt with in exactly the same way. Finally, then, Listing 11 is an exception-safe implementation of insert.

The other member functions that insert elements into a vector raise no new issues. The range version of insert is a minor variation on the three-argument insert in Listing 10, and push_back, which inserts an element at the end of a vector, is just a special case of the two-argument insert shown in Listing 9.

Closely related to insertion is the reserve member function, (Listing 12), which increases the size of a vector's memory block without actually inserting any new elements. That is, reserve increases end_of_storage - start but does not increase finish - start. This member function mainly exists for the sake of performance tuning.

Reserve requires some attention, but not very much. The only operations that can fail are the allocation in line 4 and the uninitialized_copy in line 5. A failure in line 4 requires no cleanup, and a failure in line 5 merely leaves a block of uninitialized storage that must be deleted. A simple try block around line 5 suffices.

Erasing Elements

Vector has three member functions for removing elements: pop_back, which removes the last element, and two overloadings of erase, one of which removes a single element and one of which removes a range. The third of these member functions is shown here; the other two, which are merely special cases, may be omitted:

```
void vector<T>::erase(iterator first, iterator last) {
    iterator i = copy(last, end(), first);
```

Listing 11. Exception-Safe Implementation of the Version of insert That Inserts n Copies of an Element into a vector.

```
void vector<T>::insert (iterator position, size_type n, const T& x) {
   if (n == 0) return;
   if (end_of_storage - finish >= n) {
      T x_copy = x;
      const size_type elems_after = finish - position;
      const iterator old_finish = finish;
      if (elems_after > n) {
         uninitialized_copy (finish - n, finish, finish);
         finish += n;
         copy_backward (position, old_finish - n, old_finish);
         fill(position, position + n, x_copy);
      }
      else {
         uninitialized_fill_n (finish, n - elems_after, x_copy);
         finish += n - elems_after;
         uninitialized_copy (position, old_finish, position + n);
         finish += elems_after;
         fill(position, old_finish, x_copy);
      }
   }
   else {
      const size_type old_size = size();
      const size_type len = old_size + max(old_size, n);
      const iterator new_start = data_allocator::allocate(len);
      iterator new_finish = new_start;
      try {
         new_finish = uninitialized_copy(start, position, new_start);
         new_finish = uninitialized_fill_n(new_finish, n, x);
         new_finish = uninitialized_copy(position, finish, new_finish);
   }
   catch(...) {
      destroy(new_start, new_finish);
      data_allocator:: deallocate(start, len);
      throw;
   }
   destroy(start, finish);
   deallocate();
   start = new_start;
   finish = new_finish;
   end_of_storage = new_start + len;
   }
}
```

```
3:     destroy(i, finish);
4: finish = finish - (last - first);
5: }
```

Line 2 of this code overwrites the range that is being erased, by shifting elements from the back of the vector. Line 3 destroys the elements that were shifted, and line 4 adjusts the finish pointer. Only line 2 can throw any exceptions: Lines 3 and 4 consist only of pointer manipulation and destructor calls, which cannot be permitted to fail.

An exception thrown within line 2 of erase is harmless. Line 2 simply copies elements from one part of the vector to another, and there is no point at which any of vector's class invariants might be violated. Erase, without modification, already provides Level 3 exception-safety.

The Assignment Operator

Vector's assignment operator could, in principle, be implemented in terms of member functions that we have already examined: insert and erase. That would be inefficient, though, and the actual implementation is shown in Listing 13.

The first clause in Listing 13, lines 4–8, ought to be familiar by now: It reallocates the vector's memory block, and it is very similar to the same operation in lines 10–21 of Listing 9 and lines 18–29 of Listing 10. Again, either the allocation itself (line 6) or the construction of the new elements (line 7) could fail. If line 7 fails we must delete the new memory that was allocated in line 6, and if either line fails then we must restore the vector to some stable state. The easiest way to do this would be to defer destruction of the old elements until after line 7.

Listing 12. The reserve Member Function.

```
void vector<T>:: reserve(size_type n) {
   if (capacity() < n) {
      const size_type old_size = size();
      const iterator tmp = data_allocator::allocate(n);
      uninitialized_copy (begin(), end(), tmp);
      destroy(start, finish);
      deallocate();
      start = tmp;
      finish = tmp + old_size;
      end_of_storage = start + n;
   }
}
```

Listing 13. Vector's Assignment Operator

```
1:  vector<T>& vector<T>::operator=(const vector& x) {
2:     if (&x == this) return *this;
3:     if (x.size() > capacity()) {
4:        destroy(start, finish);
5:        deallocate();
6:        start = data_allocator:: allocate(x.end() - x.begin());
7:        end_of_storage = uninitialized_copy(x.begin(), x.end(), start);
8:
9:     }
10:    else if (size() >= x.size()) {
11:       iterator i = copy(x.begin(), x.end(), begin());
12:       destroy(i, finish);
13:    }
14:    else {
15:       copy(x.begin(), x.begin() + size(), begin());
16:       uninitialized_copy (x.begin() + size(), x.end(),
17:             begin() + size());
18:    }
19:    finish = begin() + x.size();
20:    return *this;
21: }
```

The second clause (lines 11–12 of Listing 13) presents no difficulty at all—a failure in copy cannot endanger the vector's class invariants—and neither does the third (lines 15–17). Line 15 never affects vector's class invariants, and line 16 is guaranteed to have no effect if it fails. Lines 19–20, which are common to all three clauses, are simply pointer manipulation and therefore cannot throw exceptions.

WHAT ABOUT ALLOCATORS?

You might have noticed an important omission from all of this discussion: I have implicitly assumed that the pointers start, finish, and end_of_storage are of type T*. Similarly, I have been pretending that vector has only a single template parameter.

In reality, though, vector has two template parameters; the second one, an allocator, parameterizes the vector by memory model. In general, then, start, finish, and end_of_storage need not be of type T* but might be of any arbitrary pointer-like type. How does this change the analysis of vector's exception-safety?

By and large, it doesn't. This may seem like a surprising claim, since all of vector's member functions make heavy use of pointer manipulation. How can this analysis be unchanged when every pointer assignment, every increment or dereference, is some arbitrary user-defined function?

It is the very ubiquity of pointer manipulation that renders this analysis unchanged. The clearest demonstration of that is in the one non-const member function that we have not yet examined: swap. This member function exchanges the contents of two vectors in constant time, and the implementation, shown here, is the obvious one: A vector consists of three pointers, so it just swaps each of those pointers:

```
void vector<T>::swap(vector& x) {
    ::swap(start, x.start);
    ::swap(finish, x.finish);
    ::swap(end_of_storage, x.end_of_storage);
}
```

The swap member function invokes the global swap function:

```
template <class T>
inline void swap(T& a, T& b) {
    T tmp = a;
    a = b;
    b = tmp;
}
```

Swapping two vectors, then, consists of nine pointer assignments. Now suppose that the first two of these assignments succeed, but the third throws an exception.

This would be a serious error from which recovery would be impossible. Suppose that the two vectors in question are V1 and V2; that V1's data members start, finish, and end_of_storage initially have the values s1, f1, and e1; and that V2's initially have the values s2, f2, and e2. The first pointer assignment in ::swap assigns s1 to tmp, and the second assigns s2 to V1.start. If the third throws an exception, then, at that point, V1.start and V2.start will both have the value s2. The value s1, which existed only in the local variable tmp, has been lost. And without s1, it is impossible to destroy V1.

It is impossible to recover from this situation, because any recovery strategy would necessarily have to involve copying or assigning s1. This is circular: We would be trying to recover from a failure in pointer assignment by performing more pointer assignments. The only reasonable conclusion is that pointer assignment, whether of built-in pointers of type T* or of user-defined "smart pointers," may not be permitted to throw exceptions.

Similarly, by looking at the pointer operations in destroy and by noting that destroy is called by vector's destructor, it becomes clear that pointer dereference and increment may not be permitted to throw exceptions either. This, then, is the reason why user-defined pointer types do not affect the analysis of vector's exception-safety: user-defined pointers and built-in pointers may differ in many ways, but their behavior with respect to exceptions must be the same. Even Level 1 exception-safety is impossible if valid operations on valid pointers can trigger exceptions.

CONCLUSION

We have seen that it is impossible for a generic container to be exception-safe, even in the weak sense of Level 1, unless the container imposes some restrictions on its template arguments. If we do impose some reasonable restrictions, on the other hand, we have also seen that it is not too difficult to implement vector<T,Alloc> so that it has Level 3 exception-safety.

1. T's destructor doesn't throw an exception under any circumstances.
2. No operations on T, including assignment, can ever put an object of class T into a corrupted state. That is, T is itself exception-safe at Level 3.
3. Alloc::deallocate may not throw an exception.
4. Operations on objects of type Alloc::pointer and Alloc::const_ pointer do not throw exceptions.

None of this should be surprising, since generic programming always relies on a sort of "programming by contract": Generic components require that their template parameters satisfy specific properties, and guarantee that they behave as documented only if those requirements are met. Exceptions are no exception.

REFERENCE

1. Cargill, T. "Exception Handling: A False Sense of Security," *C++ Report*, 6(9), 1994.

WHAT'S IN A CLASS?

HERB SUTTER

In this article, Herb challenges the standard view of what a class, and what an object, are. Indeed, this is quite timely. For as we have grown more comfortable with object-oriented techniques we have come to realize that the concept of class and objects goes beyond the simple concept used by the language. What's more, to take the narrow view of the language is to limit ourselves from some powerful techniques. Herb describes some of those techniques in this article.

In this article, Herb defines something that he calls "The Interface Principle" (IP). The Interface Principle states that any function that is part of the interface of a class, regardless of whether that function is declared as a member of that class, is logically *part of that class. That is, a global function, not declared within a class, may be considered a true part of the class if it meets certain criteria.*

Just the other day I was reading something by Scott Meyers. Scott was referencing this article and expanding upon the concepts within it. He was making the point that functions and data do not need to be declared within a class in order to behave as though they are part of the class.

I'LL START OFF with a deceptively simple question:

- What's in a class? That is, what is "part of" a class and its interface?

The deeper questions are:

- How does this answer fit with C-style object-oriented programming?
- How does it fit with C++'s Koenig lookup? With the Myers Example? (I'll describe both.)

- How does it affect the way we analyze class dependencies and design object models?

SO, "WHAT'S IN A CLASS?"

First, recall a traditional definition of a class:

> *A class describes a set of data, along with the functions that operate on that data.*

Programmers often unconsciously misinterpret this definition, saying instead: "Oh yeah, a class, that's what appears in the class definition—the member data and the member functions." But that's not the same thing, because it limits the word "functions" to mean just "member functions."

Consider:

```
//*** Example 1(a)
class X { /*...*/ };
/*...*/
void f( const X& );
```

The question is: *Is f part of X?* Some people will automatically say "No," because f is a nonmember function (or "free function"). Others might realize something fundamentally important: If the Example 1(a) code appears together in one header file, it is not significantly different from:

```
//*** Example 1(b)
class X { /*...*/
public:
   void f() const;
};
```

Think about this for a moment. Besides access rights,* f is still the same, taking a pointer/reference to X. The this parameter is just implicit in the second version, that's all. So, if Example 1(a) all appears in the same header, we're already starting to see that even though f is not a member of X, it's nonetheless strongly related to X. I'll show what exactly that relationship is in the next section.

On the other hand, if X and f do not appear together in the same header file, then f is just some old client function, not a part of X (even if f is intended to augment X). We routinely write functions with parameters whose types

* Even those may be unchanged, if the original f was a friend.

come from library headers, and clearly our custom functions aren't part of those library classes.

The Interface Principle

With that example in mind, I'll propose the Interface Principle:

For a class X, all functions, including free functions, that:

- *"mention" X, and*
- *are "supplied with" X*

are logically part of X, because they form part of the interface of X.

By definition every member function is "part of" X:

- every member function must "mention" X (a nonstatic member function has an implicit this parameter of type X* or const X*; a static member function is in the scope of X); and
- every member function must be "supplied with" X (in X's definition).

Applying the Interface Principle to Example 1(a) gives the same result as our original analysis: Clearly, f mentions X. If f is also "supplied with" X (for example, if they come in the same header file and/or namespace[†]), then according to the Interface Principle f is logically part of X, because it forms part of the interface of X.

So the Interface Principle is a useful touchstone to determine what is really "part of" a class. Do you find it unintuitive that a free function should be considered part of a class? Then let's give real weight to this example by giving a more common name to f:

```
//*** Example 1(c)
class X { /*...*/ };
/*...*/
ostream& operator<<( ostream&, const X& );
```

Here the Interface Principle's rationale is perfectly clear, because we understand how this particular free function works: If operator<< is "supplied with" X (for example, in the same header and/or namespace), then operator<< is logically part of X because it forms part of the interface of X. That makes sense, even though the function is a nonmember, because we know that it's common practice for a class'

[†] We'll examine the relationship with namespaces in detail later in the article, because it turns out that this Interface Principle acts exactly the same way as Koenig lookup.

author to provide operator<<. If instead operator<< comes, not from X's author, but from client code, then it's not part of X because it's not "supplied with" X.[Δ]

In this light, then, let's refer back to the traditional definition of a class. That definition is exactly right, for it doesn't say a thing about whether the "functions" in question are members or not.

IS THE IP AN OO PRINCIPLE, OR JUST A C++-SPECIFIC PRINCIPLE?

I've been using C++ terms like "namespace" to describe what "supplied with" means, so is the IP C++-specific? Or is it a general OO principle that can apply in other languages?

Consider a familiar example from another (in fact, a non-OO) language—C:

```
/*** Example 2(a) ***/
struct _iobuf { /*...data goes here...*/ };
typedef struct _iobuf FILE;
FILE*  fopen ( const char* filename,
               const char* mode );
int  fclose( FILE* stream );
int  fseek ( FILE* stream,
             long offset,
             int origin );
long ftell ( FILE* stream );
   /* etc. */
```

This is the standard "handle technique" for writing OO code in a language that doesn't have classes: You provide a structure that holds the object's data and functions—necessarily nonmembers—that take or return pointers to that structure. These free functions construct (fopen), destroy (fclose), and manipulate (fseek, ftell, etc.) the data.

This technique has disadvantages (for example, it relies on client programmers to refrain from fiddling with the data directly), but it's still "real" OO code—after all, a class is "a set of data along with the functions that operate on that data." In this case of necessity the functions are all nonmembers, but they are still part of the interface of FILE.

[Δ] The similarity between member and nonmember functions is even stronger for certain other overloadable operators. For example, when you write a+b you might be asking for a.operator+(b) or operator+(a,b), depending on the types of a and b.

Now consider an "obvious" way to rewrite Example 2(a) in a language that does have classes:

```
//*** Example 2(b)
class FILE {
public:
   FILE( const char* filename,
         const char* mode );
   ~FILE();
   int fseek( long offset, int origin );
   long ftell();
      /* etc. */
private:
   /*...data goes here...*/
};
```

The FILE* parameters have just become implicit this parameters. Here it's clear that fseek is part of FILE, just as it was in Example 2(a), even though there it was a nonmember. We can even merrily make some functions members and some not:

```
//*** Example 2(c)
class FILE {
public:
   FILE( const char* filename,
      const char* mode );
   ~FILE();
   long ftell();
      /* etc. */
private:
   /*...data goes here...*/
};
int fseek( FILE* stream,
           long offset,
           int origin );
```

It really doesn't matter whether or not the functions are members. As long as they "mention" FILE and are "supplied with" FILE, they really are part of FILE. In Example 2(a), all of the functions were nonmembers because in C they have to be. Even in C++, some functions in a class' interface have to be (or should be) nonmembers: operator<< can't be a member because it requires a stream as the left-hand argument, and operator+ shouldn't be a member to allow conversions on the left-hand argument.

INTRODUCING KOENIG LOOKUP

The Interface Principle makes even more sense when you realize that it does exactly the same thing as Koenig lookup.[ß] Here, I'll use two examples to illustrate and define Koenig lookup. In the next section, I'll use the Myers Example to show why this is directly related to the Interface Principle.

Here's why we need Koenig lookup, using an example right out of the standards document:

```
//*** Example 3(a)
namespace NS {
   class T { };
   void f(T);
}
NS::T parm;
int main() {
   f(parm);  // OK: calls NS::f
}
```

Pretty nifty, isn't it? "Obviously," the programmer shouldn't have to explicitly write NS::f(parm), because just f(parm) "obviously" means NS::f(parm), right? But what's obvious to us isn't always obvious to a compiler, especially considering that there's nary a "using" in sight to bring the name f into scope. Koenig lookup lets the compiler do the right thing.

Here's how it works: Recall that "name lookup" just means that, whenever you write a call like f(parm), the compiler has to figure out which function named f you want. (With overloading and scoping there could be several functions named f.) Koenig lookup says that, if you supply a function argument of class type (here parm, of type NS::T), then to find the function name the compiler is required to look, not just in the usual places like the local scope, but also in the namespace (here NS) that contains the argument's type.[#] And so Example 3(a) works: The parameter being passed to f is a T, T is defined in namespace NS, and the compiler can consider the f in namespace NS—no fuss, no muss.

It's good that we don't have to explicitly qualify f, because sometimes we *can't* easily qualify a function name:

[ß] Named after Andrew Koenig, who nailed down its definition and is a longtime member of both AT&T's C++ team and the C++ standards committee. See also Koenig, A. and Moo, B., *Ruminations on C++* (Addison–Wesley, 1997).

[#] There's a little more to the mechanics, but that's essentially it.

```
//*** Example 3(b)
#include <iostream>
#include <string> // this header
  // declares the free function
  // std::operator<< for strings
int main() {
  std::string hello = "Hello, world";
  std::cout << hello; // OK: calls
}     // std::operator<<
```

Here the compiler has no way to find operator<< without Koenig lookup, because the operator<< we want is a free function that's made known to us only as part of the string package. It would be disgraceful if the programmer were forced to qualify this function name, because then the last line couldn't use the operator naturally. Instead, we would have to write either std::operator<<(std::cout, hello); or using namespace std;. If those options send shivers down your spine, you understand why we need Koenig lookup.

Summary: If in the same namespace you supply a class and a free function that mentions that class,†† the compiler will enforce a strong relationship between the two.** And that brings us back to the Interface Principle, because of the Myers Example:

More Koenig Lookup: The Myers Example

Consider first a (slightly) simplified example:

```
//*** Example 4(a)
namespace NS {       // typically from some
  class T { };       // header T.h
}
void f( NS::T );
int main() {
  NS::T parm;
  f(parm);           // OK: calls global f
}
```

†† By value, reference, pointer, or whatever.

** Granted, that relationship is still less strong than the relationship between a class and one of its member functions. (See the sidebar *"How Strong Is the 'Part Of' Relationship?"*)

Namespace NS supplies a type T, and the outside code provides a global function f that happens to take a T. This is fine, the sky is blue, the world is at peace, and everything is wonderful.

Time passes. One fine day, the author of NS helpfully adds a function:

```
//*** Example 4(b)
namespace NS {        // typically from some
   class T { };       // header T.h
   void f( T );       // <— new function
}
void f( NS::T );
int main() {
   NS::T parm;
   f(parm);           // ambiguous: NS::f
}                     // or global f?
```

Adding a function in a namespace scope "broke" code outside the namespace, even though the client code didn't write using to bring NS's names into its scope! But wait, it gets better—Nathan Myers†† pointed out the following interesting behavior with namespaces and Koenig lookup:

```
//*** The Myers Example: "Before"
namespace A {
   class X { };
}
namespace B {
   void f( A::X );
   void g( A::X parm ) {
      f(parm);        // OK: calls B::f
   }
}
```

This is fine, the sky is blue, etc. One fine day, the author of A helpfully adds another function:

```
//*** The Myers Example: "After"
namespace A {
   class X { };
   void f( X );                 // <— new function
}
```

†† Nathan is another longtime member of the C++ standards committee, and the primary author of the standard's locale facility.

```
namespace B {
   void f( A::X );
   void g( A::X parm ) {
      f(parm);                    // ambiguous: A::f or B::f?
   }
}
```

"Huh?" you might ask. "The whole point of namespaces is to prevent name collisions, isn't it? But adding a function in one namespace actually seems to 'break' code in a completely separate namespace." True, namespace B's code seems to "break" merely because it mentions a type from A. B's code didn't write a using namespace A; anywhere. It didn't even write using A::X;.

This is not a problem, and B is not "broken." This is in fact *exactly* what should happen.[ΔΔ] If there's a function f(X) in the same namespace as X, then, according to the Interface Principle, f is part of the interface of X. It doesn't matter a whit that f happens to be a free function; to see clearly that it's nonetheless logically part of X, again just give it another name:

```
//*** Restating the Myers Example: "After"
namespace A {
   class X { };
   ostream& operator<<( ostream&, const X& );
}
namespace B {
   ostream& operator<<( ostream&, const A::X& );
   void g( A::X parm ) {
      cout << parm;  // ambiguous:
   }                 //  A::operator<< or
}                    //  B::operator<<?
```

If client code supplies a function that mentions X and matches the signature of one provided in the same namespace as X, the call *should* be ambiguous. B *should* be forced to say which competing function it means, its own or that supplied with X. This is exactly what we should expect, given the IP:

ΔΔ This specific example arose at the Morristown meeting in November 1997, and it's what started me thinking about this issue of membership and dependencies. What the Myers Example means is simply that namespaces aren't quite as independent as people originally thought, but they are still pretty independent and they fit their intended uses.

> *For a class X, all functions, including free functions, that both:*
>
> - *"mention" X, and*
> - *are "supplied with" X*
>
> *are logically part of X, because they form part of the interface of X.*

In short, it's no accident that the Interface Principle works exactly the same way as Koenig lookup. Koenig lookup works the way that it does fundamentally *because* of the Interface Principle.

(The sidebar "How Strong Is the 'Part Of' Relationship?" shows why a member function is still more strongly related to a class than a nonmember.)

WHAT DOES A CLASS DEPEND ON?

"What's in a class?" isn't just a philosophical question. It's a fundamentally practical question, because without the correct answer we can't properly analyze class dependencies.

To demonstrate this, consider a seemingly unrelated problem: *What's the best way to write* operator<< *for a class?* There are two main ways, both of which involve tradeoffs. I'll analyze them, and in the end we'll find that we're back to the Interface Principle and that it has given us important guidance to analyze the tradeoffs correctly.

Here's the first way:

```
//*** Example 5(a) — nonvirtual streaming
class X {
   /*...ostream is never mentioned here...*/
};
ostream& operator<<( ostream& o, const X& x ) {
   /* code to output an X to a stream */
   return o;
}
```

Here's the second:

```
//*** Example 5(b) — virtual streaming
class X { /*...*/
public:
```

```
    virtual ostream& print( ostream& o ) {
        /* code to output an X to a stream */
        return o;
    }
};
ostream& operator<<( ostream& o, const X& x ) {
    return x.print();
}
```

Assume that in both cases the class and the function appear in the same header and/or namespace. Which one would you choose? What are the tradeoffs? Historically, experienced C++ programmers have analyzed these options this way:

- Option (a)'s advantage [*we've said until now*] is that X has fewer dependencies. Because no member function of X mentions ostream, X does not [*appear to*] depend on ostream. Option (a) also avoids the overhead of an extra virtual function call.
- Option (b)'s advantage is that any DerivedX will also print correctly, even when an X& is passed to operator<<.

This analysis is flawed. Armed with the Interface Principle, we can see why—the first advantage in Option (a) is a phantom, as indicated by the comments in italics:

1. According to the IP, as long as operator<< both "mentions" X (true in both cases) and is "supplied with" X (true in both cases), it is logically part of X.
2. In both cases operator<< mentions ostream, so operator<< depends on ostream.
3. Since in both cases operator<< is logically part of X and operator<< depends on ostream, therefore in both cases X depends on ostream.

So what we've traditionally thought of as Option (a)'s main advantage is not an advantage at all—in both cases X still depends on ostream anyway! If, as is typical, operator<< and X appear in the same header X.h, then both X's own implementation module and all client modules that use X physically depend on ostream and require at least its forward declaration to compile.

With Option (a)'s first advantage exposed as a phantom, the choice really boils down to just the virtual function call overhead. Without applying the Interface Principle, though, we would not have been able to analyze the true dependencies (and therefore the true tradeoffs) in this common real-world example as easily.

Bottom line, it's not always useful to distinguish between members and nonmembers, especially when it comes to analyzing dependencies, and that's exactly what the Interface Principle implies.

Some Interesting (and Even Surprising) Results

In general, if A and B are classes and f(A,B) is a free function:

- If A and f are supplied together, then f is part of A and so A depends on B.
- If B and f are supplied together, then f is part of B and so B depends on A.
- If A, B, and f are supplied together, then f is part of both A and B, and so A and B are interdependent. This has long made sense on an instinctive level ... if the library author supplies two classes and an operation that uses both, the three are probably intended to be used together. Now, however, the Interface Principle has given us a way to rigorously prove this inter-dependency.

Finally, we get to the really interesting case. In general, if A and B are classes and A::g(B) is a member function of a:

- Because A::g(B) exists, clearly A always depends on B. No surprises so far.
- If A and B are supplied together, then of course A::g(B) and B are supplied together. Therefore, because A::g(B) both "mentions" B and is "supplied with" B, then according to the Interface Principle it follows (perhaps surprisingly, at first!) that A::g(B) is part of B and, because A::g(B) uses an (implicit) A* parameter, B depends on A. Because A also depends on B, this means that A and B are interdependent.

At first, it might seem like a stretch to consider a member function of one class as also part of another class, but this is only true if A and B are also *supplied together*. Consider: If A and B are supplied together (say, in the same header file) and A mentions B in a member function like this, "gut feel" already tells us (usually) A and B are probably interdependent. They are certainly strongly

How Strong Is the "Part Of" Relationship?

While the Interface Principle states that both member and nonmember functions can be logically "part of" a class, it doesn't claim that members and nonmembers are equivalent. For example, member functions automatically have full access to class internals, whereas nonmembers only have such access if they're made friends. Likewise for name lookup, including Koenig lookup, the C++ language deliberately says that a member function is to be considered more strongly related to a class than a nonmember:

```
//*** NOT the Myers Example
namespace A {
  class X { };
  void f( X );
}
class B {              // <— class, not namespace
  void f( A::X );
  void g( A::X parm ) {
     f(parm);          // OK: B::f, not ambiguous
  }
};
```

Now that we're talking about a class B, rather than a name space B, there's no ambiguity: When the compiler ˆnds a member named f, it won't bother trying to use Koenig lookup to ˆnd free functions.

So in two major ways—access rules and lookup rules—even when a function is "part of" a class according to the Interface Principle, a member is more strongly related to the class than a nonmember.

coupled and cohesive, and the fact that they are supplied together and interact means that: a) they are intended to be used together, and b) changes to one affect the other.

The problem is that, until now, it's been hard to prove A and B's interdependence with anything more substantial than "gut feel." Now their interdependence can be demonstrated as a direct consequence of the Interface Principle.

Note that, unlike classes, namespaces don't need to be declared all at once, and what's "supplied together" depends on what parts of the namespace are visible:

```
//*** Example 6(a)
//—-file a.h—-
namespace N { class B; } // forward decl
```

```
namespace N { class A; } // forward decl
class N::A { public: void g(B); };
//—-file b.h—-
namespace N { class B { /*...*/ }; }
```

Clients of A include a.h, so for them A and B are supplied together and are interdependent. Clients of B include b.h, so for them A and B are not supplied together.

CONCLUSION

I'd like you to take away three thoughts:

- The Interface Principle: For a class X, all functions, including free functions, that both a) "mention" X, and b) are "supplied with" X are logically part of X, because they form part of the interface of X.
- Therefore both member *and nonmember* functions can be logically "part of" a class. A member function is still more strongly related to a class than is a nonmember, however.
- In the Interface Principle, a useful way to interpret "supplied with" is "appears in the same header and/or namespace." If the function appears in the same header as the class, it is "part of" the class in terms of dependencies. If the function appears in the same namespace as the class, it is "part of" the class in terms of object use and name lookup.

PIMPLES—BEAUTY MARKS YOU CAN DEPEND ON

HERB SUTTER

How can you resist article with a name like that? When I first saw the article, I chuckled a little and passed it right on to the production folks at SIGS. A few days later, they sent me back the proofs of the magazine. As I read through them I came to this article. Now at the top of each article there is a picture of the author. And on Herb's face, there was a flaw. A big dot, right on his forehead.

I don't know whether this was intentional or not. But I liked the idea so much that I called the production manager and told her that I thought, flaw or not, it should be repeated in the magazine. She chuckled and said she would do it. Then I told her that I wanted a big red dot on my picture in the Editors Corner. She chuckled again and said she would do it.

But when the magazine came out, the pictures were clean—what a shame. I bet those issues would be selling for big bucks now!

MANAGING DEPENDENCIES WELL is an essential part of writing solid code. As I've argued before,[1] C++'s greatest strength is that it supports two powerful methods of abstraction: object-oriented programming and generic programming. Both are fundamentally tools to help manage dependencies. In fact, all of the common OO/generic buzzwords (encapsulation, polymorphism, type independence), and all of the design patterns I know of, really describe ways to manage interdependencies within a software system.

When we talk about dependencies, we usually think of runtime dependencies like object interactions. In this column, I'll focus on how to analyze and manage compile-time dependencies.

A HEADER THAT COULD USE SOME WORK

In C++, when anything in a header file changes, all code that includes that header either directly or indirectly must be recompiled. To show how to reduce this kind of dependency, I'll present an example header and show how it can be improved step-by-step. Along the way I'll examine and apply three major ways to reduce compile-time dependencies:

- *Avoid gratuitous #includes*. Use forward declarations whenever a definition isn't required. (This may sound obvious to experienced programmers, but it's trickier than you might think for templates.)
- *Avoid unnecessary membership*. Use the Pimple Idiom to fully hide the private implementation details of a class.
- *Avoid unnecessary inheritance*.

So let's begin. Here is the initial version of a "problem" header file. Before reading on, take a little time to look at it and decide how it could be improved. Note: The comments are important!

```
// x.h: original header
//
#include <iostream>
#include <ostream>
#include <list>
// None of A, B, C, D or E are templates.
// Only A and C have virtual functions.
#include "a.h"                  // class A
#include "b.h"                  // class B
#include "c.h"                  // class C
#include "d.h"                  // class D
#include "e.h"                  // class E
class X : public A, private B {
public:
   X( const C& );
   B f( int, char* );
   C f( int, C );
```

```
    C&  g( B );
    E h( E );
    virtual std::ostream& print(std::ostream& ) const;
  private:
    std::list<C> clist_;
    D d_;
  };
  inline std::ostream& operator<<(std::ostream& os, const X& x )
    { return x.print(os); }
```

Do you see a few things you'd do differently?

Remove Gratuitous Headers, Use Forward Declarations

Right off the bat, x.h is clearly including far too many other headers. This is a Bad Thing, because it means that every client that includes x.h is also forced to include all of the other headers mentioned in x.h. While this probably isn't much of an overhead for a relatively small standard header like list, it could be a substantial overhead for class headers like c.h (after all, who knows what else gets pulled in by c.h?).

Of the first two standard headers mentioned in x.h, one can be immediately removed because it's not needed at all, and the second can be replaced with a smaller header:

- *Remove* iostream. Many programmers #include <iostream> purely out of habit as soon as they see anything resembling a stream nearby. X does make use of streams, that's true; but it doesn't mention anything specifically from iostream. At the most, X needs ostream alone, and even that can be whittled down.
- *Replace* ostream *with* iosfwd. Parameter and return types only need to be forward-declared, so instead of the full definition of ostream we really only need its forward declaration. In the old days, you could just replace #include <ostream> with class ostream, in this situation, because ostream used to be a class. Alas, no more—ostream is now typedef'd as basic_ostream <char>, and that basic_ostream template gets a bit messy to forward-declare. All is not lost, though; the standard library helpfully provides the header iosfwd, which contains forward declarations for all of the stream templates (including basic_ ostream) and their standard

typedefs (including ostream). So all we need to do is replace #include <ostream> with #include <iosfwd>.*

There, that was easy. We can only get...

... what? "Not so fast!" I hear some of you say. "This header does a lot more with ostream than just mention it as a parameter or return type. The inlined operator<< actually uses an ostream object! So it must need ostream's definition, right?"

That's a reasonable question. Happily, the answer is: No, it doesn't. Consider again the function in question:

```
inline std::ostream& operator<<( std::ostream& os, const X& x )
   { return x.print(os); }
```

This function mentions an ostream as both a parameter and a return type (which most people know doesn't require a definition), and it passes its ostream parameter in turn as a parameter to another function (which many people *don't* know doesn't require a definition either). As long as that's all we're doing with the ostream object, there's no need for a full ostream definition. Of course, we would need the full definition if we tried to call any member functions, for example, but we're not doing anything like that here.

So, as I was saying, we can only get rid of one of the other headers just yet:

- *Replace* e.h *with a forward declaration.* E is just being mentioned as a parameter and as a return type, so no definition is required, and x.h shouldn't be pulling in e.h in the first place. All we need to do is replace #include "e.h" with class E;.
- *Leave* a.h *and* b.h *(for now).* We can't get rid of these because X inherits from both A and B, and you always have to have full definitions for base classes so that the compiler can determine X's object size, virtual functions, and other fundamentals. (Can you anticipate how to remove one of these? Think about it: Which one can you remove, and why/how? The answer will come shortly.)
- *Leave* list, c.h, *and* d.h *(for now).* We can't get rid of these right away because a list<C> and a D appear as private data members of X. Although C appears as neither a base class nor a member, it is being used to instan-

* Once you see iosfwd, you might think that the same trick would work for other standard library templates like list and string. However, there are no comparable stringfwd or listfwd standard headers. The iosfwd header was created to give streams special treatment for backwards compatibility, to avoid breaking code written in years past for the "old," nontemplated version of the iostreams subsystem.

tiate the list member, and most current compilers require that when you instantiate list<C> you be able to see the definition of C.

Here's how the header looks after this initial clean-up pass:

```
// x.h: sans gratuitous headers
//
#include <iosfwd>
#include <list>
// None of A, B, C or D are templates.
// Only A and C have virtual functions.
#include "a.h"        // class A
#include "b.h"        // class B
#include "c.h"        // class C
#include "d.h"        // class D
class E;
class X : public A, private B {
public:
   X( const C& );
   B  f( int, char* );
   C  f( int, C );
   C&  g( B );
   E  h( E );
   virtual std::ostream& print( std::ostream& ) const;
private:
   std::list<C> clist_;
   Dd_;
};
inline std::ostream& operator<<( std::ostream& os, const X& x )
   { return x.print(os); }
```

This isn't bad, but we can still do quite a bit better.

The Beauty of Pimples

C++ lets us easily encapsulate the private parts of a class from unauthorized *access*. Unfortunately, because of the header file approach inherited from C, it can take a little more work to encapsulate *dependencies* on a class's privates. "But," you say, "the whole point of encapsulation is that the client code shouldn't have to know or care about a class's private implementation details, right?" Right, and in C++ the client code doesn't need to know or care about access to a class's privates (because unless it's a friend it isn't allowed any), but because the privates are visible in the header the client code does have to depend upon any types they mention.

How can we better insulate clients from a class's private implementation details? One good way is to use a special form of the handle/body idiom[2] (what I call the Pimple Idiom because of the intentionally pronounceable pimpl_ pointer[†]) as a compilation firewall.[3-5]

A "pimple" is just an opaque pointer used to hide the private members of a class. That is, instead of writing:

```
// file x.h
class X {
   // public and protected members
private:
   // private members; whenever these change,
   // all client code must be recompiled
};
```

We write instead:

```
// file x.h
class X {
   // public and protected members
private:
   class XImpl* pimpl_;
      // a pointer to a forward-declared class
};

// file x.cpp
struct XImpl {
   // private members; fully hidden, can be
   // changed at will without recompiling clients
};
```

(Yes, it's legal to forward-declare XImpl as a class and then define it as a struct.)

Every X object dynamically allocates its XImpl object. If you think of an object as a physical block, we've essentially lopped off a large chunk of the

† I always used to write impl_. The eponymous pimpl_ was actually coined several years ago by Jeff Sumner (chief programmer at CNTC), due in equal parts to a penchant for Hungarian-style "p" prefixes for pointer variables and an occasional taste for horrid puns.

block and in its place left only "a little bump on the side"—the opaque pointer, or pimple.

The major advantages of this idiom come from the fact that it breaks compile-time dependencies:

1. Types mentioned only in a class's implementation need no longer be defined for client code, which can eliminate extra #includes and improve compile speeds.
2. A class's implementation can be changed—that is, private members can be freely added or removed—without recompiling client code.

The major costs of this idiom are in performance:

1. Each construction/destruction must allocate/deallocate memory.
2. Each access of a hidden member can require at least one extra indirection. (If the hidden member being accessed itself uses a back pointer to call a function in the visible class, there will be multiple indirections.)

I'll talk more about these and other pimple issues in my next column. For now, in our example, there were three headers whose definitions were needed simply because they appeared as private members of X. If instead we restructure X to use a pimple, one of these headers (c.h) can be replaced with a forward declaration because C is still being mentioned elsewhere as a parameter or return type, and the other two (list and d.h) can disappear completely:

```
// x.h: after converting to use a pimple
//
#include <iosfwd>
#include "a.h"                    // class A (has virtual functions)
#include "b.h"                    // class B (has no virtual functions)
class C;
class E;
class X : public A, private B {
public:
   X( const C& );
   B  f( int, char* );
   C  f( int, C );
   C&   g( B );
   E  h( E );
   virtual std::ostream& print( std::ostream& ) const;
```

```
private:
   class XImpl* pimpl_;
      // opaque pointer to forward-declared class
};
inline std::ostream& operator<<( std::ostream& os, const X& x )
   { return x.print(os); }
```

The private details go into X's implementation file where client code never sees them and therefore never depends upon them:

```
// Implementation file x.cpp
//
struct XImpl {
   std::list<C>              clist_;
   D          d_;
};
```

REMOVE UNNECESSARY INHERITANCE

In my experience, many C++ programmers still seem to march to the "It isn't OO unless you inherit!" battle hymn, by which I mean that they use inheritance more than necessary. I'll save the whole lecture for another time and place, but my bottom line is simply that inheritance (including but not limited to *is-a*) is a much stronger relationship than *has-a* or *uses-a*. When it comes to managing dependencies, therefore, you should always prefer composition/membership over inheritance, wherever possible. To paraphrase a well-known mathematician: "Use as strong a relationship as necessary, but no stronger."

In this example, X is derived publicly from A and privately from B. Recall that public inheritance should always model *is-a* and satisfy the Liskov Substitution Principle (LSP).[Δ] In this case X *is-a* A and there's naught wrong with it, so we'll leave that as it is. But did you notice the interesting thing about B? The interesting thing is this: B is a private base class of X, but B has no virtual functions. Now, the only reason you would choose private inheritance over

[Δ] For many good discussions about applying the LSP, see the papers available online at www.oma.com, and the book *Designing Object-Oriented C++ Applications Using the Booch Method* by Robert C. Martin (Prentice-Hall, 1995). Yes, Bob is now also the editor of this magazine, but I've been recommending the papers and the book since long before that.

composition/membership is to gain access to protected members—which most of the time means "to override a virtual function." Because B has no such function, there's probably no reason to prefer the stronger relationship of inheritance.[ß] Instead, X should probably have just a plain member of type B. Because that member should be private, and to get rid of the b.h header entirely, this member should live in X's hidden pimpl_ portion:

```
// x.h: after removing unnecessary inheritance
//
#include <iosfwd>
#include "a.h" // class A
class C;
class E;
class X : public A {
public:
   X( const C& );
   B f( int, char* );
   C f( int, C );
   C&  g( B );
   E h( E );

   virtual std::ostream& print( std::ostream& ) const;
private:
   class XImpl* pimpl_; // this now quietly includes a B
};
inline std::ostream& operator<<( std::ostream& os, const X& x )
   { return x.print(os); }
```

The Bottom Line

x.h is still using other class names all over the place, but clients of X need only pay for the #includes of a.h and iosfwd. What an improvement over the original!

In the next column, I'll conclude my focus on the Pimple Idiom. I'll analyze how it can best be used, and then demonstrate how to overcome its main disadvantage.

ß Unless X needs access to some protected function or data in B, of course, but for now I'll assume that this is not the case.

REFERENCES

1. Sutter, H. "C++ State of the Union," C++ *Report*, 10(1): 51–54, Jan. 1998.
2. Coplien, J. *Advanced C++ Programming Styles and Idioms*, Addison–Wesley, Reading, MA, 1992.
3. Lakos, J. *Large-Scale C++ Software Design*, Addison–Wesley, Reading, MA, 1996.
4. Meyers, S. *Effective* C++, 2nd ed., Addison–Wesley, Reading, MA, 1998.
5. Murray, R. C++ *Strategies and Tactics*, Addison–Wesley, Reading, MA, 1993.

External Polymorphism

Chris Cleeland and Douglas C. Schmidt

I have had the pleasure of placing this article, and its ancestor into a magazine and two anthologies. Its ancestor was published in the PLOPD3 book (Pattern Languages of Programming 3, Addison Wesley, 1996), and I published it in the C++ Report, *and now in this book. So this must be a pretty good article, despite the authors' claim that it is not destined for the design patterns hall of fame.*

External polymorphism is a pattern that allows classes that are not related by inheritance and/or have no virtual methods to be treated polymorphically.

This article describes the External Polymorphism pattern, which allows classes that are not related by inheritance and/or have no virtual methods to be treated polymorphically. This pattern combines C++ language features with patterns like Adapter and Decorator[1] to give the appearance of polymorphic behavior on otherwise unrelated classes. The External Polymorphism pattern has been used in a number of C++ frameworks such as ACE[2] and the OSE class library.

This article is organized as follows: First, we describe the External Polymorphism pattern in much greater detail than an earlier version appearing in *Pattern Languages,*[3] then we describe an example implementation using C++, and finally, we present concluding remarks.

An earlier subset of this article appeared as a chapter in the book *Pattern Languages of Program Design,* edited by Robert Martin, Frank Buschmann, and Dirke Riehle, and published by Addison–Wesley, 1997.

THE EXTERNAL POLYMORPHISM PATTERN

INTENT

The pattern allows classes that are not related by inheritance and/or have no virtual methods to be treated polymorphically.

MOTIVATION

Debugging applications built using reusable class libraries can be hard. For example, when an error occurs in the library, developers often don't know the names of all the relevant objects comprising their application. This makes it hard to display the current state of these objects in a debugger or in print statements.

It is often useful, therefore, for class libraries to enable applications to dump the content of some or all objects that are "live" at any given point. In object-oriented languages like C++, live objects include (1) all global objects, (2) initialized static objects, (3) dynamically allocated objects that have not yet been freed, and (4) all automatic objects that are in valid activation records on the run-time stack of active threads.

To motivate the External Polymorphism pattern, consider the following code that uses the SOCK_Stream, SOCK_Acceptor, and INET_Addr library classes, which encapsulate the socket network programming interface within type-safe C++ wrappers[4]:

```
1. // In-memory Singleton object database.
2. class Object_DB { /* ... */ };
3. SOCK_Acceptor acceptor;          // Global storage
4.

5. int main (void) {
6.    SOCK_Stream stream; // Automatic storage
7.    INET_Addr *addr =
8.       new INET_Addr  // Dynamic storage;
9.    Object_DB::instance ()->dump_all (cerr);
```

If the state of this program were dumped when reaching line 13, we might get the following output:

```
Sock_Stream::this = 0x47c393ab,handle_ = {-1}
SOCK_Acceptor::this =0x2c49a45b,handle_ = {-1}
INET_Addr::this =   0x3c48a432,port_ = {0},addr_ = {0.0.0.0}
```

This output is a dump of the current state of each object.

Object_DB is an in-memory database Singleton,[1] i.e., there's only one copy per process. To preserve encapsulation, the Object_DB::dump_all method could access the state information of the SOCK_Stream, SOCK_Acceptor, and INET_Addr objects by calling a dump method defined by these classes. These objects register and unregister with Object_DB in their constructors and destructors, respectively, as illustrated below:

```
SOCK_Stream::SOCK_Stream (void)
{
   Object_DB::instance()-> register_object ((void *) this);
   // ...
}

SOCK_Stream::~SOCK_Stream (void)
{
   // ...
   Object_DB::instance()->remove_object
      ((void *) this);
}
```

Implementing Object_DB in a statically typed language like C++ requires the resolution of the following forces that constrain the solution:

1. *Space efficiency*—the solution must not constrain the storage layout of existing objects. In particular, classes having no virtual methods, i.e., "concrete data types,"[5] must not be forced to add a virtual table pointer (vptr).
2. *Polymorphism*—all library objects must be accessed in a uniform manner.

The remainder of this section describes and evaluates three solutions for implementing the Object_DB facility. The first two exhibit several common traps and pitfalls. The third employs the External Polymorphism pattern to avoid the problems with the first two approaches.

Common Traps and Pitfalls

The limitations with two "obvious" ways of implementing the functionality of Object_DB for statically typed, object-oriented programming languages (such as C++ or Eiffel) are presented below.

TREE-BASED CLASS LIBRARY SOLUTION.

"Tree-based" class libraries[6] have a common class, such as class Object, that forms the root of all inheritance hierarchies. For these types of class libraries, the typical polymorphic solution is to add a pure virtual method called dump into the root class. Each subclass in the library could then override the dump method to display subclass-specific state, as shown in Figure 1. Using this approach, implementing Object_ DB::dump_all is straightforward*:

```
void
Object_DB::dump_all (void)
{
  struct DumpObject {
    void operator()(const Object &obj) {
      obj->dump ();
    }
  };
  // Dump all the objects in the table.
  for_each (this->object_table_.begin (),
          this->object_table_.end (),
          DumpObject ());
}
```

There are several drawbacks to the tree-based solution, however:

1. It requires access to the source code. It also requires the ability to modify it, and the ability to maintain the modified code. Languages like C++ that do not allow methods to be added transparently to base classes are hard to extend in this manner. Other OO languages, such as Smalltalk and Objective-C, do not require programmers to have the source code to augment an interface or modify existing behaviors.
2. It requires all classes to inherit from a common root class. Conventional wisdom deprecates single-root, tree-based class library design strategy in languages like C++.[6,7] For instance, inheriting from a common root object complicates integration with third-party libraries. Moreover, the tree-based approach makes it hard to use subsets of library functionality without including many unnecessary headers and library code modules. For these reasons, the Standard Template Library[7] from the ISO/ANSI C++ draft specifically avoids inheriting from a single root class.

* Standard Template Library[7] classes are used wherever possible in examples, based on information in Musser's work.[8]

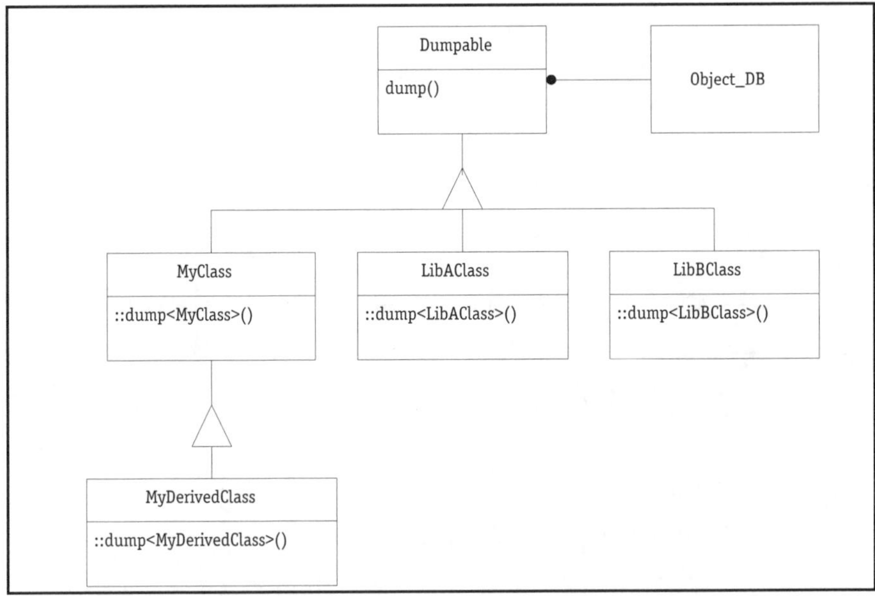

Figure 1. Object model for tree-based solution.

3. It may require changes to storage layout. For C++ libraries, all objects with virtual methods must contain vptrs in their storage layout. This extra vptr may not be feasible for class libraries that contain "concrete data types," such as classes for complex numbers, stacks and queues, and interprocess communication (IPC) interfaces.[4] The complicating factor for concrete data types is that they do not contain any virtual methods. Because virtual methods and inheritance are the C++ language mechanisms that support polymorphism, a concrete data type is—*by definition*—precluded from using those mechanisms to specialize the dump method.

Concrete data types are commonly used in C++ libraries like STL to enhance:

- *Performance*—e.g., all method dispatching is static rather than dynamic (static dispatching also enables method inlining);
- *Storage efficiency*—e.g., some objects cannot afford the space required for a virtual pointer for each instance;
- *Storage compatibility*—e.g., ensure object layouts are compatible with C; and
- *Flexibility*—e.g., to facilitate the placement of concrete data objects in shared memory.

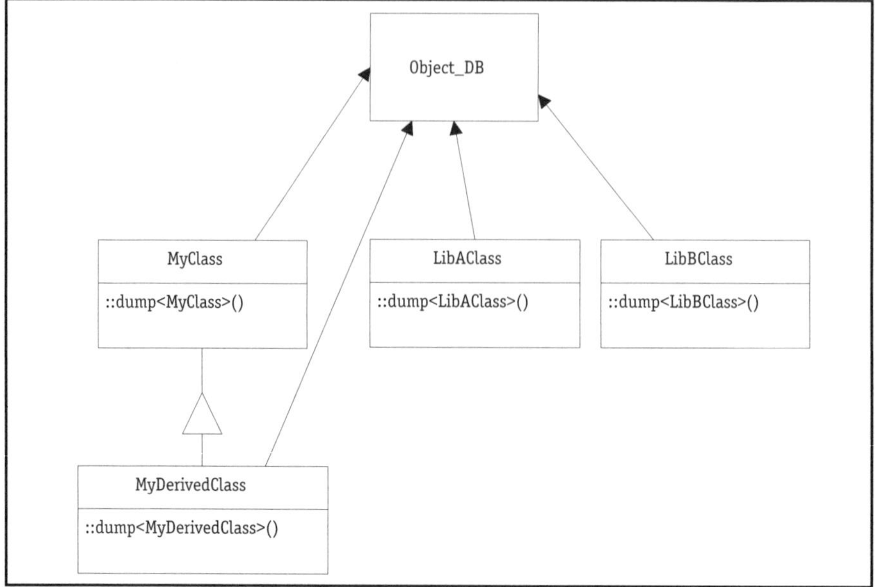

Figure 2. Object model for brute-force solution.

Therefore, for libraries that have concrete data types, it may not be feasible to implement Object_DB by using a common root class.

Of the three drawbacks described above, the first two are relatively independent of the programming language. The third is specific to C++.

Static-type encoding solution (brute-force). One way to avoid the drawbacks with the tree-based class library design is to modify the interface of Object_DB. The revised approach is shown in Figure 2. As shown below, the brute-force approach explicitly allows objects of each different type in the class library to register and remove themselves, as follows:

```
class Object_DB
{
public:
    void register_SOCK_Stream (SOCK_Stream*);
    void register_SOCK_Acceptor (SOCK_Acceptor*);
    void register_INET_Addr (INET_Addr *);
    // ...

private:
    list<SOCK_Stream> SOCK_stream_table_;
```

```
    list<SOCK_Acceptor> SOCK_Acceptor_table_;
    list<INET_Addr> INET_Addr_table_;
    // ...
};
```

In this scheme the Object_DB::dump_all method could be written as follows:

```
void
Object_DB::dump_all ()
{
    template <class T>
    struct Dump {
        void operator ()(const T &t) {
            t->dump ();  // virtual method call
        }
    };

    for_each  (SOCK_stream_table_.begin (),
               SOCK_stream_table_.end (),
               Dump<SOCK_Stream> ());

    for_each  (SOCK_Acceptor_table_.begin (),
               SOCK_Acceptor_table_.end (),
               Dump<SOCK_Acceptor> ());

    for_each  (INET_Addr_table_.begin (),
               INET_Addr_.end (),
               Dump<INET_Addr> ());

    // ...
}
```

Although it eliminates the need for a common ancestor used by the tree-based solution, the brute-force approach of enumerating all types in the system is clearly tedious and fragile. Thus, by eliminating the common ancestor, the following problems arise:

- *Tedious maintenance*—Any time a class is added or removed from the library, the interface and implementation of Object_DB must change. Considerable effort is required to maintain this scheme for large class libraries that evolve over time.
- *Error-prone*—This approach is potentially error-prone if a developer forgets

to add the necessary class-specific dump code to the Object_DB::dump_all method.

- *Integration difficulties*—The brute-force solution does not simplify integrating separately developed libraries because Object_DB must be rewritten for each combination of libraries.

SOLUTION: THE EXTERNAL POLYMORPHISM PATTERN

A more efficient and transparent way to extend concrete data types is to use the External Polymorphism pattern. This pattern allows classes that are not related by inheritance and/or have no virtual methods to be treated polymorphically. It resolves the forces of object layout efficiency (e.g., no vptrs in concrete data types) and polymorphism (e.g., all library objects can be treated in a uniform way) that rendered the previous solutions inadequate. By using this pattern, we'll be able to reclaim the conceptual elegance of the polymorphic solution we discusssed earlier, while still maintaining the storage efficiency and performance benefits of the solution we discussed in the section about the static-type encoding solution.

Figure 3 shows the object model for the External Polymorphism solution. Notice that it combines the best aspects of the strategies discussed previously. Using the External Polymorphism pattern, Dumpable and Dumpable_Adapter combine to form the tree model's Dumpable (see Fig. 1). The template function ::dump<*AnyType*> (shown in Fig. 3 as a globally scoped member function on each class) replaces the overloading of the virtual dump method in the tree model, thus eliminating the vtbl for *AnyType*.

The key to applying the External Polymorphism pattern is to define an abstract base class called Dumpable that contains a pure virtual dump method:

```
// Define the external polymorphic functionality.

class Dumpable
{
public:
   virtual void dump (void) = 0;
   virtual ~Dumpable (void);
};
```

This class provides an abstract base class interface that can be used uniformly for all objects that are "dumpable." A subclass of this base class then provides a "concrete dumpable" type defined by the following template wrapper function:

```
template <class T> void
dump (const T *t)
{
   t->dump ();
}
```

This template function forwards the **dump** method call to the object. This allows the **dump** method to be used if it is defined on template class T. Otherwise, we can define a new **dump<>** function for a class and overload or supply missing functionality to dump the state of T.

The following Adapter makes any class with a **dump** method accessible through **Dumpable**'s interface:

```
template <class T>
class Dumpable_Adapter : public Dumpable
{
public:
   Dumpable_Adapter (T *t): this_ (t) {}
```

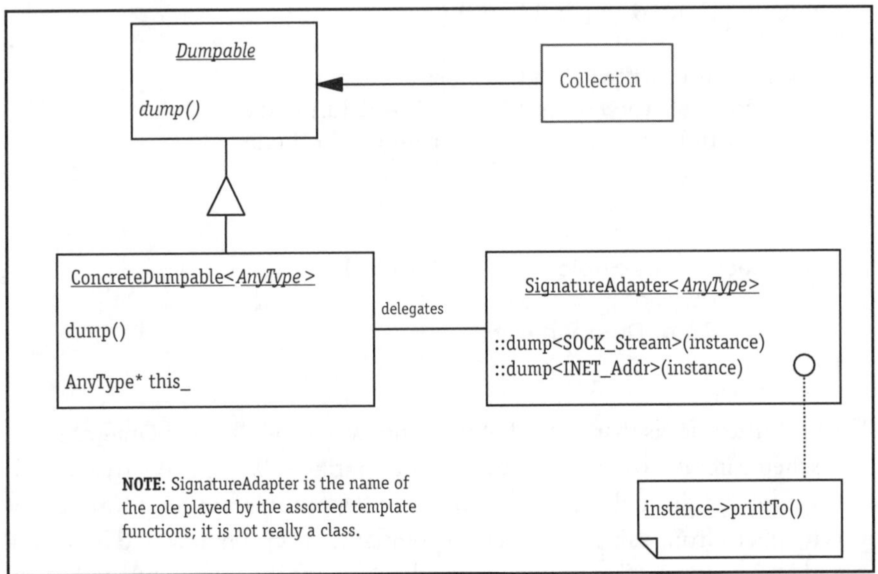

Figure 3. Object model of External Polymorphism solution.

```
    virtual void dump (void) {
      // Delegate to the global dump<T> function
      dump<T> (this_);
    }

  private:
    T *this_;
  };
```

This solution uses C++ templates for the following reasons:

- *To ensure type safety*—the compiler can detect type mismatches at template-instantiation time.
- *To eliminate the need for class* T *to inherit from a common base class*—this is useful for integrating third-party classes, where it is not possible to modify the code.
- *To improve performance*—e.g., by allowing the dump<T> template function (and the T::dump method) to be inlined to eliminate forwarding overhead.

By applying the External Polymorphism pattern, the Object_DB ::dump_all method looks almost identical to the original polymorphic one shown earlier:

```
voidObject_DB::dump_all (void)
{
  struct DumpDumpable {
    void operator() (const Dumpable &dump_obj) {
      dump_obj->dump ();// virtual method call
    }
  };

  for_each  (this->object_table_.begin (),
             this->object_table_.end (),
             DumpDumpable ());
}
```

The key difference is that instead of iterating over a collection of Object*s, this new scheme iterates over a collection of Dumpable*s. We can now treat all objects uniformly through a common ancestor (Dumpable) without forcing objects to inherit from a single root class. Essentially, the vptr that would have been stored in the target object is moved into the Dumpable object. The key benefit is that the flexibility provided by a vptr can be added transparently without changing the storage layout of the original objects.

Applicability

Use the External Polymorphism pattern when:

1. Your class libraries contain concrete data types that cannot inherit from a common base class that contains virtual methods; and
2. The behavior of your class libraries can be simplified significantly if you can treat all objects in a polymorphic manner.

Do not use the External Polymorphism pattern when:

1. Your class libraries already contain abstract data types that inherit from common base classes and contain virtual methods; and
2. Your programming language or programming environment allows methods to be added to classes dynamically.

Structure and Participants

The following describes the roles of the participants illustrated in Figure 4.

Common (**Dumpable**): This abstract base class defines an abstract interface that defines the common pure virtual **request** method(s) that will be treated polymorphically by clients.

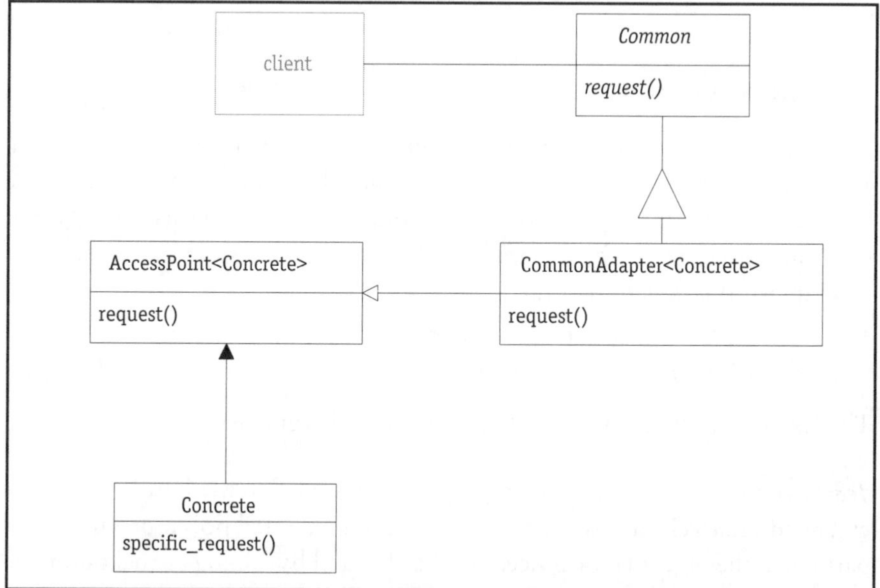

Figure 4. Structure of participants in the External Polymorphism pattern.

Common_Adapter<Concrete> (Dumpable_Adapter): This template subclass of Dumpable implements the pure virtual request method(s) defined in the Common base class. A typical implementation will simply forward the virtual call to the specific_request method in the parameterized class. If the signatures of methods in the Concrete class don't match those of the Common, it may be necessary to use the Adapter pattern[1] to make them conform.

Access Method (::dump<>): The template function forwards requests to the object. In some cases, e.g., where the signature of specific_request is consistent, this feature may not be needed. However, if specific_request has different signatures within several Concrete classes, the access method can be used to insulate such differences from the Common_Adapter.

Concrete (SOCK_Stream, SOCK_Acceptor): The Concrete classes in this pattern define one or more specific_request methods that perform the desired tasks. Although Concrete classes are not related by inheritance, the External Polymorphism pattern makes it possible to treat all or some of their methods polymorphically.

Collection (Object_DB): The Collection maintains a table of all the Common objects that are currently active in the program. This table can be iterated over to "polymorphically" apply operations to all Common objects (e.g., to dump them).

Collaborations

The External Polymorphism pattern is typically used by having a function call a virtual request method(s) through a polymorphic Common*. Each of those methods, in turn, forwards to the corresponding specific_request method of the Concrete class via the Common_Adapter. Figure 5 shows an interaction diagram for this collaboration.

Consequences

The External Polymorphism pattern has the following benefits:

Transparent: Classes that were not originally designed to work together can be extended relatively transparently so they can be treated polymorphically. In particular, the object layouts need not be changed by adding virtual pointers.

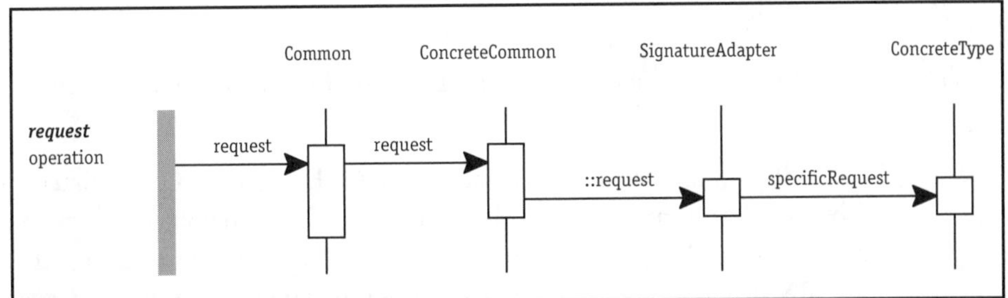

Figure 5. Interaction diagram for collaborators in External Polymorphism pattern.

Flexible: It's possible to polymorphically extend otherwise nonextensible data types, such as int or double, when the pattern is implemented in a language supporting parameterized types (e.g., C++ templates).

Peripheral: Because the pattern establishes itself on the fringes of existing classes, it's easy to use conditional compilation to remove all traces of this pattern. This feature is particularly useful for frameworks that use the External Polymorphism pattern solely for debugging purposes.

However, this pattern has the following drawbacks:

Unstable: All of the methods in the Common and Common_ Adapter must track changes to methods in the Concrete classes.

Obtrusive: It may be necessary to modify the source code of existing library classes to insert/remove pointers to Common classes.

Inefficient: Extra overhead is increased due to multiple forwarding from virtual methods in the Common_Adapter object to the corresponding methods in the Concrete object. However, using inline methods for the Concrete class will reduce this overhead to a single virtual-method dispatch.

Inconsistent: Externally polymorphic methods are not accessible through pointers to the "polymorphized" classes. For instance, in the object model in Figure 3, it's impossible to access dump through a pointer to SOCK_Stream. In addition, it is not possible to access other methods from the "polymorphized" classes through a pointer to Dumpable_Adapter.

KNOWN USES

The External Polymorphism pattern has been used in the following software systems:

- The ACE framework uses it to allow all ACE objects to be registered with a Singleton in-memory "object database." This database stores the state of all live ACE objects and can be used by debugger to dump this state. Because many ACE classes are concrete data types it was not possible to have them inherit from a common root base class containing virtual methods.
- The External Polymorphism pattern also has been used in custom commercial projects in which code libraries from disparate sources were required to have a more common, polymorphic interface. The implementation of the pattern presented a unified interface to classes from a locally developed library, the ACE library, and various other "commercial" libraries.
- The idea for the "access method" ("see Implementation Steps") came from usage in the OSE class library, by Graham Dumpleton.[†] In OSE, template functions are used to define collating algorithms for ordered lists, etc.

RELATED PATTERNS

The External Polymorphism pattern is similar to the Decorator and Adapter patterns from the Gang of Four (GoF) design patterns catalog.[1] The Decorator pattern dynamically extends an object transparently without using subclassing. When a client uses a Decorated object it thinks it's operating on the actual object, when in fact it operates on the Decorator. The Adapter pattern converts the interface of a class into another interface clients expect. Adapter lets classes work together that couldn't otherwise because of incompatible interfaces.

There are several differences between these two GoF patterns and the External Polymorphism pattern. The Decorator pattern assumes that the classes it adorns are already abstract, i.e., they have virtual methods, which are overridden by the Decorator. In contrast, External Polymorphism adds polymorphism to concrete classes, i.e., classes without virtual methods. In addition, because the Decorator is derived from the class it adorns, it must define all the methods it inherits. In contrast, the `ConcreteCommon` class in the External

† The OSE class library is written and distributed by Graham Dumpleton. Further information can be found at www.dscpl.com.au.

Polymorphism pattern need only define the methods in the `Concrete` class it wants to treat polymorphically.

The External Polymorphism pattern is similar to the GoF Adapter pattern. However, there are subtle but important differences:

Intents differ: An Adapter *converts* an interface to something directly usable by a client. External Polymorphism has no intrinsic motivation to convert an interface, but rather to provide a new substrate for accessing similar functionality.

Layer vs. Peer: The External Polymorphism pattern creates an entire class hierarchy outside the scope of the concrete classes. Adapter creates new layers within the existing hierarchy.

Extension vs. Conversion: The External Polymorphism pattern extends existing interfaces so that similar functionality may be accessed polymorphically. Adapter creates a new interface.

Behavior vs. Interface: The External Polymorphism pattern concerns itself mainly with behavior rather than the names associated with certain behaviors.

Finally, the External Polymorphism pattern is similar to the *Polymorphic Actuator* pattern documented and used internally at AG Communication Systems.

Implementing External Polymorphism in C++

The steps and considerations necessary to implement the External Polymorphism pattern are described below.

Implementation Steps

This section describes how to implement the External Polymorphism pattern by factoring behaviors into an abstract base class, implementing those behaviors in a descendant concrete class, and then performing the following steps:

1. Identify common polymorphic functionality and define it in an abstract base class. The key to polymorphic behavior is a common ancestor. Inheritance is typically used when polymorphic behavior is desired. It's not always possible or desirable, however, to use the implementation language's

inheritance to achieve polymorphism. For instance, in C++, polymorphic behavior generally requires addition of a vptr to a class' internal data structure. To avoid this, the External Polymorphism pattern can be applied.

In either situation, one must first determine the desired shared behaviors and factor them into an abstract base class. This class simply specifies an *interface* for the behaviors, not an implementation, as follows:

```
class Polymorphic_Object
{
public:
   virtual void operation1 () = 0;
   virtual void operation2 () = 0;
   ...
}
```

In some cases it may be desirable to define more than one abstract class, grouping related behaviors by class.

2. Define an access method for each behavior method. The abstract base defined in step 1 above defines the signatures of the behaviors. The actual implementation of the behavior will differ (as one might expect) from concrete class to concrete class. Likewise, names of the interfaces to actual implementations may differ. In all cases, access to the implementation of each shared behavior is provided through a template wrapper function, such as

```
template <class T> void
operation1 (const T *t)
{
   t->operation1_impl (...someargs...);
}
```

which provides a generic, default access method to an implementation named operation_impl. Likewise, the approach would be applied for operation2, and any other shared behaviors defined in the Polymorphic_Object class. Names of the interface may differ as well. In situations in which operation_impl is not the correct interface name for some class T, a special-case access method can be provided. Consider a class T1 implementing the required functionality through an interface named some_impl. The special-case access method would be defined as:

```
void
operation1<T1> (const T1 *t)
{
  t->some_operation1_impl (...args...);
}
```

3. Define a parameterized adapter, inheriting from the abstract base. Step 1 defines an abstract base class to aggregate desired polymorphic behaviors. As in language-based inheritance, concrete descendant classes provide behavior implementation. In the External Polymorphism pattern, a concrete, parameterized adapter serves this purpose.

The parameterized adapter specifies an implementation for each interface defined in the base class Polymorphic_Object. Each implementation calls the corresponding access method defined in step 2, delegating to the access method the task of calling the actual implementation.

The adapter for Polymorphic_Object might be written as:

```
template <class T>
class Polymorphic_Adapter : public Polymorphic_Object
{
public:
  Polymorphic_Adapter(T *t) : this_(t) { }

  virtual void operation1(void) {
    // delegate!
    operation1<T>(this_);
  }

  virtual void operation2(void) {
    // delegate!
    operation2<T>(this_);
  }

  ...

private:
  // Make the constructor private to ensure
  // that this_ is always set.
  Polymorphic_Adapter();

  T *this_;
}
```

4. Change application to reference through the abstract base. All facilities are now in place for the application to treat disparate classes as if they share a common ancestor. This can be done by creating instances of Polymorphic_Adapter that are parameterized over different types T, and managing those instances solely through a pointer to the abstract base, Polymorphic_Object.

It should be noted that the External Polymorphism pattern is no different from managing concrete descendants in "normal" inheritance/polymorphism. The main difference is that the parameterization and additional layer of indirection is provided by the access-method template function.

IMPLEMENTATION CONSIDERATIONS

The following issue arises when implementing the External Polymorphism pattern.

Transparency: The scheme shown in this pattern is not entirely transparent to the concrete class T. In particular, the SOCK_Stream's constructor and destructor must be revised slightly to register and deregister instances with Object_DB, as follows:

```
SOCK_Stream::SOCK_Stream(void)
{
   Object_DB::instance ()->register_object
      (new Dumpable_Adapter<SOCK_Stream>(this));
   // ...
}

SOCK_Stream::_SOCK_Stream(void)
{
   // ...
   Object_DB::instance()->remove_object
      ((void*) this);
}
```

Therefore, this solution isn't suitable for transparently registering objects in binary-only libraries.

Note, however, that the changes shown above don't require the SOCK_Stream to inherit from a common class. Nor do they change the storage layout of SOCK_Stream instances. Moreover, it's possible to use macros to conditionally include this feature at compile-time, as follows:

```
#if defined (DEBUGGING)
#define REGISTER_OBJECT(CLASS) \
   Object_DB::instance ()->register_object \
      (new Dumpable_Adapter<CLASS> (this))
#define REMOVE_OBJECT \
   Object_DB::instance ()->remove_object \
      ((void*) this)
#else
#define REGISTER_OBJECT(CLASS)
#define REMOVE_OBJECT
#endif /* DEBUGGING */

SOCK_Stream::SOCK_Stream (void)
{
   REGISTER_OBJECT (SOCK_Stream);
   // ...
}

SOCK_Stream::~SOCK_Stream (void)
{
   //...
   REMOVE_OBJECT (SOCK_Stream);
}
```

Sample Code

The following code was adapted[Δ] from the ACE framework, which is an object-oriented toolkit for developing communication software.[2] This code illustrates how to use the External Polymorphism pattern to implement a mechanism that registers all live ACE objects with a central in-memory object database. Applications can dump the state of all live ACE objects, e.g., from within a debugger.

There are several interesting aspects to this design:

- It uses the External Polymorphism pattern to avoid having to derive all ACE classes from a common base class with virtual methods. This design is crucial to avoid unnecessary overhead and to maintain binary-layout compatibility. In addition, there is no additional space added to ACE objects.
- This mechanism can be conditionally compiled to completely disable External Polymorphism entirely. Moreover, by using macros there are relatively few changes to ACE code.

[Δ] The original code does not utilize STL in its operations.

- This mechanism copes with single-inheritance hierarchies of dumpable classes. In such cases we typically want only one dump, corresponding to the most-derived instance.[ß] Note, however, that this scheme doesn't generalize to work with multiple-inheritance or virtual base classes.

The Dumpable Class

The Dumpable class defines a uniform interface for all object dumping:

```
class Dumpable
{
friend class Object_DB;
friend class Dumpable_Ptr;
public:
   Dumpable (const void *);

   // This pure virtual method must be
   // filled in by a subclass.
   virtual void dump (void) const = 0;

protected:
   virtual ~Dumpable (void);

private:
   const void *this_;
};
```

The implementations of these methods are relatively straightforward:

```
Dumpable::~Dumpable (void) {}

Dumpable::Dumpable (const void *this_ptr)
   : this_ (this_ptr)
{
}
```

The Dumpable_Ptr Class

The Dumpable_Ptr is a smart pointer stored in the in-memory object database Object_DB. The pointee (if any) is deleted when reassigned.

[ß] Thanks to Christian Millour for illustrating how to do this.

```
class Dumpable_Ptr
{
public:
   Dumpable_Ptr (const Dumpable *dumper = 0);

   // Smart pointer delegation method.
   const Dumpable *operator->() const;

   // Assignment operator.
   void operator= (const Dumpable *dumper) const;

private:
   // Points to the actual Dumpable.
   const Dumpable *dumper_;
};
```

The Dumpable_Ptr is defined to cope with hierarchies of dumpable classes. In such cases we typically want only one dump, corresponding to the most-derived instance. To achieve this, the handle registered for the subobject corresponding to the base class is destroyed. Therefore, on destruction of the subobject its handle won't exist anymore, so we'll have to check for that.

The Dumpable_Ptr methods are implemented below. Once again, these are not tricky:

```
Dumpable_Ptr::Dumpable_Ptr (const Dumpable *dumper)
   : dumper_ (dumper)
{
}

const Dumpable *
Dumpable_Ptr::operator->() const
{
   return this->dumper_;
}

void
Dumpable_Ptr::operator= (const Dumpable *dumper) const
{
   if (this->dumper_ != dumper) {
      delete (Dumpable_Ptr*) this->dumper_;
      ((Dumpable_Ptr*) this)->dumper_ = dumper;
   }
}
```

THE OBJECT DATABASE (OBJECT_DB) CLASS

The Object_DB class is the Singleton object database that keeps track of all live objects. Instances must be registered with the database using the register_object method, and subsequently removed using remove_object. The entire database can be traversed and registered objects dumped using dump_objects.

```
class Object_DB
{
public:
   // Iterates through the entire set of
   // registered objects and dumps their state.
   void dump_objects(void);

   // Add the tuple <dumper, this_> to
   // the list of registered objects.
   void register_object(const Dumpable *dumper);

   // Use 'this_' to locate and remove
   // the associated 'dumper' from the
   // list of registered ACE objects.
   void remove_object (const void *this_);

   // Factory method to get the singleton database
   static Object_DB *Object_DB::instance (void);

private:
   // Singleton instance of this class.
   static Object_DB *instance_;

   // Ensure we have a Singleton (nobody
   // can create instances but this class)
   Object_DB (void);

   struct Tuple
   {
      // Pointer to the registered C++ object.
      const void *this_;

      // Smart pointer to the Dumpable
      // object associated with this_.
      const Dumpable_Ptr dumper_;
   };
```

```
  typedef vector<Tuple> TupleVector;

  // Holds all registered C++ objects.
  TupleVector object_table_;
};
```

The instance method, along with the private constructor, enforces the policy that Object_DB is a Singleton. Note that this implementation does not protect itself against concurrent access; however, we can easily apply the *Double-Checked Locking pattern*[9] to achieve that.

```
Object_DB *Object_DB::instance (void)
{
  // For thread safety we would employ
  // double-checked locking, but not now.
  if (Object_DB::instance_ == 0)
    Object_DB::instance_ = new Object_DB;
  return Object_DB;
}
```

The dump_objects method traverses the database and calls the dump method on each registered instance.

```
// Dump all the live objects registered
// with the Object_DB Singleton.
void
Object_DB::dump_objects (void)
{
  // A "funcstruct" to dump what's in a tuple
  struct DumpTuple {
    bool operator ()(const Tuple &t) {
      t.dumper_->dump ();
    }
  };
  for_each  (this->object_table_.begin(),
         this->object_table_.end(),
         DumpTuple());
}
```

An object's life cycle with respect to the database is managed by the following methods, which register and remove instances from the database. An STL-style predicate function is used to compare for equality (see code comments for details).

```
// STL predicate function object to determine
// if the 'this_' member in two Tuples is
// equal. This will be useful throughout.
struct thisMemberEqual :
        public binary_function<Tuple, Tuple, bool> {
    bool operator ()    (const Tuple &t1,
                         const Tuple &t2) const {
        return t1.this_ == t2.this_;
    }
};

// This method registers a new <dumper>. It
// detects duplicates and simply overwrites them.
voidObject_DB::register_object (const Dumpable *dumper)
{
    TupleVector::iterator slot;

    slot = find_if (this->object_table_.begin (),
                    this->object_table_.end (),
                    bind2nd (thisMemberEqual (), dumper));

    if (slot == this->object_table_.end ())
        // Reached the end and didn't find it, so append
        this->object_table_.push_back (*dumper);
    else
        // Found this already—replace
        *slot = *dumper; // Silently replace the duplicate
}

void
Object_DB::remove_object (const void *this_ptr)
{
    Dumpable d (this_ptr);

    (void) remove_if    (this->object_table_.begin (),
                         this->object_table_.end (),
                         bind2nd (thisMemberEqual (), d));
}

Object_DB *Object_DB::instance_ = 0;
```

THE DUMPABLE_ADAPTER CLASS

This class inherits the interface of the abstract Dumpable class and is instantiated with the implementation of the concrete component class Concrete. This design is similar to the Adapter and Decorator patterns.[1] Note that class Concrete need not inherit from a common class because Dumpable provides the uniform virtual interface.

```
template <class Concrete>
class Dumpable_Adapter : public Dumpable
{
public:
   Dumpable_Adapter (const Concrete *t);

   // Concrete dump method (simply delegates to
   // the <dump> method of <class Concrete>).
   virtual void dump (void) const;

   // Delegate to methods in the Concrete class.
   Concrete *operator->();

private:
   // Pointer to <this> of <class Concrete>
   const Concrete *this_;
};
```

The Dumpable_Adapter methods are implemented as follows:

```
template <class Concrete>
Dumpable_Adapter<Concrete>::Dumpable_Adapter
   (const Concrete *t)
   : this_ (t), Dumpable ((const void*) t)
{
}

template <class Concrete> Concrete *
Dumpable_Adapter<Concrete>::operator->()
{
   return (Concrete*) this->this_;
}
```

```
template <class Concrete> void
Dumpable_Adapter<Concrete>::dump (void) const
{
   this->this_->dump<Concrete> (this_);
}
```

The critical "glue" between the external class hierarchy and the existing class hierarchy is the *access method*, which is defined for the dump method as follows:

```
template <class Concrete> void
dump<Concrete> (const Concrete* t)
{
   t->dump ();
}
```

Because it may not always be desirable to have this debugging hierarchy compiled in, we created some useful macros for conditionally compiling this implementation of External Polymorphism into an application or framework:

```
#if defined (DEBUGGING)
#define REGISTER_OBJECT(CLASS) \
        Object_DB::instance()->register_object
          (new Dumpable_Adapter<CLASS> (this));
#define REMOVE_OBJECT \
        Object_DB::instance()->remove_object
          ((void*) this);
#else
#define REGISTER_OBJECT(CLASS)
#define REMOVE_OBJECT
#endif /* DEBUGGING */
```

The Use Case

The following code illustrates how the Dumpable mechanisms are integrated into ACE components like the SOCK_ Acceptor and SOCK_Stream.

```
class SOCK
{
public:
   SOCK (void) { REGISTER_OBJECT (SOCK); }
   ~SOCK (void) { REMOVE_OBJECT; }
```

```
   void dump(void) const {
      cerr << "hello from SOCK = "
            << this << endl;
   }

   // ...
};

class SOCK_Acceptor : public SOCK
{

public:
   SOCK_Acceptor (void) {
      REGISTER_OBJECT (SOCK_Acceptor);
   }
   ~SOCK_Acceptor (void) { REMOVE_OBJECT; }

   void dump (void) const {
      cerr << "hello from SOCK_Acceptor = "
            << this << endl;
   }

   // ...
};

class SOCK_Stream : public SOCK
{
public:
   SOCK_Stream(void) {
      REGISTER_OBJECT (SOCK_Stream);
   }
   ~SOCK_Stream (void) { REMOVE_OBJECT; }

   void dump (void) const {
      cerr << "hello from SOCK_Stream = "
            << this << endl;
   }

   // ...
};

intmain (void)
{
```

```
    SOCK sock;
    // Note that the SOCK superclass is *not*
    // printed for SOCK_Stream or SOCK_Acceptor.
    // because of the smart pointer Dumpable_Ptr.
    SOCK_Stream stream;
    SOCK_Acceptor acceptor;
    Object_DB::instance ()->dump_objects ();
    {
      SOCK sock;
      // Note that the SOCK superclass is *not*
      // printed for SOCK_Stream or SOCK_Acceptor.
      SOCK_Stream stream;
      SOCK_Acceptor acceptor;
      Object_DB::instance ()->dump_objects ();
    }
    Object_DB::instance ()->dump_objects ();
    return 0;
  }
```

VARIANTS

The Object_DB that maintains the live objects can be implemented using the GoF Command pattern. In this case, the Object_DB::register_object method is implemented by "attaching" a new Command. This Command contains the object and its dump method. When an Object_DB::dump_all is invoked, all the Commands are "executed." This solution allows the Command executor to iterate through a collection of unrelated objects with no vtables and pick out the right method for each one.

For example, assume that the Object_DB had a Command_List, as follows:

```
class Object_DB
{
public:
  void register_object (Command_Base *base) {
    dumpables_.attach (base);
  }

  void dump_all (void) {
    dumpables_.execute ();
  }
  // ...
```

```
private:
  // List of Commands_Base *'s.
  Command_List dumpables_;
};
```

Individual objects can be registered as follows:

```
SOCK_Stream *ss = new SOCK_Stream;
SOCK_Acceptor *sa = new SOCK_Acceptor;

Object_DB::register_object
  (new Command0<SOCK_Stream>
    (ss, &SOCK_Stream::dump));

Object_DB::register_object
  (new Command0<SOCK_Acceptor>
    (sa, &SOCK_Acceptor::dump));
```

This implementation is more flexible than the one shown in the "Sample Code" section because it allows the other methods besides dump to be invoked when iterating over the Object_DB.

Conclusion

External Polymorphism is not likely destined for the design patterns "Hall of Fame." In particular, it is not as broadly applicable as the *Singleton* or *Adapter* patterns.[1] However, External Polymorphism does solve a subtle, real-world problem encountered by developers implementing complex software in statically typed languages like C++.

Reuse, and thus integration, typically occurs at source level. While patterns cannot change fundamental linkage styles of languages or environments from "source" to "binary," the External Polymorphism pattern enforces software integration at a different conceptual level. In particular, it encourages a component-like "black-box" style of development and integration, as opposed to a "white-box" approach.[10] Therefore, substituting one set of library components for another can be simplified. Likewise, bringing in new, externally produced libraries is also easier.

The following analogy is offered in closing: Automobiles are complex interworking systems. Many repairs or maintenance tasks can be performed by using general-purpose tools such as screwdrivers or a socket set. However, there are some automotive subsystems such as mounting a tire or performing a wheel alignment that require the application of highly specialized tools and techniques to efficiently complete the job. In the world of design patterns, External Polymorphism is definitely a special-purpose tool. Hopefully, our description of this pattern will enable you to apply it and "effectively complete the job."

Acknowledgments

Many people have given comments on earlier versions of this article including: Alex Maclinovsky, Ralph Johnson, Jody Hagins, Christian Millour, Phil Brooks, Phil Mesnier, and Bill Hess. The authors also wish to thank everyone from PLoP '96 who provided substantive comments on content and form for this pattern.

References

1. Gamma, E. et al. *Design Patterns: Elements of Reusable Object-Oriented Software*, Addison–Wesley, Reading, MA, 1995.
2. Schmidt, D. C. "ACE: An Object-Oriented Framework for Developing Distributed Applications," in *Proceedings of the 6th USENIX C++ Technical Conference*, Cambridge, MA, USENIX Association, Apr. 1994.
3. Cleeland, C., D. C. Schmidt, and T. Harrison. "External Polymorphism—An Object Structural Pattern for Transparently Extending Concrete Data Types," in *Pattern Languages of Program Design*, R. Martin, F. Buschmann, and D. Riehle, Eds., Addison–Wesley, Reading, MA, 1997.
4. Schmidt, D. C. "IPC_SAP: An Object-Oriented Interface to Interprocess Communication Services," *C++ Report*, Nov./Dec. 1992.
5. Stroustrup, B. *The C++ Programming Language*, 2nd ed., Addison–Wesley, Reading, MA, 1991.
6. Lea, D. "libg++, the GNU C++ Library," in *Proceedings of the 1st C++ Conference*, Denver, CO, pp. 243–256, USENIX, Oct. 1988.
7. Stepanov, A. and M. Lee. "The Standard Template Library," Tech. Rep. HPL-94-34, Hewlett-Packard Laboratories, Apr. 1994.
8. Musser, D. L. and A. Saini. *STL Tutorial and Reference Guide: C++ Programming with the Standard Template Library*, Addison–Wesley, Reading, MA, 1995.

9. Schmidt, D. C. and T. Harrison. "Double-Checked Locking—An Object Behavioral Pattern for Initializing and Accessing Thread-Safe Objects Efficiently," in *3rd Pattern Languages of Programming Conference* (Washington University technical report #WUCS-97-07), Feb. 1997.

10. Hueni, H., R. Johnson, and R. Engel. "A Framework for Network Protocol Software," in *Proceedings of OOPSLA '95*, Austin, TX, ACM, Oct. 1995.

A Technique for Safe Deletion with Object Locking

Jeff Grossman

If, in your programming career, you have had the good fortune to work in a multithreaded environment, you know the complication that creates. The problems of concurrent update and deadlock are very real, and very very difficult to debug.

In this article Jeff fully explores the problem of deleting objects in one thread that are used in other threads. Without great care, this could lead to the use of stale pointers. Jeff explores the various failure scenarios and provides a strategy for safe deletion.

TODAY'S APPLICATIONS DEMAND we get the best possible performance with limited resources. One technology for accomplishing this is multithreading. More and more, applications are introducing threading to provide enhanced features. Background spellchecking in word processors is one example. However, the applications with which I work are more intense than single-user GUI programs. This environment I call *aggressive multithreading*, requiring applications with these characteristics:

- These applications have multiple threads of the same type. They can be called transaction threads, worker threads, or background threads. The key point is that, except for state, these threads are identical. Of course, such an application may also have other, nontransactional threads.
- Multithreading is being used for the express purpose of minimizing "response time" and maximizing parallelism and resource utilization.

Note that aggressive multithreading does not necessarily imply real time. Real-time applications have additional hard constraints on response time. And the line between real time and transaction processing often is a philosophical discussion.

In these applications we often find ourselves required to maintain a group of objects in a container[*] in such a way that individual objects may be locked while being operated upon. If this group of objects is static throughout the lifetime of the application, the solution is simple. But when existing objects can be deleted, the twin objectives of safety and efficiency cause the solution to be challenging.

We place the following requirements on the solution:

1. It must be theoretically safe under all conditions. This is obvious. If the algorithm doesn't have to work reliably, we can make it arbitrarily fast.
2. It must provide maximum parallelism in that threads will not block unnecessarily. If a safe solution defeats the advantages of multithreading, it has no value.
3. Objects need to be exclusively locked when in use. A thread using an object must be certain the object is not modified while in use, even if that thread is not going to modify it.
4. An object must be deleted as soon as possible. In an aggressively multithreaded environment, resources need to be freed quickly when no longer needed. These resources include not only those used by the object itself, but threads as well. If any threads are waiting for an object that is intended for deletion, these threads should be released quickly to perform other tasks.
5. The first thread to request object deletion must have positive confirmation that deletion has taken place. Other actions may depend on an object's deletion.

It is requirements 4 and 5 that create difficulties.

To support development of a solution, we require only the existence of a mutual-exclusion primitive (mutex).

The straightforward approach to object locking and deletion might be[†]:

```
{
        enter container mutex
        locate object
```

[*] In actual applications, I typically use STL list<> or map <> containers that store pointers to objects. Some call this usage a "collection."

[†] In these pseudocode examples, "failure to locate the object" has been omitted for clarity.

```
        remove object from container
        leave container mutex
    }
    [use or delete object]
```

If not deleted, the object can be returned to the container with:

```
    {
        enter container mutex
        return object to container
        leave container mutex
    }
```

This is entirely safe and quite efficient, because the time spent in the container mutex is likely to be small compared to the time the object is in use, and the other, unused, objects are available for other threads to access. Unfortunately, many complex applications will require that multiple threads contend for access to the same object. This solution removes the object from view while it is being used, and provides no mechanism for those other threads to queue up while waiting for the object to be available.

Our second attempt at a solution looks like this:

```
    {
        enter container mutex
        locate object
        obtain object's mutex
        leave container mutex
    }
    [use the object]
    release the object's mutex
```

As with the first solution, this is entirely safe. But it lacks efficiency. Note that a thread could block on an object's mutex while owning the container's mutex. This locks out all other threads from the container, even those intending to use different objects, thus serializing access. This certainly is not desirable in a highly parallel multithreaded application.

Our third attempt at a solution is:

```
    {
        enter container mutex
        locate object
        leave container mutex
    }
```

```
{
    obtain object's mutex
    [use the object]
    release the object's mutex
}
```

Now we have solved the efficiency issue: The container is not tied up while we wait for an object lock. It's just that this solution is no longer safe. Why? Look carefully. This is multithreading, and paranoia is a key developer personality trait.[Δ]

Suppose our thread is preempted by another thread immediately after we exit the container's mutex. And suppose that other thread enters the container mutex and *deletes* the object (remember our original problem domain?). When we attempt to obtain the object's mutex, we find it has disappeared out from under us. Depending on the implementation, the result could be an operating-system error, because the mutex is bad. Or it could be an exception, because the memory for the object no longer is accessible.

Okay, let's make a fourth try:

```
{
    enter container mutex
    locate object
    leave container mutex
}
{
    try { obtain object's mutex }
    catch { proceed as if the object was not found }
    [use the object]
    release the object's mutex
}
```

Well, we're still efficient, and it looks as if we've solved our stale-object problem. However, looks are deceiving. In the real world, it is theoretically possible for the object to have been deleted, and a new one to have been created at the exact same memory location. Unlikely, but possible.[ß] If we try to be clever by storing the mutex in a local variable before leaving the container's mutex, we run

Δ Just because you think that all other threads are out to "get" yours doesn't mean it isn't true!

ß However, if this new developer has overridden the class' `new` operator to take advantage of the efficiencies of fixed block-size memory allocators, this situation could become likely.

into problems such as the fact that operating systems like Win32 recycle handles. There's no guarantee that the mutex handle has not been deleted and reused. We want an invalid handle error, but may not get one.

Because we're in the business of writing theoretically safe code, rather than code that should work "almost all of the time," we need a better solution.

Solution five:

```
Lock Requester
   {
      enter container mutex
      locate object
      leave container mutex
   }
   {
      obtain object's mutex
      if object is marked for deletion
         release object's mutex and proceed
         as if object was not located
      [use the object]
      release the object's mutex
   }

Deletion Requester
   {
      enter container mutex
      locate object
      mark object for deletion
      remove object from container
      leave container mutex
   }
   {
      obtain object's mutex
      delete the object
   }
```

To create this last ounce of safety, we establish procedures for both lock requesters and deletion requesters. We add a helper in the form of a deletion marker for each object. For this solution we also add a requirement that the underlying implementation of the object's mutex is such that if the mutex is deleted while a thread is blocked, the thread will wake up with a notification that is distinct from the case in which the mutex is successfully obtained. This is needed in the case in which a lock requester is blocked on the object mutex and a deletion requester arrives, marks and removes the object from the container, enters the object mutex, and deletes the object.#

By deleting an object only after having obtained its mutex, we seem to have solved the stale-object problem. Any pending lock requesters will either note the object is marked for deletion (if they obtain the object's mutex), or will receive a mutex-deleted error (if the deletion requester obtains the mutex first). Also, once an object is marked for deletion, all new lock requesters and new deletion requesters will leave the object alone because the object was removed from the container, and they will be unable to locate it.

So let's consider the scenario in Figure 1:

It looks like we correctly dealt with multiple deletions, but not multiple lock requesters. The problem is that after thread 2 locates the object, but before it can obtain the object lock, the object is deleted. Now this is the most obvious of the race conditions. For example, another scenario could have thread 2 check the deletion marker, and not attempt to lock the object if marked. However, the act of checking the deletion marker can result in a stale-object reference. Even if the deletion-marker test indicated the object was lockable, during the interval between the test and the actual lock attempt, the object could be deleted. This brings us to our sixth and last solution:

```
Lock Requester
   {
      enter container mutex
      locate object
      increment lock reservation counter
      leave container mutex
   }
   {
      obtain object's mutex
      decrement the lock reservation counter
      if object is marked for deletion,
         leave object's mutex and
         proceed as if object was not located
      [use the object]
      release the object's mutex
   }
```

Remember, there is no requirement that the mutex operate in a strictly FIFO manner (and a Win32 mutex doesn't).

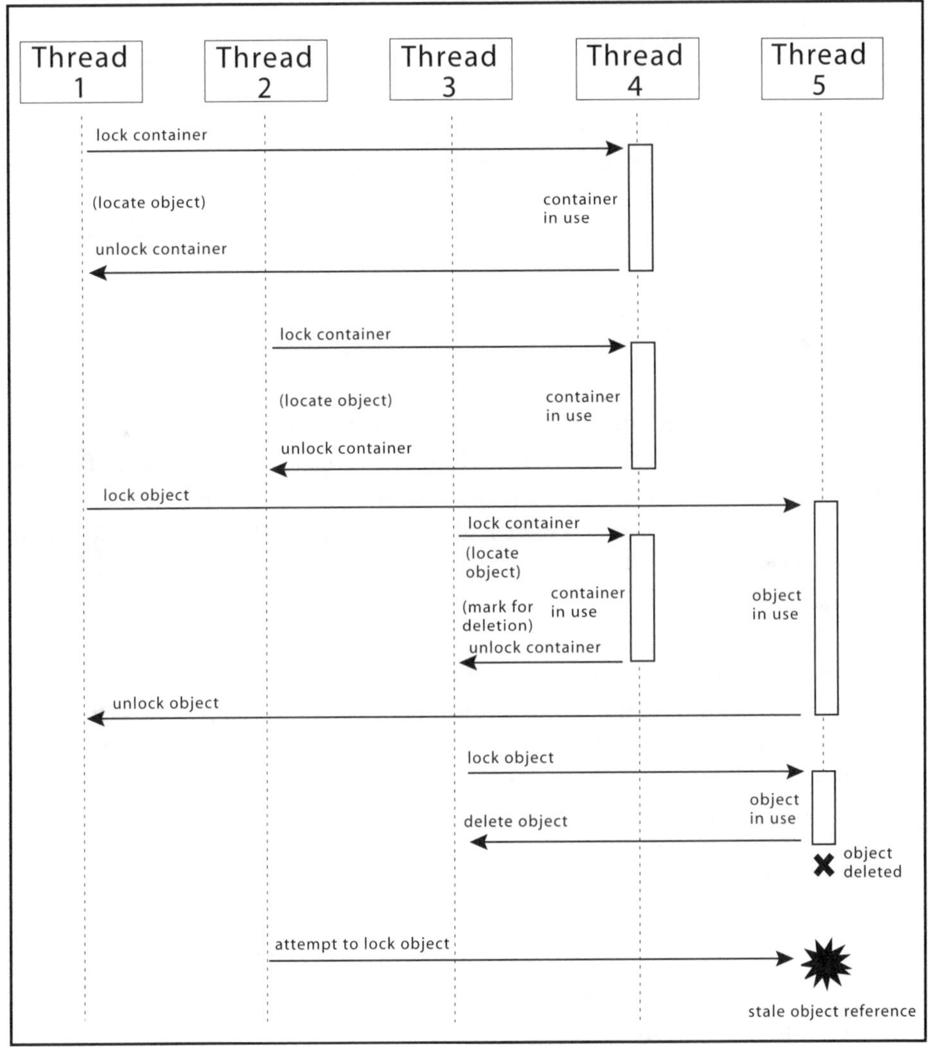

Figure 1. Stale-object reference.

```
Deletion Requester
   {
      enter container mutex
      locate object
      if already marked for deletion,
         leave container mutex and proceed
         as if object was not found
      mark object for deletion
```

```
        remove object from container
        leave container mutex
    }
    {
        obtain object's mutex
        while ( lock reservation counter > 0 )
        {
            release the mutex
            obtain object's mutex
        }
        delete the object
        }
```

By introducing the object's lock-reservation counter, we present the opportunity to all lock requesters to obtain the object's mutex, recognize that it is marked for deletion, and walk away from it. The deleting thread will back off until all requesters have had their chance to do this. We know that no new requesters will appear once the object has been removed from the container. If we reexamine the previous scenario, we see that thread 2 does not use a stale-object reference because thread 3 has deferred deleting it, because there was a pending lock reservation. However, thread 2 does not use the object, but immediately releases it, because there is a pending deletion. This is shown below in Figure 2.

Doesn't it seem as if we merely reinvented simple reference counting, but with mutual exclusion added? Not really. Examine the following:

```
Lock Requester
    {
        enter container mutex
        locate object
        increment the object's reference count
        leave container mutex
    }
    {
        obtain object's mutex
        [use the object]
        decrement the object's reference count
        if the reference count is zero,
            delete the object
        else
            release the object's mutex
    }
```

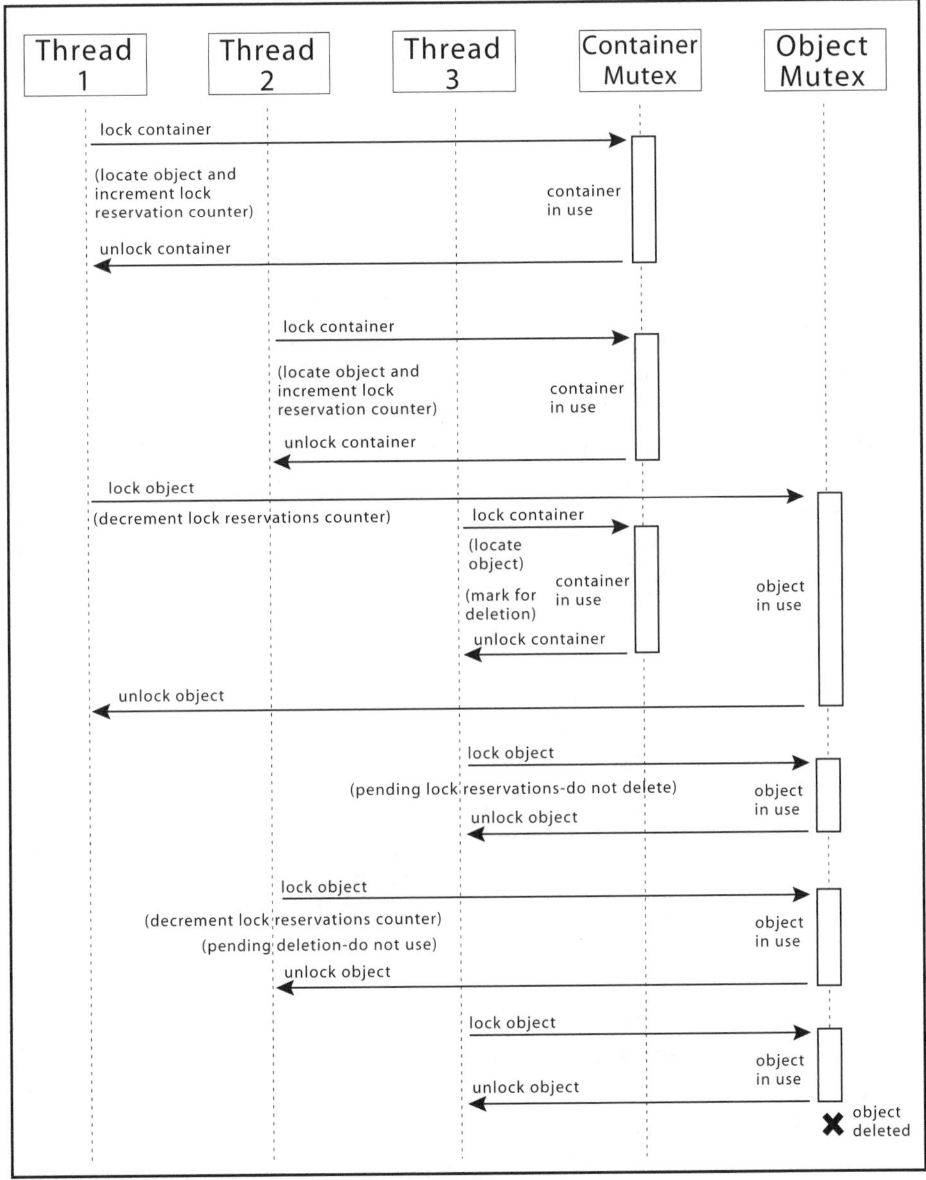

Figure 2. Safe-object deletion.

Deletion Requester

```
{
    enter container mutex
    locate object
    remove object from container
    leave container mutex
}
```

```
{
   obtain object's mutex
   decrement the object's reference count
   if the reference count is zero,
      delete the object
   else
      release the object's mutex
}
```

First, we note that all lock requesters will get access to the object, even after it is intended that deletion should take place. These lock requesters will be unaware that deletion is pending. In addition, deletion is not synchronous. If other threads have incremented the reference count and are waiting for the mutex, the thread requesting object deletion cannot know when deletion has taken place. This fails to meet our two original requirements of rapid and synchronous deletion.

Second, we observe that reference counting as shown above is not even safe. The reference count is not incremented within the object's mutex, thus creating race conditions for lock requesters and deletion requesters. If we increment the reference count within the object's mutex, we destroy all opportunities for parallelism (see our second attempt at a solution).

Reference counting is intended to control object lifetime. In fact, two common usages are to enable safe object deletion (as in COM), or to nail down shared data (as in the underlying implementation of MFC's `CString` class). Ordinary reference counting does not meet all of the requirements of aggressive multithreading.

It should also be noted that if we try to optimize a reference-counting-with-mutexes solution by deleting the mutex while deletion requester owns it, we have an unsafe situation. The mutex handle could be recycled before the lock requester has a chance to determine that it was deleted.

Interestingly, if we had started out with reference counting, added mutexes, and then tried to fix the shortfalls in that solution, we would have reached pretty much the same result as in solution six. The reservation counter is, after all, a kind of reference counter. However, the path we took exposes some subtle issues when designing algorithms for multithreading.

Solution six is safe, meets all of our requirements, and is fairly efficient. Only when deleting an object with a queue of requesters is there is a performance penalty (paid in context switches). While this solution meets all of our requirements, there are some additional real-world issues to be addressed:

- Insertion and deletion operations on the container may involve the heap, and could cause error returns or throw exceptions. You should be pre-

Win32

IN WIN32 there are two mutual-exclusion primitives: critical sections and mutexes. Critical sections are much faster than mutexes. On a Pentium II 300MHz, a round trip (enter/leave) without any context switching takes 0.29us. With a mutex it takes 5.3us. However, critical sections have severe restrictions. A thread cannot specify a wait time-out, nor can it determine if the owning thread was terminated before releasing the critical section, or if the critical section was deleted. With a Win32 mutex, a waiting thread can specify a time-out and can determine if the owning thread terminated, or if the mutex was deleted.

Because of the significant difference in overhead, a careful consideration of the mutex features will drive the decision as to which exclusion primitive to use. I use the following criteria:

- To use a critical section, the protected operation must be "short." Of course, defining "short" depends a lot on the application context. Some applications may define short as 10us; others might define short as 500us.
- To use a critical section, the operation should be nonblocking. For example, I don't use critical sections involving socket functions. If a protected operation can block, it implies a waiting thread might need to specify a time-out.
- If there's a chance that the thread might be terminated unexpectedly, a critical section is not a good choice. Waiting threads cannot be properly notified. This also means that while in a critical section, an owning thread must not permit exceptions to be propagated without releasing the critical section.
- There are some cases in which neither a mutex , nor a critical section will work. These primitives have a "thread affinity." Only the thread "owning" the object can release it. This presents a problem when you have an RPC or free-threaded COM server that maintains one of these managed lists, and you want locks to persist across RPC or COM calls.« There is no way to ensure the call to release the object will arrive on the same thread that locked it. The solution here is to use a 0/1 semaphore to achieve exclusion. The tradeoff is that a semaphore has no thread affinity, hence, abandonment is not detectable. Fortunately, in this context, abandonment is not an interesting event. On the other hand, this means you might want to consider a watchdog thread with the RPC or COM server to detect locked objects that might be considered abandoned.

In Win32, mutexes are not strictly FIFO. In fact, I've observed everything from FIFO to LIFO and completely random orders. This has implications for the case of a deletion thread leaving and reentering the object's mutex, while waiting for other threads to release their lock reservations. The deleting thread can loop, releasing and reacquiring the mutex, without causing other threads to be dispatched. A work-around to this problem is to insert a `Sleep(0)` call before reentering the mutex, forcing other threads to be dispatched.

In NT 4.0 a new synchronization primitive was introduced: `SignalObjectAndWait`. This primitive atomically signals one object and waits for another. Using this API, it is

« Unless the COM object is free threaded, locking is not needed.

possible to signal one mutex and wait for a second, without any other thread running between these two actions. Remember that race conditions in our locking algorithm were caused by exiting the container mutex, and then trying to acquire the object mutex.

SignalObjectAndWait solves these problems, but introduces another issue. We no longer need the lock-reservation counter because a deleting thread can simply delete the object once it gets ownership. Any waiting threads will wake up with a WAIT_FAILED error, assume the object was deleted, and react accordingly. However, SignalObjectAndWait can wait only for a single object. In real-world multithreaded applications, there is some value in being able to cancel threads. One strategy for supporting thread cancellation is to associate a "cancel" event with each thread. Whenever a thread waits on an object, it also waits on its cancel event. When the thread wakes up and its cancel event was signaled, it can gracefully clean up and exit. Without the ability to wait for multiple objects, the cancel feature is lost. Canceling is also possible with an asynchronous procedure call (APC), which is supported with SignalObjectAndWait. However, APCs were originally intended for overlapped I/O and cause an ambiguous return code.

pared to deal with these without leaving the container's mutex permanently locked.

- Threads could be deleted while owning objects. In Win32, if this happens with a mutex, a WAIT_ABANDONED error is returned to the next entering thread. You should be prepared to deal with this.
- In some applications, all pending requesters might need to operate on the object before it is deleted. If so, the algorithm will need to be modified so as to "use" the object, even if it is marked for deletion.
- To ensure this algorithm is enforced, it might be necessary to make an object's destructor protected and provide a delete *method*. If multiple threads use an object's delete *operator*, there is no way to prevent memory from being freed multiple times. Note that making the destructor protected will make it impossible to construct the object on the stack. This shouldn't be much of a problem because stack-based objects don't need to use this algorithm anyway. An alternative is overriding the object's delete operator.
- Exclusion primitives have implications for class design. Even if otherwise unnecessary, the presence of an exclusion primitive as a data member of a class will drive the requirement for an explicit copy constructor and an assignment operator. The default compiler-generated, bit-wise operations will generally give incorrect results, and normally you will want to create a distinct exclusion primitive for the new object.

GPERF: A PERFECT HASH FUNCTION GENERATOR

DOUGLAS C. SCHMIDT

I attended the COOTS conference this year ('99) and sat in on Doug's talk on the performance of TAO. During his presentation, he related the difficulty with performing fast lookups of object and method names in TAO (the open-source ORB I talked about a few articles ago). Doug said that in order to do the lookups as fast as possible he needed to have perfect hash functions.

Now, anybody who has written a hash table knows the problem with the hash generator. Unless you pick a generator that is well tuned to the kind of data you are going to put in to the table, your performance will suffer mightily.

So, since this is an ORB, and he has the opportunity to read IDL files and to therefore know exactly what the incoming data set is, Doug decided to write a program that generates perfect *hash functions. And I felt that this should be published in a book somewhere so that it would be logged in the Library of Congress and never be lost.*

PERFECT HASH FUNCTIONS are a time and space-efficient implementation of *static search sets*. A static search set is an abstract data type (ADT) with operations *initialize*, *insert*, and *retrieve*. Static search sets are common in system software applications. Typical static search sets include compiler and interpreter-reserved words, assembler instruction mnemonics, shell interpreter built-in commands, and CORBA IDL compilers. Search set elements are called *keywords*. Keywords are inserted into the set once, usually off line at compile-time.

gperf is a freely available perfect hash function generator written in C++ that automatically constructs perfect hash functions from a user-supplied list of keywords. It was designed in the spirit of utilities like lex[1] and yacc[2] to remove the drudgery associated with constructing time and space-efficient keyword recognizers manually.

gperf translates an n element list of user-specified keywords, called the *keyfile*, into source code containing a k element lookup table and the following pair of functions:

- hash uniquely maps keywords in the *keyfile* onto the range $0..k-1$, where $k \geq n$. If $k = n$ hash is considered a *minimal* perfect hash function.
- in_word_set uses hash to determine whether a particular string of characters occurs in the *keyfile*, using at most one string comparison in the common case.

gperf is designed to run quickly for keyfiles containing several thousand keywords. gperf generates efficient ANSI and K&R C and C++ source code as output. It has been used to generate reserved keyword recognizers in lexical analyzers for several production and research compilers and language-processing tools, including GNU C/C++[3] and the TAO CORBA IDL compiler.[4]

STATIC SEARCH SET IMPLEMENTATIONS

There are numerous implementations of static search sets. Common examples include sorted and unsorted arrays and linked lists, AVL trees, optimal binary-search trees, digital search tries, deterministic finite-state automata, and various hash table schemes, such as open addressing and bucket chaining.[5]

Different static search structure implementations offer trade-offs between memory utilization and search-time efficiency and predictability. For example, an n element sorted array is space efficient. However, the average- and worst-case time complexity for retrieval operations using binary search on a sorted array is proportional to $O(\log n)$.[5]

In contrast, chained hash table implementations locate a table entry in constant, i.e., $O(1)$, time on the average. However, hashing typically incurs additional memory overhead for link pointers and/or unused hash table buckets. In addition, hashing exhibits $O(n^2)$ worst-case performance.[5]

A *minimal perfect hash function* is a static search set implementation defined by the following two properties:

The perfect property: Locating a table entry requires O(1) time, i.e., *at most* one string comparison is required to perform keyword recognition within the static search set.

The minimal property: The memory allocated to store the keywords is precisely large enough for the keyword set and *no larger*.

Minimal perfect hash functions provide a theoretically optimal time and space-efficient solution for static search sets.[5] However, they can be hard to generate efficiently due to the extremely large search space of potential perfect hashing functions. Therefore, the following variations are often more appropriate for many practical hashing applications, especially those involving thousands of keywords:

Nonminimal perfect hash functions: These functions do not possess the minimal property because they return a range of hash values larger than the total number of keywords in the table. However, they *do* possess the perfect property because at most, one string comparison is required to determine if a string is in the table. There are two reasons for generating nonminimal hash functions:

1. Generation efficiency—It is usually much faster to generate nonminimal perfect functions than to generate *minimal perfect* hash functions.[6,7]
2. Runtime efficiency—Nonminimal perfect hash functions may also execute faster than minimal ones when searching for elements that are *not* in the table because the "null" entry will be located more frequently. This situation often occurs when recognizing programming language reserved words in a compiler.[8]

Near-perfect hash functions: Near-perfect hash functions do not possess the perfect property because they allow nonunique keyword hash values[9] (they may or may not possess the minimal property, however). This technique is a compromise that trades increased *generated-code-execution-time* for decreased *function-generation-time*. Near-perfect hash functions are useful when main memory is at a premium because they tend to produce much smaller lookup tables than nonminimal perfect hash functions.

gperf can generate minimal perfect, nonminimal perfect, and near-perfect hash functions, as described below.

Interacting with GPERF

This section explains how end users can interact with gperf. By default, gperf reads a keyword list and optional *associated attributes* from the standard input keyfile. Keywords are specified as arbitrary character strings delimited by a user-specified field separator that defaults to ' , '. Thus, keywords may contain spaces and any other ASCII characters. Associated attributes can be any C literals. For example, keywords in Listing 1 represent months of the year. Associated attributes in this listing correspond to fields in struct months. They include the number of leap year and non-leap-year days in each month, as well as the months' ordinal numbers, i.e., january = 1, february = 2, ..., december = 12.

gperf's input format is similar to the UNIX utilities lex and yacc. It uses the following input format:

```
declarations and text inclusions
%%
keywords and optional attributes
%%
auxiliary code
```

A pair of consecutive % symbols in the first column separates declarations from the list of keywords and their optional attributes. C or C++ source code and comments are included verbatim into the generated output file by enclosing the text inside %{ %} delimiters, which are stripped off when the output file is generated, e.g.:

```
%{
#include <stdio.h>
#include <string.h>
/* Command-line options:
   -C -p -a -n -t -o -j 1 -k 2,3
   -N is_month */
%}
```

An optional user-supplied struct declaration may be placed at the end of the declaration section, just before the %% separator. This feature enables "typed attribute" initialization. For example, in Listing 1 struct months is defined to have four fields that correspond to the initializer values given for the month names and their respective associated values, e.g.:

Listing 1. An example keyfile for months of the year.

```
%{
#include <stdio.h>
#include <string.h>
/* Command-line options:
      –C –p –a –n –t –o –j 1 –k 2,3
      –N is_month */
%}
struct months {
      char *name;
      int number;
      int days;
      int leap_days;
};
%%
january,     1, 31,  31
february,    2, 28,  29
march,       3, 31,  31
april,       4, 30,  30
may,         5, 31,  31
june,        6, 30,  30
july,        7, 31,  31
august,      8, 31,  31
september,   9, 30,  30
october,     10,  31,  31
november,    11,  30,  30
december,    12,  31,  31
%%
/* Auxiliary code goes here... */
#ifdef DEBUG
int main () {
      char buf[BUFSIZ];
      while (gets (buf)) {
         struct months *p = is_month (buf, strlen (buf));
         printf ("%s is%s a month\n",
            p ? p->name : buf, p ? "" : " not");
      }
}
#endif
```

```
struct months {
    char *name;
    int number;
    int days;
    int leap_days;
};
%%
```

Lines containing keywords and associated attributes appear in the *keywords and optional attributes* section of the keyfile. The first field of each line always contains the keyword itself, left-justified against the first column and without surrounding quotation marks. Additional attribute fields can follow the keyword. Attributes are separated from the keyword and from each other by field separators, and they continue up to the "end-of-line marker," which is the newline character ('\n') by default.

Attribute field values are used to initialize components of the user-supplied struct appearing at the end of the declaration section, e.g.:

```
january,  1, 31,  31
february, 2, 28,  29
march,    3, 31,  31
...
```

As with lex and yacc, it is legal to omit the initial declaration section entirely. In this case, the keyfile begins with the first noncomment line (lines beginning with a "#" character are treated as comments and ignored). This format style is useful for building keyword set recognizers that possess no associated attributes. For example, a perfect hash function for *frequently occurring English words* can efficiently filter out uninformative words, such as "the," "as," and "this," from consideration in a *key-word-in-context* indexing application.[5]

Again, as with lex and yacc, all text in the optional third *auxiliary code* section is included verbatim into the generated output file, starting immediately after the final %% and extending to the end of the keyfile. It is the user's responsibility to ensure that the inserted code is valid C or C++. In Listing 1, this auxiliary code provides a test driver that is conditionally included if the DEBUG symbol is enabled when compiling the generated C or C++ code.

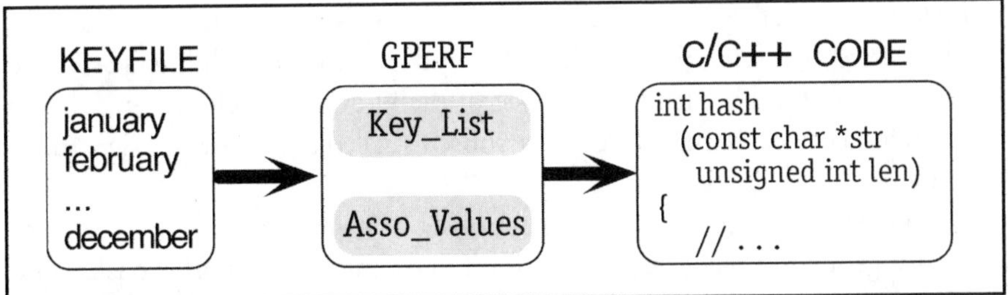

Figure 1. gperf*'s processing phases.*

Design and Implementation Strategies

Many articles describe perfect hashing[7,10,11,12] and minimal perfect hashing algorithms.[6,8,13-15] Few articles, however, describe the design and implementation of a general-purpose perfect hashing generator tool in detail. This section describes the data structures, algorithms, output format, and reusable components in gperf.

gperf is written in ~4,000 lines of C++ source code. C++ was chosen as the implementation language because it supports data abstraction better than C, while maintaining C's efficiency and expressiveness.[16]

gperf's three main phases for generating a perfect or near-perfect hash function are shown in Figure 1 and described below.

1. Process command-line options, read keywords and attributes (the input format is described in "Interacting with GPERF"), and initialize internal objects (described in "Internal Objects").
2. Perform a nonbacktracking, heuristically guided search for a perfect hash function (described in "Main Algorithm" and Collision Resolution Strategies").
3. Generate formatted C or C++ code according to the command-line options (output format is described in "Generated Output Format").

Internal Objects

gperf's implementation centers around two internal objects: the *keyword signatures* list (Key_List) and the *associated values* array (asso_values), both of which are described below.

THE KEYWORD SIGNATURES LIST. Every user-specified keyword and its attributes are read from the keyfile and stored in a node on a linked list, called Key_List. gperf only considers a subset of each keyword's characters while it searches for a perfect hash function. The subset is called the "keyword signature," or *keysig*.

The keysig represents the particular subset of characters used by the automatically generated recognition function to compute a keyword's hash value. Keysigs are created and cached in each node in the Key_List when the keyfile is initially processed by gperf.

ASSOCIATED VALUES ARRAY. The *associated values* array, asso_values, is an object that is closely related to keysigs. In fact, it is indexed by keysig characters. The array is constructed internally by gperf and referenced frequently while gperf searches for a perfect hash function.

During the C/C++ code generation phase of gperf, an ASCII representation of the associated array is output in the generated hash function as a static local array. This array is declared as u_int asso_values [MAX_ASCII_SIZE]. When searching for a perfect hash function, gperf repeatedly reassigns different values to certain asso_values elements specified by keysig entries. At every step during the search for the perfect hash function solution, the asso_values array's contents represent the current associated values' *configuration*.

When configured to produce minimal perfect hash functions (which is the default), gperf searches for an associated values configuration that maps all n keysigs onto nonduplicated hash values. A perfect hash function is produced when gperf finds a configuration that assigns each keysig to a unique location within the generated lookup table. The resulting perfect hash function returns an unsigned int value in the range 0..(k – 1), where k = (*maximum keyword hash value* + 1). When $k = n$ a *minimal* perfect hash function is produced. For k larger than n, the lookup table's *load factor* is n/k (*number of keywords/total table size*).

A keyword's hash value is typically computed by combining the associated values of its keysig with its length.* By default, the hash function adds the associated value of a keyword's first index position plus the associated value of its last index position to its length, i.e.:

```
hash_value =
   asso_values[keyword[0]]
```

* The "-n" option instructs gperf not include the length of the keyword when computing the hash function.a

```
    + asso_values[keyword[length - 1]]
    + length;
```

Other combinations are often necessary in practice. For example, using the default hash function for C++ reserved words causes a collision between delete and double. To resolve this collision and generate a perfect hash function for C++ reserved words, an additional character must be added to the keysig, as follows:

```
hash_value =
    asso_values[keyword[0]]
    + asso_values[keyword[1]]
    + asso_values[keyword[length - 1]]
    + length;
```

Developers can control the generated hash function's contents using the "-k" option to explicitly specify the keyword index positions used as keysig elements by gperf. The default is "-k 1,$", where the '$' represents the keyword's final character.

Table 1 shows the keywords, keysigs, and hash values for each month shown in the Listing 1 keyfile. These keysigs were produced using the –k2,3 option.

Keysigs are *multisets* because they may contain multiple occurrences of certain characters. This approach differs from other perfect hash function generation techniques[8] that only consider first/last characters + length when computing a keyword's hash value.

Table 1. Keywords, keysigs, and hash values for the months example.

Keyword	*Keysig*	*Hash Value*
january	an	3
february	be	9
march	ar	4
april	pr	2
may	ay	8
june	nu	1
july	lu	6
august	gu	7
september	ep	0
october	ct	10
november	ov	11
december	ce	5

The hash function generated by gperf properly handles keywords shorter than a specified index position by skipping characters that exceed the keyword's length. In addition, users can instruct gperf to include *all* of a keyword's characters in its keysig via the "–k*" option.

GENERATING PERFECT HASH FUNCTIONS

MAIN ALGORITHM. gperf iterates sequentially through the list of i keywords, $1 \leq i \leq n$, where n equals the total number of keywords. During each iteration gperf attempts to extend the set of uniquely hashed keywords by 1. It succeeds if the hash value computed for keyword i does not collide with the previous $i - 1$ uniquely hashed keywords. Listing 2 outlines the algorithm.

The algorithm terminates and generates a perfect hash function when $i = n$ and no unresolved hash collisions remain. Thus, the *best-case* asymptotic time-complexity for this algorithm is linear in the number of keywords, i.e., $\Omega(n)$.

COLLISION RESOLUTION STRATEGIES. As outlined in Listing 2, gperf attempts to resolve keyword hash collisions by incrementing certain associated values. The following discusses the strategies gperf uses to speed collision resolution.

Disjoint union: To avoid performing unnecessary work, gperf is selective when changing associated values. In particular, it only considers characters comprising the *disjoint union* of the colliding keywords' keysigs. The disjoint union of two keysigs {A} and {B} is defined as $\{A \cup B\} - \{A \cap B\}$.

To illustrate the use of disjoint unions, consider the keywords january and march from Listing 1. These keywords have the keysigs "an" and "ar," respectively, as shown in Table 1. Thus, when asso_values['a'], asso_values['n'], and asso_values['r'] all equal 0, a collision will occur during gperf's execution.† To resolve this collision, gperf only considers changing the associated values for 'n' and/or 'r'. Changing 'a' by any increment cannot possibly resolve the collision because 'a' occurs the same number of times in each keysig.

By default, all asso_values are initialized to 0. When a collision is detected gperf increases the corresponding associated value by a "jump increment." The command-line option "–j" can be used to increase the jump increment by a fixed or random amount. In general, selecting a smaller jump increment, e.g., "–j 1," decreases the size of the generated hash table, though it may increase gperf's execution time.

† Note that because the "–n" option is used in the months example, the different keyword lengths are not considered in the resulting hash function.

Table 2. Associated values and occurrences for keysig characters.

Keysig Characters	*Associated Values*	*Frequency of Occurrence*
'a'	2	3
'b'	9	1
'c'	5	2
'e'	0	3
'g'	7	1
'l'	6	1
'n'	1	2
'o'	1	1
'p'	0	2
'r'	2	2
't'	5	1
'u'	0	3
'v'	0	1
'y'	6	1

In the months example in Listing 1, the "–j 1" option was used. Therefore, gperf quickly resolves the collision between january and march by incrementing asso_value['n'] by 1. As shown in Table 2, this is its final value.

Search heuristics: gperf uses several search heuristics to reduce the time required to generate a perfect hash function. For instance, characters in the disjoint union are sorted by increasing frequency of occurrence, so that less frequently used characters are incremented before more frequently used characters. This strategy is based on the assumption that incrementing infrequently used characters *first* decreases the negative impact on keywords that are already uniquely hashed with respect to each other. Table 2 shows the associated values and frequency of occurrences for all the keysig characters in the months example.

gperf generates a perfect hash function if increments to the associated values configuration, shown in Listing 2 and described above, eliminate all keyword collisions when the end of the Key_List is reached. The *worst-case* asymptotic time-complexity for this algorithm is $O(n^3)$, where l is the number of characters in the largest disjoint union between colliding keyword keysigs. After experimenting with gperf on many keyfiles it appears that such worst-case behavior rarely occurs in practice.

Listing 2. gperf's main algorithm.

```
for i <— to n loop
    if hash (ith key) collides with any hash (1st key ... (i – 1)st key)
    then
        modify disjoint union of associated values to resolve collisions
        based upon certain collision resolution heuristics
    end if
end loop
```

Many perfect hash function generation algorithms[6,7] are sensitive to the order in which keywords are considered. To mitigate the effect of ordering, gperf will optionally reorder keywords in the Key_List if the "–o" command-line option is enabled. This reordering is done in a two-stage prepass[8] before gperf invokes the main algorithm shown in Listing 2. First, the Key_List is sorted by decreasing frequency of keysig characters occurrence. The second reordering pass then reorders the Key_List so that keysigs whose values are "already determined" appear earlier in the list.

These two heuristics help to prune the search space by handling inevitable collisions early in the generation process. gperf will run faster on many keyword sets, and often decrease the perfect hash function range, if it can resolve these collisions quickly by changing the appropriate associated values. However, if the number of keywords is large and the user wishes to generate a near-perfect hash function, this reordering sometimes *increases* gperf's execution time. The reason for this apparent anomaly is that collisions begin earlier and frequently persist throughout the remainder of keyword processing.[8,9]

GENERATED OUTPUT FORMAT

Listing 3 depicts the C code produced from the gperf-generated minimal perfect hash function corresponding to the keyfile depicted in Listing 1. Execution time was negligible on a Sun SPARC 20 workstation, i.e., 0.0 user and 0.0 system time. The following section uses portions of this code as a working example to illustrate various aspects of gperf's generated output format.

GENERATED SYMBOLIC CONSTANTS. gperf's output contains the following seven symbolic constants that summarize the results of applying the algorithm in Listing 2 to the keyfile in Listing 1:

Listing 3. Minimal perfect hash function generated by gperf.

```
#include <stdio.h>
#include <string.h>
/* Command-line options:
       -C -p -a -n -t -o -j 1 -k 2,3
       -N is_month */
struct months {
       char *name;
       int number;
       int days;
       int leap_days;
};

enum {
       TOTAL_KEYWORDS = 12,
       MIN_WORD_LENGTH = 3,
       MAX_WORD_LENGTH = 9,
       MIN_HASH_VALUE = 0,
       MAX_HASH_VALUE = 11,
       HASH_VALUE_RANGE = 12,
       DUPLICATES = 0
};

static unsigned int
hash (const char *str, unsigned int len)
{
       static const unsigned char asso_values[] =
       {
          12, 12, 12, 12, 12, 12, 12, 12, 12, 12,
          12, 12, 12, 12, 12, 12, 12, 12, 12, 12,
          12, 12, 12, 12, 12, 12, 12, 12, 12, 12,
          12, 12, 12, 12, 12, 12, 12, 12, 12, 12,
          12, 12, 12, 12, 12, 12, 12, 12, 12, 12,
          12, 12, 12, 12, 12, 12, 12, 12, 12, 12,
          12, 12, 12, 12, 12, 12, 12, 12, 12, 12,
          12, 12, 12, 12, 12, 12, 12, 12, 12, 12,
          12, 12, 12, 12, 12, 12, 12, 12, 12, 12,
          12, 12, 12, 12, 12, 12, 12, 2, 9, 5,
          12, 0, 12, 7, 12, 12, 12, 12, 6, 12,
```

(continued)

Listing 3. (continued)

```
        1, 11, 0, 12, 2, 12, 5, 0, 0, 12,
        12, 6, 12, 12, 12, 12, 12, 12,
    };
    return asso_values[str[2]] + asso_values[str[1]];
}

const struct months *
is_month (const char *str, unsigned int len)
{
    static const struct months wordlist[] =
    {
        {"september", 9, 30, 30},
        {"june",      6, 30, 30},
        {"april",     4, 30, 30},
        {"january",   1, 31, 31},
        {"march",     3, 31, 31},
        {"december",  12, 31, 31},
        {"july",      7, 31, 31},
        {"august",    8, 31, 31},
        {"may",       5, 31, 31},
        {"february",  2, 28, 29},
        {"october",   10, 31, 31},
        {"november",  11, 30, 30},
    };
    if (len <= MAX_WORD_LENGTH
            && len >= MIN_WORD_LENGTH) {
        int key = hash (str, len);
        if (key <= MAX_HASH_VALUE
                && key >= MIN_HASH_VALUE) {
            char *s = wordlist[key].name;
            if (*str == *s
                    && !strcmp (str + 1, s + 1))
                return &wordlist[key];
        }
    }
    return 0;
}
```

```
enum {
   TOTAL_KEYWORDS = 12,
   MIN_WORD_LENGTH = 3,
   MAX_WORD_LENGTH = 9,
   MIN_HASH_VALUE = 0,
   MAX_HASH_VALUE = 11,
   HASH_VALUE_RANGE = 12,
   DUPLICATES = 0
};
```

gperf produces a *minimal perfect* hash function when HASH_VALUE_RANGE = TOTAL_KEYWORDS and DUPLICATES = 0. A *nonminimal perfect* hash function occurs when DUPLICATES = 0 and HASH_VALUE_RANGE > TOTAL_KEYWORDS. Finally, a *near-perfect* hash function occurs when DUPLICATES > 0 and DUPLICATES << TOTAL_KEYWORDS.

THE GENERATED LOOKUP TABLE. By default, when gperf is given a keyfile as input it attempts to generate a perfect hash function that uses at most one string comparison to recognize keywords in the lookup table. gperf can implement the lookup table, either an array or a switch statement, as described below.

asso_values *array lookup table*: gperf generates an array by default, emphasizing runtime speed over minimal memory utilization. This array is called asso_values, as shown in the hash function in Listing 3. The asso_values array is used by the two generated functions that compute hash values and perform table lookup.

gperf also provides command-line options that allow developers to select trade-offs between memory size and execution time. For example, expanding the range of hash values produces a sparser lookup table. This generally yields faster keyword searches but requires additional memory.

The array-based asso_values scheme works best when the HASH_VALUE_RANGE is not considerably larger than the TOTAL_KEYWORDS. When there are a large number of keywords, and an even larger range of hash values, however, the wordlist array in is_month function in Listing 3 may become extremely large. Several problems arise in this case:

- The time to compile the sparsely populated array is excessive;
- The array size may be too large to store in main memory;
- A large array may lead to increased "thrashing" of virtual memory in the OS.

Listing 4. The switch-based lookup table.

```
{
  const struct months *rw;

  switch (key)
  {
    case  0: rw = &wordlist[0];     break;
    case  1: rw = &wordlist[1];     break;
    case  2: rw = &wordlist[2];     break;
    case  3: rw = &wordlist[3];     break;
    case  4: rw = &wordlist[4];     break;
    case  5: rw = &wordlist[5];     break;
    case  6: rw = &wordlist[6];     break;
    case  7: rw = &wordlist[7];     break;
    case  8: rw = &wordlist[8];     break;
    case  9: rw = &wordlist[9];     break;
    case 10: rw = &wordlist[10];    break;
    case 11: rw = &wordlist[11];    break;
      default: return 0;
  }
  if (*str == *rw->name
        && !strcmp (str + 1, rw->name + 1))
      return rw;
  return 0;
```

Switch-based lookup table: To handle the problems described above, gperf can also generate one or more switch statements to implement the lookup table. Depending on the underlying compiler's switch optimization capabilities, the switch-based method may produce smaller *and* faster code, compared with the large, sparsely filled array. Listing 4 shows how the switch statement code appears if the months example is generated with gperf's "–S 1" option.

Because the months example is somewhat contrived, the trade-off between the array and switch approach is not particularly obvious. However, good C++ compilers generate assembly code implementing a "binary-search-of-labels" scheme if the switch statement's case labels are sparse compared to the range between the smallest and largest case labels.[3] This technique can save a great deal of space by not emitting unnecessary empty array locations or jump-table

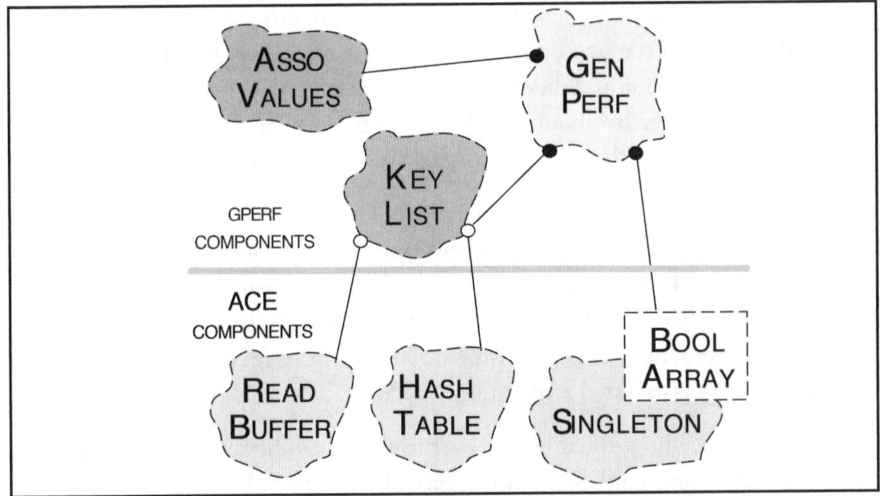

Figure 2. gperf*'s software architecture.*

slots. The exact time and space savings of this approach varies according to the underlying compiler's optimization strategy.

gperf generates source code that constructs the array or switch statement lookup table at *compile-time*. Therefore, initializing the keywords and any associated attributes requires little additional execution-time overhead when the recognizer function is run. The "initialization" is automatically performed as the program's binary image is loaded from disk into main memory.

THE GENERATED FUNCTIONS. gperf generates a hash function and a lookup function. By default, they are called hash and in_word_set, although a different name may be given for in_word_set using the "–N" command-line option. Both functions require two arguments, a pointer to a NUL-terminated ('\0') array of characters, const char *str, and a length parameter, unsigned int len.

The generated hash function (hash): Listing 3 shows the hash function generated from the input keyfile shown in Listing 1. The command-line option "–k 2,3" was enabled for this test. This instructs hash to return an unsigned int hash value that is computed by using the ASCII values of the 2nd and 3rd characters from its str argument into the local static array asso_values.† The two resulting numbers are added to calculate str's hash value.

The asso_values array is generated by gperf using the algorithm in "Associated Values Array." This array maps the user-defined keywords onto unique hash

† Note that C arrays start at 0, so str[1] is actually the second character.

values. All asso_values array entries with values greater than MAX_HASH_VALUE (i.e., all the "12s" in the asso_values array in Listing 3) represent ASCII characters that do not occur as either the second or third characters in the months of the year. The is_month function in Listing 3 uses this information to quickly eliminate input strings that cannot possibly be month names.

Generated lookup function (in_word_set): The in_word_set function is the entry point into the perfect hash lookup function. In contrast, the hash function is declared static and cannot be invoked by application programs directly. If the function's first parameter, char *str, is a valid user-defined keyword, in_word_set returns a pointer to the corresponding record containing each keyword and its associated attributes; otherwise, a NULL pointer is returned.

Listing 3 shows how the in_word_set function can be renamed to is_month using the "–N" command-line option. Note how gperf checks the len parameter and resulting hash function return value against the symbolic constants for MAX_WORD_LENGTH, MIN_WORD_LENGTH, MAX_HASH_VALUE, AND MIN_HASH_ VALUE. This check quickly eliminates many nonmonth names from further consideration. If users know in advance that all input strings are valid keywords, gperf will suppress this addition checking with the "–O" option.

If gperf is instructed to generate an array-based lookup table the generated code is quite concise; i.e., once it is determined that the hash value lies within the proper range the code is simply:

```
{
   char *s = wordlist[key];
   if (*s == *str && !strcmp (str + 1, s + 1))
      return s;
}
```

The *s == *str expression quickly detects when the computed hash value indexes into a "null" table slot because *s is the NUL character ('\0') in this case. This check is useful when searching a sparse keyword lookup table, where there is a higher probability of locating a null entry. If a null entry is located, there is no need to perform a full-string comparison.

Because the months' example generates a minimal perfect hash function, null entries never appear. The check is still useful, however, because it avoids calling the string comparison function when the str's first letter does not match any of the keywords in the lookup table.

Reusable Components and Patterns

Figure 2 illustrates the key components used in gperf's software architecture. gperf is constructed from reusable components from the ACE framework.[17] Each component evolved "bottom-up" from special-purpose utilities into reusable software components. Several noteworthy reusable classes include the following components:

ACE_Bool_Array. Earlier versions of gperf were instrumented with a runtime code profiler on large input keyfiles that evoke many collisions. The results showed that gperf spent approximately 90 to 99% of its time in a single function when performing the algorithm in Listing 2. This one function, Gen_Perf::affects_previous, determines how changes to associated values affect previously hashed keywords. In particular, it identifies duplicate hash values that occur during program execution.

Because this function is called so frequently, it is important to minimize its execution overhead. Therefore, gperf employs a novel boolean array component called ACE_Bool_Array to expedite this process. The C++ interface for the ACE_Bool_Array class is depicted in Listing 5. Because only one copy is required, BOOL_ARRAY is typedef'd to be a Singleton using the ACE_Singleton adapter. This template automatically transforms a class into a Singleton using the Singleton and Adapter patterns.[18]

The in_set method efficiently detects duplicate keyword hash values for a given associated values configuration. It returns nonzero if a value is already in the set and zero otherwise. Whenever a duplicate is detected, the reset method is called to reset all the array elements back to "empty" for ensuing iterations of the search process.

If many hash collisions occur, the reset method is executed frequently during the duplicate detection and elimination phase of gperf's algorithm. Processing large keyfiles, e.g., containing more than 1,000 keywords, tends to require a maximum hash value k that is often *much* larger than n, the total number of keywords. Due to the large range, it becomes expensive to explicitly reset all elements in array_ back to empty, especially when the number of keywords actually checked for duplicate hash values is comparatively small.

To address this issue, gperf uses a pattern called *generation numbering*, which optimizes the search process by not explicitly reinitializing the entire array. Generation numbering operates as follows:

Listing 5. The ACE boolean array component.

```
class ACE\_Bool_Array
{
public:
    // Constructor.
    ACE\_Bool_Array (void);

    // Returns dynamic memory to free store.
    ~ACE_Bool_Array (void);

    // Allocate a k element dynamic array.
    init (u_int k);

    // Checks if <value> is a duplicate.
    int in_set (u_int value);

    // Reinitializes all set elements to FALSE.
    void reset (void);

private:
    // Current generation count.
    u_short generation_number_;

    // Dynamically allocated storage buffer.
    u_short *array_;

    // Length of dynamically allocated array.
    u_int size_;
};

// Create a Singleton.
typedef ACE_Singleton <ACE_Bool_Array,
                       ACE_Null_Mutex>
     BOOL_ARRAY;
```

1. The Bool_Array init method dynamically allocates space for *k* unsigned short integers and points array_ at the allocated memory. All *k* array elements in array_ are initially assigned 0 (representing "empty") and the generation_number_ counter is set to 1.
2. gperf uses the in_set method to detect duplicate keyword hash values. If the number stored at the hash(keyword) index position in array_ is not

equal to the current generation number, then that hash value is not already in the set. In this case, the current generation number is immediately assigned to the hash(keyword) array location, thereby marking it as a duplicate if it is referenced subsequently during this particular iteration of the search process.

3. If array_[hash(keyword)] is equal to the generation number, a duplicate exists and the algorithm must try modifying certain associated values to resolve the collision.
4. If a duplicate is detected, the array_ elements are reset to empty for subsequent iterations of the search process. The reset method simply increments generation_number_ by 1. The entire k array locations are only reinitialized to 0 when the generation number exceeds the range of an unsigned short integer, which occurs infrequently in practice.

A design strategy employed throughout gperf's implementation is "first determine a clean set of operations and interfaces, then successively tune the implementation." In the case of generation numbering, this policy of optimizing performance, without compromising program clarity, decreased gperf's execution-time by an average of 25% for large keyfiles, compared with the previous method that explicitly "zeroed out" the entire boolean array's contents on every reset.

ACE_Read_Buffer. Each line in gperf's input contains a single keyword followed by any optional associated attributes, ending with a newline character ('\n'). The Read_Buffer::read member function copies an arbitrarily long '\n'-terminated string of characters from the input into a dynamically allocated buffer. A recursive auxiliary function, Read_Buffer::rec_read, ensures only one call is made to the new operator for each input line read; i.e., there is no need to reallocate and resize buffers dynamically. This class has been incorporated into the GNU libg++ *stream* library[19] and the ACE network programming tookit.[17]

ACE_Hash_Table. This class provides a search set implemented via double hashing.[5] During program initialization gperf uses an instance of this class to detect keyfile entries that are guaranteed to produce duplicate hash values. These duplicates occur whenever keywords possess both identical keysigs and identical lengths, e.g., the double and delete collision described in "Associated Values Array." Unless the user specifies that a near-perfect hash function is desired, attempting to generate a perfect hash function for keywords with duplicate keysigs and identical lengths is an exercise in futility!

EMPIRICAL RESULTS

Tool-generated recognizers are useful from a software engineering perspective because they reduce development time and decrease the likelihood of development errors. However, they are not necessarily advantageous for production applications unless the resulting executable code speed is competitive with typical alternative implementations. In fact, it has been argued that there are *no* circumstances where perfect hashing proves worthwhile, compared with other common static search set methods.[20]

To compare the efficacy of the gperf-generated perfect hash functions against other common static search set implementations, seven test programs were developed and executed on six large input files. Each test program implemented the same function: a recognizer for the reserved words in GNU g++ . The function returns 1 if a given input string is identified as a reserved word and 0 otherwise.

The seven test programs are described below. They are listed by increasing order of execution time, as shown in Table 3. The input files used for the test programs are described in Table 4. Table 5 shows the number of bytes for each test program's compiled object file, listed by increasing size (both patricia.o and chash.o use dynamic memory, so their overall memory usage depends upon the underlying free store mechanism).

- *trie.exe.* a program based upon an automatically generated table-driven search trie created by the *trie-gen* utility included with the GNU libg++ distribution.
- *flex.exe.* a flex-generated recognizer created with the "–f" (no table compaction) option. Note that both the flex.exe and trie.exe are uncompacted, deterministic finite automata (DFA)-based recognizers. Not using compaction maximizes speed in the generated recognizer, at the expense of larger tables. For example, the uncompacted flex.exe program is almost five times larger than the compacted comp-flex.exe program, i.e., 117,808 bytes versus 24,416 bytes.
- *gperf.exe.* a gperf-generated recognizer created with the "–a –D –S 1 –k 1, $" options. These options mean "generate ANSI C prototypes ("–a"), handle duplicate keywords ("–D"), via a single switch statement ("–S 1"), and make the keysig be the first and last character of each keyword."
- *chash.exe.* a dynamic chained hash table lookup function similar to the one that recognizes reserved words for AT&T's cfront 3.0 C++ compiler. The table's load factor is 0.39, the same as it is in cfront 3.0.

Table 3. Raw and normalized CPU processing time.

Executable	*Input File*					
Program	*ET++. in*	*NIH. in*	*g++. in*	*idraw. in*	*cfront. in*	*libg++. in*
control.exe	38.8|1.00	15.4|1.00	15.2|1.00	8.9|1.00	5.7|1.00	4.5|1.00
trie.exe	59.1|1.52	23.8|1.54	23.8|1.56	13.7|1.53	8.6|1.50	7.0|1.55
flex.exe	60.5|1.55	23.9|1.55	23.9|1.57	13.8|1.55	8.9|1.56	7.1|1.57
gperf.exe	64.6|1.66	26.0|1.68	25.1|1.65	14.6|1.64	9.7|1.70	7.7|1.71
chash.exe	69.2|1.78	27.5|1.78	27.1|1.78	15.8|1.77	10.1|1.77	8.2|1.82
patricia.exe	71.7|1.84	28.9|1.87	27.8|1.82	16.3|1.83	10.8|1.89	8.7|1.93
binary.exe	72.5|1.86	29.3|1.90	28.5|1.87	16.4|1.84	10.8|1.89	8.8|1.95
comp-flex.exe	80.1|2.06	31.0|2.01	32.6|2.14	18.2|2.04	11.6|2.03	9.2|2.04

5. *patricia.exe*. a PATRICIA trie recognizer, where PATRICIA stands for "Practical Algorithm to Retrieve Information Coded in Alphanumeric." A complete PATRICA trie implementation is available in the GNU libg++ class library distribution.[19]
6. *binary.exe*. a carefully coded binary search function that minimizes the number of complete string comparisons.
7. *comp-flex.exe*. a flex-generated recognizer created with the default "–cem" options, providing the highest degree of table compression. Note the obvious time/space trade-off between the uncompacted flex.exe (which is faster and larger) and the compacted comp-flex.exe (which is smaller and much slower).

In addition to these seven test programs, a simple C++ program called control.exe measures and controls for I/O overhead, i.e.:

```
int main (void) {
   char buf[BUFSIZ];

   while (gets (buf))
      printf ("%s", buf);
}
```

All of the above reserved word recognizer programs were compiled by the GNU g++ 2.7.2 compiler with the "–O2 -finline-functions" options enabled. They were then tested on an otherwise idle SPARCstation 20 model 712 with 128 megabytes of RAM.

All six input files used for the tests contained a large number of words, both user-defined identifiers and g++ reserved words, organized with one word per line. This format was automatically created by running the UNIX command "tr –cs A–Za–z_ '\012'" on the preprocessed source code for several large C++ systems, including the ET++ windowing toolkit (ET++.in), the NIH class library (NIH.in), the GNU g++ 2.7.2 C++ compiler (g++.in), the idraw figure-drawing utility from the InterViews 2.6 distribution (idraw.in), the AT&T cfront 3.0 C++ compiler (cfront.in), and the GNU libg++ 2.8 C++ class library (libg++.in). Table 4 shows the relative number of identifiers and keywords for the test input files.

Table 3 depicts the amount of time each search set implementation spent executing the test programs, listed by increasing execution time. The first number in each column represents the user-time CPU seconds for each recognizer. The second number is "normalized execution time," i.e., the ratio of user-time

Table 4. Total identifiers and keywords for each input file.

Input File	*Identifiers*	*Keywords*	*Total*
ET++.in	624,156	350,466	974,622
NIH.in	209,488	181,919	391,407
g++.in	278,319	88,169	366,488
idraw.in	146,881	74,744	221,625
cfront.in	98,335	51,235	149,570
libg++.in	69,375	50,656	120,031

CPU seconds divided by the control.exe program execution time. The normalized execution time for each technique is consistent across the input test file suite, illustrating that the timing results are representative for different source code inputs.

Several conclusions result from these empirical benchmarks:

- *Time/space tradeoffs are common*: The uncompacted, DFA-based trie (trie.exe) and flex (flex.exe) implementations are both the fastest and the largest implementations, illustrating the time/space trade-off dichotomy. Applications in which saving time is more important than conserving space may benefit from these approaches.
- gperf *can provide the best of both worlds*: While the trie.exe and flex.exe recognizers allow programmers to trade-off space for time, the gperf-generated perfect hash function gperf.exe is comparatively time *and* space efficient. Empirical support for this claim can be calculated from the data for the programs that did not allocate dynamic memory, i.e., trie.exe, flex.exe, gperf.exe, binary.exe, and comp-flex.exe. The number of identifiers scanned per-second, per-byte of executable program overhead was 5.6 for gperf.exe, but less than 1.0 for trie.exe, flex.exe, and comp-flex.exe.

Because gperf generates a stand-alone recognizer, it is easily incorporated into an otherwise hand-coded lexical analyzer, such as the ones found in the GNU C and GNU C++ compiler. It is more difficult, on the other hand, to partially integrate flex or lex into a lexical analyzer because they are generally used in an "all or nothing" fashion. Furthermore, neither flex nor lex are capable of generating recognizers for extremely large keyfiles because the size of the state machine is too big for their internal DFA state tables.

Table 5. Size of object files in bytes.

Object File	*Byte Count*				
	text	*data*	*bss*	*dynamic*	*total*
control.o	88	0	0	0	88
binary.o	1,008	288	0	0	1,296
gperf.o	2,672	0	0	0	2,672
chash.o	1,608	304	8	1,704	3,624
patricia.o	3,936	0	0	2,272	6,208
comp-flex.o	7,920	56	16,440	0	24,416
trie.o	79,472	0	0	0	79,472
flex.o	3,264	98,104	16,440	0	117,808

Listing 6. The near-perfect lookup table fragment.

```
{
    char *rw;
    ...
    switch (hash (str, len)) {
    ...
    case 46:
        rw = "delete";
        if (*str == *rw
                && !strcmp (str + 1,
                rw + 1, len - 1))
            return rw;
        rw = "double";
        if (*str == *rw
                && !strcmp (str + 1,
                rw + 1, len - 1))
            return rw;
        return 0;
    case 47:
        rw = "default"; break;
    case 49:
        rw = "void"; break;
    ...
    }
    if (*str == *rw
            && !strcmp (str + 1, rw
            + 1, len - 1))
        return rw;
    return 0;
}
```

CURRENT LIMITATIONS AND FUTURE WORK

gperf has been freely distributed for many years along with the GNU libg++ library and the ACE network programming toolkit at www.cs.wustl.edu/~schmidt/ACE.html. Although gperf has proven to be quite useful in practice, there are several limitations. This section describes the trade-offs and compromises with its current algorithms and outlines how it can be improved. Because gperf is open-source software, however, it is straightforward to add enhancements and extensions.

Trade-Offs and Compromises

Several other hash function generation algorithms utilize some form of backtracking when searching for a perfect or minimal perfect solution.[6,8,9] For example, Cichelli's[8] algorithm recursively attempts to find an associated values configuration that uniquely maps all *n* keywords to distinct integers in the range 1..*n*. In his scheme, the algorithm "backs up" if computing the current keyword's hash value exceeds the minimal perfect table-size constraint at any point during program execution. Cichelli's algorithm then proceeds by undoing selected hash table entries, reassigning different associated values, and continuing to search for a solution.

Unfortunately, the exponential growth rate associated with the backtracking search process is simply too time consuming for large keyfiles. Even "intelligently guided" exhaustive search quickly becomes impractical for more than several hundred keywords.

To simplify the algorithm in Listing 2, and to improve average-case performance, gperf does not backtrack when keyword hash collisions occur. Thus, gperf may process the entire keyfile input, *without* finding a unique associated values configuration for every keyword, even if one exists. If a unique configuration is not found, users have two choices:

1. They can run gperf again, enabling different options in search of a perfect hash function; or
2. They can *guarantee* a solution by instructing gperf to generate a *near-perfect* hash function.

Near-perfect hash functions permit gperf to operate on keyword sets that it otherwise could not handle, e.g., if the keyfile contains duplicates or there are a large number of keywords. Although the resulting hash function is no longer "perfect," it handles keyword membership queries efficiently because only a small number of duplicates usually remain.[ß]

Both duplicate keyword entries and unresolved keyword collisions are handled by generalizing the switch-based scheme described in "Interacting with GPERF." gperf treats duplicate keywords as members of an *equivalence class* and generates switch statement code containing cascading if-else comparisons within a case label to handle nonunique keyword hash values.

ß The exact number depends on the keyword set and the command-line options.

For example, if gperf is run with the default keysig selection command-line option "–k 1, $" on a keyfile containing C++ reserved words, a hash collision occurs between the delete and double keywords, thereby preventing a perfect hash function. Using the "–D" option produces a near-perfect hash function that allows at most one string comparison for all keywords except double, which is recognized after two comparisons. Listing 6 shows the relevant fragment of the generated near-perfect hash function code.

A simple linear search is performed on duplicate keywords that hash to the same location. Linear search is effective because most keywords still require only one string comparison. Support for duplicate hash values is useful in several circumstances, such as large input keyfiles (e.g., dictionaries), highly similar keyword sets (e.g., assembler instruction mnemonics), and secondary keys. In the latter case, if the primary keywords are distinguishable only via secondary key comparisons, the user may edit the generated code by hand, or via an automated script to completely disambiguate the search key.

ENHANCEMENTS AND EXTENSIONS

Fully automating the perfect hash function generation process is gperf's most significant unfinished extension. One approach is to replace gperf's current algorithm with more exhaustive approaches.[7,9] Due to gperf's object-oriented program design, such modifications will not disrupt the overall program structure. The perfect hash function generation module, class Gen_Perf, is independent from other program components; it represents only about 10% of gperf's overall lines of source code.

A more comprehensive, albeit computationally expensive, approach could switch over to a backtracking strategy when the initial, computationally less expensive, nonbacktracking first pass fails to generate a perfect hash function. For many common uses, where the search sets are relatively small, the program will run successfully without incurring backtracking overhead. In practice, the utility of these proposed modifications remains an open question.

Another potentially worthwhile feature is enhancing gperf to automatically select the keyword index positions. This would assist users in generating time or space-efficient hash functions quickly and easily. Currently, the user must use the default behavior or explicitly select these positions via command-line arguments. Finally, gperf's output functions can be extended to generate code for other languages, e.g., Java, Ada, Smalltalk, Module 3, Eiffel, etc.

Conclusion

gperf was originally designed to automate the construction of keyword recognizers for compilers and interpreter-reserved word sets. The various features described in this paper enable it to achieve its goal, as evidenced by its use in the GNU compilers. In addition, gperf has been used in the following applications:

- The TAO CORBA IDL compiler[4] uses gperf to generate the operation-dispatching tables[21]used by server-side skeletons.
- A hash function for 15,400 "Medical Subject Headings" used to index journal article citations in MEDLINE, a large bibliographic database of the biomedical literature maintained by the National Library of Medicine. Generating this hash function takes approximately 10 minutes of CPU time on a SPARC 20 workstation.
- The GNU indent C code reformatting program, where the inclusion of perfect hashing sped up the program by an average of 10%.
- A public-domain program converting double precision FORTRAN source code to/from single precision uses gperf to modify function names that depend on the types of their arguments, e.g., replacing sgefa with dgefa in the LINPACK benchmark. Each name corresponding to a function is recognized via gperf and substituted with the version for the appropriate precision.
- A speech-synthesizer system, where there is a cache between the synthesizer and a larger, disk-based dictionary. A word is hashed using gperf, and if the word is already in the cache it is not looked up in the dictionary.

Because automatic static search set generators perform well in practice and are widely and freely available, there seems little incentive to code keyword recognition functions manually for most applications.

Acknowledgments

In addition to Keith Bostic, who initially inspired gperf, special thanks is extended to Michael Tiemann and Doug Lea. Michael wrote the GNU g++ compiler. Doug gave me a forum in GNU libg++ to exhibit my creation; he also commented on drafts of this paper. Adam de Boor and Nels Olson contributed many insights that greatly helped improve the quality and functionality of

gperf. Vern Paxson provided an efficient **flex** input specification file for the GNU C++ keywords.

REFERENCES

1. Lesk, M. and E. Schmidt. *LEX—A Lexical Analyzer Generator*, Unix Programmers Manual ed., Bell Laboratories, Murray Hill, NJ.
2. Johnson, S. *YACC—Yet Another Compiler Compiler*, Unix Programmers Manual ed., Bell Laboratories, Murray Hill, NJ.
3. Stallman, R. M. *Using and Porting GNU CC*, Free Software Foundation, GCC 2.7.2 d.
4. Gokhale, A., D. C. Schmidt, and S. Moyer. "Tools for Automating the Migration from DCE to CORBA," in *Proceedings of ISS 97: World Telecommunications Congress*, Toronto, Canada, IEEE Communications Society, Sept. 1997.
5. Knuth, D. E. *The Art of Computer Programming, Vol. 1: Searching and Sorting*, Addison–Wesley, Reading, MA, 1973.
6. Cook, C. R. and R. R. Oldehoeft. "A Letter Oriented Minimal Perfect Hashing Function," *SIGPLAN Notices*, 17:18–27, Sept. 1982.
7. Tharp, A. and M. Brain. "Using Tries to Eliminate Pattern Collisions in Perfect Hashing," *IEEE Transactions on Knowledge and Data Engineering*, 6(2):329–347, 1994.
8. Cichelli, R. J. "Minimal Perfect Hash Functions Made Simple," *Communications of the ACM*, 21(1):17–19, 1980.
9. Brain, M. and A. Tharp. "Near-Perfect Hashing of Large Word Sets," *Software—Practice and Experience*, 19(10):967–978, 1989.
10. Sprugnoli, R. "Perfect Hashing Functions: A Single Probe Retrieving Method for Static Sets," *Communications of the ACM*, pp. 841–850, Nov. 1977.
11. Cormack, G. V., R. Horspool, and M. Kaiserwerth. "Practical Perfect Hashing," *Computer Journal*, 28:54–58, Jan. 1985.
12. Dietzfelbinger, M. et al. "Dynamic Perfect Hashing: Upper and Lower Bounds," *SIAM Journal of Computing*, 23:738–761, Aug. 1994.
13. Jaeschke, G. "Reciprocal Hashing: A Method for Generating Minimal Perfect Hashing Functions," *Communications of the ACM*, 24:829–833, Dec. 1981.

14. Sager, T. "A Polynomial Time Generator for Minimal Perfect Hash Functions," *Communications of the ACM*, 28:523–532, Dec. 1985.
15. Chang, C. C. "A Scheme for Constructing Ordered Minimal Perfect Hashing Functions," *Information Sciences*, 39:187–195, 1986.
16. Stroustrup, B. *The C++ Programming Language*, 3rd. ed., Addison–Wesley, Reading, MA, 1991.
17. Schmidt, D. C. "ACE: An Object-Oriented Framework for Developing Distributed Applications," in *Proceedings of the 6th USENIX C++ Technical Conference*, USENIX Association, Cambridge, MA, Apr. 1994.
18. Gamma, E. et al. *Design Patterns: Elements of Reusable Object-Oriented Software*, Addison–Wesley, Reading, MA, 1995.
19. Lea, D. "libg++, the GNU C++ Library," in *Proceedings of the 1st C++ Conference*, USENIX, pp. 243–256, Denver, CO, Oct. 1988.
20. Kegler, J. "A Polynomial Time Generator for Minimal Perfect Hash Functions," *Communications of the ACM*, 29(6):556–557, 1986.
21. Gokhale, A. and D. C. Schmidt. "Evaluating the Performance of Demultiplexing Strategies for Real-Time CORBA," in *Proceedings of GLOBECOM '97*, IEEE, Phoenix, AZ, Nov. 1997.

Uses and Abuses of Inheritance—Part I

Herb Sutter

Herb is good at writing duets. This particular series of articles discusses the various uses of inheritance in extreme depth. He talks about public inheritance, private inheritance, and multiple inheritance.

Inheritance is often overused, even by experienced developers. Always minimize coupling: If a class relationship can be expressed in more than one way, use the weakest relationship that's practical. Given that inheritance is nearly the strongest relationship you can express in C++ (second only to friendship), it's only really appropriate when there is no equivalent weaker alternative.

In this column, the spotlight is on private inheritance, and one real (if obscure) use for protected inheritance. In the next column, I'll start by covering public inheritance, and then bring things together by discussing some multiple-inheritance issues and techniques.

A Motivating Example

Here's an example to help illustrate some of the issues. The following template provides list-management functions, including the ability to manipulate list elements at specific list locations:

```
// Example 1
//
template <class T>
class MyList {
public:
   bool Insert( const T&, size_t index );
   T     Access( size_t index ) const;
   size_t  Size() const;
private:
   T*       buf_;
   size_t  bufsize_;
};
```

Consider the following code, which shows two ways to write a **MySet** class in terms of **MyList**. Assume that all important elements are shown:

```
// Example 1(a)
//
template <class T>
class MySet1 : private MyList<T> {
public:
   bool Add( const T& );      // calls Insert()
   T     Get( size_t index )  const;
                       // calls Access()
   using MyList<T>::Size;
   //...
};

<None>// Example 1(b)
//
template <class T>
class MySet2 {
public:
   bool Add( const T& );       /*calls impl_.Insert()
   T     Get( size_t index )    const;
                       /*calls impl_.Access()
   size_t Size() const;    /*calls impl_.Size();
   //...
private:
   MyList<T> impl_;
};
```

Before reading on, give these alternatives some thought, and consider these questions:

- Is there any difference between **MySet1** and **MySet2**?
- More generally, what *is* the difference between nonpublic inheritance and containment?
- Which version of **MySet** would you prefer—**MySet1** or **MySet2**?

NONPUBLIC INHERITANCE VS. CONTAINMENT

The answer to Question 1 is straightforward: There is no substantial difference between **MySet1** and **MySet2**. They are functionally identical.

Question 2 gets us right down to business:

- *Nonpublic inheritance* should always express IS-IMPLEMENTED-IN-TERMS-OF (with only one rare exception, which I'll cover shortly). It makes the using class depend upon the public *and protected* parts of the used class.
- *Containment* always expresses HAS-A and, therefore, IS-IMPLEMENTED-IN-TERMS-OF. It makes the using class depend upon only the public parts of the used class.

It's easy to show that inheritance is a superset of single containment—that is, there's nothing we can do with a single **MyList<T>** member that we couldn't do if we inherited from **MyList<T>**. Of course, using inheritance does limit us to having just one **MyList<T>** (as a subobject); if we needed to have multiple instances of **MyList<T>**, we would have to use containment instead.

That being the case, what are the extra things we can do if we use inheritance that we can't do if we use containment? In other words, why use nonpublic inheritance? Here are five reasons, in rough order from most to least common. Interestingly, the final item points out a useful(?) application of protected inheritance:

- *We need access to a protected member.* This applies to protected member functions* in general, and to protected constructors in particular.

* I say "member functions" because you would never write a class that has a public or protected member variable, right? (Regardless of the poor example set by some libraries.)

- *We need to override a virtual function.* This is one of inheritance's classic *raisons d'être.*[†] Often we want to override in order to customize the used class' behavior. Sometimes, however, there's no other choice: If the used class is abstract—that is, it has at least one pure virtual function that has not yet been overridden—we must inherit and override because we can't instantiate directly.
- *We need to construct the used object before, or destroy it after, another base subobject.* If the slightly longer object lifetime matters, there's no way to get it other than using inheritance. This can be necessary when the used class provides a lock of some sort, such as a critical section or a database transaction, which must cover the entire lifetime of another base subobject.
- *We need to share a common virtual base class, or override the construction of a virtual base class.* The first part applies if the using class has to inherit from one of the same virtual bases as the used class. If it does not, the second part may still apply: The most-derived class is responsible for initializing all virtual base classes, so if we need to use a different constructor or different constructor parameters for a virtual base, then we must inherit.

There is one additional feature we can get using non public inheritance, and it's the only one that doesn't model IS-IMPLEMENTED-IN-TERMS-OF:

- *We need "controlled polymorphism"—LSP IS-A, but in certain code only.* Public inheritance should always model IS-A as per the Liskov Substitution Principle (LSP).[Δ] Nonpublic inheritance can express a restricted form of IS-A, even though most people identify IS-A with public inheritance alone. Given `class Derived : private Base`, from the point of view of outside code, a `Derived` object IS-NOT-A `Base`, and so of course can't be used polymorphically as a `Base` because of the access restrictions imposed by private inheritance. However, *inside* `Derived`'s own member functions and friends only, a `Derived` object can indeed be used polymorphically as a `Base` (you can supply a pointer or reference to a `Derived` object where a `Base` object is expected), because members and friends have the necessary access. If instead of private inheritance you use protected inheritance, then the IS-A relationship is additionally visible to further-derived classes, which means subclasses can also make use of the polymorphism.

---

† See also Meyers, S. *Effective C++*, 2nd ed. (Addison–Wesley, 1998), under the index entry "French, gratuitous use of."

Δ See www.oma.com for several good papers describing LSP.

That's as complete a list as I can make of reasons to use nonpublic inheritance. (In fact, just one additional point would make this a complete list of all reasons to use any kind of inheritance: "We need public inheritance to express IS-A." More on that in the next column.)

So What about MySet?

All of this brings us to Question 3: Which version of MySet would you prefer—MySet1 or MySet2? Let's analyze the code in Example 1 and see whether any of the above criteria apply:

- MyList has no protected members, so we don't need to inherit to gain access to them.
- MyList has no virtual functions, so we don't need to inherit to override them.
- MySet has no other potential base classes, so the MyList object doesn't need to be constructed before, or destroyed after, another base subobject.
- MyList has no virtual base classes that MySet might need to share, or whose construction it might need to override.
- MySet IS-NOT-A MyList, not even within MySet's member functions and friends. This last point is interesting, because it points out a (minor) disadvantage of inheritance: Even had one of the other criteria been true, so that we would use inheritance, we would have to be careful that members and friends of MySet wouldn't accidentally use a MySet polymorphically as a MyList—a remote possibility, maybe, but sufficiently subtle that if it did ever happen it would probably keep the poor programmer who encountered it confused for hours.

In short, MySet should not inherit from MyList. Using inheritance where containment is just as effective only introduces gratuitous coupling and needless dependencies, and that's never a good idea. Unfortunately, in the real world I still see programmers—even experienced ones—who implement relationships like MySet's using inheritance.

Astute readers will have noticed that the inheritance-based version of MySet does offer one (fairly trivial) advantage over the containment-based version: Using inheritance, you only need to write a using-declaration to expose the unchanged Size function. Using containment, to get the same effect you have to explicitly write a simple forwarding function.

BUT WHAT IF WE DO NEED TO INHERIT?

Of course, sometimes inheritance will be appropriate. For example:

```
// Example 2: Sometimes you need to inherit
//
class Base {
public:
   virtual int Func1();
protected:
   bool Func2();
private:
   bool Func3(); // uses Func1
};
```

If we need to override a virtual function like Func1 or access a protected member like Func2, inheritance is necessary. Example 2 illustrates why overriding a virtual function may be necessary for reasons other than allowing polymorphism: Here Base is implemented in terms of Func1 (Func3 uses Func1 in its implementation), and so the only way to get the right behavior is to override Func1. Even when inheritance is necessary, however, is the following the right way to do it?

```
// Example 2(a)
//
class Derived : private Base { // necessary?
public:
   virtual int Func1();
   //... some functions use Func2,
   // some of them don't ...
};
```

This code allows Derived to override Base::Func1, which is good. Unfortunately, it also grants access to Base::Func2 *to all members of* Derived, and there's the rub: Maybe only a few, or just one, of Derived's member functions really need access to Base::Func2. By using inheritance like this, we've needlessly made all of Derived's members depend upon Base's protected interface.

Clearly inheritance is necessary, but wouldn't it be nice to introduce only as much coupling as we really need? Well, we can do better with a little judicious engineering:

```
// Example 2(b)
//
class DerivedImpl : private Base {
public:
   int Func1();
   //... functions that use Func2 ...
};

class Derived {
   //... functions that don't use Func2 ...
private:
   DerivedImpl impl_;
};
```

This design is much better, because it nicely separates and encapsulates the dependencies on Base. Derived only depends directly on Base's public interface, and on DerivedImpl's public interface. Why is this design more successful? Primarily because it follows the fundamental "one class, one responsibility" design guideline. In Example 2(a), Derived was responsible for both customizing Base and implementing itself in terms of Base. In Example 2(b), those concerns are nicely separated out.

Variants on Containment

Containment has some advantages of its own. First, it allows having multiple instances of the used class, which isn't possible with inheritance.[ß] If you need to both derive and have multiple instances, just use the same idiom as in Example 2(b): Derive a helper class (like DerivedImpl) to do whatever needs the inheritance, then contain multiple copies of the helper class.

Second, having the used class be a data member gives additional flexibility: The member can be hidden behind a compiler firewall inside a pimple[1] (whereas base class definitions must always be visible), and it can be easily converted to a pointer if it needs to be changed at runtime (whereas inheritance hierarchies are static and fixed at compile time).

ß For those who revel in unuseful obscurities: Yes, it's technically possible to have the same class appear as a base class more than once (indirectly), but it's not useful because even if you do that, there's no way to refer to any of those base's nonstatic members. At any rate, even if it were possible, it would be unmaintainable—the whole point of this article is that containment is much cleaner.

Finally, here's a third useful way to rewrite MySet2 from Example 1(b) to use containment in a more generic way:

```
// Example 1(c): Generic containment
//
template <class T, class Impl = MyList<T> >
class MySet3 {
public:
   bool Add( const T& ); // calls impl_.Insert()
   T Get( size_t index ) const; // calls impl_.Access()
   size_t Size() const; // calls impl_.Size();
   //...
   private:
   Impl impl_;
};
```

Instead of just choosing to be IMPLEMENTED-IN-TERMS-OF MyList<T> only, we now have the flexibility of having MySet IMPLEMENT*ABLE*-IN-TERMS-OF any class that supports the required Add, Get and other functions that we need. The C++ standard library uses this very technique for its stack and queue templates, which are by default IMPLEMENTED-IN-TERMS-OF a deque but are also IMPLEMENT*ABLE*-IN-TERMS-OF any other class that provides the required services.

Specifically, different user code may choose to instantiate MySet using implementations with different performance characteristics—for example, if I know I'm going to write code that does many more inserts than searches, I'd want to use an implementation that optimizes inserts. We haven't lost any ease of use, either: Under Example 1(b), client code could simply write MySet2<int> to instantiate a set of ints, and that's still true with Example 1(c) because MySet3<int> is just a synonym for MySet3<int,MyList<int> >, thanks to the default template parameter.

This kind of flexibility is more difficult to achieve with inheritance, primarily because inheritance tends to fix an implementation decision at design time. It is possible to write Example 1(c) to inherit from Impl, but here the tighter coupling isn't necessary and should be avoided.

CONCLUSION

In general, it's a good idea to prefer less inheritance. Use containment wherever possible, and inheritance only in the specific situations in which it's needed. Large inheritance hierarchies in general, and deep ones in particular, are confusing to understand and therefore difficult to maintain. Inheritance is a design-time decision and trades off a lot of runtime flexibility.

In the next installment, I'll focus on public and multiple inheritance. Public/LSP inheritance is the clearest form of inheritance to design and understand, and it should account for the vast majority of inheritance in most projects; more about that when we return.

Reference

1. Sutter, H. "More About the Compiler-Firewall Idiom," *C++ Report*, 10(7):47–51, July/Aug. 1998.

Uses and Abuses of Inheritance, Part 2

This is the second of two columns about inheritance and how to use it judiciously. In the previous column,[1] I focused on private and protected inheritance, showing how these are often abused to express IS-IMPLEMENTED-IN-TERMS-OF when plain old containment would do just as well or better, and along the way I detailed a pretty exhaustive list of the reasons to use nonpublic inheritance. Thanks to Astute Reader Alex Martelli for his follow-up remarks about two more situations when using inheritance instead of containment can be appropriate; I'll start this month's column by covering one of them. After that, I'll touch briefly on public inheritance, and then bring things together by covering some multiple inheritance issues and techniques.

Another Reason to Use Nonpublic Inheritance

Here is an addition to the previous column's list of reasons to use inheritance instead of containment:

- *We benefit substantially from the empty base- class optimization.* Sometimes the class you are IMPLEMENTING-IN-TERMS-OF may have no data members at all; that is, it's just a bundle of functions. In this case, there can be a space advantage to using inheritance instead of containment because of the empty base-class optimization. In short, compilers are allowed to let an empty base subobject occupy zero space, whereas an empty member object must occupy nonzero space even if it doesn't have any data:

```
class B { /* ... functions only, no data ... */ };
// Containment: incurs some space overhead
//
class D {
   B b;  // b must occupy at least one byte,
};       // even though B is an empty class
// Inheritance: can incur zero space overhead

//
class D : private B {
       // the B subobject need not occupy
};     // any space at all
```

For a detailed discussion of the empty base optimization, see Nathan Myers' excellent article on this topic in *Dr. Dobb's*.[2]

Having said all that, let me end with a caution for the overzealous: Not all compilers actually perform the empty base-class optimization, and even if they do you probably won't benefit significantly unless you know there will be many (say, tens of thousands) of these objects in your system. Unless the space savings are very important to your application, and you know that your compiler will actually perform the optimization, it would be a mistake to introduce the extra coupling of the stronger inheritance relationship instead of using simple containment.

THE MOST IMPORTANT THING TO KNOW ABOUT PUBLIC INHERITANCE

There is only one point I want to stress about public inheritance, and if you follow this advice it will steer you clear of the most common abuses: *Only* use public inheritance to model true IS-A, as per the Liskov Substitution Principle (LSP).* That is, a publicly derived class object should be able to be used in any context where the base class object could be used and still guarantee the same semantics.

*See www.oma.com for several good papers describing LSP.

In particular, following this rule will avoid two common pitfalls:

- *Never use public inheritance when nonpublic inheritance will do*. Public inheritance should never be used to model IS-IMPLEMENTED-IN-TERMS-OF without true IS-A. This may seem obvious, but I've noticed that some programmers routinely make inheritance public out of habit. That's not a good idea, and this point is in the same spirit as my advice last time to never use inheritance (of any kind) when good old containment/membership will do. If the extra access and tighter coupling aren't needed, why use them? If a class relationship can be expressed in more than one way, use the weakest relationship that's practical.
- *Never use public inheritance to implement "almost IS-A."* I've seen some programmers, even experienced ones, inherit publicly from a base and implement "most" of the overridden virtual functions in a way that preserved the semantics of the base class. In other words, in some cases using the Derived object as a Base would not behave quite the way that a reasonable Base client could expect. An example often cited by Robert Martin is the usually misguided idea of inheriting a `Square` class from a `Rectangle` class "because a square is a rectangle." That may be true in mathematics, but it's not necessarily true in classes. For example, say that the `Rectangle` class has a `virtual SetWidth(int)` function; then `Square`'s implementation to set the width would also naturally set the height, so that the object remains square. Yet there may well exist code elsewhere in the system that works polymorphically with `Rectangle` objects, and would not expect that changing the width would also change the height—after all, that's not true of `Rectangles` in general! This is a good example of public inheritance that would violate LSP, because the derived class does not deliver the same semantics as the base class.

Usually when I see people doing this kind of "almost IS-A" I'll try to point out to them that they're setting themselves up for trouble. After all, someone somewhere is bound to try to use derived objects polymorphically in one of the ways that would occasionally give unexpected results, right? "But it's okay," came one reply, "it's only a little bit incompatible, and I know that nobody uses Base-family objects that way [in that particular way that would be dangerous]." Well, being "a little bit incompatible" is a lot like being "a little bit pregnant"—now, I had no reason to doubt that the programmer was right, namely that no code then in the system would hit the dangerous differences; but I also had every reason to believe that someday, somewhere, a maintenance programmer was going to make a seemingly innocuous change, run afoul of the problem, and spend hours analyzing why the class was poorly designed and then spend additional days fixing it.

Don't be tempted. Just say no. If it doesn't behave like a Base, it's NOT-A Base, so don't derive and make it look like one.

Multiple Inheritance—Nutshell Recap

This brings us to the main topic of this article—multiple inheritance (MI). Very briefly: MI means the ability to inherit from more than one direct base class. For example:

```
class Derived : public Base1, private Base2 { /*...*/ };
```

Note that allowing MI also introduces the possibility that a derived class may have the same (direct or indirect) base class appear more than once as an ancestor. For example, in the above code, say that Base1 and Base2 were previously defined as:

```
class Base1 : public Base { /*...*/ };
class Base2 : public Base { /*...*/ };
```

Then Base appears twice as an indirect base class of Derived, once via Base1 and once via Base2. This situation introduces the need for an extra feature in C++: virtual inheritance. We need to be able to answer the question, "Does the programmer want Derived to have one Base subobject, or two?" If the answer is "one," then Base should be a virtual base class; if the answer is "two," Base should be a normal (nonvirtual) base class.

The main complication of virtual base classes is they must be initialized directly by the most-derived class. For more information on this and other aspects of MI, see a good text like Bjarne Stroustrup's *The C++ Programming Language*, 3rd ed., or Scott Meyers' *Effective C++* books.

Multiple Inheritance—Boon, or Abomination?

So, here we have this wonderful feature called MI. The question is, or at least was, is this a Good Thing?†

† In part, the topic for this column was inspired by events at the SQL standards meeting this past June, because there MI was removed from the ANSI SQL3 draft standard (those of you who are interested in databases may see a revised form of MI resurrected in SQL4, once we get that far). This was mainly done because the proposed MI specification had technical difficulties, and to align with languages like Java that do not support true MI. Still,

In short, there are people who think that MI is just a bad idea that should be avoided at all costs. That's not true. Yes, if it's used thoughtlessly, MI can incur unnecessary coupling and complexity—but so does any kind of misused inheritance (see the previous column), and I think we agree that doesn't make inheritance a Bad Thing. And, yes, any program can be written without resorting to MI—but for that matter any program be written without using inheritance at all, and in fact, any program can be written in assembler.

So when is MI appropriate? In short, the answer is: only when each inheritance, taken individually, is appropriate. In this column and the previous one I've tried to give a pretty exhaustive list of when to use inheritance. Specifically, most appropriate real-world uses of MI fall into one of three categories:

1. *Combining modules/libraries.* I'm citing this point first for a reason, illustrated again below. Many classes are designed to be base classes; that is, to use them you are intended to inherit from them. The natural consequence is the question: "What if you want to write a class that extends two libraries, and each library requires you to inherit from one of its classes?"

When you're facing this kind of situation, usually you don't have the option of changing the library code to avoid some of the inheritance. You probably purchased the library from a third-party vendor, or maybe it's a module produced by another project team inside your company; either way, not only can't you change the code, but you may not even have the code! If so, then MI is necessary; there's no other (natural) way to do what you have to do, and using MI is perfectly legitimate.

In practice, I've found that knowing how to use MI to combine vendor libraries is an essential technique that belongs in every C++ programmer's toolchest. Whether you end up using it frequently or not, you should definitely know about it and understand it.

2. *Protocol classes (pure abstract base classes).* In C++, MI's best and safest use is to define protocol classes—that is, classes composed of nothing but pure virtual functions. The absence of data members in the base class avoids outright MI's more famous complexities.

Interestingly, different languages/models support this kind of "MI" through non-inheritance mechanisms. Two examples are Java and COM: Strictly speaking, Java

---

just sitting there and listening to people discussing the merits and demerits of MI was intriguing because it's something we haven't done much in the C++ world since the formative years, and it made me reminisce aloud about extended newsgroup flame wars from years ago (and some more recent than that) with subject lines like MI is evil.

has only single inheritance (SI), but it also supports the notion that a class can implement multiple "interfaces," where an interface is similar to a C++ pure abstract base class without data members. COM does not include the concept of inheritance per se (although that's the usual implementation technique for COM objects written in C++), but it likewise has a notion of a composition of interfaces, and COM interfaces resemble a combination of Java interfaces and C++ templates.

3. *Ease of (polymorphic) use.* Using inheritance to let other code use a derived object wherever a base is expected is a powerful concept. In some cases, it can be useful to let the same derived object be used in the place of several kinds of bases, and that's where MI comes in. For a good example of this, see C++PL3[3] section 14.2.2, where Stroustrup demonstrates an MI-based design for exception classes in which a most-derived exception class may have a polymorphic IS-A relationship with multiple direct base classes.

Note that #2 overlaps greatly with #3. It's frequently useful to do both at once for the same reasons.

Here's one more thing to think about: Don't forget that sometimes it's not just necessary to inherit from two different base classes, but to inherit from each one for a different reason. "Polymorphic LSP IS-A public inheritance" isn't the only game in town; there are many other possible reasons to use inheritance. For example, a class may need to inherit privately from base class A to gain access to protected members of class A, but at the same time inherit publicly from base class B to polymorphically implement a virtual function of class B.

SIAMESE TWIN FUNCTIONS

That said, I want to show you a minor pitfall that can come up with MI, and how to handle it effectively. Say that you're using two vendors' libraries in the same project. Vendor A provides the following base class BaseA:

```
class BaseA {
public:
   virtual int ReadBuf( const char* );
   /* ... */
};
```

The idea is that you're supposed to inherit from BaseA, probably overriding some virtual functions, because other parts of Vendor A's library are written to expect objects they can use polymorphically as BaseAs. This is a common and normal practice, especially for extensible application frameworks, and there's nothing wrong with it.

Nothing, that is, until you start to use Vendor B's library and discover, to your uneasy amazement:

```
class BaseB {
public:
   virtual int ReadBuf( const char* );
   /* ... */
};
```

"Well, that's rather a coincidence," you may think. Not only does Vendor B, too, have a base class that you're expected to inherit from, but it happens to have a virtual function with exactly the same signature as one of the virtuals in BaseA. But BaseB's is supposed to do something completely different—and that's the key point.

The problem becomes clear when you have to write a class that inherits from both BaseA and BaseB, perhaps because you need an object that can be used polymorphically by functions in both vendors' libraries. Here's a naive attempt at such a function:

```
// Attempt #1: Doesn't work
//
class Derived : public BaseA, public BaseB {
   /* ... */
   int ReadBuf( const char* );
      // overrides both BaseA::ReadBuf
      // and BaseB::ReadBuf
};
```

Here Derived::ReadBuf overrides both BaseA::ReadBuf and BaseB::ReadBuf. To see why that isn't good enough given our criteria, consider the following code:

```
// Counterexample 1: Why attempt #1 doesn't work
//
Derived d;
BaseA*   pba = d;
BaseB* pbb = d;
pba->ReadBuf( "sample buffer" );// calls Derived::ReadBuf
pbb->ReadBuf( "sample buffer" );// calls Derived::ReadBuf
```

Do you see the problem? ReadBuf is virtual in both interfaces and it operates polymorphically just as we expect—but the *same* function, Derived::ReadBuf, is invoked regardless of which interface is being used. Yet BaseA::ReadBuf and

BaseB::ReadBuf have different semantics and are supposed to do different things, not the same thing. Further, Derived::ReadBuf has no way to tell whether it's being called through the BaseA interface or the BaseB interface (if either), so we can't just put an "if" inside Derived::ReadBuf to make it do something different depending on how it's called. That's lousy, but we're stuck with it.

"Oh, come on," you may be thinking. "This is an awfully contrived example, isn't it?" Actually, no, it's not. For example, Astute Reader‡ John Kdllin of Microsoft reports that creating a class derived from both the IOleObject and IConnectionPoint COM interfaces (think of these as abstract base classes composed entirely of public virtual functions) becomes problematic, because: a) both interfaces have a member function with the signature virtual HRESULT Unadvise(unsigned long); and b) typically you have to override each Unadvise to do different things.

Stop a moment and think about the example above: How would you solve this problem? Is there any way that we can override the two inherited ReadBuf functions separately, so that we can perform different actions in each one, and the right actions get performed depending on whether outside code calls through the BaseA or BaseB interface? In short, how can we separate these twins?

How to Separate Siamese Twins

Fortunately, there is a fairly clean solution. The key to the problem is that the two overridable functions have exactly the same name and signature. The key to the solution, therefore, must lie in changing at least one function's signature, and the easiest part of the signature to change is the name.

How do you change a function's name? Through inheritance, of course! What's needed is an intermediate class that derives from the base class, declares a new virtual function, and overrides the inherited version to call the new function.

```
// Attempt #2: Correct
//
class BaseA2 : public BaseA {
public:
   virtual int BaseAReadBuf( const char* p ) = 0;
private:
   int ReadBuf( const char* p ) { // override inherited
```

‡ Yes, I've been shamelessly hijacking Chuck Allison's "Diligent Reader" designation. It's concise and effective—imitation is the sincerest from of flattery, Chuck!

```
        return BaseAReadBuf( p );  // to call new func
    }
};
class BaseB2 : public BaseB {
public:
    virtual int BaseBReadBuf( const char* p ) = 0;
private:
    int ReadBuf( const char* p ) {      // override inherited
        return BaseBReadBuf( p );       // to call new func
    }
};
class Derived : public BaseA2, public BaseB2 {
    /* ... */
    int BaseAReadBuf( const char* );
            // overrides BaseA::ReadBuf indirectly
            // via BaseA2::BaseAReadBuf
    int BaseBReadBuf( const char* );
            // overrides BaseB::ReadBuf indirectly
        // via BaseB2::BaseBReadBuf
};
```

BaseA2 and BaseB2 may also need to duplicate constructors of BaseA and BaseB so that Derived can invoke them, but that's it. (Often a simpler way than duplicating the constructors in code is to have BaseA2 and BaseB2 derive virtually, so that Derived has direct access to the base constructors.) BaseA2 and BaseB2 are abstract classes, so they don't need to duplicate any other BaseA or BaseB functions or operators, such as assignment operators.

Now everything works as it should:

```
// Example 2: Why attempt #2 works
//
Derived d;
BaseA*    pba = d;
BaseB* pbb = d;
pba->ReadBuf( "sample buffer" );// calls Derived::BaseAReadBuf
pbb->ReadBuf( "sample buffer" );// calls Derived::BaseBReadBuf
```

Further-derived classes only need to know that they must not further override ReadBuf itself. If they did, it would disable the renaming stubs that we installed in the intermediate classes.

Conclusion

Use inheritance wisely. If you can express a class relationship using containment alone, you should always prefer that. If you need inheritance but aren't modeling IS-A, use nonpublic inheritance. If you don't need the combinative power of multiple inheritance, prefer single inheritance.

Some people feel that "it just isn't OO unless you inherit," but that isn't really true. Large inheritance hierarchies in general, and deep ones in particular, are confusing to understand and therefore difficult to code and maintain. Use the simplest solution that works, and you'll be more likely to enjoy pleasant years of stable and maintainable code.

References

1. Sutter, H. "Uses and Abuses of Inheritance—Part I," *C++ Report*, 10(9):19–22, Oct. 1998.
2. Myers, N. "The Empty Base C++ Optimization," *Dr. Dobb's Journal*, Aug. 1997.
3. Stroustrup, B. *The C++ Programming Language*, 3rd ed., Addison–Wesley, Reading, MA, 1997.

Review: The BOOSE Programming Language

Herb Sutter

This last article in the anthology is probably the most important. These are the times that try programmers' souls. We have COM on the one side, C++ on the other, Java sliding down from above, and COOL sneaking up from below. And somewhere far far above, there are angelic creatures crying: "I-Fell, I-Fell, I-Fell."

Into this big ball of muddy confusion comes BOOSE!

Despite its strengths, the BOOSE programming language has been largely (and undeservedly) lost in the industry press amid all the recent fanfare surrounding Ada, Java, Lisp, and other new Internet-related languages. It's important to give equal coverage to some of the other viable options available to developers today, especially those directly based on C++.

BOOSE: C++ for Specialized Environments

BOOSE (pronounced as a single syllable, "booz") was originally conceived in 1997 by Robert Klarer of IBM Labs to compete with Java in the high-performance, real-time embedded market.[1] In short, BOOSE consists of the complete standard C++ language, along with a set of specialized extensions to make the language more applicable in embedded and other nonstandard environments. Insider gossip has it that BOOSE originally stood for "Bjarne's Object-Oriented

Software Environment"—a tip of the hat to the creator of the C++ language, Bjarne Stroustrup, and an indicator of BOOSE's focus on nonstandard, runtime environments.[2]

Since then, BOOSE has been expanded to become a good response to Java as an alternative portable and universal language.[3] In short, BOOSE is more potent than Java. When it comes to capturing and holding developer market share, it is also at least as addictive.

BOOSE does have some drawbacks compared to Java, however. For one thing, you get what you pay for: BOOSE costs more per developer than Java, and it isn't (yet) as widely available through 24x7 vendors. BOOSE can also have dangerous side effects if used improperly; for example, it's not appropriate for real-time automotive systems, and such use may contravene existing laws in some jurisdictions. Other national laws have prohibited early adopters, who are normally essential for the growth and acceptance of a new programming environment. All of these concerns are being addressed, either in the next release of the BOOSE specification, or as local legislative amendments.

WHY PREFER BOOSE?

In general, BOOSE's extra flexibility for liquid programming styles more than outweighs its minor disadvantages. Probably BOOSE's greatest strength is that it leverages and increases the power of C++'s existing features:

- *Generic Programming*: BOOSE offers even stronger support for generic programming than standard C++. Some developers have reported that, after only a few weeks of using BOOSE, all programs start to look the same.
- *Namespaces*: In standard C++, namespaces are a relatively new feature and still not widely used. A developer who has become proficient in BOOSE tends to use namespaces much more naturally (even offensive namespaces).
- *Exception Handling*: When using BOOSE, a developer quickly becomes more proficient in exceptions—both in raising exceptions to others, and responding to exceptions thrown at the developer. It also adds the concept of exception escalation, and (in extreme cases) it allows invoking `terminate()` on other developers' processes to recover from integrity breaches.
- *Polymorphism*: BOOSE has unparalleled support for polymorphism. No matter how well you know a developer, chances are that BOOSE will reveal another side to his or her personality.

BOOSE has unmatched strength in mixed environments:

- *Availability*: Unlike most competing products, BOOSE offers critical-systems support and continuous availability during holiday periods, although some users do need more support than usual.
- *Portability*: BOOSE provides easy options for migrating from single-user stations to heavy-duty configurations, from six-pack multiprocessors still suitable for a single power user on up to 24-way systems for serious multiuser environments, all using only a single operating system handle. Instead of requiring a notoriously slow and inefficient Java Virtual Filter (JVF) layer for each new environment, BOOSE allows true filterless operation in all environments, and even BOOSE's vitreous middleware is optional and may be omitted to avoid impeding execution flow.
- *Potability*: A clear advantage. See "Portability."

BOOSE also has advantages for large projects:

- *Improving Teamwork*: BOOSE is inherently team-oriented. It encourages greater-than-usual camaraderie on software development projects, although excessive fraternization is sometimes a problem.
- *Handling Schedule Pressure*: BOOSE has also been known to work especially well on projects that are late and/or under intense schedule pressure. Especially in such high-pressure situations, developers have been known to adopt BOOSE voluntarily on their own time without prodding by management, and the effects soon spill over into working time and their current development project.
- *Promoting Team Communication*: Many BOOSE users become more-than-ordinarily happy and communicative. Others have an improved ability to speak spontaneously, passionately, and at great length about their program designs, usually while standing on a desk or in some other visible place (note that this also improves project visibility, a common gremlin in the software development industry).

Different developers have been found to respond to BOOSE in different ways, and it's true that some developers have less-than-positive reactions: Some can become angry and irritable; others have been observed to engage in unusual and risky programming behavior; and a few become downright unpredictable. Some studies suggest that BOOSE may interfere with typing accuracy and other motor skills during and after prolonged use, and three messy keyboard cleanup incidents have been documented. (All of the latter were found to be merely gastrointestinal reflexes attributed to extreme overuse, and as isolated cases they should not be a cause for concern.)

Managers need to watch for and control these warning signs to make sure their teams get the best benefit from using BOOSE more and more extensively, but in a controlled or social setting.

BOTTOM LINE

It's important to note that hardly any of the positive effects of BOOSE use can be seen in developers using Java alone. Some early studies indicated that many Java-only developers started to talk and code more quickly, improving their general efficiency, but almost always this has been at the expense of later irritability and nervousness, and in the end they were rarely as happy, spontaneous, or passionate as frequent BOOSE users. Finally, while Java has been known to keep developers up all hours of the night, BOOSE has just the opposite effect when used in quantity.

Keep your options open. There's more than one potable portable language out there. On your next project, consider using BOOSE: It's more potent than Java.

REFERENCES

1. Klarer, R. "C++ Extensions for Real-Time and Embedded Systems," *Communications of the MCA*, 1997.
2. Stroustrup, B. *The C++ Programming Language*, third ed., Addison-Wesley, Reading, MA, 1997.
3. Klarer, R. *The BOOSE Programming Language*, Prentice-Wiley, New York, 1997.

Index

B

C

E

M

N

O

P

T

Fleming Ho